READ ALL ABOUT IT!

The history of the newspaper is a fascinating one, and newspapers have always played an important role in the lives of British people. More newspapers are bought per capita in Britain than almost anywhere else. This book traces the evolution of the newspaper, documenting its changing form, style and content as well as identifying the different roles ascribed to it by audiences, government and other social institutions.

Starting with the early seventeenth century, when the first prototype newspapers emerged, through Dr Johnson, the growth of the radical press in the early nineteenth century, the Northcliffe revolution in the early twentieth century, the newspapers wars of the 1930s and the rise of the tabloid in the 1970s, right up to Rupert Murdoch and the online revolution, Kevin Williams explores the impact of the newspaper on our lives and its role in British society.

Using lively and entertaining examples, Kevin Williams illustrates the changing form of the newspaper in its social, political, economic and cultural context. As well as telling the story of the newspaper, he explores key topics in detail, making this an ideal text for students of journalism and the British newspaper. Issues include:

- newspapers and social change
- the changing face of regional newspapers
- the impact of new technology
- development of reporting techniques
- forms of press regulation

Kevin Williams is Professor of Media and Communication Studies at Swansea University. He is author of *Get Me a Murder a Day! A History of Mass Communication in Britain* (1998), *Understanding Media Theory* (2003) and *European Media Studies* (2005).

READ ALL ABOUT IT!

A history of the British newspaper

Kevin Williams

Routledge

Taylor & Francis Group

LONDON AND NEW YORK

First published 2010
by Routledge
2 Park Square, Milton Park, Abingdon, Oxon, OX14 4RN

Simultaneously published in the USA and Canada
by Routledge
270 Madison Ave, New York, NY 10016

Routledge is an imprint of the Taylor & Francis Group, an informa business

Typeset in Garamond by
Taylor & Francis Books
Printed and bound in Great Britain by
TJ International Ltd, Padstow, Cornwall

British Library Cataloguing in Publication Data
A catalogue record for this book is available from the British Library

Library of Congress Cataloging in Publication Data
Williams, Kevin.
Read all about it! : a history of the British newspaper / Kevin Williams.
p. cm.
1. Press–Great Britain–History. 2. English newspapers–History. I. Title.
PN5114.W55 2009
072'.09–dc22
2009006219

ISBN 978-0-415-34623-8 (hbk)
ISBN 978-0-415-34624-5 (pbk)
ISBN 978-0-203-59689-0 (ebk)

CONTENTS

FIGURES

PREFACE

An exhaustive survey of how the newspaper has developed into a central cultural artefact in British society is probably impossible. There are simply too many newspapers in libraries and collections up and down the country and not enough time to read all of them. Hence the author has been dependent on secondary sources – and all the potential diversions and distortions created by individual interpretations. This is, not surprisingly, sometimes problematic. One of the revelations of examining the content of a newspaper is that empirical study often counters theoretical elucidation. Jürgen Habermas's influential study of the emergence of the 'public sphere' in eighteenth-century Britain is constructed from secondary sources, most of which are in German. Constructing a theory based on such evidence is as much an act of the imagination as it is an examination of the available data. This book relies on secondary sources but where possible attention is drawn to the problematic nature of the evidence cited, as well as the difficulties of excavating the history of an ephemeral product which is not usually held in high regard. There is much dispute over the role, power and influence of particular newspapers in history but also over the basic facts, figures and even dates pertaining to their development. Who wrote what, when and why is often shrouded in mystery, particularly as for most of its history newspaper content has been compiled with no attribution to the author.

Simply reading the vast amount of material that survives would not be enough. To understand what appears in a newspaper it is also necessary to appreciate the broader organisational, social, political, economic and cultural context within which it is produced. An historian needs to be aware of the process by which newspapers were distributed and read, and the printing and reporting practices required to reproduce them, as well as social trends, geographical, financial and political factors, to say nothing of the particular biographies of editors, owners and journalists. The aim of the book is fairly basic – to describe the evolution of the newspaper in Britain and identify some of the themes that run through this history. It is generally accepted that newspaper history is about the struggle to attain free speech and freedom of expression. The dominant motif for understanding the historical development of newspapers is political freedom. Hence most newspaper history is political history, intimately entwined with the evolution of Parliament, democracy and the British political system. There is no doubt that for most of their history the political content of newspapers was considerable, waxing and waning with the issues of the day, but generally focussed on how political decisions are arrived at. However, newspapers have never been just about politics – the multifaceted nature of their content, a characteristic which distinguishes them from other forms of printed news, illustrates their deep involvement with other parts of life and society. Newspapers have played their role in reflecting and initiating social and cultural change and acting as barometers for the societies they claim to report on. Their history incorporates the changing social, cultural and moral mores that govern society and the struggles that have surrounded them. The extent to which criticism has poured forth from intellectuals, moral entrepreneurs, social guardians and opinion formers of all shades emphasises the importance of newspapers in this respect. Newspaper history is therefore also social, cultural and moral history.

The history in this book has an overt bias – it places emphasis on the continuities that appear in the historical development of the press in Britain. Many histories emphasise change; from the birth of the first newspapers through significant moments which have transformed the course of the newspaper's development. Moments of change are important and must be highlighted, but the familiar debates, discussions and developments that run through the newspaper's history are as appealing. At the centre of the story is a tension between commerce and social responsibility. Newspapers are businesses which need to sell a product to as many people as possible to make money. Most of those involved in the production of a newspaper – printer, publisher, editor and reporter – have been there in order to earn a salary, make a profit or finance a lifestyle. This has been a major ingredient in shaping what newspapers look like, their content and how they present the news, information and opinion they carry. However, newspapers have also aggregated to themselves another role, a role whereby they discharge their responsibility to society. Whether by providing a platform for debate or acting as a check on abuses of power or serving as guardians of propriety, they have sought to give the public what they need. Social responsibility has not always fitted comfortably alongside commercial imperatives and newspapers have grappled with the effort to balance these two obligations. Different eras have resolved the balancing act in different ways and the nature of the balance has varied from newspaper to newspaper. However, this struggle is at the heart of understanding how newspapers work.

Finally the history of the newspaper is a history of censorship – what is not there is almost as important as what is. While progress has been couched in the march to a broader and more diverse representation of views and opinions in British newspapers, new forms of censorship have always accompanied the evolution of the press. Shifts from direct to indirect censorship, from controlling the individual newsman or woman to shaping the environment in which they operate, have characterised the way in which the State and other social institutions have sought to influence what people read. Tracing these shifts is an integral part of newspaper history, and reveals that newspapers have played a role in restricting the flow of information as well as promoting freedom of expression.

This book provides an introductory history of how newspapers emerged, prospered and gradually declined in the United Kingdom. It focuses on understanding the underlying economic imperatives, the changing social circumstances and the prevailing cultural and moral climate that have shaped what a newspaper is and the purposes it serves. The content, shape and style of the newspaper are profoundly influenced by economy and society, but this does not mean that there is no room for the personality disputes that, as Roy Greenslade rightly notes in his impressive tome on post-war newspapers, *Press Gang*, have had 'a profound impact on the fortunes of individual titles and entire newspaper groups'. It is perhaps unfashionable to draw attention to the role of individuals at key moments. Press history has been shaped not only by the 'great editors and owners' but also by countless 'dirty people with no names' who have at one time or another acted in a way that has had a significant impact on the development of the press. Paramount amongst these are the women and children in the nineteenth century who 'hawked' newspapers to ensure they reached their readers. Devising methods of distributing newspapers has been a vital driver in the success of the newspaper. Often the structural features that define how newspaper content appears are neglected, so some effort is made here to link the larger context in which newspapers are produced with the organisational factors that underpin their production. The book also assumes that to understand how the press operates today – as well as its social, cultural and political influence – we have to attain some knowledge of the layers of decisions made in earlier periods by newspapers as part of a process of adjusting to the conditions, issues and concerns of their times.

For helping to piece together this history I would like to thank several people, most of whom imparted interesting insights and observations that I was able to incorporate into the book. These include Tom O'Malley and Sian Nicholas at Aberystwyth, who have struggled valiantly to promote the cause of media history. Particular thanks go to Tom for his comments, corrections and insightful observations. I would also like to thank my colleagues at Swansea University and Chas Critcher, Jenny Kitzinger, David Miller, Bob Franklin, Stephanie Marriott, Hans Henrik Holm, Hanne Bruun, John Eldridge and Marianne Peters. I am also very grateful to Rhys Williams for his support and Eleanor Parker and Debbie Rideout for helping to ease administrative burdens. Particular thanks go to Noel Thompson for access to his back copies of the *Poor Man's Guardian* – as well as his willingness as a professional historian to listen to the ramblings of an amateur. Clare Hudson's comments, criticisms and corrections were again invaluable and I would like to thank her for beaming in from the outer reaches of the BBC galaxy to provide assistance and support at crucial moments. The support and continued encouragement – as well as patience – of Natalie Foster at Routledge have been vital. Thanks also to Charlie Wood for her skill and imagination, Lesley Riddle for the consistent interest she has shown and Megan Graieg for her patience and understanding. The usual suspects are still there – Ed, Marge, Alan, Fran, Barry, Pam, Griff and Ie. All of the errors in the text are mine and mine alone.

HISTORY OF THE NEWSPAPER IN BRITAIN

Key moments

1771	Press wins right to report parliamentary debates
1779	First Sunday newspaper, the *British Gazette & Sunday Monitor*, is started by Mrs E. Johnson
1785	*Daily Universal Register* – later renamed *The Times* – started
1787	Post Office sets up separate office to distribute newspapers
1791	The *Observer* founded
1792	Free distribution of newspapers by Post Office begins; Fox's Libel Act introduced
1802	William Cobbett sets up *Political Register*
1814	Koenig steam presses introduced by *The Times*
1817	Thomas Barnes appointed editor of *The Times*
1831	Birth of *Poor Man's Guardian*
1833	Advertising duty reduced
1836	Stamp duty reduced
1838	The birth of the *Northern Star*
1840s	Introduction of electric telegraph
1841	John Delane appointed editor of *The Times*
1842	*Lloyd's Weekly News* begins
1843	Launch of the *News of the World*
1848	Rotary presses first used
1850	*Reynolds Newspaper* launched
1851	Reuter opens office in London
1853	William Howard Russell appointed by *The Times* as war correspondent to report Crimean War
1855	Stamp duty abolished; launch of the *Daily Telegraph*
1868	Establishment of the Press Association (PA) as news agency
1881	George Newnes starts *Tit-Bits*
1883	The parliamentary Lobby begins
1885	W.T. Stead, editor of the *Pall Mall Gazette*, is imprisoned for reports on child prostitution in London
1888	Alfred Harmsworth (later Lord Northcliffe) starts *Answers to Correspondents*
1889	First Official Secrets Act
1896	*Daily Mail* launched by Lord Northcliffe; *Lloyd's Weekly Newspaper* reaches a circulation of one million
1900	Pearson starts the *Daily Express*
1903	*Daily Mirror* founded as first women's daily newspaper
1904	*Daily Mirror* re-launched as illustrated newspaper
1905	Northcliffe buys the *Observer*
1908	Northcliffe buys *The Times*
1911	William Waldorf Astor buys the *Observer*; Second Official Secrets Act passed
1912	*Daily Herald* begins life as strike newspapers1915
	Sunday Pictorial (renamed *Sunday Mirror*) is launched by Lord

	Rothermere; Berry brothers (later Lords Camrose and Kemsley) buy the *Sunday Times*
1917	Lord Beaverbrook takes a controlling interest in the *Daily Express*; Beaverbrook and Northcliffe join the government
1918	Beaverbrook launches the *Sunday Express*
1919	Air Ministry appoints first full-time government press officer
1922	Labour Party and the TUC take over the *Daily Herald*; John Jacob Astor buys *The Times*; Lord Northcliffe dies
1927	Kemsley Newspapers founded
1929	Odhans takes a controlling interest in the *Daily Herald*
1931	Post of Prime Minister's Press Secretary created; Audit Bureau of Circulations (ABC) formed
1933	Arthur Christiansen appointed editor of the *Daily Express*
1934	Harry 'Guy' Bartholomew becomes editorial director of the *Daily Mirror*
1940	Newsprint rationing introduced
1941	*Daily Worker* closed down
1947	First Royal Commission on the Press
1950	*News of the World* hits massive 8.5 million sales
1951	Cecil Harmsworth King becomes Chairman of Mirror and Pictorial companies; Hugh Cudlipp appointed editorial director
1953	Press Council established; Lord Thomson buys *Scotsman*
1955	Newsprint rationing ends
1959	Lord Thomson buys Kemsley Newspapers
1960	Several national newspapers, including *News Chronicle*, *Sunday Graphic*, *Evening Star* and *Empire News*, close
1961	Second Royal Commission on the Press
1962	IPC founded
1964	IPC launches the *Sun* to replace the *Daily Herald*; Lord Beaverbrook dies
1966	*The Times* puts news on the front page for the first time; Lord Thomson buys *The Times*
1969	Rupert Murdoch purchases the *News of the World* and the *Sun*
1970	Reed International acquires IPC
1971	*Daily Sketch* closes down
1974	Third Royal Commission on the Press
1976	Atlantic Richfield acquires majority shareholding in the *Observer*
1978	*Daily Star* launched in Manchester; *The Times* and the *Sunday Times* cease publication for eleven months
1981	Murdoch buys *The Times* and the *Sunday Times*; Lonrho buys the *Observer*
1984	Robert Maxwell buys *Mirror* newspapers

1985	Conrad Black assumes a controlling interest in *Telegraph* papers
1986	Murdoch newspapers move to Wapping; Eddie Shah launches *Today*; Andreas Whittam Smith sets up the *Independent*
1987	Murdoch acquires *Today*
1989	Official Secrets Act reformed
1990	First Calcutt report on privacy; launch of the *Independent on Sunday*
1991	Press Complaints Commission replaces Press Council
1992	Calcutt Committee recommends introduction of privacy laws
1993	Guardian Media Group buys the *Observer*
1995	Murdoch closes *Today*; Thomson Regional Newspapers sold to Trinity
1998	Irish entrepreneur Tony O'Reilly acquires the *Independent* newspapers
1999	Launch of the London free newspaper *Metro* by Associated Newspapers; Trinity merges with Mirror Group Newspapers (MGN)
2000	Richard Desmond, owner of top-shelf magazines, takes over Express Newspapers
2004	Black sells *Telegraph* papers to the Barclay Brothers
2005	The *Guardian* re-launches in 'Berliner' format
2005	Freedom of Information implemented

INTRODUCTION

News, newspapers and society

Newspapers are unique barometers of their age. They indicate more plainly than anything else the climate of the societies to which they belong. This is not simply for the obvious reason that they are a source of news about their time but because the conditions in which they operate, the responsibilities they are expected, or allowed to fulfil, the pressures they have to meet, their circulation and economic base, the status of those who write for them and their relationship to their readers, all provide a direct insight into the nature of their communities

Francis Williams, former editor of the *Daily Herald*[1]

Newspapers have always played an important role in the lives of British people. More newspapers are bought per capita in Britain than in most other countries. In Europe, only the Scandinavians are more committed to reading newspapers. British newspapers are best sellers, with the *Sun, Mirror, Mail, Express, Telegraph* and *Star* among the top ten of Europe's most read newspapers. They excite the passions of British people. For a long time they have played 'an important part in cultural and political life by informing, entertaining, exasperating, delighting and infuriating their readers'.[2] While newspaper reading is currently in decline, it has been a 'major time-consuming activity' for most people over the last hundred years or so.[3] As leisure hours increased so did the time people spent consuming their newspapers. Historically the newspaper was used to fill additional free time, whether travelling to work on the train, bus or tube or accompanying a cup of tea or coffee or even a cigarette. People have also accessed other popular pastimes such as sport through newspapers, and surveys have found that newspaper reading has until recently been seen as a 'status conferring activity'. Reading a newspaper, it was believed, made people 'better informed', 'more up-to-date' or 'more enlightened'.[4] Those who did not read daily papers were often seen as uninformed or 'stupid', although readers of the *Sun* have been subject to similar ridicule, usually from middle-class comedians and commentators. Newspapers are subject to conflicting views about their cultural and political value: at certain times they have been seen as midwives to democracy in Britain; at other times they have been accused of debasing political, ethical and moral standards. However the British newspaper is regarded, it has been a matter for argument and disagreement throughout its history.

1

While the newspaper has been central to people's experience for centuries, the study of newspaper history is a relatively recent phenomenon. Historians have resisted the subject, tending to see newspapers as sources of historical information rather than artefacts in their own right. Press history that has been undertaken is time bound; focussing on a particular period or a specific moment, usually one seen as a turning point in history or in the evolution of the medium. There are excellent studies of the press in the seventeenth century (for example Raymond and Sutherland), eighteenth century (for example Harris and Black), nineteenth century (for example Lee and Koss) and the last century (for example Greenslade and Tunstall).[5] There are few attempts to trace the evolution of the newspaper since the first newssheets emerged with the invention of the printing press in the late fifteenth century. Many of the efforts to provide comprehensive press histories are products of the nineteenth century (Hunt, Fox Bourne, Andrews).[6] Reflecting the spirit of their age, they are generally uncritical chronologies which focus on the impact of particular individuals on the emergence of newspapers, which are consistently seen as agents of progress. The recounting of colourful anecdotes about some of the larger than life figures in press history is favoured over attempts to offer broad social, political and economic interpretations of the rise of the newspaper. The rise of media studies has not resulted in a concerted effort to compensate for this omission in historical research. Most media scholars are preoccupied with the agenda of the media and especially its obsession with immediacy. Hans Fredrik Dahl[7] argues that the nature of the media is responsible for the reluctance to treat them as historical objects. 'They seem to resist historical exploration by their sheer and monotonous insistence of dealing with mainly contemporary moments – today's news, the situation now'.

Histories that have tried to fill the gap began to emerge in the late 1970s, coinciding with the growth of interest in popular history and popular culture. Boyce, Curran and Wingate's book[8] is the outstanding example of the efforts to trace the historical development of the British newspaper in a broader context. An edited collection, it explores the changing form of the newspaper from the seventeenth century, emphasising the 'underlying social and economic forces that have shaped the press' as a means to redress the focus in too much newspaper history on 'great personalities' and the relationship between the press and the State. As one of the contributors has said elsewhere: 'the question about any medium of communication is a question of its social structure: its actual and possible organisation and relationships'.[9] The essays also address 'ideas in newspaper history' by examining how audience expectations, the values and beliefs of newspaper producers and the attitudes and actions of other social actors influenced the emergence of the newspaper. The changing nature of the newspaper is explained by the interaction of social and cultural formations. Cultural historians such as Williams emphasise the importance of understanding the newspaper in relation to other

2

forms of writing, publishing and reading as well as other kinds of political and cultural organisation such as political movements, industrial change and educational developments. The newspaper, its content, appearance and influence are moulded by the society and culture within which it operates.

These authors focussed on the history of the newspaper in the particular context of the development of popular culture. Distinction is made between elite and popular newspapers, primarily on the basis of the community or class or the groups of readers they serve. Newspapers are conceived as having originally been written for the elite of society; the educated and better off who have access to the levers of power. Their history is the struggle to give voice to ordinary people and popular concerns and issues. This struggle produced a politically driven popular press at the end of the eighteenth century and the beginning of the nineteenth century. The high point of this press coincided with the birth of Radical politics in the 1830s and subsequently it has been gradually replaced by what Raymond Williams calls the 'simulacrum of popular journalism'.[10] Rather than representing the 'authentic voice of the people', newspapers have been transformed into providing material that diverts attention from the problems of working people and encourages them to identify with the established social order.[11] The catalyst of change was the 'commercialisation' of the press from the mid-nineteenth century onwards. The new popular newspapers brought about by market forces no longer offered what Williams[12] calls 'genuine arousal' but instead relied on 'the sensational manipulation of popular sentiment'.[13]

Subsequent historical overviews have been undertaken within an interpretative analysis that focuses on the 'growing ascendancy' of commerce and capitalism in economic and political arenas, which is mirrored in newspaper production.[14] Such an approach represents a more sophisticated explanatory framework for understanding the history of the press. Newspaper history of this kind has concentrated on institutions and the economic and social structures within which they have to operate. What has remained less visible is the changing nature of the content, character and form of the newspaper. Such studies do exist, for example Virginia Berridge's brilliant analysis[15] of popular Sunday newspapers in the nineteenth century and the examinations of layout and typographical developments by Alan Hutt and Keith Williams.[16] Content and character are also touched on in studies of particular newspapers or eras, but the systematic exploration of form and content in the context of their institutional and social development is less common.

What this book seeks to do, within the considerable limitations of space, is to map out a history of the British newspaper which connects changes in newspaper style, form and techniques with developments in institutions and social and economic structures. Writing styles, layout and design, typographical shapes and size, as well as reporting and editing techniques, have evolved since the early seventeenth-century newsbooks. This evolution is explained by many historians in terms of shifts in technology and the political and economic circumstances within which production takes place.[17] There is also an emphasis on readers' expectations of what a newspaper should be and how this has been understood by owners, editors and reporters. Satisfying perceived changing reading habits and requirements has brought about new writing styles and techniques, as well as changing the nature of what appears in newspapers. Fusing together a history of the political economy of newspaper production and organisation, the development of the style, character and content, as well as the changing social, technological and cultural context within which newspaper production and reading happens, rests on the premise that the nature of the newspaper can only be explained through an understanding of the interaction between external pressures that are brought to bear on the medium in any era and the internal mechanisms by which they are produced.

The emergence of the newspaper from a 'marginal to a central place' in British culture occurred over a long period of time.[18] Taking the early seventeenth century as a starting point, many scholars argue that the newspaper has taken nearly 400 years to develop as a particular form of printed news. This 'long revolution' can be stretched back even further to the years prior to the birth of printing, as society's need for news, the essential ingredient of the newspaper, has its roots in oral societies. The early newspapers – or 'corantos' as they were called – were born into a culture which was still overwhelmingly oral and many of the features that were incorporated into these forerunners of the modern newspaper took on the characteristics of communication in an oral society. Since the early seventeenth century the newspaper, and public understanding of the newspaper, has undergone various and numerous changes. Struggles over the social meaning of the newspaper characterise this long evolution. The modern newspaper in the process of emerging from the midst of a vast array of printed and other kinds of material that have attempted to convey news has gone through an array of different forms. The cultural form we call 'the newspaper' has not been fixed, as shown by the astounding range of names that have been used to describe news serials: for example corantos, newsbooks, diurnals, gazettes, newssheets, mercuries, intelligencers, periodicals, tabloids, newspapers and journals.

Newspaper circulations

The expansion of newspapers is usually judged in terms of circulation and readership. Trying to assess how many people read newspapers in different periods in the past is almost impossible. Newspaper readers, reading practices and the impact of reading on individuals are only captured in newspaper history by references in literature, correspondence, diaries and sometimes trade records. Circulations similarly are difficult to assess, and even after the establishment of an official body in 1931

---

to verify the circulation of individual newspapers, the means by which newspapers have calculated and reported their circulations have often served to 'puff up' sales rather than accurately capture circulation figures.

Newsbooks in the early seventeenth century are estimated to have sold between 200 and 400 copies per week; the official government news-paper the *London Gazette* in the later seventeenth century is calculated to have had a print run of between 12,000 and 15,000 copies. The early eighteenth century witnessed the first 'boom' in circulation, though there is little hard evidence to document actual circulation numbers. Newspapers such as the tri-weekly *Post Boy* and *Post Man* are reported to have sold between 3,000 and 4,000 copies per issue. The introduc-tion of press taxation in 1712 allowed more accurate calculation of the growing circulations of the newspapers who took the stamp in the eighteenth and early nineteenth century; many newspapers, however, did not take the stamp. In 1750 7.3 million stamps were recorded annually; 9.4 million in 1760 and 12.6 million in 1775. Using the guesses of contemporary critics, the total weekly circulation of the estimated six to ten unstamped papers that were distributed in the London area in the 1730s and 1740s is assumed to have been 50,000 copies. By the 1830s Radical unstamped papers such as the *Poor Man's Guardian* sold between 10,000 and 15,000 copies every week.

The nineteenth century saw a rapid expansion of the press; in 1801 16 million stamps were recorded throughout the country. The Sunday newspapers led the way, with the leading newspaper *Lloyd's Weekly News* selling between 60,000 and 70,000 copies in 1852, over 100,000 in 1854, reaching a million by 1896. Total newspaper circulation rose by 36 per cent between 1816 and 1836; by 70 per cent between 1836 and 1856; and by a staggering 600 per cent between 1856 and 1881. From the end of the nineteenth century Sunday and daily newspapers became mass circulation publications, selling in their millions. By 1920 the total daily circulation of the Fleet Street dailies stood at 5 million and the Sundays at 13 million. The circulation wars of the 1930s turned many dailies into million-selling papers and by 1949 the national dailies were sell-ing over 16 million and the Sundays 29 million. The high point was in the mid- to late 1950s, with 1957 the year that the total circulation of the national dailies reached its zenith. Since this period there has been a slow and gradual decline in newspaper circulations, with a rapid speeding up of decline in recent years. By 2007 the total for Sundays and dailies was roughly the same, at just over 11 million copies sold.

Source: O'Malley and Soley, *Regulating the Press*, 9–13;
Seymour-Ure, *The British Press and Broadcasting since 1945*, 17;
Boyce, Curran and Wingate, *Newspaper History*, 82–97, 98–117;
and Franklin, *Pulling Newspapers Apart*, 9.

The newspaper and British society

The newspaper, as Francis Williams's words at the outset of this chapter remind us, has an intimate relationship with the society in which it has developed. The peculiarities of British society, its institutions, peoples and culture, have played a central role in shaping the kinds of newspapers we have. There are several features to which attention should be drawn. Newspaper reading has permeated British society to a greater extent than almost any other in the world. Newspapers in continental Europe and to a lesser extent North America have for most of their history been confined to a particular stratum of society. Sociologist Jeremy Tunstall[19] notes that newspaper reading in comparable countries is more narrowly drawn, confined primarily to the middle classes. Why the British read newspapers so avidly is a matter of conjecture. Rationality often governs our understanding of the process of newspaper reading: we want to be informed, understand what is going on so that we can play our role in society as voters and electors. We need to have access to diverse opinions and different explanations so that we can make up our own minds on the major issues of the day. However, the power of emotion also plays its part; many read in order to have their prejudices confirmed. They seek to have their worldview validated in the pages of the newspaper they buy, whether that newspaper is the conservative *Daily Mail* or the liberal *Guardian* or the communist *Daily Worker*.

A newspaper's perception and understanding of the expectations of its readers are vital components in its success and failure in building circulation and influence. This relationship is at the heart of the newspaper's historical development. Those papers that have best understood their readers – captured the *Zeitgeist* – have generally been market leaders, influencing the nature, form and content of their competitors. Such dominance does not last for long: readership is fickle and volatile. Great titles that have cast long shadows over one era have completely vanished in another – who today has heard of *Reynolds News*, the *Daily News* or the *Daily Herald*? A large circulation is not necessarily an indicator of influence – or even survival. The *Daily Herald*, when it folded in the 1960s, had a circulation of 1.25 million, a relatively healthy figure for Fleet Street at the time, and a higher level of reader satisfaction than most contemporary newspapers.[20] The paper, however, had the wrong kind of readers. The *Daily Herald*'s readership was ageing quickly; its readers were dying out. They were also drawn from lower-income groups, which did not make them attractive to advertisers, whose expenditure has become an ever more vital component in the financial viability of a newspaper. Readership is not only a matter of how many, but also of what kind.

Geography has also played its part in shaping the British press. Britain is a small country in which the majority of people are clustered together in large conurbations. London is the largest of these and is at the centre of a web of road and rail links which tie the country's major cities close together.

Political, economic and cultural power is concentrated in the nation's capital. A highly centralised political system has played its part in ensuring that London's newspapers are distributed and read the length and breadth of the land. This distinguishes the British press from its counterparts in other liberal democracies. In America national newspapers are few and far between. America is wedded to local and city newspapers, with place names usually recognised in the titles of its leading publications, such as the *New York Times*, *Washington Post*, *Chicago Tribune* and *Los Angeles Times*. Most of the major European countries follow the US example. The leading newspaper in France is the *Ouest France*, published in Rennes. Regional newspapers dominate the French market, with the internationally renowned paper *Le Monde* selling best in its own backyard, the Paris region. In Germany, the strong regional flavour of the press is reflected in its papers' titles: for example *Frankfurter Allgemeine Zeitung*, *Hamburger Abendblatt* and *Süddeutsche Zeitung*. Some newspapers such as *Bild* have established national circulation in the post-war period, but it is really only in Britain that newspapers have a national reach and orientation and compete with each other on a national basis.

Regional newspapers have struggled to survive in such an environment. First developed in the early eighteenth century, they were almost exclusively based on news taken from the London papers. It was only from the late eighteenth century that they cultivated their own identity. Some of these newspapers, such as the *Manchester Guardian*, established themselves as national newspapers and moved their operations to London. Other regional newspapers such as the *Yorkshire Post* acquired a national reputation in their heyday. Since the 1920s there has been a steady decline in regional newspaper titles and in the number of people buying them. The London-based national papers have extended their reach into the nations and regions of Britain, consolidating their hold over the market in stark contrast to the situation in most European countries. There is one exception and that is in one of the other nations of Britain – Scotland.[21] Here London-based newspapers have hardly made an impression. Newspapers produced and edited in Scotland outsell their London counterparts by large margins. The *Daily Record*, the *Herald* and the *Scotsman* exert a strong hold over the Scottish newspaper buying and reading public. London papers, in order to compete, have had to cloak themselves in Scottishness, presenting themselves as Scottish editions of the London publication, such as the *Scottish Daily Express*.[22] It is interesting to note that since the establishment of a Scottish Parliament in 1999 the London press, particularly the Scottish edition of the *Sun*, has thrived at the expense of the local newspapers.[23]

While the historical development of the British newspaper is dominated by the London press, what has happened outside the nation's capital should not be neglected. Key innovations in the British press have taken place in the other nations and regions. Newspapers in Scotland, Ireland and to a lesser extent Wales have contributed to the development of national self-awareness in these nations, sometimes rejecting London as a focus for the centre of the expression of views and opinion. Newspapers in the English provinces have also played a role in building regional, local and urban identities and affiliations.[24] Provincial newspapers have at times exerted political influence: Prime Minister William Gladstone stated in 1877 that 'there was more political power in the provincial press than in the whole of the London press'.[25] It should also be recognised that the Scots, Welsh and Irish provided a disproportionate number of the personnel who played a crucial role in the editorial and commercial development of the London press. The lack of respectability that accompanied the growth of newspapers encouraged men and women from the periphery and margins of British society to make their way into the industry. The success of personalities such as Jonathan Swift and Hugh Cudlipp in different eras illustrates the view of one late nineteenth-century editor that newspapers are sufficiently meritocratic that 'even an Irishman or a Scotsman could reach the top if he had sufficient wit and intellect'.[26] The marginal nature of newspaper work has also encouraged the participation of women and other disadvantaged groups in society. The anonymous nature of writing for newspapers in the nineteenth century provided an opportunity for some of those hidden from history to put their views into the public domain.

The British press is also distinguished by Sunday newspapers which sell in large numbers and traditionally are separate publications from the daily press. This contrasts with Western Europe, where there is no tradition of such newspapers, and the United States, where Sundays are the same publications that appear on every other day of the week. The Sunday papers took a longer time to establish themselves as reputable publications, the first Sunday newspaper appearing in the late 1770s. The early Sunday papers were serious publications. It was the format of sex, gossip and crime developed by papers such as the *News of the World*, *Reynolds News* and *Lloyd's Weekly News* which enabled the Sundays to become Britain's best-selling newspapers from the mid-nineteenth century. The sales of the Sunday paper have traditionally dwarfed those of their daily counterparts: the *News of World* reached its sales peak in June 1950, when the number of people buying the newspaper was calculated at 8.44 million.[27] The highest calculated circulation of a daily newspaper was the *Daily Mirror* in 1967, at 5.27 million.[28] There was no link between the Sundays and dailies. The *Sunday Times* launched in 1822 had no connection with the daily paper, *The Times*, established nearly forty years earlier. Some daily papers launched Sunday versions in the early twentieth century but it was not until the latter part of the century, when merger mania hit Fleet Street, that Sundays and dailies became associated with one another.[29] The role of Sunday newspapers is often neglected in standard histories of the British press, where they appear in a secondary role to the exploits of the daily newspaper.[30] They were the first newspapers to establish the new printing technology that revolutionised the production of newspapers in the nineteenth century and sought to maximise their appeal to as broad a readership as possible. They laid the foundations for the development of the modern newspaper with their focus on sensation, crime, sport and illustrations. Their role in the political struggles of working-class Radical newspapers in the early nineteenth century to free themselves from government control and persecution is particularly neglected. Radical in their politics, the Sunday newspapers' roots lay in popular street literature, which has led many to see them as a distraction from the noble political causes promoted by the more serious papers such as the *Poor Man's Guardian*. This underestimates their position, and that of popular papers in general, in the development of popular education and culture as well as the struggle for political emancipation.

There is a strong correlation between newspaper reading and social class in Britain. National newspapers have been, and continue to be, strongly divided along class lines; with demarcations between 'upmarket' or 'broadsheet', 'middle-market' or 'middle-brow' and 'popular' or 'tabloid' newspapers. Those with higher levels of income, educational attainment and social status tend to read the upmarket or broadsheet papers, while those at the other end of the spectrum read the tabloids in large numbers. From a historical viewpoint it is argued that middle-market newspapers such as today's *Daily Mail* and *Daily Express* have been buffeted by competitive pressures, their numbers and readership dwindling over the years. Whether or not this is the case they have been part of the history of the newspaper. Each of these segments of the market operates in slightly different ways, with different social, economic and cultural pressures being brought to bear. This is reflected in their content: they combine news and comment, information and entertainment, text and pictures in a way which satisfies their kind of readers. Crucial to their product differentiation is the economics of newspaper production. The balance between sales and advertising revenue differs in each segment of the market, with broadsheets relying more on the latter source of revenue and tabloids on the former, which has a considerable impact on the presentation and content of newspapers.

The size and shape of the newspaper has changed throughout its history but it took on a tabloid size in the first decade of the twentieth century. Tabloid-size newspapers are a feature of press systems throughout the world. However, it is in Britain that the tabloid newspaper has thrived. Lord Northcliffe, the founder-owner of the *Daily Mail*, produced a tabloid version of the New York newspaper the *Daily World* in 1901, when he was invited to edit it for a day on a visit to the United States.[31] Northcliffe emphasised the economy of style not the size of the newspaper in defining the term 'tabloid'. Brevity and simplicity were the virtues that he sought, in the form of short sentences and succinct words; they would enable the reader 'by glancing down the subjoined list of contents and following the arrangement of the pages' to gain an 'outline of the day's news ... in sixty seconds'.[32]

Northcliffe's journalism gradually spread throughout the British newspaper market at the expense of the 'vanishing serious press'.[33] The process of 'tabloidisation', seen as more virulent in Britain than elsewhere in the world, is used to describe not only an emphasis on visual material, shortened articles and bold headlines but also a shift in content, away from information and analysis and toward sensational copy focussing on scandal, celebrities and popular entertainment. It is a euphemism for 'declining standards' in the press, sometimes conceived in cultural terms but as often labelled as a 'degradation in political discourse'.[34] 'Tabloidisation' is seen as slowly developing from the popular end of the newspaper market into the middle and upmarket newspapers as well as the provincial press throughout the twentieth century. For many scholars, commentators and workers in the newspaper industry this development is a 'downward spiral' into the production of something which is the antithesis of good newspaper journalism. The debate about the role of the newspaper in devaluing public discourse and 'dumbing down' society has a long lineage. One of the earliest voices raised against the failure of newspapers to inform their readers was that of the dramatist Ben Jonson. He wrote a number of plays and masques, such as *News from the New World* (1620) and *The Staple of News* (1626), in which he compared the 'false information of the rapidly expanding news culture with the truth of poetry' and criticised the recording of trivialities to 'fatten the book'.[35]

Role of newspapers

Newspapers mean different things to different people. A variety of functions can be attributed to the different needs of advertisers, readers, owners, editors, politicians, governments, amongst others. However, it is possible to argue that the newspaper carries out two distinct communication functions. According to cultural theorist James Carey,[36] newspapers, like other news media, work by transmitting information *and* bringing readers together as part of a community. He labels these two functions: the *transmission* model and the *ritual* model. The former model is more familiar to us. We all accept that the newspaper's 'most important and exacting task … is the provision of a daily … supply of news'.[37] However, more careful scrutiny indicates that the pages of newspapers have historically included a variety of often conflicting and contradictory material. The 'indeterminate nature of their content and form' is a feature of newspapers.[38] The *Daily Universal Register*, which became *The Times*, drew attention in its first issue in 1785 to the need to cater for a wide variety of interests: 'A newspaper', it stated, 'ought not to be engrossed by any particular object, but, like a well covered table; it should contain something for every palate'.[39] The incorporation of other types of publication is an essential ingredient in the development of the newspaper. Advertisements are one obvious example of content that has nothing to do with the supply and analysis of news. Editorial and leading articles can be traced back to the handwritten newsletters of the seventeenth century which provided commentary on contemporary events. Puzzles and pastimes such as crosswords have helped readers while away the time spent with their newspaper. The serialisation of fiction, stories and novels in nineteenth-century newspapers is a further example of how non-news and non-information content has always been an essential ingredient of the newspaper. Media theorist Denis McQuail[40] draws attention to the *multiple purpose* of the newspaper. Thus to see the historical development of the newspaper through the prism of the conveyance of news and information is to exclude a variety of content newspapers serve up.

The provision of news nevertheless has had a considerable impact on the form and content of the newspaper. It has been responsible for several factors that have shaped its production, distinguishing it from other forms of printed news. *Regular and frequent publication* is one feature. Newspapers have been published throughout history at different intervals; monthly, weekly, tri-weekly and daily have been the most common forms. Attempts at other intervals have been tried but proven ineffective. Printed news began as a one-off publication; a single account of an event written much longer after it had happened, it was labelled a 'relation' and the lapse between the occurrence and its reporting was so long that it was only sufficient to 'mention the year in which the event took place'.[41] Subsequently the newspaper established the regularity of publication we associate with the modern daily paper. The regularity of publication, whether daily, weekly or monthly, has implications for what appears in a newspaper and how it operates. The gathering of news and information ceases to be a casual operation and becomes a more systematic and deliberate attempt to collect and process the latest information. The new formats and methods devised to respond to regular publication determine the content and presentation of newspapers.

Closely related to regular publication is an emphasis on *newness and recency* of the content of a newspaper. The timeliness of what appears in a newspaper has developed in response to the increasing speed with which news and information can be gathered and transmitted. The development of technology has provided the impetus to immediacy, which has increasingly been identified as a crucial element in the production of the newspaper. Developments such as the telegraph, telex, telegram, telephone and typewriter have all augmented the speed with which news can be gathered and processed, and advances such as the steam-driven press and the railways have increased the number of copies and speed at which newspapers can be distributed. However, the emphasis on immediacy pre-dates the technological developments of modern, industrial society. Early newspapers operated under a cultural imperative to produce the earliest possible report of events. This focus on topicality underlines the newspaper's reputation for ephemerality, something technological change accentuated. Inclined to the coverage of the immediate, consumed instantly, on the spot, and reproduced on a regular daily basis, the newspaper could be discarded without too much anxiety. Yesterday's newspaper, it was said, was only good as wrapping for today's fish and chips. This perception of newspapers as ephemeral is responsible for shunting their study into the margins of academic research.

The *public character* of the newspaper has differentiated it from other forms of printed news. An important source of news and information in the seventeenth and early eighteenth centuries was the handwritten newsletter. Newsletters continued to be produced in the nineteenth century but by that time had been superseded by newspapers. They first appeared during the Wars of the Roses to supply political, practical and commercial information on a private basis; a luxury good, they were only available to the elites of the day – although subscription widened access in later years. The newsletters played a role in the development of news consciousness, but the lack of an essential public character limited their influence. The capacity to function in the public domain and the sense of serving the population at large are essential ingredients of the newspaper. This is associated with another feature of the newspaper: it is a commodity, *openly for sale* to anyone who can afford it. Unlike posters and newssheets, which could be read on the walls of most towns and cities, or in the windows of shops, pubs, taverns, coffee houses and barbers shops, and unlike ballads and songs that could be sung in the streets and places of entertainment, newspapers were for sale. That the newspaper was sold shaped the nature of what it produced. Coming to know readers and their wants and needs is a feature of the history of the newspaper. However, not all readers are equal in the pressure they bring on the newspaper to shape how it covers the world.

A newspaper is a 'complex, sensitive mechanism subject to an immense range of influences and pressures'.[42] Providing insights into the diversity of expectations readers bring to their newspapers and how these have changed has proven difficult in historical terms. Just establishing how many people read newspapers, let alone discovering who they were and why they read them, is a challenge. Perhaps more pertinent – and easier to extrapolate from history – is the view newspapers have of their readers. The nature, form and content of a newspaper are often shaped by the perception that the newspaper has of its readers and what they want and how they should be addressed. The *Daily Mail* was launched as the busy man's newspaper, and much of its layout reflected the desire to appeal to a reader who had little time to consume the paper. Market research has enabled newspapers over time to know more about their readers and their habits and desires and direct their content to satisfy them. This is vital if the newspaper is to survive – and the history of the newspaper shows that more newspapers fail than succeed. Newspaper history is an examination of the shifting balance between differing expectations, influences and pressures.

The relationship with readers is often encapsulated into a discussion of binary opposites. In historical terms the newspaper is part of a broader struggle between moral instruction and popular amusement. Crudely put, and the former word is stressed here, there have been, at least since the emergence of prototype newspapers in the seventeenth century, two broad approaches to communicating what is going on: one which seeks to instruct and educate people by 'giving them what they need' and another which aims to entertain and represent people by 'giving them what they want'. These approaches have competed and collided with each other as newspapers have developed. Mark Hampton,[43] in his groundbreaking book on press history, documents the two visions that have propelled the growth of the newspaper: the 'educational ideal' and the newspaper as a form of 'representation'. From the very early days the newspaper has sought to educate and entertain. The attempt to attain a balance between these is a continuous feature of newspaper history.

While many writing about the newspaper, in historical and contemporary terms, emphasise what it imparts to its readers – news, knowledge, education or entertainment – the newspaper throughout its history has also played a role in forging group identities. According to Carey, 'a ritual view of communication is directed not towards the extension of messages in space but toward the maintenance of society in time'.[44] He emphasises the role of newspapers and other forms of mass communication in bringing people together by mobilising a range of rituals which call attention to what they have in common. This has led several scholars to focus on the role of the newspaper in the creation of national identity.[45] Benedict Anderson argues that the book and the newspaper, which he regards as a larger but ephemeral form of the book, enabled their readers to imagine that they were part of a broader national community.[46] Michael Billig[47] emphasises how newspapers and other media flag up the taken-for-grantedness of national identity and association in everyday life, while Martin Conboy has examined how the tabloid press in Britain provides 'an explicit sense of place, a textual focus for a popular national community'.[48] Making people feel connected with a nation is not the only form of collective identity newspaper reading is seen as encouraging. Forging a sense of class identity is emphasised by many students of the nineteenth-century press, including the Radical press, which is seen as assisting the development of a class consciousness amongst working people.[49] Historians have also shown how newspapers have reinforced other kinds of identities.[50] Newspapers have sought to cater for women, young people, trade and professional groups, political parties, regional and local interests, as well as other national communities in Wales, Scotland and Ireland. Newspaper layout and design, as well as the language used, have been targeted to appeal to readers newspapers are seeking to reach, reinforcing their values and the way in which they see the world and themselves.

Evolution of the newspaper

The orthodox view of the evolution of the newspaper is encapsulated in what is labelled the 'Whig' tradition of history. Newspapers are portrayed as locked into a political struggle with the State to gain their independence and right to freedom of expression. The fight for liberty, freedom from censorship and the right to report without restriction is seen as a long drawn-out conflict which was eventually won in the middle of the nineteenth century when the 'taxes' imposed on the press were finally revoked. Key dates in the successful struggle for the liberty of the press include the end of licensing in 1695, the granting of the right to report Parliament in 1771 and Fox's Libel Act in 1792, which allowed juries instead of judges to adjudicate. With the lifting of the final press tax in 1861 the British newspaper is seen as attaining its freedom. The subsequent years are seen as ones in which the newspaper consolidated its role as the 'fourth estate', by representing the people and holding the government and State to account. Newspapers have acted as the voice of the people, vehicles for the extension of democracy, watchdogs of those in authority and platforms for political debate. Newspaper history is thus an account of the steady progress that has been made to achieve this situation, emphasising the importance of the newspaper in the strengthening of political freedom and democracy. This view of the historical development of the British newspaper has been criticised, in particular by James Curran, who has dismissed Whig press history as 'political mythology' which serves to legitimate the role of the press in British society and ward off those who seek to change the ways in which newspapers operate. His re-evaluation of the development of the newspaper turns orthodoxy on its head, by stressing the role of the newspaper as an agent of social control. Rather than initiate a new era of freedom the repeal of press taxation in the mid-nineteenth century ushered in a 'new system of press censorship more effective than anything that had gone before'.[51] In this account the struggle for press freedom is lost. Newspaper history is not a tale of progress but one of changing forms of censorship. The most influential theorist of press history, Jürgen Habermas,[52] emphasises progress and deterioration in his account of the evolution of the newspaper in British society. He argues that the newspaper played a crucial role in the rise of what he labels the 'public sphere' in eighteenth-century Britain, encouraging rational and critical debate that fashioned public opinion and had an effect on government policy and action. Confined to the political elite, the public sphere nevertheless represented an advance in democratic activity. However, it did not last; the commercialisation of the newspapers and the bureaucratisation of public life polluted the public sphere. Newspapers no longer expressed critical opinion or encouraged debate; they simply served up conventional political wisdoms and fostered consumer passivity. This is what Habermas describes as the 'refeudalisation' of the public sphere. Many of those influenced by Habermas discuss the deterioration of the performance of the press in a number of respects.

To assume that matters can only get better and/or worse is to simplify the nature of newspaper history. Curran identifies several historical narratives that have shaped the interpretation of the role and development of media history.[53] Each adopts a linear perspective of historical development: things can only get better or worse. Calls for the reassessment of how media history is conducted draw attention to the need for more complexity.[54] Thus the growing importance of news in the nineteenth-century newspaper needs to be seen as part of the struggle between news and comment that has permeated newspaper history. Similarly 'tabloidisation' in the twentieth century should be contextualised by the clash between education and entertainment apparent since the early forerunners of the newspaper appeared in Britain. To capture the ebb and flow of history, this account of the newspaper's development attempts to understand the newspaper in the particular historical periods in which it has existed. To paraphrase Curran, newspaper history should be conceptualised in terms of opening and closure, advances and reverses that have occurred simultaneously within certain historical periods.

Stages of evolution

History is often divided into particular periods, categories or stages. Arbitrary dates are selected to represent a point when history is supposed to have changed course. These dates are seen as breaks in the progress of history, taking developments in another direction or ushering in a new period or era. Such categorisation is subjective; schemas which divide historical development into different phases often have more to do with hindsight than with charting contemporaneous development. Emphasising change also ignores the way in which history waxes and wanes, and undervalues the continuity of issues, problems and circumstances that confront individuals and society. Historians of the newspaper sometimes ascribe to the medium fabulous powers to change society and bring about a revolution in daily life. Seduced by the technology, we often believe that the media cause social change. Gutenberg's printing press, for example, is sometimes credited with changing the whole course of Western civilisation. Such analysis should be situated in the ways in which every medium of mass communication is located and 'institutionalised' in the society within which it operates.[55] Newspapers, like other media, are often portrayed as 'creating themselves out of nowhere' without any reference to the social conditions in which they are introduced.[56] The newspaper has been born, developed and institutionalised within a set of social circumstances, which vary across time. Different eras have their own cultural, social, economic and political imperatives which impact on the newspaper and determine form and appearance, what appears in the pages, how content is produced, the way in which people understand its role in society and its relationship with other social actors. Several scholars have emphasised that we can only understand the evolution of the media in terms of a technology and the set of social conditions that shape its application.[57] Privileging social conditions that select technological innovations rather than respond to them should be emphasised.

15

Acknowledging the difficulties and limitations of dividing history into stages, this book is organised around particular periods in the history of the newspaper. Within these periods newspapers have evolved in particular ways, shaped by the conditions in which they have functioned. Their development has been neither uniform nor consistent but part of a struggle between competing understandings. New media forms do not simply replace old ones; they grow and develop within a context determined by older forms. However, it is possible to identify factors which are common to particular periods and distinct from others. In doing so the focus is not only on dates but on the changing structural features that define how content, the coverage and representation of the period in question, appears in the newspaper. This categorisation draws on the work of John Nerone and Kevin Barnhurst, who have classified the growth of the American press according to the development of form, appearance and style, changing systems of news production and ways of conceptualising the role of the newspaper in society.[58] They identify four timelines in the historical formation of the newspaper – printerly, partisan, Victorian and modern – positing that we are perhaps now entering a new stage of development in the digital age. Their typology is based on an 'internalist' perspective, focussing on the organisation and production of the newspaper. This contrasts with 'external' histories of the press which are located in the broader transformations of society. Jeremy Black, in discussion of the internal and external dimensions of newspaper histories of the eighteenth century, points out that it is not really possible to separate them out.[59] They have interacted to shape the evolution of the newspaper. It is possible to differentiate between four types of newspaper formation on the basis of organisation and culture. The British newspaper has evolved in a manner in which four key actors have had a substantial role at certain times in determining its organisation and culture. These actors are the printer, editor, proprietor and reader, now often known as the consumer.

Chapters 1 and 2 of this book look at the emergence of the newspaper from amongst a range of other printed material imparting news, information and comment that was spawned in the wake of the invention of the printing press. The newspaper in this period developed as a distinct cultural form and the key figure was *the printer*. Although editors and others whose job it was to produce the paper had existed from the very early days of the newspaper, they did not become an established feature until later. Generally it was the printer who oversaw the entire operation. Newspapers were part of a portfolio of printed material that the printer produced, and given the importance of the book to the printer's business the early newspapers resembled books in their form and appearance. The marginal position of the newspaper in the world of printing is highlighted by the haphazard way in which newspapers were laid out, items being placed onto the page as they were acquired. The lack of a systematic means to gather news was complemented by the problems of distribution. Methods by which the newspaper could be placed in the hands of individual readers emerged, such as the postal service, mail coach and eventually news agents. However, the primary way in which readers got their newspapers was in the coffee houses, taverns and barbers' shops. Newspaper reading was a more collective and shared experience. Newspaper shops emerged where those with sufficient income could purchase a newspaper, but more usually people read them in the windows of these shops or had them read to them in the streets outside. Politics and foreign news dominated the content of the newspaper in this period. This reflects the intervention of the State in the operation of the press as much as the interests of readers. Direct censorship gave way to indirect control in the form of press taxation in the State's attempts to influence what the newspapers could report. As they became more profitable, newspapers became increasing involved in the struggle to establish political rights. The great struggle of the time was for the right to report the proceedings of Parliament, eventually won in 1771.

Chapters 3 and 4 cover a period from the latter part of the eighteenth to the mid-nineteenth century when the printer's pre-eminence gave way to that of *the editor*. The rise of the editor is associated with the emergence of class politics. Newspapers and periodicals in the eighteenth century were associated with one man, who often wrote and compiled much of what appeared. To survive, the newspaper became associated with political causes, factions and parties as recipients of official subsidies from government and 'paid servants of political parties and personages'.[60] 'Suppression' and 'contradiction' fees thrived as the press sought to survive. Such commitments in an era in which party politics was in its early days were lukewarm, suiting the needs of the newspaper as much as politics. Newspapers became the paid polemicists of political interest, often writing for those who coughed up the highest fee. Towards the end of the century the newspaper morphed into a political organ which served the needs of the classes or sub-classes that emerged following the Industrial Revolution. Unlike their eighteenth-century predecessors these newspapers were committed to the causes and interests of their class. Radical newspapers serving working people were pitted against respectable papers serving the middle classes. The radical newspaper the *Northern Star* acted as the voice for the Chartist movement but it did this by generating debate between the different opinions, factions and interests which constituted the movement. It let 'every rival speak' and its comprehensive coverage of the politics of the movement made it a newspaper.[61] A similar range of coverage emerged in respectable newspapers such as *The Times*. In articulating class interests these newspapers grasped the importance of an editor who could 'speak' for his or her class as well as attend to the organisation of the newspaper, which as a result of technological and economic change was becoming more complex. Layout and design, organisation of news gathering and developing effective means of distribution were increasingly pressing matters. Innovations in printing technology meant more pages could be produced more quickly. Editors not only had to be gifted polemicists but also had to have the skills to oversee the production process.

Editors of the early nineteenth century had to have strong opinions. News-papers operated in a world of politics, partisanship and opinion. Editors were the 'links between Party leaders and their supporters in the country'.[62] They organised their newspapers to attack political foes and defend political friends. Newspapers acted as political advocates and the main advocate was the editor, who used the leader column as the primary means of communication. News – much of which was made up with the speeches of politicians – was secondary to the articulation of opinion. However, the strength of opinion was tied to the quality of news and information.[63] The battle for political hearts and minds in which the press was engaged increasingly came to rest on the superiority of the information and intelligence that a newspaper amassed. Papers expanded in order to carry more news and comment, the balance between them chan-ging as newspapers became more sophisticated in their news gathering. John Delane, who edited *The Times* and oversaw its attainment of a position of pre-eminence in the mid-Victorian newspaper market, was called 'the best informed man in Europe'.[64] The editor acquired greater power, likened to 'the oracle whom no one in or out of the office denied the right to print or omit what seemed to him best'.[65] This led editors such as Delane to assert their independence in the daily conduct of the newspaper and the framing of policy. The notion of the 'sovereign editor' who exercised absolute control over the editorial side of the newspaper and remained separate from the business of the newspaper was established. The extent to which editors exercised such control is disputed. However, what is incontestable is that editorship became the crucial component in the operation of the newspaper in the nineteenth century.

The power of editors was usurped with the growth of market forces. Chapters 5 and 6 explore the industrialisation of the newspaper from the late nineteenth century onwards. The amount of money required to enter the newspaper market and continue to run a newspaper in a competitive envir-onment shifted attention to the men and women who had sufficient capital to invest in the press. The *owner or proprietor* came to the fore in what has been described as the era of the press barons. The newspaper was now a large-scale undertaking; more reporters were required, copy could be bought from numerous national and international news gathering agencies, advertising departments expanded as newspapers carried display ads for the growing range of products available in the emerging consumer society and technology speeded up the gathering, processing and distribution of the newspaper. The industrialisation of the press changed the ways in which newspapers were produced and the kinds of things that appeared on their pages by privileging the position of capital. Rising costs of production, expanding pages to fill, growing competition and the increasing importance of advertising to the financial success of the newspaper enhanced the power of owners. Deep pockets were called for and in return the press barons demanded more control over the product. Newspapers became vehicles for the idiosyncratic beliefs of individual owners; men like Northcliffe, Rothermere and Beaverbrook used their newspaper to promote their own causes. These causes were diverse but in general terms the newspapers of the press barons supported the commercial interests of their owners and the system of business within which they operated. Radical newspapers disappeared and the range of opinion in the press contracted. Newspapers sought to mould opinion in an era in which propaganda thrived. Public suspicion about the power of these owners increased; calls for reform to encourage greater responsibility transpired. Mechanisms were developed inside newspaper organisations to counter the growing power of owners; journalists formed unions and developed professional techniques to allay public concerns and resist proprietary intervention.[66] Objectivity was one such technique incorporated into the British newspaper – although the commitment of British newspapers to the concept never attained the levels it did in the United States. Mark Hampton has traced the 'limited extent to which objectivity has been embraced as an ideal by practicing journalists' in this country.[67]

Under the press barons the newspaper became more commercial. Fuelled by competition and the need to make returns on investments, owners expanded the content of their newspapers, increasingly introducing a broader range of content designed to appeal to as wide a range of readers as possible. Pictures, typographical innovation, shorter and more readable stories on a wide range of topics replaced the focus on politics and foreign news that had dominated the newspaper of earlier periods. New ways of promoting the newspaper were adopted, including dispensing with anonymity of reporting, which had characterised the newspaper of the nineteenth century. News stories became more central, although they now were focussed on human interest and entertainment value. Politicians found new ways of influencing the press. Fearing the growing influence of newspapers under the control of the 'press barons', they no longer sought to control the press through direct and indirect measures but rather attempted to shape the environment in which newspapers operated. Exploiting the newspaper's demand for a regular, reliable and daily supply of news and information, government and politicians used their position as sources of information to manage and manipulate the news agenda. A range of techniques were adopted, including the Lobby system, press officers, news conferences and press releases, to influence what appeared. The formalisation of arrangements whereby newspapers employed specialist correspondents to cover bodies such as the courts, police and the City, which provided regular stories, confirmed the newspaper's dependence on official sources of information. The result was the poor performance of the British press in covering some of the great, controversial issues of the inter-war years.

The era of the press barons was swept away in the Second World War, which radically changed British society. The issue of ownership did return in the form of the debate about the power of Murdoch and Maxwell in the 1980s, but by this time the nature of ownership had changed. Less individualistic and more focussed on commercial rather than political considerations, owners were now part of large conglomerates whose interest lay well beyond those of the press barons. The newspaper in the post-war period has been driven by commerce, competition and profit. Chasing readers, advertisers and revenue was the primary objective of the *consumerist newspaper*. The number of people reading newspapers has fallen steadily since the 1950s and the press has adopted, in an increasingly frenzied way, more and more means to make its product attractive. This is part of the debate about 'tabloidisation', which is seen as spreading from the popular press through to the quality newspapers as competition has intensified. Price wars and advertising drives have accelerated the 'dumbing down' process, with newspapers increasingly packaged to maximise advertising potential. The increase in the size of the newspaper is to contain more advertisements and more advertising-driven copy. The division of the newspaper into sections is to better target the audience advertisers are seeking to reach. Chapters 7 and 8 describe the commercialisation of the newspaper industry since the end of the Second World War. The concentration of ownership has been a feature of an increasingly competitive industry. The relationship between national newspapers and their regional counterparts has changed, with large companies such as Trinity Mirror owning national and regional titles. News stories have dwindled further as features, soft news, entertainment and comment have taken up more space. More engaging ways of telling and presenting the story emerged with the use of colour, larger font sizes, pictures and bigger headlines. More space to fill has not been matched by the employment of more people to fill the space. Job cuts, downsizing, retrenchment and standardisation were features of newspaper production in the last decades of the twentieth century. Technological innovation has resulted in the removal of a whole swathe of people who previously were essential to the compiling and printing of the newspaper. Profits were increasing, but sales, titles and staff declined. Advertising – and the requirement to produce an audience for advertisers to direct their wares at – drives the finances of the modern newspaper. The precarious nature of this economic situation was exposed with the advent of competition for advertising revenue from television and the internet. However, it was the consumer – or rather newspapers' perception of their consumers – that drove the industry and shaped the nature of the newspaper.

Technological and economic changes in the early twenty-first century have led to speculation that the 'end of the newspaper' is nigh. Declining newspaper circulation has coincided with more people turning to the internet for news. Newspapers have responded to the perceived threat from web news sites by launching their own online editions. The internet 'de-forms' the newspaper by changing the way in which people read it.[68] Web versions of the newspaper enable readers to browse not just the content but the main providers of that content. Reading a newspaper on the web allows readers to enter a portal which gives them access to a much broader world. They are afforded some form of response beyond the traditional letter to the editor, with greater autonomy and interactivity provided. Reading can be more selective, and targeting readers is more difficult in a digital world in which readers are more elusive. New ways have to be found of reaching the consumer. Consumers are also converted into producers as the new technology allows individuals to contribute to the text of the web newspaper, thereby threatening to usurp the traditional function of the journalist and editor. There is also a threat to one of the basic characteristics that shapes a newspaper – its voice.[69] The editorial function of identifying a newspaper as a particular kind of 'brand' that is distinct from its competitors could be submerged amongst the growing array of opinions that make up a digital newspaper. The increasing prevalence of opinion and comment in the world of blogging, surfing and the online newspaper has led to speculation about the 'death of news'.[70] The internet also poses a challenge to the economics of the traditional newspaper; which is today more heavily dependent on advertising than ever before. The internet is drawing – and is likely to continue to do so – revenue away from the hard-copy newspaper. In response the newspaper has yet to devise an effective strategy to make a profit from online editions by developing ways to make people pay for the content.[71] The final chapter (Chapter 9) explores the shift from the consumerist newspaper into the as yet undefined world of the online newspaper; evidence about the impact of the internet on the newspaper and its primary function of gathering news remains confused and contradictory. Throughout its history the newspaper has shown the capacity and versatility to adapt to circumstances, redefining what it does as well as its relationship with its readership. The newspaper survived the advent of the photograph, cinema, radio and television and promises to evolve into a new form in response to the internet.

Nouem. 7. 1622.   *Numb. 6.*

A Coranto.

RELATING

DIVERS PARTICV-
LARS CONCERNING
THE NEWES OVT OF *ITALY,*

Spaine , *Turkey* , *Persia* , *Bohemia* , *Sweden* ,
Poland , *Austria* , the *Pallasinates* , the *Grisons* , and
diuers places of the Higher and Lower
GERMANIE.

Printed for *Nathaniel Butter* , *Nicholas Bourne* ,
and *William Shefford* , 1622.

A Coranto, 7 November 1622

SPREADING THE WORD

The pre-history of the British newspaper, 1486–1660

News (plus the printing press) created the newspaper[1]

It took nearly two centuries for a publication devoted to the regular dissemination of news to emerge as a distinct form out of the variety of printed material that flowed from the development of the printing press in the late fifteenth century. These were the formative years of the British newspaper and the structure and content of modern newspapers were influenced by a number of things that happened in this period. Newspapers are a relatively recent invention but their basic ingredient is 'one of humanity's oldest pleasures'.[2] People have always had the desire to know about what is happening around them, and the spreading of news, or 'tydings' as it was referred to in the medieval era, responds to what the anthropologist Claude Lévi Strauss[3] labels a basic human trait. Long before people could read and write they exchanged news and information. The advent of the printing press was an essential catalyst in the emergence of the newspaper but many of the features we associate with the newspaper pre-date printing. They can be traced back to the era of handwritten manuscripts and even further back to when societies were dominated by oral communication. Printed news material developed within the context of – and was influenced by – the communication of news by word of mouth and handwritten manuscript. The early newspapers not only had to survive in a predominantly oral culture but also had to compete with other forms of printed news material, such as posters, ballads and handbills. Understanding the history of the newspaper requires some knowledge of the struggles of these forerunners of today's newspaper to establish themselves.

Word of mouth

Prior to the printing press the dissemination of news and information was dominated by word of mouth. Most towns and communities in medieval Europe gained their news from passing travellers. Merchants and mercenaries, drovers and peddlers, singers and seasonal workers spread the news of occurrences in the outside world. Certain kinds of people specialised in the oral dissemination of news and stories. Town criers had responsibility for announcing deaths, decrees and royal proclamations. Balladeers and travelling players, poets and troubadours would carry stories throughout the countryside, playing at fairs and usually embellishing their accounts to attract a larger audience. Much of what they imparted would be familiar to us today. Death, war and destruction figured prominently. People then as today sought news not only for practical reasons but also for pleasure and entertainment,[4] but unlike now ordinary people relied on face-to-face communication. Song, poetry and storytelling were the predominant forms of popular expression. The centrality of oral communication was acknowledged in the titles of many of the early newspapers, whose names – such as *Herald*, *Messenger* and *Mercury* – reflected the oral form of communication which dominated the world into which they were born. Oral communication did not disappear with the appearance of handwritten manuscripts or the arrival of the printing press and continues to play a role in the imparting of news up to the present day. Recent research suggests the resurgence of the spreading of news by word of mouth in Britain's newly emerging digital world.[5]

Newspaper titles

It is possible to argue that newspaper titles in different periods reflect the generally accepted role of a newspaper in society. Early newspaper titles incorporated the predominant view that newspapers were messengers conveying accounts of events, hence names such as *Herald*, *Messenger* and *Mercury*. Later in the seventeenth century the involvement of the newspapers in gathering information in a world turned upside down by ideological conflict was reflected in titles such as *Intelligencer*, *Scout*, *Spy* and *Informer*. The accurate and faithful reproduction of news and information was considered significant to the early newsbooks of the Civil War period – hence *Perfect Diurnall*, *True and Perfect Diurnall* and *Perfect Passages*. Speed, time, technology, methods of distribution and production and nature of readership have been central to other stages of the development of newspapers. The early eighteenth century placed emphasis on the importance of means of getting the newspaper to readers, with terms such as *Post*, *Flying Boy*, *Mail*, *Courier*, *Dispatch* and *Packet* in the titles. Fascination with new technology in the nineteenth century was manifested in titles such as the *Telegraph* and *Telegram*, although the *Abergavenny Telephone* never caught on. *Times*, *Express*, *Courant* and *Journal* reflect the newspaper's obsession with speed and deadlines, while *Observer*,

Guardian, Sentinel, Independent, Moderator, Tribune, Monitor, Record, Recorder, Examiner, Ledger, Register, Spectator, Tatler and *Standard* suggest basic dispositions to society or guiding properties. *Gazette, Reporter, Chronicle, Review, Sketch, Advertiser, Correspondent, News* and *Bulletin* incorporate notions of what are believed to be the functions of a newspaper. *Star, Sun, Comet* and *Lantern* can be seen as representing what many papers in the late eighteenth and early nineteenth centuries believed was one of their main objectives, to enlighten their readers. The growing importance of the visual components of the newspaper from the end of the eighteenth century is reflected in titles such as *Pictorial, Graphic* and *Mirror*.

Handwritten manuscripts and printed forms of news emerged into a world in which oral communication was pre-eminent. Scholars, most notably Walter Ong[6] and Marshal McLuhan,[7] have drawn attention to the differences between oral and written cultures. The time- and space-bound nature of oral communication is emphasised; speaker and audience have to be co-present and recall is limited to those present. The reliability of what is communicated is a crucial matter of concern in oral cultures. Human memory is far from infallible and spoken news is open to manipulation and miscommunication. Inevitably, after much telling and retelling, the news becomes completely distorted. In oral cultures, free from the capacity to provide a permanent record of knowledge which written cultures supply, rumour abounds. Magic and superstition could prevail in such conditions and news of the fantastic and phantasmagorical was commonplace. As news was primarily spoken, sung or recited, attention was paid to dramatisation to ensure people listened. However, as Mitchell Stephens[8] points out, the limitations of the oral communication of news and information went beyond the problems of inaccuracy, embellishment and dramatisation. Oral communication is only capable of sustaining and supplying local communities. The oral transmission of news and information proved increasingly inadequate with the growth of more sophisticated forms of social and economic organisation. The rise of urban communities, nations and empires in the late Middle Ages increased the demand for a reliable flow of news and information that could reach more people more quickly. Particular sections of medieval society sought news and information of greater reliability. Miscommunication of what was going on at court or what had happened in foreign wars or about the price of commodities could have profound consequences for monarchs, mercenaries and merchants. The need to manage and understand the more sophisticated and complex society that was emerging led to more value being placed on specialist writers, scribes and copyists, who could document knowledge and communicate more reliable forms of news and information.

The rise of the written word

Handwritten newssheets had appeared in China about 200 years before the birth of Christ. Produced by the government, they circulated primarily amongst officials. In the Western world the handwritten communication of news and information can be traced back to the early days of Rome. News was disseminated more widely than in China, travelling along the roads and seaways of the Roman Empire to most major centres of population. For nearly 300 years these handwritten manuscripts, *acta diurna*, would be posted in public places displaying details of the major political and military events of the day as well as news of births, deaths, marriages, ceremonies and human interest stories. They contained accounts of the proceedings of the Senate and the pleadings in the courts of law,[9] as well as much trivial and erroneous information. The philosopher Cicero complained about the quality of what appeared in the handwritten dispatches sent out from Rome, which he found too full of 'tittle-tattle' and 'reports of gladiatorial pairs and the adjournments of trials'.[10] Historians emphasise the social value of these publications. They are seen as helping to hold the Empire together, playing a key role in the socialisation of the Empire's citizens and the effective dissemination of official information and decrees throughout the Empire.[11] Published 'by authority', they represent an early written form of promulgating the news, spread from above to the rest of the population.

Following the collapse of the Roman Empire transportation and communication networks across Europe withered and the forward march of written news was temporarily halted. Literacy declined in the so-called 'Dark Ages' and written material became more inaccessible due to the ornate handwriting employed in its reproduction and to the use of Latin, a language which most ordinary people in Europe could not read.[12] They spoke only their vernacular languages. The dominance of Latin was a reflection of the cultural monopoly of the Church, which was an obstacle to the dissemination of news and information and the development of reading and writing. Medieval life was deeply embedded within the Church. Most people gained news through the pulpit. Gothic cathedrals have been called 'encyclopaedias of stone and glass'.[13] Papal control over the institutions of mental production was virtually complete, and by managing the means of mass communication of the day, the pulpit, altar and religious rituals and imagery, the Papacy was able 'to transmit not merely its claims of church leadership but an ideological perspective of the world that legitimated its domination of Christendom'.[14] To ensure that only ideas that conformed to the doctrines and desires of the religious establishment were communicated, the Church propagated its message through an elaborate system of non-verbal communication reinforced by the spoken words of priests, who, from the pulpit, promoted their interpretation of the Bible. The written word was a potential threat and had to be carefully policed by the religious authorities. Hence the use of ornate styles and Latin to ensure that knowledge was maintained in the hands of the approved few. The copying of material was dominated by the Church. The monasteries had a virtual monopoly over the means of manuscript production; most scribes learned their trade in the shadows of the Church. They worked in scriptoria for free, serving the interests of their masters and superiors. The Church's hegemony over the supply of written material placed restrictions on the exchange of ideas, which acted as a barrier to the freedom of public expression and an impediment to the development of public forms of news.

The Church's influence over the transmission of literate culture slowly diminished from the thirteenth century. The waning of the Middle Ages corresponded with the expansion of the numbers of those interested in gaining knowledge and information. The balance between information which could be 'passed on freely' and that which could only be 'whispered in confidence' slowly began to change.[15] Public communication was enhanced by the growth of independent centres of learning and knowledge in the form of universities, first established in the twelfth century.[16] Centres of secular learning in medicine and the law, these bodies increased the demand for reliable and accurate information. They also promoted 'disputation'; establishing that opinions could diverge on a given topic or matter. However, the majority of teachers and students in medieval universities were members of the clergy and the disputations between them took place within parameters laid down by the Church.[17] The outcome was the growth of demand for a wide range of non-papal texts on medicine, law, astronomy, travel, mathematics and Greek philosophy. Responding to the growth in demand for books and material from the universities and mendicant orders, lay stationers gradually began to replace monastic scribes. Copyists were employed in greater numbers to produce parts of texts for payment as a mean of speeding up production.[18] The process of manuscript production was transformed as paper replaced parchment. Costs of production fell and output rose. There was a substantial increase in the number of manuscripts as the laborious preparation involved in the use of parchment was replaced by the 'simpler, quicker and cheaper techniques of paper production'.[19] Commercial and university scriptoria emerged as the copying of manuscripts became an industry. The growth of lay influence over cultural production as well as the development of lay consciousness not only eroded the Church's monopoly over knowledge but undermined papal authority. The result was the publication of a wider range of material in spite of the efforts of the Church to proscribe and regulate the reproduction of what it saw as undesirable. The extension of scribal culture is also associated with the rising demand for secular education and literacy. The late medieval period witnessed the 'gradual penetration' of reading and writing into everyday life, the emergence of unorthodox opinion, the establishment of the foundations of a publishing industry and the birth of a broader 'reading public'.[20] These changes were to be crucial to developing and sustaining news as a form of public communication.

The gradual emergence of a group of people and institutions devoted to the pursuit of learning and knowledge was accompanied, if not promoted, by the expansion of the dynastic order across Europe. Pressure for access to information from kings, princes and merchants was a crucial factor in the rise of the written word. Political rulers required information to pursue their efforts to centralise government, gain legitimacy and, above all, pursue war. Feudalism as a system of government was 'heavily dependent on the co-operation and voluntary services of the governed'.[21] Europe's medieval monarchs used heralds to provide accounts of battles but the search for faithful and accurate reproduction of what they wished to communicate to their subjects led them to employ the written word in the form of bulletins, ballads, writs and proclamations. As the value of favourable publicity increased, more and more scribes and copyists were employed to ensure royal propaganda reached the public domain. However, handwritten manuscripts as a form of public communication were rare, turning into a flurry only at times of crisis such as the Hundred Years War, and then as a secondary means of support to prayers and the pulpit which began to act as a type of royal propaganda agency.[22] Political information, dynastic struggles and the activities and ambitions of princes were generally seen as the preserve of the State, something not suitable for public consumption. It was commonly held that ordinary men and women were 'no fit guides' to interpreting public events, which was best left to 'ministers and great officers to judge', who had 'handled the helm of government, and been acquainted with the difficulties and mysteries of statecraft'.[23] The view the philosopher and statesman Francis Bacon had of ordinary people reflects what many in government and authority have believed over successive centuries. Such opinion was a major obstacle to the development of written news.

Handwritten newsletters

News in the late medieval and early modern period was most often communicated privately through handwritten letters. From the early fourteenth century 'intelligence' became an essential component of politics, diplomacy and, above all, finance and trade. The Church and State developed mechanisms to gain intelligence; diplomats were sending back political and economic news in private letters to their paymasters. The Church pioneered the use of scribal techniques for administration, while the State gathered information to react to specific problems such as sedition, plague and war.[24] Religious and political networks of pre-print communication were added to with the development of commerce.[25] Merchants required more and better information about a range of mercantile activity such as shipping times, interruptions in the supply of goods and the state of the harvest. Their need for reliable information made news an increasingly valued commodity in its own right – a departure from the medieval view that knowledge was a gift from God not be sold.[26] Financiers and merchants established their own postal systems as well as networks of correspondents. Perhaps one of the most advanced networks was developed by the banking family the Fuggers. By the late sixteenth century they were copying reports from agents and contacts around the world and distributing them in manuscript form to their clients.[27] The content of these manuscript newsletters was not simply about exchange rates, insolvencies and financial and commercial information. It was also about current affairs, reports of battles, disasters, plots, births, deaths and marriages and ceremonies – in fact, news of anything that might interrupt regular patterns of trade.[28] They also contained accounts of bizarre and 'weird happenings'.[29] Much of this material was speculative, based on gossip and rumour, and often false. Yet, the importance of these handwritten news manuscripts to the development of the newspaper was the emphasis they placed on factual accuracy. They were regarded as less susceptible to the embellishments and alterations that characterised spoken news as their compilers had a 'continuing responsibility' to their clients to ensure the reliability of the material they provided, which meant checking sources of information.[30] In an age where facts appeared 'vaporous', the handwritten word was 'prized for its relative weight'; it represented the difference between 'flying rumours' and 'certain knowledge'.[31]

The growth of manuscript newsletters reflected the development of a 'single information community' across Europe. They were not usually regular publications but a service provided for those who could employ someone to gather news and to carry messages over great distances. They circulated amongst a small number of people, the elite of their time, princes, statesmen, nobles and the emerging traders and financiers. Only the elite had the financial resources to support and sustain such an enterprise; newsletters were a 'luxury only obtainable by the rich'.[32] To sustain this form of communication a system of distribution developed which was of crucial importance to the later growth of the press. The establishment of a regular postal service contributed to building up the expectation of a regular flow of news. The service developed on an ad hoc basis from the middle of the sixteenth century. There were two forms of public carriage: royal posts and common carriers.[33] The royal posts were unreliable, frequently disrupted by warfare, legal entanglements and the collapse of royal subsidies. Hence the elite of late medieval and early modern Europe relied on special couriers to deliver their newsletters. The reluctance of printers throughout the sixteenth century to regularly produce printed news was a consequence of the lack of security and the high cost of postal distribution. From the 1590s the improvement in postal services made the flow of news more reliable. The growing interconnectedness of weekly posts across Europe resulted in the expectation of statesmen and merchants of regular reports, a feature that distinguishes the character of the newspaper. By the mid-seventeenth century the efficiency of posts and couriers and the growing expectation of regular reports from Europe and beyond made it more feasible and profitable for printers to produce regular printed news. The authorities saw the value of a postal monopoly to control the gathering and flow of information; letters were detained and examined well into the eighteenth century.[34]

The birth of printing

The advent of the printing press was vital to the development of the newspaper. It was in many respects 'the extension of previous innovations, and its effects ... merely the reinforcement of the consequences of the development of scribal culture'.[35] Printing consolidated the expansion of the written word which had begun in the late medieval period. Much of the material that rolled off the presses in the late fifteenth and early sixteenth centuries was the 'staple products of scribal culture' and it is estimated that it took about fifty years for new material to appear.[36] What the printing press did was to produce a revolutionary increase in the amount of material available. The laborious process of copying by hand limited the amount of material produced. Printing speeded up the process of copying, resulting in more material reaching a larger audience. For every single copy produced by the scribe the press could produce over a thousand copies.[37] Speeding up the process of reproduction increased the amount of information and knowledge available and ensured that other people's ideas were more readily and widely accessible. The furthering of the exchange of ideas, opinions, theories and conjectures assisted the advancement of science. The preservative capacity of print allowed technological, intellectual and scientific advances to be recorded for others to access when and where they wanted. This not only revolutionised Western culture but ultimately swept away the remaining vestiges of papal control over knowledge, encouraging the notion of free speech.

The capacity of the printing press to increase the amount and speed of information was matched by an increase in demand for knowledge at the beginning of the sixteenth century. This was brought about by the Reformation. Religious material such as bibles, psalters, hymnals and prayer books dominated the output of the early printers, with the majority of books printed before 1500 devoted to religious literature. The Reformation produced a huge schism in the religious order that had underpinned the medieval world. As Catholics and Protestants battled with each other to establish the true faith, the printing press responded to an exponential growth in the public thirst to hear more about the convulsions that were bringing about fundamental change. Unlike religious movements of previous centuries, the Reformation found in the printing press a potent channel of communication.[38] Martin Luther's message was distributed further and farther than that of his predecessors as a result of the new invention, which for the rebellious German priest was 'the medium by which God, through Gutenberg, chose to liberate the German people from the corruption of Rome'.[39] The mass

dissemination of religious texts, particularly of the Bible in vernacular languages, challenged the clergy's monopoly over the interpretation of religious
knowledge and provided the possibility of alternative readings of the word of
God.[40] The Church responded by attempting to ban Bible reading and to
proscribe the printing of religious material in languages that ordinary people
could understand. The printing press also enabled more people to learn about
the excesses and corruption of the Papacy. Thousands of handbills, posters
and broadsheets were churned out; described by Lucien Febvre and Henri-Jean
Martin[41] as the 'first literature of information, the ancestor of the modern
newspaper'. Protestantism was intimately linked to the rise of print culture.
Protestant churches deliberately sought to remove traditional modes of religious communication; rituals and rites were suppressed or simplified, murals
were painted over and sculptures destroyed, stained glass was replaced by pane
glass, superstition was discouraged and the role of the priest demystified.[42]
In the process Protestants defended their right to be heard.

The relationship between printing and the vast social changes associated
with the Reformation is a matter of debate.[43] Printing was a necessary but
not sufficient development in accounting for the changes that brought medieval society to an end; but without the religious and social upheavals and
disputes there would not have been the demand for information that fuelled
the expansion of printing. Unravelling the relationship between print and
social change in the early modern period is beyond the scope of this book.
However, printing and social change in the early sixteenth century were
crucial to the rise of printed news. The growth of print culture is closely
linked with the rise of vernacular languages in Europe.[44] The Reformation
fuelled the translation of the Bible, previously accessible only in Latin, into
the vernacular languages of Europe. The requirement of Protestant reformers
to spread their word was accompanied by the emergence of centralising national
monarchies. A process of standardisation, codification and unification took
place which 'established fairly large territories throughout which a single
language was written'.[45] The desire of Luther and his fellow reformers to
reach ordinary people played a significant role in the formation of language
blocks which provided the foundations for the emergence of national consciousness. Europe was divided behind language barriers as print incorporated
Europe's cultural elite into national cultures.[46] In Britain Tyndale and Cov-
erdale's translation into English of the Bible and Scriptures paved the way
for the multiplication of texts in the English language and the development
and systemisation of the literary language of the English nation.[47]

The growing availability of printed material and its accessibility for a
greater number of people were accompanied by the extension of literacy.
Printing was initially 'integrated into the needs of those who were socially
ascendant, rather than used to democratise knowledge'.[48] It was seen as an
essential tool of good governance and by the end of the sixteenth century it
was expected that every noble could read and write; William Herbert, Earl

of Pembroke, who died in 1570, was the last illiterate member of the 'cabinet' in Britain.[49] It was in this period that the development of the 'reading public' began, which was essential for the growth of literature and newspapers. The reproduction of school textbooks was to result in 'a spectacular increase in literacy at all levels of English society in the period 1560–1640'.[50] According to Marshal McLuhan,[51] rising literacy levels and access to more and more printed material represented the death of oral culture and the triumph of print culture. However, printed material did not immediately replace oral communication. While the traditional storyteller began to disappear, the majority of people continued to receive news and information orally. The spoken word continued to play a crucial role in the process of public communication and the hearing public co-existed alongside the emerging reading public. Oral culture only now began to take the form of a literate person reading aloud to those who could not read. Ong refers to 'oral residue' being retained in the printed form: phrases, grammatical constructions or constructions more suited to speech than writing, to the ear instead of the eye. Silent reading struggled to emerge and printed news, including newspapers, was written to be read aloud well into the nineteenth century.

The rise of printed news

Printed news did not at first figure amongst the books, pamphlets, primers, tracts, ballads and songs, almanacs, handbills, posters, periodicals and journals that started to roll off the presses across Europe in the early sixteenth century. As the religious wars sparked by the Reformation waned in their intensity, printers turned to other material to keep themselves in business. From the middle of the century a variety of printed forms were published in the British Isles. Educational primers concerned with practical guidance appeared.[52] Reading was associated with self-improvement and, as the old feudal order collapsed, many people sought instruction and knowledge on what was considered good behaviour and character in the wake of the social changes brought about by the Reformation. Traders were exhorted to read 'forasmuch as it behoveth every good discreet merchant to have knowledge and cunning in reading and writing'.[53] Popular literature – often labelled street literature – in the form of the chapbook, jest book, ballads and pamphlets emerged.[54] Sex and violence were a staple part of the output of the printing press. Stories of the exploits of notorious villains sold well. In 1566 Thomas Harman's pamphlet on the criminal world in London became a 'best seller'.[55] Scandal sheets, 'lewd ballads', 'merry tales of Italie' and 'corrupted tales in Inke and Paper' satisfied a curiosity in 'the worldly society'.[56] The law and medicine provided further opportunities, and almanacs were another profitable area. Out of this miasma of printed material came the first products devoted to imparting news.

Printed news first appeared as single-sheet broadsides or small books indistinguishable from books on other material. These formats represented a continuation of what had previously circulated in manuscript form. For most of the sixteenth century news usually appeared in this form. Sold at fairs or outside churches, these publications tended to take one of two forms: ballads and proclamations.[57] Both these forms of news have their roots in oral culture and are associated with minstrels, heralds and criers. Proclamations were simply government propaganda, promoting the monarch's interpretation of events. As a single sheet, so that they could be easily affixed to walls, and in an era of limited literacy their contents would be disseminated further by word of mouth.[58] What was gleaned from proclamations was fairly restricted compared to the contents of ballads. These were usually printed songs which represented a direct connection between the oral and printed dissemination of news, information and entertainment. They emerged from the practice of the medieval period when songs were composed to comment on and commemorate events such as battles, feuds, murders, executions, tragedies and cataclysmic occurrences. Comical, political, romantic or simply lewd, these broadside ballads reflected the lives, attitudes and mores of ordinary people and were 'churned out in their thousands by anonymous hacks often working from dingy rooms at the back of print shops'.[59] They were purchased for domestic use or to be used in taverns for singing or recitation. Unlike the folk ballads of the medieval period they placed emphasis on current events. Whether it was the 'last words' and confessions of a condemned criminal or accounts of recent disasters, or marking the change in seasons or recounting the sexual exploits of a jilted suitor, ballads would turn topical events into rhyme to be sold by peddlers travelling throughout the realm. Unlike the minstrels before them, most of these sellers of ballads had little or no musical ability. Some may have received vocal training but mostly they were, in the words of one contemporary, 'idle youths, loathing honest labour', who printers would dispatch around the country 'with a dozen groatsworth of ballads' on a sale or return basis.[60]

While popular songs abounded, there were also narrative ballads which were 'recited rather than sung'.[61] As stories of current events these ballads can be said to be an early form of news communication. One of the earliest known publications of printed news in this form was a contemporary account of the Battle of Flodden between the English and Scots published in 1513. Such ballads were less a record of what had happened and more the expression of opinion about what had happened. Rather than relate details or provide a true account, they were used to provide interpretations of popular impressions or reactions to what had happened. Thus the account of the Battle of Flodden, while imparting some information about the military encounter, is primarily a celebration of the crushing of the Scots.[62] Notwithstanding their 'bias', the topicality of news ballads, their account of events and the kind of subject matter they dealt with, singles them out as precursors of the newspaper. Aimed at ordinary people, they were the 'lowest form of printing', requiring the 'minimum of equipment and of forethought and editorial judgement' and 'sold to the least critical class of reader'.[63] Deprived of the ability to print the most highly demanded books, which were the monopoly of a small number of officially sanctioned printers, ballads were an important source of revenue for many printers in the sixteenth and seventeenth centuries.

The vast amount of the news material published in the sixteenth century was *sensational* in tone, presentation and content. 'Wonderful and Strange Newes' in the form of murders, monsters, witches, dragons and spectacular occurrences prevailed.[64] Whether it was the 'true reporte of ... a monstrous childe borne at Muche Horkesley' or 'the tragicall and desperate end of Sir John Fites', printers sought to satisfy popular demand. Such stories did not have the immediacy of modern news, often being published months after the events were supposed to have happened, but they did produce a reaction we are familiar with today. The more educated and literate in society complained that the 'slightest pamphlet is nowadays more vendable than the works of the learnedest men'.[65] Disapproval of popular news stories was strongly expressed, with a clear distinction made between the quality of popular and serious works. Some of the characteristics of newsworthiness emerged, such as the qualities of being extraordinary, sensational and prodigious.[66]

Sensationalism

The extent to which sensational copy has formed part of the output of newspapers is a matter of conjecture within the literature. Jean Chalaby, in his influential book *The Invention of Journalism*, argues that sensationalism is the product of the increasing influence of the market and commercial criteria on the production of newspapers. Such copy originates from 'the urgent necessity for editors to attract readers and divert them from rivals'; to compete, newspapers had to embrace sensationalism, even if they were uneasy or critical of its uses and effects. For Chalaby, the emphasis on the sensational is a 'modern phenomenon', which contrasts with the view of press historian Mitchell Stephens, who sees it as timeless, citing examples from the early newsbooks in the late sixteenth and early seventeenth century, which carried reports of grisly murders, supernatural happenings, monstrous apparitions and catastrophic occurrences. Chalaby believes historians such as Stephens overstate their case and sensational copy was never as prevalent as they suggest. To support his point he cites the example of the radical press in the early nineteenth century, which carried a relatively small number of sensational-type stories and treated them in a very matter of fact, non-sensational way. Chalaby is correct to highlight the greater emphasis placed on sensational copy as a result of the increasing commercialisation of the newspaper industry. However, to characterise what appeared in the press prior to its commercial development in the mid-nineteenth century as serious and matter of fact is to ignore the substantial number of sensational reports that appeared. Much of what was 'sensation' in the sixteenth and seventeenth centuries was not the spectacle, shock and scandal we associate with the Victorian period but more connected to popular beliefs, superstition and the low levels of education of the day. It also ignores the fact that newspapers were a business activity before their industrialisation and commercialisation. Business and commerce have existed alongside moral instruction, information provision and political enlightenment throughout the history of newspapers. The balance has differed as a result of the prevailing social, economic and political conditions.

Source: Chalaby, *The Invention of Journalism*, 148 et passim;
Stephens, *A History of News*, 102–7.

Printed news ballads and newssheets were not newspapers. They were not published regularly and usually commented on a single event. As Mitchell Stephens[67] states, 'they each appeared only once. To report on one story, and they each had no identity separate from the particular news story they told'. The news they printed was not as perishable a commodity as it is with contemporary newspapers. Old stories turned up time and again: 'the taste for it (news) seems to have kept its zest rather longer'.[68] These publications also tended to focus on news from abroad, although ballads did relate domestic events such as the Northern Rising of 1569, the fate of Mary Queen of Scots, the Armada and the earthquake of 1580.[69] They were responding to the growing demand for news in the latter part of the sixteenth century. According to Sommerville,[70] nearly a quarter of all publications in England between 1591 and 1594 were devoted to current affairs. These irregular accounts were unable to satisfy the 'general thirst after news' that characterised the growth of post-Elizabethan Britain. In particular they failed to meet the requirement for information from the rapidly developing merchant class, whose influence rose with Britain's expansion as a commercial and trading power.[71]

 ## Censorship

The content of these 'relations' can be accounted for by the controls exercised over printers and presses. The growth in printed material was at first ignored by those who had most to lose through the communication of falsehoods. European monarchs initially saw the printing press as a 'harmless novelty'.[72] It was not long before the authorities recognised the threat posed and the opportunity presented by the new invention. They sought to control and manipulate what was printed. Censorship and licensing were their chosen instruments. The Tudors – as a result of the weaknesses of their claim to the throne of England – were quick to introduce a system of censorship. To stamp out dissenting opinion, especially the claims of the pretenders, Henry VII introduced in 1486 an edict against 'forged tidings and tales'.[73] His son was even more draconian. In the guise of 'defender of the faith' he introduced a list of prohibited books as well as a ban on all translations of the Bible into English. Henry VIII soon fell out with Rome and in his battle with the Pope to gain his divorce from Catherine of Aragon he is credited as mounting the 'first mass communications campaign of modern times', using the printing press as its agent.[74] Under his successors control of the printing press was extended. Initially a licensing and pre-publication censorship system operated under the jurisdiction of the Church. By the end of the century the State had usurped this role. To ply their trade printers had to be licensed by the Stationers' Company, which was granted a Royal Charter in 1557. Under Elizabeth I the number of printers, the content of all printed material and the number of copies of a publication printed were carefully controlled by the Company. Licences were granted only to those known for their 'skill, ability and good behaviour'.[75] The Tudors were highly effective in their efforts to control the flow of information. Printers shied away from controversy, religious and political. Some attempted to print works clandestinely; but most chose to 'take the hand of the monarch and respectfully, if occasionally rambunctiously, follow along'.[76] To avoid getting on the wrong side of the authorities they began to publish a wider array of material, in particular news.

Newsletters as public communication

The main vehicle for the dissemination of news and information in the sixteenth and for much of the seventeenth century was the handwritten newsletter. The transmission of news in this form remained an important form of written news until the eighteenth century: 'it was more plentiful than printed news; it was more accurate, less censored, and regarded as more authoritative'.[77] Its continued presence is seen as a significant factor in accounting for the slowness of the development of the newspaper between 1450 and 1650.[78] The fear of 'licentious discourse' worked in favour of the private newsletter. There was deep unease at the selling of news in case the affairs of State were hawked on the streets like any other commodity, available to anyone who wanted to purchase them.[79] Private newsletters were more acceptable. Their limited circulation and confinement to the better educated made them less susceptible to censorship.

These newsletters began to transmogrify from private correspondence into a public form of communication. Throughout the sixteenth century the generation of newsletters expanded enormously and newsletters writers began to be able to earn a living through providing the service. Venice was at the centre of the news business. There is a dispute amongst historians as to the exact nature of the newssheets that circulated in the city at this time but the earliest newssheets compiled for public consumption were in manuscript form. It is possible to argue that these publications played a crucial role in shaping the format of the first newspapers. Venice's importance as a centre of information was the result of its trading and diplomatic activity. The Venetian newssheet, referred to as a *gazette*, was 'a sheet of paper written by hand with a simple style of handwriting'.[80] They appear to have been produced regularly, once a month, and consist of accounts of events that took place outside Venice, dated and with an identified place of origin.[81] These might not have been newspapers as we know them, but the gazettes did influence the printed newsbooks that began to appear in Germany, Holland and Britain in the early seventeenth century. The roots of the newspaper lie as much in the emergence of newsletters as a public form of communication as in the arrival of the printing press.

The importance of newsletters declined as other forms of printed news appeared. At times of crisis and clampdowns on the printed press, there was a resurgence in their fortunes. For example, during the Restoration, when the Surveyor of the Press took monopoly control over the printing of news in Britain, newsletters became the only form of uncensored news. Henry Muddiman, the writer of what is often described as Britain's first newspaper, the officially sanctioned London *Gazette*, reverted to sending newsletters through the post to his clients when he lost his official position. His enterprise proved highly lucrative. Muddiman's subscribers could receive his letters as often as three times a week. Begun as a semi-official enterprise – the term 'Whitehall' appeared in the heading of each newsletter – Muddiman's correspondence became more critical of government policy.[82] Compared with previous newsletters, Muddiman's were cheap enough to be purchased by a broad cross-section of society; they could be bought at fairs or markets. The man appointed as the King's Surveyor of the Press, Sir Roger L'Estrange, who also took Muddiman's position at the *Gazette*, was also a celebrated and successful newsletter writer. The popularity of the newsletter remained after the Restoration, primarily to satisfy the demand from the provinces for news from London. The continued importance of the handwritten newsletter as a means to disseminate news is indicated by the effort of one news writer, Icabod Dawks, to reproduce the handwritten newsletter in printed form. (See Figure 1.1) Such imitation shows that printed news was often seen as a secondary form of news; as were the words of scorn poured on the handwritten newsletters by early newspaper and journal writers such as Joseph Addison, who could not believe that his fellow countrymen and women continued to read such an inferior form of news when printed publications were available.[83] The work routines of these early compilers of newsletters resembled the activities of modern journalists. They are described as men who 'rambled from coffee-room to coffee-room collecting reports, squeezed into ... the Old Bailey if there was an interesting trial ... obtained permission to the gallery of Whitehall and noticed how King and Duke looked'.[84]

DAWKS's News-Letter.

Sr London, August 3. 699.

Last night we received an Holland Mail, with some of these particulars following.

Lemberg, July 22. The Bassa Capigi, Treasurer General to the Grand Seignior, arrived at Caminieck on the 6th. instant, and gave Orders to the Governour to prepare to March out with his Garrison, and evacuate that Fortress to the Poles; whereupon the Turks have already begun to pack up their Baggage. The Hospodar of Walachia is also arrived upon the Frontiers, and is laying a Bridge over the Dniester, for the more convenient carrying of the Baggage. The Field Marshal of the Crown has sent to acquaint the King herewith.

Warsaw, July 28. The Diet is now like to have a good Issue, the King having Declared that he will maintain the Liberties of the People; that his Saxon Troops were all on their March homewards; That he will keep no Regiments by his Person, but only a Guard of 1200 Men at his own Charge, all of them Poles and Lithuanians: That if the Saxons do not March out of the Kingdom within the time limited, or return again on any Pretence whatsoever, without consent of the Republick, it shall be lawful for the Nobility to Assemble on Horseback without his Order, and Treat them as Publick Enemies. And in return hereof the Diet have obliged themselves to secure his Majesties Person with their utmost Power; that they will Severely Punish all that Act or but Speak against him: That all Libels against him shall be Burnt by the Hand of the Hangman; and the Authors of them serv'd in the same manner, if they can be apprehended. His Majesty will hold a Diet in Saxony in September; and its said he will bring his Queen hither with him when he returns.

Hamburg, August 4. Dr. Meyer, the Minister having Printed his Latin Oration upon the Marriage of the King of the Romans, on Cloth of Silver and Gold, and edg'd every Leaf of it with Point of Venice, which altogether cost this City 500 Crowns, he sent the same to the Emperour and King of the Romans, who have thereupon made the Doctor a Palsgrave, and given him his Patent free.

Hague, August 8. They write from Nieuenheusen in the County of Benthem, that 300 Neuburgers came to put the Countrey under Military Execution, for not submitting to the Popish Count; but that a Body of Dutch Soldiers advancing, who were sent by the States to support the Protestant Count, put the Neuburgers to flight, having kill'd a Lieutenant and wounded three others. Letters from Hungary say, that General Nehm, who was impower'd to be present at adjusting the Frontiers, falling into some Difference with the Bassa of Temeswaer, Struck him Dead from his Horse; whereupon some other Turkish Officers taking up the Quarrel, there were 30 or 40 Men Killed on both sides; however the Commissioners went on with adjusting the Frontiers. Admiral Aylmer with his Squadron is Sail'd from Messina to Leghorn: The French Gallies shunn'd meeting him, because they knew he would oblige them to Strike. A Million of Crowns has been collected at Rome by way of Alms, for the Irish Papists as is given out. The refreshing Rains we have had of late, have in some manner dissipated the Fevers which raged in this Country, especially at Amsterdam, where People suffered

very

Figure 1.1 Dawks's Newsletter, 3 August 1699

38

The resemblances between newspapers and newsletters should not be taken too far. Newsletters were the '*samizdat*' of their era, satisfying the thirst for news in an era where information was heavily circumscribed. Handwritten newsletters enabled the circulation of news that governments sought to keep secret. Subscribers were often urged to destroy their newsletters after they had consumed them. They were for the most part accessible to the few, and the few who had the wealth and resources to pay for the service they provided. Their flexibility enabled them to be tailored to individual subscribers and variations were produced to satisfy the needs, interests and prejudices of those who bought them. Above all, they were forms of private communication. Their popularity over printed news declined as political controls were relaxed and tolerance increased. They were also not able to respond to the growing public demand for more frequent news.

The first newspapers?

It was at the beginning of the seventeenth century that something which could be said to resemble a newspaper appeared. These early newspapers reflected the growing importance attached to the regular communication of events and happenings. This focus on imparting information within a time-based framework was an aspect of the rise of modern society. Time was not a significant feature of medieval life. It took many days, even weeks, for news of what we today know as crucial events in history to reach the cities, towns, villages and rural communities. For example, it is said news of the fall of Constantinople in 1453 took a month to reach Venice and three months to filter through to the rest of Europe. The growing interest in recording and 'telling' time led to the growth of time-based publications such as almanacs, astrological material and newspapers.[85] *Corantos* were the first attempt to devote a printed form of communication to the regular and timely publication of reports of and commentaries on the events of the day. The first *corantos* published in Britain supposedly came from the Netherlands. They were English translations of Dutch publications with stories about Britain removed to avoid the possibility of causing offence to the authorities. Much of their content was devoted to foreign news. What distinguished them from the one-off news ballads or newssheets was the emphasis they placed on the regularity of publication. As with handwritten newsletters, they sought to provide a continuous flow of news and information which updated what had previously been reported. They were published more or less weekly. News ballads and sheets were occasional publications, usually published by those with religious, ideological or political motives. *Corantos* were inspired by commercial considerations; regular publications concerned with practical and commercial information were seen as a means of making money. They had titles, a recognisable format and were dated with accompanying serial numbers. The importance of dates is illustrated by the changes to English-language versions to make the news appear as up-to-date as possible. Regular publication was not without its obstacles. The struggle for news was a precarious business and many *corantos* failed to find enough material to fill their pages, often missing their deadline. One of the earliest known *corantos* in the English language opened with an apology: 'The new tidings out of Italie are not yet com'.[86] Establishing and meeting the expectation of regular news was a major challenge.

Coranto

The word *coranto* is derived from the French world *'courante'*, which literally means 'running' and was used to describe a publication in which different items of news were run together to provide an account of events over a particular period of time. News of these events was 'current'. The notion of providing a constant flow of news appears to have originated in what is now Germany. In 1594 the *Mercurius Gallobeligus* was published in Cologne; written in Latin, it appeared biannually and lasted several decades, closing down in 1635. It was read throughout Europe, including in Britain. Similar publications began to appear elsewhere: Strasbourg and Augsburg in 1609, Basel in 1610, Frankfurt and Vienna in 1615, Hamburg in 1616, Berlin in 1617, Amsterdam in 1618 and Antwerp in 1619. Amsterdam, as a major port and trading centre, became the 'global nerve centre of the gathering and dissemination of news'.[87] The liberal environment of seventeenth-century Holland tolerated a wide diversity of ideas and opinions, which encouraged the growth of the news industry. By 1619 the city was publishing two weekly *corantos* and by 1620 was exporting others to France and Britain. The first known *coranto* published in Britain was Pieter van den Keere's single sheet which appeared in December 1620 and was published weekly until September 1621. The single black-letter folio sheets which characterised the first *corantos* in Britain were soon transformed into quarto roman letter newsbooks. Their quality was low, made up of four, eight, twelve, sixteen or even twenty-four poorly printed pages. Their circulation was very low; estimates put the maximum print run at 400 or 500 copies. It is not clear who bought and read them. At two pence a copy the price was too high for most people; they were primarily read by 'the principal gentry, lords, courtiers and men of all professions'. Often they were distributed alongside handwritten newsletters to those who subscribed. Their printers realised that serialisation would help them to sell more copies by retaining the loyalty of readers.

Source: Williams, *The English Newspaper*, 7–8; Herd, *The March of Journalism*, 12; Thompson, 1996, 66; Sommerville, *The News Revolution in England*, 28.

It was not long before home grown *corantos* emerged. The first known indigenous dated *coranto* is supposedly from September, 1622. *Corante, or Newes from Italy, Germanie, Hungaria, Bohemia, the Palestinate, France and the Low Countries* was a collection of articles translated from Dutch and German publications. (See Figure 1.2) *Coranto* printing was an uncertain occupation and a short-lived phenomenon, lasting for a couple of decades prior to the Civil War. During this time their format, style and regularity of publication underwent considerable changes.[88] But one characteristic remained constant: they were devoted to foreign events, primarily wars. The concentration on foreign at the expense of domestic news is often attributed to the desire to avoid conflict with the authorities. There is some debate about this. The extent to which *corantos* were subject to licensing and censorship is questioned. Their foreign origins led to the expectation that domestic events would receive limited attention.[89] There was also strong public demand for information about events in Europe, which was engulfed in the Thirty Years War.[90] According to one news writer of the period, 'the subject of Newes most enquired for, is for the most part of *Wars*, *Commotions* and *Troubles*, or the *Composing* of them'.[91] The pressure of filling pages was assisted by the availability of material that could be translated from foreign journals and publications.

The publisher of the oldest surviving indigenous *coranto* printed in Britain was only identified by his initials, N.B. – either Nathaniel Butter or Nicholas Bourne. Both men were printers and played a critical role in the development of Britain's first newspapers. The 'stubborn dedication' of *coranto* printers to putting out regular news is often singled out by commentators, who refer to the 'excitements and challenges' of 'what must have seemed the most hopeless of causes'.[92] There was little status in what they did: dismissed as 'newsmongers' and 'dishonest swindlers', they were pilloried by playwrights such as Ben Jonson, who accused them of a 'dereliction, a degradation of the proper function of a writer'.[93] It was unlikely that they gained or even sought any political influence by what they did. Printers such as Butter and Bourne attempted to secure official approval only because that could enable them to obtain the monopoly to publish certain material, a potentially lucrative enterprise. The more likely motivation of these printers was monetary reward. Publishing newspapers by themselves provided little reward, but printers such as Bourne, Butter and Thomas Archer did not limit themselves to printing news. The *corantos* were never more than a small part of their wider publishing and business activities.

The title page of the *corantos* hid the lack of organisation that greeted the reader on their inside pages. The printer was responsible for their production, content and distribution; journalism would remain a 'mere appendage of printing' until well into the eighteenth century.[94] The lack of editorial intelligence meant that the *coranto* was a hodgepodge of unedited translations of material from continental publications, laid out randomly, attributed to other publications and presented in no order of importance. There were no

The 30. of May.

WEEKLY
NEVVES FROM
ITALY, GERMANIE,
HVNGARIA, BOHEMIA,
the Palatinate, France, and
the Low Countries.

*Tranſlated out of the Low
Dutch Copie.*

LONDON:
Printed by E. A. for *Nicholas Bourne* and *Thomas Archer,*
and are to be ſold at their Shops at the *Exchange,*
and in *Popes-head Pallace.*
1622.

Figure 1.2 *Weekly Newes from Italy,* 30 May 1622

42

headings provided to assist the reader to navigate through the pages. Some attempts can be detected to turn *corantos* into an 'attractive and reasonably coherent publication', with the provision of more personal accounts orga-nised around stories that appealed to the reader.[95] Thomas Gainsford is credited with this transformation; as the first editor, between 1622 and 1624 he brought a 'sense of organisation and of perspective' to the news by initi-ating the compilation of 'a "digest" of discreet items into a continuous smooth narrative'.[96] Gainsford introduced a more conversational style into his editorials and the presentation of news, drawing diverse accounts into con-tinuous stories.[97] He attempted to engage with critics, responding to accu-sations of editorial bias,[98] and tailored his output to the expectations and demands of his audience. He wanted 'every weeke to please or pleasure you and afford such novelty as the season affordeth us'.[99] Gainsford realised that for news to flourish readers had to believe in it and buy it; his innovations in presentation and content reflected this. However, his effort to make news engaging and acceptable was not long lasting. The publishing syndicate that employed him, which included Bourne and Butter and held a monopoly of printed news production between 1622 and 1624, broke up when changes in foreign policy led to foreign news becoming less lucrative.[100] Gainsford's death from the plague in the summer of the same year brought to an end the attempts to change presentation and style to get closer to the reader. Whether it was a matter of cost or the inability to find someone who matched Gainsford's skills and talent, a successor was not appointed and *corantos* reverted back to a more literary style and relied again on the simple translation of foreign news and letters.[101]

Corantos were produced on a small, wooden hand press which had hardly altered since the day William Caxton introduced the printing press into Britain. An advantage of these presses was that they could easily be dismantled, so that a printer was able to quickly escape detection by the authorities. Official hostility made the distribution of *corantos* a challenge. Men and women were employed as 'news boys' to hawk bundles of papers through the narrow streets of London, avoiding the clutches of government agents.[102] By 1628 the efforts of the printers were beginning to wilt. The number of issues fell and in 1630 the rate was one every three weeks.[103] The reversal of for-tunes is attributed to the declining interest in the Protestant cause and the German wars.[104] Censorship was tightened in the early 1630s and Bourne and Butter's publications were banned, following the alleged slander of the Duke of Olivares. Declining public trust as a result of the publication of false reports of Protestant successes in Germany was also a factor. In 1632 *coranto* publication was halted by the Star Chamber, at a time when Bourne was complaining that he was losing considerable sums of money. Revived in 1638, the days of the *coranto* were already numbered. Bourne had abandoned the market, Archer ended up as a pauper and only Butter attempted to continue the business. The Civil War finally swept away the market for the *coranto* and publication was discontinued in 1641. It was superseded by newsbooks which responded to the growing public thirst for domestic news.[105] Newsbooks differed very little in format from the *corantos* they succeeded; except that their 'periodicity of publication was more constant' and they contained domestic as well as foreign news.[106]

✳ The Civil War and the rise of the newsbook

The year 1641 was the beginning of a period of major upheaval in society which included the Civil War (1640–5), the execution of the King (1649) and the establishment of the Protectorate (1655–60). The collapse of the ability and capacity of the State to regulate and control the publication of printed material corresponded with a boom in printed news. The breakdown of absolute monarchy fuelled the unprecedented growth of political expression and debate. In a time of considerable political strife people desired news and information and sought out political ideas and opinions to make sense of events. The vast outpouring of printed news, information, comment and opinion reflected the urgency with which the parties involved in the Civil War attempted to convince people of the rightness of their cause. The printed material that was churned out – and it is estimated that 30,000 pamphlets, journals and folio sheets were published in a single year – took many forms. The 'newsbook' was one of these forms and it is described by historians as the 'immediate predecessor of the newspaper'.[107]

The first newsbook appeared in November 1641, published by a book-seller named John Thomas. *Heads of Severall Proceedings in this Present Parliament from the 22 November to the 29, 1641* presented a weekly account of parliamentary debates and speeches. Later renamed *A Perfect Diurnall of the Passages in Parliament*, it was the first printed periodical to contain domestic news – previously this had only appeared in manuscript newsletters. It was written by Samuel Pecke, who, unlike his predecessors working for *corantos*, would 'go out and find his own news'.[108] Thomas's publication spawned a vast number of competitors; within seven weeks five weeklies reporting the proceedings of Parliament were on sale in London.[109] There were 'many newsbooks produced by different publishers, competing with and counter-feiting each other, struggling to find a foothold in a potentially lucrative market', including, by August 1642, several different *Perfect Diurnalls* and one *True and Perfect Diurnall*.[110] By 1644 it is estimated that Londoners could pick from a dozen weekly newsbooks made up of eight or more pages.[111] There is dispute amongst historians over the reasons for the rapid emergence of the newsbook,[112] but it had a profound impact on the development of the newspaper.

The newsbook gradually evolved throughout the 1640s. The early newsbooks, such as *A Perfect Diurnall*, were 'sober' and provided the 'driest and most matter-of-fact' accounts of parliamentary events.[113] The printing of parliamentary speeches and texts was news and it was controversial. It was also facilitated by a 'revolution in information technology ... which radically expanded the possibilities of reportorial journalism'.[114] Forerunners of short-hand – systematically developed as a reportorial device in the nineteenth century – developed during the Civil War. Systems of symbolic representation enabled a small number of people to take down a speech nearly at the rate at which it was spoken. Most of these people were employed as secretaries to those in power, but they began to publish their accounts of the proceedings of trials, scaffold speeches, sermons, as well as other events to which they were eye-witnesses. These accounts appeared in the newsbooks, distinguishing them from the *corantos*. Claims to give a factual account of events were made. While some form of accurate reporting was aspired to, the newsbooks were not impartial. Most of the early publications were supportive of Parliament, which was happy for them to relate what was said and what happened within their confines, as long as the accounts of speeches were approved by the speaker. *A Perfect Diurnall* informed its readers that they would be 'informed onely of such things that are of credit, and of some part of the proceedings of one or both houses of Parliament fit to be divulged or such other news that has been certified by Letters from the Army, and other parts from persons of speciall trust'.[115]

Newsbooks may have initially sought some form of neutrality in the struggle between Crown and Parliament but their content was primarily an extension of politics and diplomacy. As political debate descended into out-right warfare, notions of neutrality disappeared. The appearance of the 'mer-curies' reflected the desire to 'influence public opinion by providing partisan commentary on the news'.[116] Britain's political elite were divided and they sought to mobilise the public to support their cause. The vehicle they used was the newsbook. Publications such as the *Mecurius Aulicus*, *Mercurius Poli-ticus* and *Mecurius Britanicus*,[117] The *Scotish Dove* and the *Moderate* were established as official or semi-official mouthpieces of the parties and factions that were emerging within the ranks of both sides, particularly Parliament. Presbyterians, Baptists, Ranters, Levellers, and Fifth Monarchists required out-lets for their version of what had occurred and what should occur. The two most famous 'mercuries' were the *Mercurius Aulicus*, a leading royalist news-book edited by Sir John Berkenhead, and the strongly pro-Parliament *Mer-curius Britanicus*, edited by one of the early pioneers of modern journalism, Marchamont Nedham. The newsbooks were an essential ingredient in the development of popular politics in this era, which was conducted by placard, petition and demonstration as people from all walks of life had an opportu-nity to participate in public discourse and debate, thereby assisting the emergence of a democratic culture in Britain.[118]

Most of the output of the newsbooks was propaganda, part of the struggle between the King and Parliament. However, elevated discussion of freedom, rights and duties co-existed alongside 'low trivialities and gross personal abuse'.[119] For example, Nedham and Berkenhead not only challenged the veracity of each other's accounts but also demonised opponents by focussing on atrocities, exaggerating sinister schemes, identifying personal scandals and corruption as well as the foibles of individuals.[120] Nedham described Berkenhead as 'a mathematicall liar, that framest lies of all dimensions long, broad and profound lies ... the quibbling prick louse ... a knowne notorious forger ... an underling pimpe to the whore of Babylon and thy conscience an arrant prostitute for base ends'.[121] Intemperate, full of invective and highly polemical, these newsbooks were happy to carry personal slights alongside high politics. News of the Civil War was subsumed within propaganda, political intrigue and personal abuse.

The competition between newsbooks was intense; over 300 titles were purportedly launched in the 1640s and 1650s, most lasting a very short period of time.[122] To retain readers they would appeal to specific audiences, seeking to attract their loyalty. It is important to stress that the publishers and contributors to newsbooks were not solely motivated by their political principles. Making money was also an inducement, as illustrated by the career of John Crouch, whose publications combined news with smut and sexual innuendo.[123] Newsbooks became a major source of information in the mid-seventeenth century but it is important to point out that news still reached the people in a plethora of other ways. The Civil War galvanised the dissemination of manuscript newsletters, ballads and pamphlets, which played a crucial role in furnishing people with news. The intensity of political debate also led to the development of 'pictorial propaganda' in the form of political prints; as many as 150 such prints from 1641 survive.[124] There was an upsurge in political graffiti, and oral communication still held considerable sway, as shown in the Putney Debates of 1647. However, the emergence of the newsbook represented a crucial step forward in the establishment of the newspaper. It was the first regular publication dedicated to domestic news and comment, establishing periodicity which would differentiate the newspaper. Appearing on a specific day, usually once a week newsbooks displayed a strong sense of continuity. They laid down some of the key features that would distinguish the modern newspaper – for some commentators 'regular English journalism began with the Civil War'.[125]

The physical appearance of the newsbooks did not differ significantly from that of the *corantos*. They remained small-format book-like publications usually composed of eight pages.[126] One significant change in their appearance occurred on the title page. Newsbooks incorporated news into the title page. What was innovative was to be found inside the covers of the newsbooks. Not only did domestic news reports and comment appear regularly, but so did many of the features we associate with the modern newspaper, such as leading articles, advertisements, illustrations and even an agony column. According to Joseph Frank, many of the basic techniques of political journalism, such as the planted item, the inadequately denied rumour and the inside story, were developed.[127] The newsbooks thrived in the 1640s but their existence was precarious. They faced problems of production and an intensely competitive market for news. But the pressures brought to bear on editors and publishers by the authorities were the most serious obstacle they encountered. The system of State censorship that collapsed in 1640 did not disappear altogether, as some historical accounts of the period imply. Parliament had an interest in encouraging the reporting of its proceedings and critical commentaries of the Crown and its authority. However, the Stationers' Company continued to lobby for Parliament to restrict the number of printing presses and enforce copyright through prosecution. It was particularly anxious to reinstate the monopoly it had over the presses and printing. Parliament began to respond to such demands as the popularity of the royalist newsbook *Mecurius Aulicus* increased and as more dissenting voices and opinions began to emerge from within the ranks of the parliamentary cause. Attempts were made to reintroduce pre-publication censorship in 1643, only to fail because of the disorder of the period. Printers, publishers and editors were nevertheless subjected to more pressure; fines and prison sentences were dished out, making the life of the men and women of the newsbooks increasingly precarious. Parliamentary purges brought a sudden end to some newsbooks, not always to the dismay of their competitors, who sometimes welcomed weekly pamphlets being 'contracted into a shorter number'.[128]

The pressures also influenced the style, tone and rhetoric of the newsbooks. Discretion often prevailed and language and political argument were sometimes moderated. Jason Peachey[129] describes how the content and style of *Mercurius Britanicus* was shaped by parliamentary intervention. The editor of *Mercurius Britanicus* was Marchamont Nedham, one of the most independent voices of the period and someone who revelled in his attempts to avoid prosecution and jail. *Mercurius Britanicus* throughout its existence operated under a licensing system which meant that its content was perused and vetted by an appointee of Parliament.[130] The licenser regularly changed copy, although the ability of Parliament to enforce its decisions waxed and waned. *Mercurius Britanicus* – as other newsbooks – often shifted its stance on crucial matters of the day, changing political direction, including the occasional *volte-face* on particular issues as pressure was exerted by the political authorities.[131] Civil War newsbooks were the product of their authors and editors but they operated within the constraints imposed by the shifting controls exercised by licensers and the political grandees of the day. These controls were tightened with the passing in 1649 of the Act against Unlicensed and Scandalous Books and Pamphlets and became almost absolute in 1655 when Oliver Cromwell banned all newsbooks and used the army to rigorously enforce their proscription. Censorship became effective. No new newsbooks were published in the remaining years of Cromwell's military dictatorship except those officially sanctioned by the regime. Official newsbooks recognised that the public thirst for news had to be satisfied as well as Cromwell's desire to see his view of events prevail. Ironically the officially sanctioned newsbooks were run by none other than Marchamont Nedham.[132]

The Daily Courant.

Wednesday, March 11. 1702.

From the Harlem Courant, Dated March 18. N. S.

Naples, Feb. 22.

ON Wednesday last, our New Viceroy, the Duke of Escalona, arriv'd here with a Squadron of the Galleys of Sicily. He made his Entrance drest in a French habit; and to give us the greater Hopes of the King's coming hither, went to Lodge in one of the little Palaces, leaving the Royal one for his Majesty. The Marquis of Grigni is also arriv'd here with a Regiment of French.

Rome, Feb. 25. In a Military Congregation of State that was held here, it was Resolv'd to draw a Line from Ascoli to the Borders of the Ecclesiastical State, thereby to hinder the Incursions of the Transalpine Troops. Orders are sent to Civita Vecchia to fit out the Galleys, and to strengthen the Garrison of that Place. Signior Casali is made Governor of Perugia. The Marquis del Vasto, and the Prince de Caserta continue still in the Imperial Embassador's Palace; where his Excellency has a Guard of 50 Men every Night in Arms. The King of Portugal has desir'd the Arch-Bishoprick of Lisbon, vacant by the Death of Cardinal Sousa, for the Infante his second Son, who is about 11 Years old.

Vienna, Mar. 4. Orders are sent to the 4 Regiments of Foot, the 2 of Cuirassiers, and to that of Dragoons, which are broke up from Hungary, and are on their way to Italy, and which consist of about 14 or 15000 Men, to hasten their March thither with all Expedition. The 6 new Regiments of Hussars that are now raising, are in so great a forwardness, that they will be compleat, and in a Condition to march by the middle of May. Prince Lewis of Baden has written to Court, to excuse himself from coming thither, his Presence being so very necessary, and so much desir'd on the Upper-Rhine.

Francfort, Mar. 12. The Marquis d'Uxelles is come to Strasburg, and is to draw together a Body of some Regiments of Horse and Foot from the Garisons of Alsace; but will not lessen those of Strasburg and Landau, which are already very weak. On the other hand, the Troops of His Imperial Majesty, and his Allies, are going to form a Body near Germesheim in the Palatinate, of which Place, as well as of the Lines at Spires, Prince Lewis of Baden is expected to take a View, in three or four days. The English and Dutch Ministers, the Count of Frise, and the Baron Vander Meer, and likewise the Imperial Envoy Count Lowenstein, are gone to Nordlingen, and it is hop'd that in a short time we shall hear from thence of some favourable Resolutions for the Security of the Empire.

Liege, Mar. 14. The French have taken the Cannon de Longie, who was Secretary to the Dean de Mean, out of our Castle, where he has been for some time a Prisoner; and have deliver'd him to the Provost of Maubeuge, who has carry'd him from hence, but we do not know whither.

Paris, Mar. 13. Our Letters from Italy say, That most of our Reinforcements were Landed there; that the Imperial and Ecclesiastical Troops seem to live very peaceably with one another in the Country of Parma, and that the Duke of Vendome, as he was visiting several Posts, was within 100 Paces of falling into the Hands of the Germans. The Duke of Chartres, the Prince of Conti, and several other Princes of the Blood, are to make the Campaign in

Flanders under the Duke of Burgundy; and the Duke of Maine is to Command upon the Rhine.

From the Amsterdam Courant, Dated Mar. 18.

Rome, Feb. 25. We are taking here all possible Precautions for the Security of the Ecclesiastical State in this present Conjuncture, and have desir'd to raise 3000 Men in the Cantons of Switzerland. The Pope has appointed the Duke of Berwick to be his Lieutenant-General, and he is to Command 6000 Men on the Frontiers of Naples: He has also settled upon him a Pension of 6000 Crowns a year during Life.

From the Paris Gazette, Dated Mar. 18. 1702.

Naples, Febr. 17. 600 French Soldiers are arriv'd here, and are expected to be follow'd by 3400 more. A Courier that came hither on the 14th. has brought Letters by which we are assur'd that the King of Spain designs to be here towards the end of March; and accordingly Orders are given to make the necessary Preparations against his Arrival. The two Troops of Horse that were Commanded to the Abruzzo are posted at Pescara with a Body of Spanish Foot, and others in the Fort of Montorio.

Paris, March. 18. We have Advice from Toulon of the 5th instant, that the Wind having long stood favourable, 12000 Men were already sail'd for Italy, that 2500 more were Embarking, and that by the 15th it was hoped they might all get thither. The Count d'Estrees arriv'd there on the Third instant, and set all hands at work to fit out the Squadron of 9 Men of War and some Fregats, that are appointed to carry the King of Spain to Naples. His Catholick Majesty will go on Board the *Thunderer*, of 110 Guns.

We have Advice by an Express from Rome of the 18th of February, That notwithstanding the pressing Instances of the Imperial Embassadour, the Pope had Condemn'd the Marquis del Vasto to lose his Head and his Estate to be confiscated, for not appearing to Answer the Charge against him of Publickly Scandalizing Cardinal Janson.

ADVERTISEMENT.

IT will be found from the Foreign Prints, which from time to time, as Occasion offers, will be mention'd in this Paper, that the Author has taken Care to be duly furnish'd with all that comes from Abroad in any Language. And for an Assurance that he will not, under Pretence of having Private Intelligence, impose any Additions of feign'd Circumstances to an Action, but give his Extracts fairly and Impartially; at the beginning of each Article he will quote the Foreign Paper from whence 'tis taken, that the Publick, seeing from what Country a piece of News comes with the Allowance of that Government, may be better-able to Judge of the Credibility and Fairness of the Relation: Nor will he take upon him to give any Comments or Conjectures of his own, but will relate only Matter of Fact; supposing other People to have Sense enough to make Reflections for themselves.

This Courant (as the Title shews) will be Publish'd Daily: being design'd to give all the Material News as soon as every Post arrives: and is confin'd to half the Compass, to save the Publick at least half the Impertinences, of ordinary News-Papers.

LONDON. Sold by E. Mallet, next Door to the *King's-Arms* Tavern at *Fleet-Bridge.*

The *Daily Courant*, 11 March 1702

2

NEWSPAPERS FOR THE FEW

Politics, the press and partisanship, 1660–1789

They did not grub about for news stories, hovering in the extremities of favoured places where the latest rumours, scandals, and hints at forthcoming Government policy were likely to be bandied injudiciously about. Their forte was the social and/or political essay, an experimental trial and testing of an argument in a public setting – a form of newspaper literature today preserved in the leading article or editorial.[1]

The daily newspaper first appeared in 1702. Newspapers thrived as people enjoyed their newly found freedom of expression following the collapse of state censorship in 1695. Weekly, tri-weekly and daily newspapers arrived and departed at a rapid rate in London, but by the 1750s the London press had established itself at the heart of national life and politics. Weekly newspapers outside the capital city began to emerge: between 1714 and 1725, 22 provincial newspapers were born and the total number is estimated to have increased from 25 in 1735, rising to 35 in 1760 and around 50 in 1780.[2] This led the *British Observer* in 1733 to report 'a general complaint that there is already such a glut of newspapers and weekly pamphlets'.[3] Scotland produced another nine newspapers by the end of the century, although Wales had to wait until the start of the nineteenth century for its first home-grown newspaper. More significantly, the annual consumption of newspapers rose dramatically, from an estimated 2.5 million in 1712–13 to 7.3 million in 1750 and 12.6 million in 1775. This expansion represented the birth of the modern newspaper and many of the features we associate today with the newspaper.

A leading historian of the eighteenth-century press emphasises that the 'form and character of the newspaper' were established by 'a series of adjustments focused in the first half of the century'.[4] The first adjustment was to the State, which, following the 'inundation' of newspapers in the late seventeenth and early eighteenth centuries, resorted to the law and taxation to damp down the flow of news and information in the press. The laws of blasphemy, sedition and libel were used by successive governments to influence what was reported. The system of press taxation introduced in 1712

49

remained the main tool to control the press until the mid-nineteenth century. These taxes had a profound impact on the newspaper, the kind of reporting it undertook, as well as its shape and appearance. The aim of the government was to put newspapers out of business by taxing them beyond the means of ordinary people. This did not happen – as the thirst for news propelled the press forward. What contemporaries called the 'furious itch for novelty' could not be contained. Nevertheless the growth of the press was arrested and the kind of newspaper that emerged was strongly shaped by these taxes. They ensured that many newspapers operated at the financial margins, relying on individual or party bribes to print 'puffs' or suppress gossip to keep on publishing. Operating at the margins meant that there were insufficient resources for news gathering, so opinion, comment and essays were important components of these newspapers. It also ensured the press was closely allied to politics, with individual titles usually serving the interests of a politician or political party or political faction. Newspapers in eighteenth-century Britain were organs of political opinion and their publishers and contributors were men – and sometimes women – who could be bribed, bought and paid off.

Newspapers also had to adjust to the demands of the marketplace. The rise of the 'leisured' class increased the purchasing power of a section of British society. As the century progressed, newspapers became increasingly profitable ventures, so much so that an effective newspaper entrepreneur could, as Jeremy Black[5] observes, counteract fiscal constraints imposed by the State by increasing readership and/or advertising revenue. Advertising gradually became an important source of revenue; as early as 1705 one of the leading newspaper figures of the period, Daniel Defoe, could comment that 'the principal support of all the public papers now on foot depends on advertisements'.[6] More advertisements were carried and newspapers started to specialise in particular kinds of advertising. The organisation of the newspaper changed as sales, profits and revenues rose. The early eighteenth-century newspaper was typically a one-man operation; at most it involved a handful of people. By the end of the century more and more people were participating in the production of the newspaper, with the employment of specialist writers and news gatherers. The content diversified as news and politics were complemented by other kinds of stories. A more dynamic entrepreneurial culture pervaded the business, with a corresponding shift from politics to profits in determining the content and composition of the newspaper.

The term 'newspaper' was first used in the 1670s but what constituted the 'newspaper' took on a variety of formats, styles and content for most of the eighteenth century.[7] It is not until the 1780s that it is possible to see the basic shape of the modern British newspaper emerge. Regular publication, a particular appearance and a specific mix of stories developed from responses to the political, social, economic and cultural change in eighteenth-century Britain. Standardisation in the form and character of the newspaper was a response to commercialisation. Newspapers became businesses in their own right, transforming the relationship between them and their readers. Newspapers increasingly claimed to speak on behalf of the public, defined as their readers, rather than parties, factions or sectional interests.

The collapse of censorship

The starting point for the proliferation of printed news, including newspapers, newssheets and pamphlets, is usually seen as the demise of direct censorship. Following the restoration of the monarchy in 1660, strong control was exerted over the dissemination of newspapers and other printed material. Oliver Cromwell's rigid system of censorship was retained by the returning Stuarts and gradually tightened. Sir Roger L'Estrange was appointed Surveyor of the Press, exercising control over the printing and licensing of newspapers. An ardent Royalist who had been sentenced to death by Parliament, L'Estrange had a clear view of his duty – to hunt down heretical and seditious publications and make an example of those who sought to publish them. His zealous prosecution of unlicensed printing led in 1663 to the execution of John Twyn for seditious libel. In passing sentence on unlicensed publishers that same year, the Lord Chief Justice emphasised the need for examples to be made: 'The press is grown so common, and men take the Boldness to print whatever is brought to them, let it concern whom it will; it is high time Examples be made'.[8] L'Estrange's efforts to suppress the press were supported by the Licensing Act passed in June 1662. The Act sought to prevent the 'frequent Abuses in printing seditious, treasonable and unlicensed Books and Pamphlets' and regulate 'Printing and Printing Presses'. Printing was restricted to the Universities of Oxford and Cambridge and to the master printers of the Stationers' Company in London. No new printers would be licensed unless the number fell below a stipulated level and no book or pamphlet could be printed unless it was entered into the Stationers' Register with a full disclosure of its content.[9] Licensers were appointed to assess the loyalty of all printed material; copy had to be submitted and approved by a licenser before it could be published and every printer had to put his name to what he printed and provide the name of the author if so required by the licenser. To enforce the licensing system the Act granted general warrants which enabled the government 'to search all houses and shops where they shall know, or upon some probable reasons suspect, any books or papers to be printed, bound or stitched'.[10] Such power enabled L'Estrange to exercise a considerable hold over what appeared in Restoration newspapers.

Not that many newspapers appeared in this period. L'Estrange, as remuneration for his work, requested from the King 'the right to publish all news, and all bills and advertisements'.[11] On his return to Britain, Charles II had appointed Henry Muddiman as his official news writer. Muddiman's publications, *Mercurius Publicus* and *Parliamentary Intelligencer*, became the officially sanctioned newspapers of the early years of the Restoration. They were 'Published by Authority' and had access to the corridors of power. Their content reflected their official status. They were full of official proclamations, notices and statements. Bob Clarke[12] outlines the content of the edition of the *Mercurius Publicus* of the first week of February 1661, which opened with the 'Proclamation for the Restraint of Killing, Dressing and Eating of Flesh in Lent or on Fish-Days' followed by notes of sermons preached before the Scottish Parliament, the text of two Acts of Parliament and a proclamation of the Lords and Council of Ireland. The official pronouncements were broken up by a page of advertisements, including for 'those so famous lozenges or Pectorals' made by 'Theophilius Buckworth of Mile-end Green', and the sixteen pages concluded with what could be considered the only piece of news, that the heads of the three main regicides were placed on poles in Westminster Hall.

The output of Muddiman's official newspapers did not mean he had no interest in the news. More newsworthy items appeared in his manuscript newsletters service which he set up for subscribers at the same time. Exempt from proscription by the law, these newsletters contained 'any items that he could not risk publishing in his newspapers'.[13] He set up a nationwide network of correspondents to provide a regular supply of information, incorporating the most newsworthy into the newsletters, which were sent free through the post[14] – a privilege of his official position – to subscribers for £5 per annum. His enterprise was highly lucrative and continued to be the main source of news at this time. However, his official monopoly did not last for long. It was taken over by L'Estrange in 1662. A struggle between L'Estrange and Muddiman ensued which led Muddiman to take advantage of the Court's withdrawal to Oxford to escape the plague in London and launch the bi-weekly *Oxford Gazette*, a direct challenge to L'Estrange's monopoly. Muddiman's venture succeeded as long as the King remained at Oxford. The Surveyor of the Press had to be in London to do his job and the Court was reluctant to take his newspapers for fear of catching the plague.[15] With the plague receding in 1666 and the Court returning to London, Muddiman's involvement came to an end and for the rest of his career he confined his activities to the running of his newsletters. However, his legacy is seen as the production of Britain's first newspaper.

Renamed the *London Gazette*, it was the first news periodical to break from the format of the newsbooks. It did this in terms of its appearance rather than its content. Muddiman concentrated on foreign and shipping news as well as the usual official notices. Foreign news was an important component of newspapers throughout the eighteenth century. Much of it was gained by the *Gazette* from official sources such as ministries and ambassadors. Material would continue to be taken from foreign papers which arrived in the ports of

Britain. Storms could stop such news, often leaving papers short of material. Shipping news was commonly gained from interviews with sea captains, crews and passengers, a source many considered uncertain.[16] One innovation of Muddiman's *Gazette* was the inclusion of weekly Bills of Mortality which listed all the deaths in London and their causes, something which became a regular feature of the popular press.[17] The radical innovation was in the layout. The *Gazette* was printed on a single sheet of paper and divided its reports into two columns which could be read quickly. The reader no longer had to turn over the pages to follow stories but could scan the news columns quickly. This reflected Muddiman's awareness of his readers, who he believed devoted only limited time to examining his newspaper. The *Gazette* may have given rise to the first recorded use of the word 'newspaper' but it was a 'most unsatisfactory newspaper'; a 'dull read whose only saving grace was its brevity'.[18] It remained Britain's sole newspaper for thirteen years, promoting social harmony after the years of turmoil represented by the Civil War and Protectorate. However, increasingly it ceased to satisfy the growing demand for news, which was by the end of Charles's reign the prerogative of the newsletters.

The Licensing Act and the post of Surveyor of the Press remained in place until 1695 but the ability of the authorities to control and censor the printed word began to unravel from 1679. This was due as much to the ineffectiveness of the system in dealing with the growing volume of printed material as it was to any increase in the commitment to press freedom. James Curran[19] draws attention to the State's lack of the necessary apparatus 'to control production, monitor output, regulate distribution, stop the import of prohibited printed material and neutralize or destroy dissident elements in society'. Direct censorship as championed by L'Estrange became unenforceable. The inability of the system to cope was apparent in 1679 when Parliament in an astonishing oversight allowed the Licensing Act to lapse. This is accounted for by the confusion surrounding the struggle for the right of succession to the throne. To prevent the passing of legislation excluding his brother's succession Charles dissolved Parliament, forgetting that it had not renewed the Licensing Act.[20] Between 1679 and 1685 several unlicensed newsbooks and newssheets appeared. Attempts to restrict their publication failed. With James's accession in 1685 licensing and the state monopoly of the press were reintroduced, only to be swept away with his overthrow by the Glorious Revolution of 1688. The new monarch, the Dutchman William of Orange, commanded the popular support his predecessor lacked. L'Estrange was removed but his office remained. However, William was secure enough to allow greater freedom for the printers and publishers and in 1695 the Licensing Act died a natural death; 'it died of senility and neglect'.[21] The criticism levelled by contemporaries at the system did not dwell on its restriction of liberty but on the commercial unfairness of the monopoly and the inefficiency of censorship. This reflected the views of the readers of printed news and newspapers, who were increasingly drawn from the ranks of those involved in commerce, business, trade and manufacturing.

The arrival of the daily newspaper

The first decade of the eighteenth century witnessed an exponential increase in the number of newspaper titles as anyone could print and publish material without permission. By 1709 eighteen papers were published regularly in London, of which the most significant was the *Daily Courant*, Britain's first daily newspaper. The advent of tri-weeklies and dailies quickened the pace of regular publication. Launched in 1702 by an E. Mallet, presumed by some to be Elizabeth Mallet, the initial version did not last very long. Revived under Samuel Buckley, the *Daily Courant* was not very different from most of the newspapers of the period other than in its daily appearance. It was a single-sheet folio with advertisements printed on the reverse side, except on exceptional news days.[22] Many of the news stories were translated from Dutch and French journals and newspapers. Buckley was a bookseller and gifted linguist, which was helpful in getting stories from abroad.[23] Perhaps what was different was Buckley's keenness to ensure that his newspaper reported factual news. Despite being a Whig, he placed emphasis on ensuring the credibility of what appeared. His was the first newspaper to consistently identify the place and source of publication of reports. He stated:

> at the beginning of each Article he will quote the Foreign Paper whence it is taken, that the Publick, seeing from what Country a piece of News comes with the Allowance of that Government, may be better able to Judge of the Credibility and Fairness of the Relation … Nor will he take it upon him to give any Comments or Conjectures of his own, but will relate only Matter of Fact; supposing other People have Sense enough to make reflections for themselves.
>
> (*Daily Courant*, 21 April 1702)[24]

Buckley's professed desire to establish the factual basis of his reports singled him out from his competitors, who were inclined to 'provide a variety of versions of unproven material for the benefit of ideological factions'.[25] He gave up running the *Courant* in 1714 but during his tenure he showed that newspaper publishing could be a profitable venture. The daily newspaper increased in popularity during the eighteenth century as the demand for more up-to-date news developed. The *Daily Courant* eventually became a four-page publication with a circulation of around 800, surviving until 1735.[26]

Newspapers of 1709: day of publication and title

Daily

The Daily Courant

Monday, Wednesday and Friday

The Supplement
The British Apollo
The General Remark
The Female Tatler
The General Postscript

Wednesdays only

The Observator

Tuesday, Thursday and Saturday

The London Gazette
The Post Man
The Postboy
The Flying Post
The Review
The Tatler
The Rehearsal
The Evening Post
The Whisperer
The Postboy Junior
The City Intelligencer

The rapid growth of newspapers, the lure of making money and the promise of regular work attracted a number of talented writers into the business. Richard Steele, Joseph Addison and Daniel Defoe were three outstanding individuals who played a key role in shaping the practice of journalism in Britain. While they reflected the spirit of their times, each of them exploited his skills and abilities to have a lasting impact on the character of the British newspaper. Richard Steele's first newspaper job was as the editor of the *London Gazette*. Losing sales as a result of the increased competition created following the collapse of licensing, the newspaper was in need of a revamp. Steele was given the task but his efforts to improve the newspaper's image foundered on the restrictions placed on him.[27] Unable to publish many things in the official organ of the State, he launched in 1709 his own newspaper, the *Tatler*, to serve as an outlet for such stories. Published three times a week the *Tatler* initially contained news, advertisements, poetry and anecdotes as well as some politics.[28] However, news and politics declined, to be replaced by essays on morals, manners and social behaviour. The conversion to 'views' instead of 'news' is attributed to Steele's assertion that in the absence of news he would not 'present you with musty foreign edicts or dull proclamations'.[29] The problems of providing up-to-date information, fear of causing affront to the authorities, as well as the growing popularity of essay papers, were practical reasons for the decision to drop news. His desire to avoid conflict with the government proved unrealistic and in 1710 Steele lost his post at the *Gazette* because of a critical article published in the *Tatler*, which closed the following year.

Steele had co-operated with Addison in the production of the *Tatler* and together they founded the *Spectator* in 1711, which lasted a little over two years. Despite its short existence – and the fact that it was not a newspaper as we would understand it today but rather an essay-type periodical published regularly[30] – the *Spectator* had an impact which outlived its times. Steele and Addison aimed to 'enliven morality with wit and to temper wit with morality'.[31] Writers of great skill, they penned essays on a variety of topics, including affectation, Ladies head-dresses, Lottery Adventurers and Coffee-House Politicians.[32] Essays were accompanied by letters and occasional poems as the journal sought to express opinions on morals, manners and literature. John Brewer[33] describes how the journal promoted the values of 'polite' society in a fractious era: 'in opposition to political divisiveness and religious bigotry, politeness proposed a more harmonious ideal'. Social improvement, education and self-help were the essence of polite society and the *Spectator* sought to bring 'philosophy out of the closet and libraries, to dwell in the clubs and assemblies, at tea-tables and in coffee-houses'.[34] Combining entertainment and instruction with wit and subtlety, the *Spectator* was an instant success. By its tenth issue Addison was claiming a circulation of 3,000, with as many as twenty people reading each copy; readers were found as far away as New England and Sumatra.[35] Above all, the *Spectator* established itself as the favourite publication of the coffee houses and taverns that had come to dominate social and cultural life in early eighteenth-century London.

The coffee houses of London provided the primary readership base for the newspapers, journals and pamphlets of the early eighteenth century. Coffee shops had been introduced into Britain in the 1650s, becoming popular in London in the last decade of the seventeenth century.[36] Estimates of their number vary enormously, but, according to one contemporary account, by 1739 there were more than 550 such premises.[37] They were centres of gossip, rumour, political debate and commercial exchange as well as places to down coffee and other kinds of beverages. 'They were places of pleasure and business, catering to customers from all walks of life, centres of rumour, news and information ... of conversation and conviviality' where people met to 'drink, gossip, talk, debate and intrigue'.[38] There was almost an umbilical connection between the coffee houses and the newspaper – for the price of a cup of coffee, access to newspapers was provided for those who could not afford to purchase them.[39] Those unable to read could have the newspapers read to them. The newspaper still had to compete with other sources of news in such places, with popular ballads and songs being recited as well as news-sheets affixed to the walls of the premises. Newspaper reading spread to ale houses, inns, taverns and barbers shops. In 1739, in addition to the coffee shops, there were 207 inns and 447 taverns in London.[40] The dependence of these establishments on the newspaper is highlighted by the *Lloyd's Evening Post*, which commented in 1780 that '[w]ithout newspapers our Coffee-houses, Ale-houses and Barber shops would undergo a change next to depopulation'.[41]

Coffee houses

Coffee houses offered their customers chocolate, wine, brandy and punch as well as coffee, all served from a small bar in a corner of the main room. They had benches and tables where anyone could sit, and some had booths or snugs ... their chief attraction was that they became centres of conversation and 'intelligence', commercial premises and places of private exchange where deals were cut and money, goods and information traded ... The coffee house was the precursor of the modern office, but once you were there you were likely to talk about matters of general interest – the latest play, sexual scandal or political quarrel – as well as carry on business. Besides being meeting places, coffee houses were *postes restantes*, libraries, places of exhibition and sometimes even theatres ... provided a wide range of newspaper and pamphlets, whose contents often provoked coffee house debate.

Source: Brewer, *The Pleasures of the Imagination*, 34–6.

At the outset coffee houses had been controversial, attracting criticism from those in authority as centres of 'the most seditious, indecent and scandalous discourses'.[42] There was an attempt to close them down in 1675, only for the government to back down in the face of a general public outcry. It was following the Glorious Revolution that they came to be praised as centres of free expression. This image was promoted by Addison and Steele, who romanticised the coffee house in the pages of the *Spectator* as a place of polite conversation and moral enlightenment. Others were more sceptical of their benefits. Radical journalist William Cobbett believed they were places where ordinary men, rather than gaining education, were driven to drink. They had 'become sots through the attraction of these vehicles of novelty and false-hood'.[43] The coffee houses had a profound impact on the content of the newspapers; 'assumptions about the expectations of such outlets helped shape the product'.[44] A socially diverse clientele frequented the coffee houses – more diverse if ale houses and barbers shops are included. Their vast numbers forced these outlets to specialise in serving particular audiences; scholars, men interested in trade with the colonies, the theatre and literature and so on would go to a specific coffee shop to indulge their interests and pastimes.[45] However, it was primarily the interests and concerns of the emerging middle classes which shaped what people were reading. Essays on society, literature and politics were what the middle-class reader wanted; that is, information and instruction on questions of social behaviour, moral etiquette and political change. In the Age of the Enlightenment people desired guidance on the great conversation issues around the tables of the coffee houses. The *Spectator* educated, informed and instructed its readers about 'what to think'. Steele outlined in the first issue of the *Tatler* his view that the role of a newspaper

> should be principally intended for the Use of Publick Persons, who are so publick-spirited as to neglect their own Affairs and to look into the Transactions of the State. Now these gentlemen for the most Part, being Persons of strong Zeal and weak Intellects, it is both a Necessary and Charitable Work to offer something, whereby such worthy and well-affected Members of the Commonwealth may be instructed after their Reading, what to think: Which shall be the end and Purpose of this my Paper.
>
> (*Tatler*, 12 April 1709)[46]

Steele and Addison developed an intimate relationship with their readers. Their essays are described as the 'public version of a private conversation'.[47] To this end they sought to adopt a writing style that was 'nearer ... to that of common talk than any other writers'.[48] The *Spectator* was careful

> not to speak for sectional interests; encouraging readers of the first issue to send in their contributions they called on 'all manner of Persons, whether Scholars, Citizens, Courtiers, Gentlemen of the Town or of Country, and all Beaux, Rakes, Smarts, Prudes, Coquets, Housewives, and all sort of Wits, whether male or Female, and however distinguished ... and of what Trade, Occupation, Profession, Station, Country, Faction, Party, Persuasion, Quality, Age or Condition soever, who have ever made Thinking a Part of their Business or Diversion'.[49]

The essay form they developed, which instructed people and attempted to lead them to think in a particular way, became the basis for the editorial or leader, which became a prominent feature in most types of newspaper in later years.[50] More crucial was the emphasis placed on the readership. By attempting to reach the general population, the *Spectator* initiated the refrain that became common to most British newspapers, the claim to reach beyond particular interests to speak to and for a community or nation of readers.

The *Spectator*'s capacity to speak for the broader public was facilitated by the focus on cultural and literary aesthetics, which for those in power was 'comparatively harmless'.[51] It was the political commentaries in publications such as Jonathan Swift's *Examiner* which excited the authorities. Swift was a Tory and contemptuous of Addison and Steele's journal, writing that he 'will not meddle with the *Spectator*, let him fair sex it to the world's end'.[52] Swift was a brilliant polemicist and propagandist, celebrated for satires such as *A Modest Proposal*. His voice was one of many in a world which was the antithesis of that found in the *Spectator*. Writers were able to make a living for the first time in the early eighteenth century and they did this primarily by acting as 'hired hands' or advocates for a politician, party or faction.[53] Out of office politicians would use the press to agitate for change, while those in government used it to defend and promote policy. Swift and his adversaries in print revelled in the presentation and articulation of polemical opinion, the lineage of which can be traced back to the newsbooks of the Civil War. The political invective that poured out of the pages of these publications gained them notoriety and excited strong feelings: Swift believed it was safer for him not to walk out at night, while others such as Daniel Defoe received anonymous letters threatening murder.[54] These newspapers and journals were seen as a threat to political stability and social order, encouraging disobedience and heresy and undermining good governance. It was publications such as the *Examiner* and Defoe's *Weekly Review* that Chief Justice Holt had in mind when he complained in 1702: 'if people should not be called to account for possessing the people with an ill opinion of the government, no government can subsist. For it is very necessary for all governments that the people should have a good opinion of it'.[55]

Defoe's impact on the British newspaper was not merely as a polemicist. He was an enigmatic figure who sought to maintain his anonymity – for professional as much as personal reasons. He is nevertheless described as the 'father' or 'founder' or 'early master' of 'modern journalism'.[56] Defoe is credited with developing many of the techniques that we associate with the practice of reporting, including the gathering of eyewitness accounts. Andrew Marr[57] argues that Defoe created a journalistic style that has lasted: 'he wrote excellent, clear, uncluttered, reported English full of relatively short sentences of plain description'. Defoe himself stated that 'if any man were to ask me what I would suppose to be a perfect style of language, I would answer that in which a man speaking to five hundred people all of common and various capacities ... should be understood by them all'.[58] However, Defoe was similar to most of his contemporaries in this respect: there was a general consensus about the need for good writing and clear prose. Rather, Defoe is singled out by his commitment to reporting. He believed in going and seeing for himself and providing eyewitness accounts of events. He would attend the execution of notorious criminals to report their dying words, interviewing the highwayman Jack Sheppard in the condemned cell in 1724. His commitment to covering 'events in the here and now' was a major contribution to the development of newspaper journalism.

What constituted news in the 1700s was 'heavily political, the reports derivative, anonymous and impersonal'.[59] Plagiarism was rife as newspapers copied material from one another and items were put together by a 'cut and paste' method. The poor communications infrastructure meant that nothing could be verified quickly and many of the items that appeared were 'inaccurate, unchecked and conjectural'.[60] The items were not put together in any systematic or orderly fashion, often put into the paper as they came in. It was not unusual to have contradictory accounts in one edition of the newspaper. Such an approach was dictated by the technology of the hand presses.[61] Time was required to manually typeset and let pages dry before distribution, which militated against the systematic ordering of reports. The strength of newsletters, and what made them effective competitors of the newspaper, was that they were better able to order stories and include late news. Filling pages was a continual challenge, and printers and publishers often turned to their readers to supply information. Correspondence from readers, and the paper's response, became a fundamental means by which to fill space. The printer and publisher, often the same person, were primarily responsible for what went into the newspaper and there was an absence of 'a profession occupational group whose task was to provide an unblemished version of events'.[62] The result was considerable public mistrust of the content of the newspapers. Addison expressed this concern when he stated that the newspapers 'all received the same advices from abroad and very often in the same words; but their way of cooking it is so different that there is no citizen, who has an eye to the public good, that can leave the coffee-house with peace of mind, before he has given every one of them a reading'.[63] According to Andrew Marr, Defoe 'understood, as no one before him seems to have done, that the news business would only thrive if the public developed a basic trust in its sources and truthfulness'.[64]

Defoe expressed his disquiet with the credibility of what was published. The *Weekly Review*'s first number stated it was 'purged from the Errors and Partiality of News-writers and Petty Statesmen of all Sides'. In his preface to his account of the great storms in Britain in the winter of 1703 he wrote: 'if a book printed obtrudes a falsehood, if a Man tells a Lye in Print, he abuses Mankind, and imposed upon the whole World, he causes our Children to tell Lyes after us and their children after them'.[65] Defoe emphasised the importance of seeing things for oneself, interviewing those who were present and sourcing the information he wrote up in his news stories. He believed in using quotations, gathering a variety of views on what had happened and providing some background information in order that readers could understand the context within which events took place – Jenny McKay shows how he used these devices in his account, *The Storm*.[66] While Defoe might have pioneered many of the techniques we associate with modern newspaper journalism, his motives for developing these techniques remain a matter of conjecture. What he meant by credibility and accuracy is problematic. Horst Pottker[67] reports that Defoe saw no contradiction in claiming journalistic accuracy for his fictional text *Robinson Crusoe*, which was based on the experience of a Scottish sailor: 'journalists of the Enlightenment did not seem to use the criterion of verifiable factuality ... to differentiate journalism from literature'. Defoe's search for the truth occurred in a world in which he was familiar with seeing and presenting issues from many perspectives. An agent in the pay of government, he acted as an advocate of Whig beliefs while defending the Toryism of his paymaster, Sir Robert Harley. He wrote for both Tories and Whigs and his anonymity in print was maintained partly to facilitate his espionage. His travels coincided with his work as a spy. Tours of the country, asking questions of men in positions of influence and making their acquaintance in a variety of settings, enabled him to inform his paymasters who could be useful to their cause.[68] For many of his contemporaries Defoe was a 'mean and mercenary prostitute'[69] and his commitment to impartiality was simply a device to disguise his political allegiances.

Whether Defoe's journalism was facilitated by his espionage is a moot question. Much of his writing, the referencing of others, and the exploration of problems and events from several angles can be seen as a product of the secretive and highly political world in which he had to operate. Anonymity allowed him to pen critical pieces for oppositional papers such as *Mist's Weekly Journal* (see p. 64) and there is evidence that Defoe had an awareness of the problematic nature of truth. He wrote that no story could perfectly reflect the event it claims to represent: 'nothing is more common than to have two Men tell the same Story quite differing from one another, both of them Eye-witness to the Fact-related'.[70] Yet his emphasis on the rhetoric of factuality and his ability to write from both, if not all, sides laid the foundations for the development of newspapers that, in the words of press historian Henry Fox Bourne,[71] 'would be critical and instructive, exposing follies and falsehoods, enforcing truths, and elucidating principles'; in other words, acting as a 'fourth estate'.

Steele and Addison may have shaped the manners of an age but it was Swift and Defoe who stirred its politics and it was their reporting that brought forth the reintroduction of press control. Following the collapse of the Licensing Act there were several attempts to bring back censorship. Each attempt failed due to parliamentary divisions or the lack of time to consider the matter.[72] However, new scandals and more withering political and satirical attacks in the press strengthened the calls for a return to censorship and licensing. Scandals were increasingly a feature of the newspapers. The *Female Tatler*, under the editorship of Mrs Mary de la Riviere Manley, known as 'Mrs Crakenthorpe, a Lady that knows everything', was launched in 1709 as a competitor to Steele's publication. Described as a 'trenchant journalist' and referred to as 'Scandalosissima Scoundrelia' by other papers, Mrs Manley published a 'gossip' sheet. The *Female Tatler* was successful in developing the 'problem page', which had been pioneered by John Dunton in his *Athenian Mercury* published in the 1690s.[73] Printing answers to readers' questions, Mrs Manley is credited with being the first 'agony aunt' in the British press.[74] The flood of material critically commenting on matters of Church and State and those who conducted them was seen as undermining popular faith in public institutions. It incensed many in authority, including Queen Anne, who continually called on Parliament to take action against seditious material. But the lobby for the reintroduction of licensing also came from within the printing trade. Many of the master printers who had been granted favour under the Stationers' monopoly pined for the return of such privileges. Booksellers had also petitioned Parliament for more legal protection from the widespread reprinting of material. In 1712 Parliament acted.

Parliament's decision to introduce press taxation was motivated by several considerations. The urgent necessity of raising revenue arose from the cost of the wars fought with France – and when other forms of taxation were high the press provided a new source. Traditional fears of the power of the press to stir up political dissatisfaction and dissent also drove them. By raising the price of newspapers Parliament sought to deny people access to negative opinion. The decision to adopt a more sophisticated mechanism than censorship and the law to constrain the press is attributed to Robert Harley, the benefactor of Swift and Defoe. Harley was one of the first politicians to fully appreciate the value of the newspaper as a vehicle for propaganda.[75] Taxation raised revenue for the Exchequer but did not impair the newspaper as a propaganda device. It also forced the press into depending on subsidies and payouts, tying them to the government of the day.

Indirect censorship

The passing of the First Stamp Act in 1712 meant that fiscal constraints were used to control what newspapers reported and what pamphleteers opined for the next 140 years. Between 1712 and 1815 taxes on newspapers were to increase by nearly 800 per cent.[76] Paper, pages and advertisements were taxed. The 1712 Act taxed printed news material at a halfpenny per copy on half a sheet of paper, a penny on a full sheet, and a duty of one shilling was placed on every advertisement.[77] The impact of taxation was immediate and savage. The *Spectator* disappeared; other newspapers were merged and some were published less frequently. Several of London's newspapers closed down and about twenty-four provincial newspapers in England folded.[78] Swift observed that 'Grub-street is dead and gone ... no more Ghosts or Murders now for Love or Money'.[79] His assessment was a little premature but the introduction of taxes on newspapers, the so-called 'taxes on knowledge', slowed down the growth of newspapers and caused a significant shift in what they looked like and what they reported.

The most obvious change wrought by the imposition of taxation was on the physical appearance of the newspaper. From the 1720s onwards, the size of the average newspaper was extended, particularly at times of disorder or war when news was in greatest demand. The number of pages basically remained the same but they were larger, containing more columns, with most newspapers carrying three columns, and with a corresponding decrease in typeface.[80] The attempt to cram in more material at times of crisis led to complaints from readers about the 'injury done to the Sight and of the difficulty ... in reading so minute a Character'.[81] The 1712 Act – as well as its successor in 1725 – had left a loophole in that no limit was placed on the size of the sheet that was taxed. The broadsheet newspaper was a response to the system of taxation deployed by the government. The increase in columns which accompanied the larger page size meant that there was more space to fill. Filling it was a major headache. Increased comment and opinion, long editorials, were one means, but the risks of offending powerful figures made this a precarious option. Finding a regular supply of material to fill the newspapers became the order of the day and the kind of material that found its way into the pages of a newspaper expanded. By 1730 there were 'collectors' who were paid to 'furnish material for the Dayly papers'.[82] They were reported by the *Grub Street Journal* in 1737 to be 'sent all over the City, suburbs and surrounding villages, to pick up articles of News'.[83] Scraping material together from jails, and from ale houses and gin-shops to find news of those 'such as dye from excessive Drinking' became a source of information. Coffee houses were also haunts of the collectors, where they 'could thrust themselves into Companies where they are not known; or plant themselves at a convenient Distance, to overhear what is said, in order to pick up Matter for the Papers'.[84] As casual employees, collectors were paid on a piecemeal basis according to the length and number of stories they provided. There was no incentive to ensure that their stories were true. They worked for several different papers and had little loyalty to any publication. By the end of the century newspapers retained their own news gatherers on a permanent basis, to ensure exclusivity and greater reliability of the material they collected.

The need to attract more readers to meet the increased costs of production led to a shift towards news that would attract a wider audience. The *Examiner*, the *Tatler* and the *Spectator* were by and large read by members of the upper and middle classes, the elite of eighteenth-century Britain. This is not to say that newspapers were not read by other elements of society. From the 1720s there was a commercial incentive to expand readership to other parts of society that newspapers had up until then not regularly reached. Nathaniel Mist's *Weekly Journal* widened the appeal of the newspaper to embrace the interests of the lower classes. Mist held strong Jacobin views which brought him into conflict with Britain's Hanoverian rulers. The *Weekly Journal* published anti-ministerial essays which immediately got Mist into trouble. Within a few months of the first issue in 1716 he was arrested for printing libel against the government. Fined, pilloried, imprisoned and sentenced to hard labour, Mist was subjected, like most of the newspaper publishers who chose to be politically adversarial, to a variety of harassments, including the threat of further libel action, general warrants and denial of the use of the postal service. Mist's publication was popular, selling between 8,000 and 12,000 copies per issue.[85] Such sales brought in readers and advertisers, enabling Mist to sustain the fines levied on him and continue his fight against authority. The success of the *Weekly Journal* was, according to one of its competitors, due to it being 'mightily spread about among the vulgar'.[86] The coverage of home news was more extensive than in previous newspapers and journals; aware of the entertainment value of certain kinds of domestic stories, Mist posted men at ale houses, jails and notorious spots around the city so that they could overhear scurrilous gossip or observe disturbances. The paper announced that '[d]eaths, executions and discoveries of the most audacious and unheard of villainies can be read over a whole page in a weekly journal' (*Mist's Weekly Journal*, 14 May 1726). Non-political news such as crime and other human interest stories regularly featured. However, the toll of Mist's battles against the authorities mounted up and he eventually fled to France, from where he continued to edit the paper under a new title, *Fog's Weekly Journal*.[87] Mist made an important contribution to the principle of the liberty of the press, writing in one of his leaders that 'English men have always looked on it as part of their right to speak and write on public affairs',[88] but he also played his role in broadening the appeal of the newspaper.

To increase sales newspapers started to pay more attention to publicity and distribution. New newspapers placed advertisements as well as distributed handbills to promote themselves from the 1730s onwards.[89] Fanfares, processions with bands and streamers, as well as handing out free copies, were all part of the campaigns to sell papers. The men hired to distribute the newspaper were sometimes supplied with uniforms to distinguish them.[90] Means of distribution improved and costs fell throughout the second half of the century. Up until the 1730s the primary way in which newspapers reached their audience was through hawkers. Usually destitute or semi-destitute itinerants, they would carry newspapers around to the coffee houses, post office, booksellers, as well as sell them to individuals on their 'walk'. All kinds of goods were sold on the street and the 'cry for news' tended to exaggerate the product to gain a sale.[91] Hawkers would be allowed a financial margin on each paper and given a certain number of copies free per bundle. Sometimes they would hire them out to individuals who could not afford to buy a copy. While many newspapers, especially those who sought to avoid paying the stamp, continued to use hawkers, by the middle of the century a more organised system of distribution began to emerge. Shops were set up, usually run by the wives of the printer, to sell cheap printed material. By the 1720s Mrs Nutt, Mrs Smith and Mrs Dodd were the main sellers of newspapers in London, managing large operations which distributed copies of various newspapers and pamphlets. Any newspaper they disliked would struggle to survive. As distribution networks developed, such as the stagecoach service in the 1760s, newspapers expanded their reach. The postal service had always been subject to interruptions. London newspapers began to reach the provinces in large numbers, and 'country news', previously unreliable and spasmodic, began to be taken from the provincial papers, which were rapidly increasing with the growth of urban communities.

News walk

Advertisement, The Times, 15 April 1792

An Old established NEWS WALK to be disposed of that brings in £1.12s per week clear profit; situate in the best part of London, and capable, with care and assiduity, of great improvement; such opportunity seldom offers for an industrious person. Enquire tomorrow at No. 14, Portugal Street, Lincoln's-Inn-Fields.

While devising ways to raise revenue through increased advertising and sales, most newspapers were forced to rely on political actors to cover increased costs of production resulting from press taxation. Under Sir Robert Walpole, who was Prime Minister for ten years, considerable resources were devoted by government to the financing of the press. It is estimated that he spent over £50,000 from the Treasury setting up new newspapers, supporting established ones and buying off opposition writers.[92] Some newspapers sought to avoid the stamp to make them less vulnerable to political subsidy but a 1743 Act which imposed heavy fines and imprisonment for unstamped newspapers put many of these out of business. However, political subsidies were 'spasmodic, reflecting differing political circumstances and the attitude of individual politicians'.[93] It was also an expensive business, which did not guarantee favourable coverage. Between 1742 and the early 1760s there was little ministerial intervention in the press 'on a continuous or substantial basis'.[94] The more politically charged atmosphere of the latter part of the century led to a return of ministerial sponsorship of newspapers, but often, as the Earl of Bute found, with limited success (see p. 69).[95] Politicians could be a source of income in other ways – blackmail, for example. One of the most notorious episodes was the blackmail of the Prince of Wales by the *Morning Post* in 1789 to suppress a story about his irregular marriage to a Catholic widow.[96] Politicians were not the only people to pay 'suppression fees' – theatre managers would do so to avoid hostile criticism.[97] Money could buy you good reviews or favourable comments. Such was the capacity to buy good copy that 'by 1780 there was scarcely a paragraph in (the *Morning Post*) which had not been paid for by someone'.[98]

Bribes and subsidies were a feature of the newspaper business throughout the eighteenth century. Besides supplying newspapers with money, politicians also furnished copies of their speeches. Newspapers that carried stories of which government approved were circulated free by government and often sent to editors in the provinces for their use. This reached a high point in the 1780s under William Pitt the Younger. He used intimidation, Secret Service subsidies, the withholding of official news and advertisements as well as threats of 'trouble at the Stamp Office' to manipulate the newspapers.[99] Two-thirds of London's morning newspapers were in his pay, the key to his victory in the 1788 elections. By the eve of the French Revolution political intervention and involvement in the operation of newspapers in Britain had reached a high point.

The growth of the newspaper in the eighteenth century was sustained by the changing social and economic conditions in early Hanoverian society. The demand for up-to-date news was sustained by the rise of a prosperous middle class who sought news and information not only to pursue their commercial and business interests but also to better themselves. The emergence of an increasingly literate population expanded interest in the newspaper as well as extended the nature of what appeared as news and how it was written and presented. The evolution of the two-party political system required a competitive press to convey the views and opinions of the Whigs and Tories, and the coffee house culture provided the audience which was responsible for the newspaper serving up particular kinds of news, information and analysis. The intellectual curiosity of the Enlightenment was also a driving force as rational discussion and scientific enquiry came to play a more prominent role in social discourse.[100] Perhaps more significantly, newspapers were better organised, produced and distributed. Newspapers were put together in a more orderly and more systematic fashion, which reflected how the news was gathered. Sub-headings came to be used more regularly to identify different kinds of stories: London, Port News, Ireland, Bankrupts.[101] There was increasingly recognition of the need to check the veracity of what was printed. By the 1750s a broad range of items appeared in the pages of the newspapers and most noticeably they were bigger, better laid out and more up-to-date. If some of the features of the modern newspaper had been put into place, it is important to emphasise that the demand for news was met by the supply of a variety of different kinds of newspapers and other publications. There was also no consistency in the ways in which different newspapers packaged, presented, promoted and distributed themselves. However, the style and form that characterised a modern newspaper were emerging. Essay newspapers had become less popular by the mid-eighteenth century, although they were to regain some popularity later when Dr Samuel Johnson's journals the *Rambler* and the *Idler* gained critical recognition if not large sales.

Local press

Newspapers spread their tentacles to most corners of the British Isles during the eighteenth century. The earliest regional newspapers are usually identified as emerging in the 1690s with publications such as *Berrow's Worcester Journal* and the *Rutland and Stamford Mercury*. The content of the local newspapers that developed in the early eighteenth century was almost exclusively based on news taken from the London papers. These newspapers simply copied material and did nothing to check the veracity of the stories they provided. The *Northampton Mercury* apologised to its readers in 1721 for the 'many falsities that of late have been therein', asking for their forgiveness as 'we took them all out of the London Printed Papers, and those too the most creditable'.[102] The early provincial papers were small, poorly printed and of rudimentary design; published weekly, they had little that was original or locally derived.[103] They simply claimed to provide a complete and accurate 'collection' of the news in the London papers and their only claim to being local was that they were printed locally.[104] Reports of national and international events figured prominently and they crammed as much news as possible into their pages about wars that were in progress.[105] They tried as much as possible to steer clear of controversial matters, not on political grounds but due to financial considerations. Taking a firm political position could estrange customers and induce a rival publication to launch. As the *Derby Mercury* stated in the issue of 21 February 1734, 'as it is undoubtedly my Interest to be equally willing and faithful in serving all Parties, so I hope all who read my News Paper may be convinced that I am so far from being a Bigot as to act contrary to that Interest'.[106]

The lack of local news and political partisanship did not inhibit the expansion of provincial newspapers. By 1760 130 had been started up as regular publications; not all stayed the course, with only 35 surviving until the nineteenth century.[107] However, circulation grew steadily and profits were made – although never at the level of the London papers. The latter was derived from the number of ads that these papers carried, which for many local businesses was their only outlet. The quality of the provincial newspapers increased and their content expanded to take in what the *Gloucester Journal* referred to as 'some pleasant Amusements in Prose or Verse' as well as essays. They also became less timid politically as the politics of the period became more acrimonious. Above all, they started to pay more attention to what was happening in their local community. Such links were to remain relatively weak until the end of the century, but as the Wilkes Affair (see below) developed, many provincial papers sought to articulate local opinion on the great matters of the day. Local papers tended in the eighteenth century to be confined to towns and cities where printers were located – Bristol and Norwich, the second and third largest towns in England at the time, were two places that were able to attract and sustain printers and were major centres of newspaper activity in the eighteenth century. Soon newspapers were established in market towns, sea ports and county capitals. However, it was not until the late eighteenth century that a more rapid expansion of provincial newspapers occurred, mainly in the Midlands and the North of England, as a result of the Industrial Revolution.[108]

Wilkes and liberty of the press

The second half of the eighteenth century did not see any significant shift in the content and appearance of the newspaper. These decades concerned the struggle of newspapers to adjust to a new kind of politics that was emerging in Britain. This struggle is often represented as centring on one man, John Wilkes, and one newspaper, the *North Briton*. However, his battle was symbolic of a greater battle, the struggle for the liberty of the press and the individual's freedom of expression. As important to the struggle were the battles over copyright and libel which were won in the passing of the 1770 Copyright Law and Fox's Libel Law in 1792. Improvements in the quality of journalism and the press were also apparent during this period, and the gradual incorporation of a variety of material that had previously appeared elsewhere was a feature of the newspaper's development. Such material included sports, literary reviews, serials and novels and sex.[109] The most significant inclusion was the increase in the amount of space devoted to advertising as well as the prominence of advertisements in the composition of the papers. By 1783 when Pitt the Younger became Prime Minister there were five daily newspapers in London devoted to advertising: *Daily Advertiser, Public Advertiser, General Advertiser, Public Ledger* and *London Gazetteer*.[110] The growth of advertising alongside the increase in sales transformed the newspaper from being 'a printer's sideline, ancillary to his other interests', into 'a business in its own right'.[111] From the 1730s advertisements began to appear on the front pages of most newspapers. In the process politics had become less central to the operation of the newspaper as well as increasingly a smaller portion of a newspaper's content, except at times of heightened conflict.

Wilkes and his campaign for the right to publish the forty-fifth issue of his newspaper, the *North Briton*, is well documented.[112] As an MP he fought through the courts, Parliament and the ballot box to establish the 'birthright of a Briton', a free press. The *North Briton* was launched in 1762 with a clear statement of principle:

> The Liberty of the press is the birthright of a Briton, and is justly esteemed the finest bulwark of the liberties of the country. It has been the terror of all bad ministries; for their dark and dangerous designs, or their weakness, inability or duplicity, have been detected, and shown the public.[113]

Such words were perhaps no different from what other papers had declared; what was different was Wilkes's campaign to defend his right to criticise government. It began with his attack in issue number 45 on the Earl of Bute, who had succeeded Pitt the Elder in 1762. A former tutor of King George III, Bute was deeply unpopular with the country. To redress this feeling he used the press to promote his cause. Wilkes launched the *New Briton* as a vehicle for anti-Bute propaganda, which was not out of keeping with most newspapers at that time. Few could, however, match his tone of invective.[114] Issue number 45 was a vituperative attack on the King's Speech, and Wilkes, together with forty-eight other persons, including writers, printers, proof-readers, hawkers and the publishers associated with the newspaper and its distribution, were arrested on a general warrant. Wilkes claimed privilege as an MP and was soon released, and he and his co-defendants won £100,000 damages, much to the chagrin of the government. The case condemned the use of general warrants, which as a result fell out of use, to be declared illegal in 1765.[115] The government then sought to strip immunity from MPs on matters of seditious publications and expelled Wilkes, whom they also attempted to re-arrest. He had fled to France, returning in 1768 to win back a parliamentary seat in Middlesex. He was again arrested, which led to riots in which several people lost their lives. By this time Wilkes's personal crusade against Bute, who had long since departed, had become a popular struggle for the liberty of all Britons.

This row between press and government mobilised people in a way never seen before. Hannah Barker[116] draws attention to the modern campaigning techniques associated with Wilkes's cause: badges, pictures, cartoons, porcelain buttons, rings and glassware decorated with the number 45 were used to show support for Wilkes. Wilkes, an accomplished self-publicist with excellent contacts in the press, used the printed word to build 'a popular movement on a national scale'. This was the first significant occasion on which the press defined central issues on the political agenda in defiance of the elite consensus that ran Parliament.[117] Wilkes articulated the claims of the growing middle classes for a greater say in the running of society, particularly Parliament, which had been controlled by the few, the landed gentry, monarchy and aristocracy, for most of the century through rotten boroughs, bribery and political clientelism. Excluded from the political process, the eighteenth-century press was part of the struggle to give greater visibility to the middle classes in the political life of the nation. The Wilkes affair was a watershed in the growth of political consciousness. Party politics up to the mid-eighteenth century was operating in an embryonic form; Whigs and Tories were divided along the lines of their attitude to the power and legitimacy of the Crown. Newspapers represented shifting factions within this world and there was no systematic or organised opposition.

Opposition to the Crown and elite began to emerge in the early 1730s. This was expressed through appeals to the 'public', the 'people' or the 'common voice'.[118] Politics gradually shifted from being primarily about debates between those with access to the corridors of power, focussing on claims to the Crown, to being a public discussion between 'Crown' and 'country'. The nature of liberty, government, patriotism and power became central to the political discourse that was developing. Newspapers began to claim to speak for the country and the rights of its people, articulating the rights of the multitude to meddle in the affairs of state. The *Craftsman* criticised the corruption and abuse of power of Walpole's government, accusing him of putting self-interest above the national interest, to the disadvantage of those people the newspaper said it represented, the middling orders of society.[119] The paper attracted considerable advertising revenue, with an estimated half of its costs covered from this source, which enhanced the ability of the paper to take a political line that distanced itself from parties and factions. Commercial sources became as important as political ones in providing finance for the press and, as a result, newspapers appealing to the national interest became more common. They did not replace the 'party paper' in the eighteenth century but they did indicate the new politics that was emerging which positioned newspapers as voices of particular classes of society. This struggle was manifest in the campaign waged for the right to report Parliament.

Reporting Parliament

Despite politics being a major ingredient of eighteenth-century newspapers, they were unable to report what was said in Parliament. It had been a long established convention that the reporting of parliamentary debates and proceedings should be kept secret, mainly to prevent the sovereign finding out what members were saying as they could be arrested for sedition.[120] Parliament broke with the condition during the Civil War but as an instrument of the landed gentry it had no long-term interest in letting the press cover its activities. In 1660 a resolution was passed banning the printing of any votes or proceedings of the House.[121] The newsletters ignored this edict, continuing to provide accounts of what was said in Parliament – although letter writers who overstepped what Parliament believed was acceptable were summoned to appear before the House of Commons and reprimanded. In 1680 the Commons agreed to the publication of the motions carried, the votes for and against, but not how individuals voted. The newspapers remained silent, although provincial newspaper sometimes attempted to print extracts of debates copied from the newsletters. Parliament was less concerned about what appeared in the provincial newspapers, but occasionally clamped down on these newspapers to prevent them from becoming too free in their coverage.[122] The first systematic effort to report the proceedings of Parliament came at the start of the eighteenth century in the magazines that appeared at this time. They sought to get around the ban by reporting debates when the House was in recess, presenting them as history rather than news. Prevented in 1738 from doing this, the *Gentlemen's Magazine, London Magazine* and the *Political State of Britain* resorted to covert means such as presenting the dealings of Parliament as the proceedings of the Senate of Lilliputia, where speakers were identified by Roman names or by anagrams of their real names.[123] 'Allusions, allegory and innuendo' prevailed in the accounts that appeared, as magazines and now newspapers attempted to report what their readers' elected representatives were saying.

Parliament's antagonism to the press ostensibly stemmed from fears of being misreported; Walpole, winding up the debate in 1738 which banned reporting in the recess, stated that press coverage of parliamentary proceedings was 'a forgery of the worst kind'.[124] However, what was at stake was the balance of power between Parliament and the people. If Parliament was reported it would make parliamentarians accountable and the 'balance of power between Parliament and the public would shift'.[125] The struggle for the right to report Parliament that the press embarked on in the 1760s was a fundamental part of the struggle for democracy in Britain. Emboldened by rising circulation, several newspapers started to publish extracts from debates between 1760 and 1765, with Parliament censuring and fining them for their misdemeanours. Their challenge to parliamentary privilege appears to have been motivated as much by their desire to respond to public demand as by a commitment to democratic principles. Galvanised by Wilkes and his clashes with authority, public demand for news and information increased and it became clear to newspapers that 'if they did not transgress the prohibition on the reporting of Parliament, they would lose readers to their less timorous counterparts'.[126] Wilkes's role in the campaign that eventually overturned the ban in 1771 is well documented.[127] His victory was not complete as it took many years for the right of newspapers to be established in practical terms by allowing reporters some form of direct access to the Lords and Commons. Severe restrictions, such as not being allowed to take notes of speeches or having anywhere to sit to record them, were imposed on reporters until well into the nineteenth century. However, from 1771 parliamentary reports became a staple feature of newspapers; in the words of one editor in 1782, the 'speeches and debates ... are of such importance, as to engross the greatest part of our newspapers, and necessarily become of utmost consequence to all our readers'.[128]

The increasing reliance on parliamentary reports to make up the pages of the newspapers led to the development of techniques to ensure that full and accurate accounts of what happened in Parliament were forthcoming. Verbatim reporting did not regularly appear until the mid- to late nineteenth century when shorthand was perfected and the conditions under which the press reported Parliament were accepted as trustworthy by both parties. In the meantime what the press reported was subject to the covert manipulation of politicians. Newspapers were also selective in how they reported parliamentary debates, politicised by the Wilkes affair and the controversy over the government's handling of the American War of Independence. Reports of what members said may have been accurate but 'the weight given to various speeches and speakers differed between different newspapers, as in some cases, did the language used by some of the speakers'.[129] Newspapers had become re-politicised in the wake of the new national politics initiated by the Wilkes affair. Politics was more public than it had been at the start of the century as a result of the growth of newspapers. It was also acknowledged that the public's right to know was a legitimate, if not fully accepted, part of political debate in Britain.

Public opinion may have become part of political thought and debate in the late eighteenth century but, as Jeremy Black[130] notes, there was 'uncertainty about what constituted such opinion'. Wilkes and the press represented the frustrations and discontent of the middle classes and industrial bourgeoisie at the dominance of the landed elite who controlled Parliament. Newspaper coverage of politics as well as society reflected the demands for greater representation of the views of this emerging stratum of society. The rise of the commercial press was accompanied by the growth of political associations and other forms of extra-parliamentary activity which laid down the foundations for the extension of the vote in the nineteenth century. Wilkes's campaign was always supported at crucial times by popular demonstrations. The call for change stretched beyond the middle classes. Many of those who marched for Wilkes, crying 'Wilkes and Liberty', came from outside the usual ranks of those involved in politics. Weavers, glass-grinders and hatters marched for Wilkes. This was what Stanley Harrison[131] labels the stirrings of a 'half blind movement ... of the workers for wages'. They were not the long-established class of artisans, journeymen and the urban poor, but the emerging proletariat which had been created by the onset of industrialisation and urbanisation in the late eighteenth century. Their calls for political and press reform would constitute a radical departure from the emerging bourgeois order, and divided the press into two broad camps, 'radical' and 'respectable' newspapers.

THE

POOR MAN'S GUARDIAN.

A Weekly Paper

FOR THE PEOPLE.

PUBLISHED, IN DEFIANCE OF "LAW," TO TRY THE POWER OF "MIGHT" AGAINST "RIGHT."

" IT IS THE CAUSE; IT IS THE CAUSE."

| No. 7. | Saturday, August 20, 1831. | Lent to Read, without deposit, CHARGE ONE PENNY. |

Friends, Brethren, and Fellow-Countrymen,

We have taken the above for our motto, and must justify our adoption of it; do we not deserve it? do we not, on all occasions, seek out the *cause* of the evil, and suggest a cure for *that* rather than waste our time in supplying vain remedies for an endless and inevitable *effect?* and is it not clear to reason that it is both kind and wise to do so? "*Prevention's* better than *cure*," says the proverb!—if we content ourselves with merely curing a bad *effect*, so long as we allow the *cause* to remain, we do not *prevent* a repetition of the evil, and thus are useless pain and unnecessary trouble perpetuated,—nay, indeed, *increased*, for *causes* are contagious; to simply pluck the leaves from the tree which intercepts the light, is only to provide a yearly repetition of the same office and offence,—better to cut off the branch which bears the leaves, or cut down the whole tree itself which bears the branch; to simply allay the symptoms of a disease is but to ensure a continuation of suffering, and to render necessary the constant attendance of the physician,—whereas, to eradicate the *cause* of the disease itself, would be a prevention of both further pain and necessity of cure; and thus in all things; who will not say it were better to prevent disease than cure it? who will not say, for the same reasons, it were better to prevent crime than punish it—to destroy ignorance itself rather than cure and restrain the numberless effects of it? who can call himself christian, and not own this? what man, having a disease, would not rather it had been prevented than have it cured—and who, wishing as much for himself, can withhold the same charity from others! and yet, alas! how little do we find this simple wisdom practised! let us cast our eyes around and see our lofty prisons—and our spacious hospitals;—let us see the thousands of armed slaves ready, at the word of command, to butcher, in cold blood, their very kindred—and still think it " honourable duty;" let us see in every street a doctor, in every square a judge, and at every corner a minister of " law;" and, last not least, let us count, if possible, our numberless churches and multitudes of " teachers of the truth;"—WHY all this? why, to punish innumerable crimes, *correct* and *suppress* innumerable evil propensities, and to cure innumerable accidents and diseases!—now these things are *mere effects*,—and yet are the energies of all men directed to the cure and correction of *them*, while—even by the very remedies employed for that purpose—by the severest penalties of the " law"—the actual *cause* of them is nourished and protected! Now, *what* is the one great CAUSE of all these evils?—have we not often declared it, but can it be declared too often? "PROPERTY!"—Yes "*Property*"—the means of possessing wealth and possessing it not together *cause* the crimes and evils which make this earth the bitter *hell* it is,—which render *necessary*—*prisons* and *hospitals*, and *armies* and *judges*, and *physicians* and *churches*, and " LAWS!"—Why groans that sufferer in yonder bed? " Poor soul !" his limbs are fractured by a fall from " Lord " ———'s lofty mansion !"—What is the disease of this " living ghost? " Consumption; he is a water *gilder*—and water *gilders* never live long !"—Why are we beckoned away from yonder room? " A dreadful fever rages there; caused by bad living and uncleanliness; we call it the *poor disease* !"—Why are those soldiers hurrying along?—and why this tumult? " The people are demanding more wages: they say they are starving, and some of them have attacked a waggon of provisions ; the soldiers are going to protect property, and put the rioters down !"—What are these preparations for? " Oh! only a man going to be hung; he robbed our parson in the king's highway; he was a poor man, and had a large family; but there's no hope for him !"—What a splendid funeral ! " It is " Lord " ———'s; he was murdered in resisting some villains who entered his house to rob; however, *they* will be hung !"—Another funeral—a double one ! " Yes, the beautiful wife and young sister of the Squire; poor things ! their tenants and the working people were sick of what we call the " poor fever," and they caught it ;—ah ! it always kills gentle folks when it *does* catch them !—the Squire himself has had a narrow escape of it."—Why do those brothers quarrel? " The father has left all his property to the younger

The *Poor Man's Guardian*, 20 August 1831

3

KNOWLEDGE AND POWER

The Radical press, 1789–1850

Some simpletons talk of knowledge as rendering the working classes more obedient, more dutiful ... But such knowledge is trash; the only knowledge which is of any service to the working people is that which makes them more dissatisfied and makes them worse slaves. That is the knowledge we shall give them.

James Bronterre O'Brien, *Destructive*, 7 June 1834[1]

The end of the eighteenth century was a period of cataclysmic change. One event in particular had a profound impact on society: the French Revolution. In a world turned upside down by the outpouring of new ideas, the French Revolution swept away the cosy world of 'politics for the few' which had shaped the development of the press in Britain and throughout Europe. Radical politics began to emerge from the 1750s onwards. The Wilkes affair represented the beginning of a shift in the political order in which the bourgeoisie united with working people and agitated for change in a political system dominated by the landed gentry and upper classes. Press freedom was a central issue in this struggle, and the first edition of the *North Briton* in 1762 referred to the 'good old days' of the Civil War.[2] The French Revolution broke the link between the bourgeoisie and the working classes and brought about class conflict across Europe. Fear of working people, the masses of the nations of Europe, led the upper and emerging middle classes into allegiance in the face of the threat posed to the political and economic order. Calls for greater representation for working people were resisted as the ruling classes attempted to prevent a political revolution taking place in Britain. The response of those in positions of political and economic power was twofold: the *suppression* of all forms of agitation for change and the *substitution* of radical ideas by values that upheld the status quo, most clearly promoted through the development of a State-run education system. Knowledge was central to the class struggle: the masthead of one of the leading radical newspapers of the period, the *Poor Man's Guardian*, trumpeted the slogan 'Knowledge is Power'.

Traditional histories of the press represent the first half of the nineteenth century as the era in which newspapers attained their freedom from the State and political control. The repeal of the 'taxes on knowledge', ending direct government intervention in the running of the press, occurred between 1836 and the 1850s. The midwife of this victory is seen as the ability of newspapers to attain economic independence. Advertising 'provided the material base for the change of attitude from subservience to independence'.[3] By the mid-nineteenth century the foundations had been laid down for the press to act as the 'fourth estate', challenging and holding to account government and those in positions of authority. Newspapers, free from their political shackles, could now provide the platform on which citizenship and democracy could be built. They would give the people the information they needed to make informed judgements. Radical newspapers are seen as marginal or secondary to the efforts of newspapers such as *The Times* in the struggle for press freedom. Their role is acknowledged but it is often portrayed as 'colourful and strident' and not as 'wholesome' as that of the more respectable newspapers.[4] For some commentators, advertising did not help to liberate the press but operated as a new method of control, acting as a patronage system which influenced the editorial strategies of newspapers.[5] Newspapers took up the cause of their class, serving as 'mouthpieces' for competing values and viewpoints. Their presentation and content reflected the interests they served. Radical newspapers, catering for the political, industrial and cultural needs of working people, were unable to attract the advertising revenue which was necessary for them to survive in a market system. 'Market forces' rather than 'legal suppression', it is argued, were able to conscript the press to support the established social order.

The form and style of the newspaper underwent a considerable transformation during this period. The widening demand for reading material was accompanied by a profound revolution in print technology. The introduction of mechanised paper-making in 1803, steam-powered presses in 1814 and multiple-cylinder stereotype printing in 1827 facilitated the low-cost and high-speed dissemination of the printed word.[6] Cheap literature flooded the market, and newspapers, according to one contemporary observer, progressed from the 'old region of enormous expenditure and fiscal restraint to an age when journalism may be said to be universal as air or light'.[7] The composition of newspapers was enhanced by the advent of new typefaces, better print type and the ability to reproduce drawn visual images, which extended their appeal. At a time when the reproduction of knowledge was a site of political struggle newspapers became more accessible and plentiful throughout the country.

Industrial change and class consciousness

In order to understand the development of the newspaper in the late eighteenth and early nineteenth centuries it is important to outline the political, industrial and cultural circumstances of the period. Political agitation, primarily in the form of the rise in the 1840s of Chartism, Britain's first organised political movement of working people, developed from growing unrest in the workplace brought about by the rapid economic, social and industrial changes sparked by the Industrial Revolution. The capitalist organisation of society that emerged from industrialisation produced a growing awareness of class allegiance in Britain. People's lives changed enormously, and not only in their work relationships but also in their daily existence. Relations between capital and labour underwent a transformation, but other areas of social relations such as the status of women began to fundamentally alter. Such radical change heightened antagonism throughout society. Initially this conflict took place between those who benefited from the established aristocratic order, the landed gentry and nobility, and the new classes that were beginning to emerge: the middle and working classes. Competition ensured that conflicts also occurred within classes; but by the outbreak of the French Revolution struggle between owners and workers, between the proletariat and the bourgeoisie, came to the fore. Class conflict meant that politics became the concern of a large section of the population as they attempted to make sense of and adjust to the profound changes that were going on around them. People were mobilised into continued political debate and activity. There was considerable pressure to articulate attitudes and opinions in response to political and economic change. The values, beliefs and explanation of the old order were unsatisfactory and new forms of understanding, as well as a new language of politics, were needed. New ideas and new forms of communication arose in response to this demand. The development of the novel in the nineteenth century and its emphasis on the individual hero could be seen as one such example. More significant was the emergence of newspapers as 'voices' of class consciousness and class analysis.

Newspapers were spokespersons for the emerging classes and sub-classes. It is possible to make a distinction between two broad kinds of newspapers: 'respectable' and 'radical'. The former group of papers took the stamp, indicating that they had paid the taxes levied on the press. Operating within the law, they represented the variety of shades of opinion within the bourgeoisie. They supported the campaigns of the middle classes for political change, including the extension of the vote, free trade, reform of the civil service and military. Supporting such causes, the respectable newspapers provided the middle class with a sense of identity. They trumpeted the virtues of the class: as the *Leeds Mercury* wrote in 1821, 'never in any country under the sun was an order of men more estimable and valuable, more praised and praiseworthy than the middle class of society in England'.[8] While praising the virtues of the middle classes, the respectable press were keen to highlight the vices of other classes. Aristocrats and workers were both represented as idle, debauched, drunk, dissolute and feckless.

The majority of radical newspapers rejected the stamp and operated clandestinely. They appealed to the working classes and associated themselves with the growth of political agitation and trade unionism. Some of these news-papers sought to act as the organs of the first attempts to organise working people through corresponding societies, political associations and trade unions. Hetherington, in the first issue of the *Poor Man's Guardian*, emphasised the paper's allegiance with working people: 'it is the cause of the rabble we advocate, the poor, the suffering, the industrious, the productive classes ... we will teach this rabble their power – we will teach them that they are your master instead of being your slave'.[9] The break in the link between the bourgeoisie and the working classes forged during Wilkes's struggle for parliamentary reform and a free press laid down the foundation for the dis-tinction between radical and respectable newspapers. Newspapers took sides in what was a battle of the mind, a struggle to control public opinion which had started to take shape at the end of the eighteenth century. Church and State and the ruling classes united to prevent what at the time was described as the 'march of the intellect' and the extension of education, which they saw as spreading knowledge that would destabilise society and usher in a new English revolution. Reformers sought to extend knowledge so that the lot of ordinary men and women could be improved and society become more just.

The politics of reading

The struggle for working-class demands for political reform corresponded with the growing efforts of working people to read and write and acquire some learning. Reading was seen by those living through the eighteenth century as having expanded, to the extent that Dr Johnson could conclude in 1779 that 'general literature now pervades the nation through all its ranks'.[10] Modern historical research contests the view expressed by Johnson and his contemporaries that 'all ranks and degrees now READ'.[11] The evidence avail-able points to reading levels remaining static, with the growth in the con-sumption of printed material attributed to those who could read simply reading more. There are also indications that pronounced regional differences existed, with literacy rising in London but actually declining elsewhere in Britain. Literacy was higher in urban than rural communities, in which 'superstitious consciousness' continued to hold sway well into the nineteenth and some would say even the twentieth century.[12] The 'reading public' was primarily drawn from those connected with commerce, such as shopkeepers, skilled journeymen, clerical workers and artisans. It was the tastes and pre-ferences of the middle classes that determined the output of booksellers, publishers, printers as well as newspapers during the eighteenth century.[13] Most working people are seen as excluded from the emerging bourgeois culture because of their lack of literacy.

Judging levels of literacy is a 'notoriously difficult' job[14] and the notion of a 'reading public' is 'extremely slippery'.[15] Reading has always been present amongst the ranks of the so-called ordinary people. Newssheets, almanacs, ballads and other forms of cheap literature were consumed by ordinary people from Tudor times. It is also worth pointing out that much of the reading material published throughout the eighteenth century presented old super-stitions and beliefs rather than the new and progressive ways of thinking of the Enlightenment.[16] The appetite to read and write rapidly spread across society at the beginning of the nineteenth century: 'never before in British history had so many people read so much'.[17] Greater social prestige was attached to the ability to read and write. Economic necessity was also a driving force. Industrial and urban society places a premium on literacy; working people had to acquire the skills to operate in the workplace as well as meet the challenges presented by living in cities. Schooling became important and a variety of such institutions were established: charity, Sunday and workhouse schools, schools of industry and 'adventure' or 'dame' schools run by private individuals.[18] Working people also systematically sought to educate them-selves through 'Free Schools' or through Sunday schools set up by the dis-senting churches such as the Methodists or Baptists. Technological advances also assisted reading. The arrival of gaslight made reading after work in homes and public reading rooms an easier and more pleasurable experience. The opportunity to read increased as reading matter appeared in many more places. Walls, shop windows, book stalls were plastered with printed mate-rial; advertisers promoted their wares on a variety of products and discarded printed material was used as wrapping paper, extending the printed word into the hands of people who could not afford to purchase it.[19] Circulating libraries, first developed in Scotland, opened up access to literature to more people.

The combination of rising levels of literacy and new kinds of reading material produced a complex response. The pre-eminent feeling in an era of political unrest was that of anxiety. In 1832 a representative of the Society for the Promotion of Christian Knowledge (SPCK) stated that 'the popula-tion of this country (was) for the first time a reading population, actuated by tastes and habits unknown to preceding generations, and particularly susceptible such an influence as that of the press'.[20] The extension of reading was seen as facilitating the dissemination of ideas that would contribute to political instability and moral corruption. The spread of knowledge through the 'the more ignorant classes' would, according to one commentator of the time, be the 'tune to which one day or the other a hundred thousand tall fellows with clubs and pikes will march against Whitehall'.[21] Reading was regarded by those in authority as a subversive act, as more people would be open to the 'ill impressions' conveyed by newspapers. The *Anti Jacobin Review* articulated this fear when it wrote in 1801 that 'we have long con-sidered the establishment of newspapers in this country as a misfortune to be regretted; but since their influence has become predominant by the uni-versality of their circulation, we regard it as a calamity most deeply to be deplored'.[22]

The dissemination of newspapers was not dependent on more people being able to read. Illiteracy was not a barrier to the consumption of what was written in a newspaper or any other form of printed material. It was common for people who could not or did not want to read to have newspapers, pamphlets and books read out aloud to them. Reading was up until the 1850s as much a social as a solitary experience. Newspapers attempting to reach a wider audience were aware of this. Radical newspapers not only assisted in the promotion of literacy but also compiled and presented their product so that it could be read aloud. Cobbett addressed the audience for his *Political Register* as 'my readers and hearers', while the *Northern Star* was written in a 'highly rhetorical style' to facilitate reading it out aloud.[23] Venues where working people congregated, such as pubs or working men's halls or clubs, were used to read out newspapers to assembled groups; people would also meet in one another's houses to read and talk about what was in the newspapers. Political meetings would often start with a newspaper or extracts from newspapers being read aloud. The collective process of reading and discussion helped to politicise working people, as people would discuss and debate what they had heard.

Reading in the early nineteenth century was a political battleground. Suggestions were made that reading and writing should only be taught to those children whose parents would guarantee their future behaviour and that schooling should inculcate values that were not injurious of social order and supportive of national endeavour.[24] Working people were suspicious of the educational efforts of the Church, religious societies and their employers, often not taking up offers from proprietors to pay for their children to attend school.[25] Their preference for self-education led to the founding of study groups, reading societies and informal schools, utilising cheap fiction, tracts and newspapers which many educationalists of the period regarded as 'the worst kind of schoolbook for young and old'.[26] This was a different type of literature from what had been previously available. Following the French Revolution political tracts, pamphlets and materials of all sorts started to circulate throughout Britain. Perhaps the most significant political publication was Tom Paine's *Rights of Man*, which first appeared in 1791. Within two years the book had sold over 200,000 copies, attesting to the appeal that his ideas on republicanism, democracy and individual rights had for many working people. The dissemination of radical literature was furthered by the setting up of corresponding societies in the 1790s. Those seeking to promote political and parliamentary reform established such groups to exchange material and ideas. The London Corresponding Society was formed in 1792, followed by similar groups in Sheffield, Manchester and Derby. The attempt to spread radical literature and ideas caused consternation amongst the upper and middle classes, who made strenuous efforts to suppress such ideas and material. The *Rights of Man* was banned as seditious libel in 1793 and legislation was enacted to limit public assembly and restrict what was printed.

To further minimise public discontent, a battle was launched for the hearts and minds of working people. Cheap, anti-radical literature was distributed which sought to 'train up the lower classes in the habits of industry and piety'.[27] Hannah More's *Cheap Repository Tracts* were first published in 1795, selling almost two million copies by 1797, swamping Paine's works.[28] A monthly publication, they included stories, addresses and ballads and freely discussed political and religious matters, speaking out against the ideas of the French Revolution. Great efforts were made to ensure the tracts conformed to popular tastes. Catchy titles and suggestive woodcuts were incorporated into the format of popular literature to attract working-class readers, but they were 'political pamphlets in pious dress, reactionary in content and patronising in tone'.[29] There is some evidence of resentment amongst the people who received them. More successful as an anti-radical publication was Charles Knight's *Penny Magazine* (1832–45). Knight was a member of the Society for the Diffusion of Useful Knowledge (SDUK), which was established in 1826 to combat the dissemination of 'dangerous Science [and] more dangerous History' amongst the new reading public.[30] A self-educated working man, he was motivated by two factors. First, there was his desire 'of checking the progress and the sale' of radical publications and newspapers which he regarded as 'shameful'.[31] He believed such publications were responsible for discontent amongst working people and the basis of social instability. The *Penny Magazine* sought to 'divert audiences away from dangerous political knowledge to useful knowledge of a harmless nature'.[32] Second, he wanted to improve the quality of the literature and imagery available to working people. The *Penny Magazine* was a vehicle for the dissemination of general knowledge, addressing what Knight believed was the main problem facing British working people, 'their want of mental culture and material worth'.[33] He sought to 'awaken the reason and lead the imagination into innocent and agreeable trains of thought'.[34] Facts and pictorial illustrations abounded in the magazine and by 1832 its circulation had reached 200,000.[35] Some historians of the radical press see the *Penny Magazine* and similar publications as 'diversionary tactics' to draw readers away from the radical newspapers.[36] Their emphasis on harmless novelty, facts and slick illustrations highlights that a popular desire for entertainment existed alongside the public thirst for knowledge and instruction. The 'War on the Unstamped', as the efforts to suppress radical newspapers in the 1830s is often labelled, was not simply a political engagement but also a cultural struggle.[37] It was in the midst of this political and cultural conflict that newspapers in the first half of the nineteenth century operated.

Respectable newspapers

The newspapers that emerged from the eighteenth century were evolving into successful commercial operations. Profits were booming; James Perry's

Morning Chronicle is reported to have been making £12,000 per annum by 1820 and Daniel Stuart sold the *Morning Post* for £25,000 in 1803.[38] Advertising was the basis for the commercial success of these papers. Stuart stated that he 'encouraged the small and miscellaneous advertisements in the front page. ... numerous and various advertisements attract numerous and varied readers, looking for employment, servants, sales, and purchasers etc ... Advertisements act and react. They attract readers, promote circulation and circulation attracts advertisements'.[39] Such profitability brought about changes in the production of newspapers which 'increased specialisation and demarcation'. By the 1820s newspapers were becoming complex organisations, moving beyond the management of one man and his team.

Newspaper organisation in the 1820s

Employed on each morning newspaper, there are an editor, a sub-editor, from ten to fourteen regular reporters, at salaries of four to six guineas a week, each; from thirty to thirty five compositors in the printing office, some of whom being what is called full hands, that is, men who work the whole of their day, receive £2 8s each, as wages, with some additions for over hours; whilst others, who are called supernumeraries, and who compose only a limited portion of matter called a galley, receive £1 3s 6d each; one or two readers who correct the proofs as they come from the compositors, and who receive from two and a half to three and a half guineas per week; a reading boy whose duty it is to read copy aloud, whilst the reader makes his corrections upon the proof; a printer, who receives from four to six, or even eight guineas per week; and a certain number of men and boys who attend the printing machine, and to take off the papers as they fall from the cylinders; a publisher and sub-publishers; two or more clerks in the office to receive advertisements and keep accounts; a porter, a number of errand boys etc. ... besides the regular reporters ... there are occasional, or as they are called 'penny a line' reporters from the circumstance of their furnishing articles of intelligence, at a fixed price per line.

Source: Gibbons Merle (1829) 'The newspaper press'
Westminster Review, 10, reproduced in
King and Plunkett, 2005, 342–5.

Perry and Stuart – together with John Walter I of the *Times* – played a key role in the professionalisation of the production and management of the newspaper. In particular, they paved the way for the development of the role of the editor as the person who oversees the composition of the newspaper.

They turned the newspaper into 'an organisation presided over by a man (sic) skilled in delegation, arrangement and judgements about the world of various kinds' and separated the function from that of the owner.[40] Editors began to preside over an office which was now large enough to have staff gathering news on a variety of subjects and from a number of places as well as laying out the paper with the stories supplied. Decisions about which stories to run and how to present them became the editor's responsibility. From 1802 the post had developed into deciding the overall composition, content and commentary of the newspaper.

The daily newspaper became more prevalent in the early nineteenth century. Tri-weeklies and weeklies started to fade away with the growing demand for up-to-date news, the arrival of a daily postal service and the improved capacity to provide a regular supply of information. The availability of increased capital to invest in the business encouraged daily publication. Morning newspapers were soon joined by evening counterparts. The first daily evening newspaper was the *Star*, launched in 1788. The paper took advantage of the opening of a newspaper distribution office by the inventor of the mail coach, John Palmer, who agreed that if the copies reached his office by six o'clock he would distribute them to various parts of London and the South East.[41] Dailies slowly started to be distributed from London to other parts of the United Kingdom. They were also joined by Sunday newspapers, the first of which was launched in 1779, Mrs E. Johnson's *Sunday Monitor and British Gazette*. Sunday papers confronted more obstacles to publication than their daily counterparts; the sale of everything but milk and mackerels on Sundays was against the law.[42] Sundays were aimed at those who had neither money nor leisure to buy and consume a daily newspaper.[43] The Sabbath was a day on which working men and women had some spare time, which Mrs Johnson appears to have believed could be filled by reading moral essays, matters of instruction and entertainment and some news.

John Bell's *Weekly Messenger* developed family reading matter on Sundays, leaving out advertisements to avoid offending lady readers.[44] 'Disencumbered from advertisements', the *Messenger* provided 'useful instruction ... relative to the Sciences and the Fine Arts ... calculated to help the pen of the historian, to assist the artists, to entertain the curious, the grave and volatile, to gratify the politician, courtier and the mechanic, the soldier and the churchman, lawyer and doctor; and above all, to afford an innocent amusement to the fair sex, and to improve their knowledge' (*Weekly Messenger*, 3 January 1802).[45] The *Weekly Messenger* was one of the best-selling newspapers in the early nineteenth century, breaking records for sales of certain issues, such as the 14,405 copies sold at the time of Nelson's funeral.[46] By 1812 at least eighteen Sunday papers were sold in London and by the mid-nineteenth century they were the most popular newspapers, catering for a mass working-class readership.[47] Their content had now changed; typical were the *Weekly Dispatch* and *Bell's Life in London*, which mainly covered boxing, crime (usually involving rape) and was written in slang.[48] Blood, gore and crime became a feature of the Sunday newspaper. It is estimated that by the 1830s a typical issue of the *Sunday Times* devoted over half of its news reports to crime.[49]

The leading respectable newspaper of the early nineteenth century was *The Times*. Starting life in 1785 with a loan from the Treasury, the newspaper grew to exert considerable influence over the Victorian press. Its early years reflected the way in which most respectable newspapers functioned in this period. They were usually established by payments from government and continued to operate through a system of bribes and subsidies. In 1803 *The Times* turned its back on such subsidies, developing its own independent system of news gathering. It was able to do this as a result of commercial success. The paper introduced new printing technology which increased the number of copies that could be printed. In 1812 *The Times* printed 250 copies per hour, on one side of the page only; by 1827 this had risen to 4,000 printed on both sides.[50] The speed of its Koenig steam presses was matched by the business acumen of the paper's owner, John Walter II. He succeeded in attracting advertising to *The Times* which freed his paper from government and political parties. By 1829 *The Times* was paying more advertising duty than its nearest rival and its advertising revenue was underwriting its political independence.

The Times used its economic independence to establish a reputation as Britain's leading newspaper, claiming to speak on behalf of the whole nation at times of crisis. Under the editorship of Thomas Barnes, *The Times* developed a news service envied by newspapers around the world and the quality of its commentary made it an essential read for all those in positions of power. Its political influence grew so much that by the 1850s the Prime Minister of the day could refer to the 'vile tyranny' that *The Times* exerted over the conduct of public affairs. Barnes developed the role of a newspaper as the intermediary between the governed and the government. Appointed editor in 1817, he sought to align the newspaper not with one man or one party or one political faction or the government of the day but with public opinion. The duty of a newspaper was to search out what the public thought on the issues of the day and articulate it clearly in its newspaper columns. To this end he deployed a team of shorthand reporters to cover public meetings and events. The paper's formidable news gathering team enabled it to do away with accepting news and prior intelligence from government sources, given in return for editorial support.[51] Barnes, by asserting his paper's independence from political and party connections and seeking to speak on behalf of the public, sometimes for and sometimes against the government, increased the sales of his paper fourfold and, according to the then Lord Chancellor, made him 'the most powerful man in the country'.[52]

The Times under Barnes was a newspaper of record. Reports, debates, speeches, proceedings and inquests were the primary accounts of what was happening. Eight pages, each consisting of six columns of closely typeset copy, were

divided into three pages of advertisements and five pages of news, correspondence, features and comment.[53] Parliamentary debates, Select Committee hearings, government departments' annual reports, coroners' inquests,
court reports and financial intelligence from the City were familiar fare.
Accounts from overseas in the form of correspondence from *Times* men situated around the world sat alongside reports from country papers around
Britain and letters from readers. The latter were distributed around the
paper, fitted in where space was available. Most papers of the early Victorian
period – apart from the front-page advertisements and leading articles –
would not have regular slots for certain kinds of items. The lack of attention
paid to the layout of the pages did not make *The Times* or its rivals easy to
read.

The newspaper's commitment to the public did not extend to British
working people. Like its main competitors – *Morning Post*, *Morning Chronicle*,
Globe, *Standard* and *Morning Advertiser* – *The Times* was firmly wedded to the
interests of the middle classes, as clearly manifested through its dependency
on advertising revenue. It championed reform against revolution; the 1819
Peterloo massacre of protesting workers had been vividly reported by a *Times*
correspondent present. Previously the paper had been hostile to the Peterloo
meeting and calls for reform but its leader on the morning after the massacre
made reform a respectable cause. Its support for the 1832 Reform Act – which
earned it the nickname the 'Thunderer' as a result of the paper 'urging ...
people everywhere ... [to] ... come forward to petition, ay, thunder for
reform'[54] – did not extend to the right for working people to have the vote.
Speaking for Britain did not mean giving voice to the working people of
Britain – that rested with the radical press.

Radical newspapers

A press devoted to the causes of the working classes emerged at the end of
the eighteenth century. Despite concerted efforts to ban, penalise or tax these
newspapers out of business, the 'radical' or 'pauper' or 'unstamped' press thrived:
'a stream of news pamphlets and newssheets, handbills and embryonic newspapers grew into a torrent' by the 1830s.[55] Neglected in traditional histories
of the British press, these newspapers played a crucial role in extending
freedom of the expression to working people as well as reinforcing their sense
of class consciousness. They enabled disparate members of the labouring
classes to see that their predicament was something they had in common.[56]
They were closely associated with the rise of working-class politics; the
world's best-selling newspaper in the middle of the nineteenth century, the
Northern Star, was the mouthpiece of Chartism. They also played a key role
in the development of working-class culture and literature as well as
extending the nature of popular journalism. For cultural historian Raymond
Williams,[57] the editors of the leading radical newspapers, Cobbett and

Carlile, Wooler and Hetherington, are the 'real heroes of popular journalism', representing the authentic voice of working people, which was diminished and subsumed into the commercial popular press in the twentieth century. Radical newspapers were both a catalyst for and a component of the rise of the 'popular press' in Britain.

The first wave of radical newspapers corresponded with the disturbances that occurred in the immediate aftermath of the French Revolution. Strongly influenced by the radical wing of the bourgeoisie, and embracing the philosophy of Tom Paine, early radical newspapers had much in common with the liberalism of some of their respectable counterparts. Their emphasis was on individual liberty rather than class solidarity and collectivist action. The most renowned newspaper of this phase was William Cobbett's *Political Register*. Cobbett's newspaper began life as a pro-government publication in 1802 with a grant from the Treasury to support the government's war against France. Within a couple of years it had undergone a conversion. Cobbett declared in the edition of 1 September 1805 that the main danger to Britain was not from abroad but from 'despotism at home'.[58] The government's efforts to gerrymander a by-election had disgusted him, making his paper more critical of government, and in particular of the methods it adopted to finance its continental war. He denounced the profits made by bankers from Britain's wars and wrote of the plight of agricultural workers who had suffered the greatest hardship in meeting the costs of Britain's struggles with Napoleon. Gradually the *Political Register* came to articulate the interests of labouring men and women whom Cobbett believed were ill served by the British press. He argued that most newspapers were 'enslaved' by those who commanded the resources to purchase space in their pages for their advertisements. The *Political Register* attempted to convince ordinary people that the cause of their suffering was political. His most famous political message was the two-headed monster he referred to as 'The Thing'. The two heads represented the 'old corruption', the privileges of the Church and State, which had a deep-seated hatred for the poor, and the 'war-profiteers, the merchants and bankers' who placed intolerable burdens on the poor labourers of Britain. He preached that only reform of Parliament could defeat the monster.

Cobbett's weekly newspaper faced considerable difficulties – as a stamped newspaper it sold at a price which most working people could not afford. He found a way around paying stamp duty in 1816 when he discovered that if a sheet was folded and contained comment but not news it could not be considered a newspaper and was exempt from stamp duty. He therefore published reprints from his paper in folded form at 2 pence a copy, referred to by his critics as 'Twopenny Trash'. Published as a booklet in 1816 the *Address to Journeymen and Labourers* sold around 200,000 copies in two months. Cobbett's main contribution to the development of the British newspaper was his punchy prose and crude invective, which helped him to reach ordinary men and women. He was able 'to master the art of writing for the working class',

86

his coarseness and invective helping him to translate Paine's ideas into a language that working people could understand.[59] It was hard-hitting political commentary that enabled the *Political Register* to achieve a weekly circulation of between 40,000 and 50,000.[60] He realised the importance of distribution, developing a sophisticated system, signing up small shopkeepers across the country to act as his selling agents.[61] Regular orders were sent to him and parcels of the *Political Register* were delivered by coach, with discounts available for larger numbers. The suspension of Habeas Corpus in 1817 led Cobbett to flee to America, and the popularity of his newspaper was never again to reach the same heights. He returned to Britain in 1819 and toured the country advocating reform; he then published his account of these trips in his collection *Rural Rides*. His lobbying was rewarded in 1832 with the passing of the Great Reform Act, which extended the franchise, and he directly benefited, becoming MP for Oldham. He died soon after.

Cobbett's contemporary Richard Carlile exhibited even more dedication to the cause of a free press. He suffered more than nine years of imprisonment; 'You have done your duty bravely, Mr Carlile, if everyone had done it like you, it would be all very well', remarked Cobbett.[62] Carlile's 'whole and sole object, from first to last ... has been a Free Press and Free Discussion'.[63] A tinplate worker, his involvement with the press began as a hawker of Wooler's *Black Dwarf*, a paper which proclaimed itself to be 'the greatest object of ministerial hatred'.[64] He soon held a more precarious job. He became the publisher of Sherwin's *Political Register*, which he eventually took over and renamed the *Republican*, as well as of cheap versions of seditious works, namely Paine's writings. Prosecuted on several occasions, Carlile realised the sales potential of the publicity surrounding his arrest. Writing from jail he stated: 'I hear from London that the prosecution of Mrs Carlile produces just the same effect as my prosecution did – it quadruples the sales of all her publications'.[65] To take advantage of such publicity the Carliles – mother, father and daughter all served prison sentences for seditious publication – established an effective distribution system. 'General Carlile's Corps' constituted 150 volunteer shopmen and vendors who together served over 200 years of imprisonment.[66] Carlile's analysis of the plight of the workers did not extend to accepting that there was a fundamental conflict between capital and labour, nor to accepting that the political system worked in the interest of capital. He believed that associations and clubs were an infringement of the rights of the individual, but his attempts to organise the distribution of radical literature impressed other radicals such as John Wade, who used the pages of his paper, the *Gorgon*, to advocate the need for the working people to organise.

The great unstamped

The heyday of the radical newspaper was between 1831 and 1836, when it is estimated that 560 papers were started up.[67] These papers, often referred to as the 'great unstamped press', were more radical in their critique of society than their predecessors. They were hostile to the 1832 Act for its limited extension of the franchise and were active in the efforts to organise working people. Hetherington's *Poor Man's Guardian* was affiliated to the National Union of the Working Classes and Others, one of the earliest attempts in Britain to form a trade union movement. Like many of his colleagues, Hetherington's journalism was secondary to his politics. He used his publications to build a sense of solidarity between working people the length and breadth of Britain. The *Poor Man's Guardian* wanted to show the weavers of Lancashire, the fishermen of Cornwall and the cabinet makers of London that in spite of their different experiences they were members of one working class as a result of their labour. He, like many of his fellow radical editors, believed the role of their newspapers was to provide knowledge that would help their readers to understand better the reasons for their plight and thereby be better able to organise themselves to bring about political change. James Bronterre O'Brien, who edited the *Poor Man's Guardian* and its sister publication, the *Destructive*, and was the radical press's most gifted polemicist, put it like this:

> The knowledge most wanted by the people is a knowledge of their rights and duties as members of society, and the wrongs committed on them by those who have usurped the Government to their exclusion ... why a man, who works all day, and whose grandfather and father did the same, should be poorer than another, who never worked at all, nor his father and grandfather before him; why the working man should have no vote in the laws, while the idle and mischievous man has a vote; why the most useful classes of society are always the most degraded, and the most useless the most honoured; why the wealth of society should be produced exclusively by one class of persons, while another class, producing nothing but crime and misery, should almost as exclusively possess and enjoy it ... Now this is the sort of knowledge that people require.
>
> (*Destructive*, 7 June 1834)

The columns of radical newspapers were full of propaganda and information about political struggle. Their analysis reflected the broad and varied range of political objectives that was to be found at the time. An eight-page quarto printed on flimsy paper and in rough type, the typical radical newspaper in the early 1830s would contain accounts of trials of political activists, reports of public meetings, addresses of celebrated orators, articles on religious abuses, critiques of parliamentary debates, correspondence from readers, extracts from other radical papers as well as collections for political causes, the amount raised and the names of those who had made what donations. The first page would be a leading article, usually a polemic calling readers to arms. The back page would be made up of notices of meetings, events and occasions, advertisements (often from radical booksellers) and now and then employment ads such as that in the issue of 16 June 1832: 'WASHING: Wanted by an Experienced Laundress ... a family's or single gentlemen's washing. Terms moderate. Address (post paid) to ... ' The occasional poem would creep in but the output of the paper was relentlessly political and uncompromisingly austere in layout.

Poor Man's Guardian, 17 August 1832

The middle classes are the real tyrants of society. All that is mean, and grovelling, and selfish, and rapacious, and harsh, and cold and cruel, and usurious, belongs to this huckstering race. To screw all they can out of poverty and seduce all they can out of powerful vice is the grand wish of their lives ... All these are the men to whom the Whigs have entrusted the guardianship of our liberties and industry. It was not enough that we were exposed for centuries to prowling oligarchs. These noble beasts of prey were too good for us. So, to keep the Whigs in power, the lion must give place to the rat, and the tiger to the leech ... Oh, may we die as we have lived, a race of despised outlaws, if we submit to it a moment longer than it may please God and our right arms.

In the period of high political tension leading up to the 1832 Reform Act political coverage resonated with readers. The 'unstamped' newspapers by refusing to submit to press taxation were in open opposition to the government. Workers bought them to gain information, to mobilise their political activities and to defend them against official sanction. The masthead of the *Poor Man's Guardian* stated that it was published 'Contrary to the Law, to try the power of Right against Might'. The words 'contrary to' were soon replaced by 'in defiance of' as the conflict with the forces of law and order intensified. By not taking the stamp radical newspapers were cheaper than their 'respectable' rivals. They were outselling them. The *Poor Man's Guardian*, a weekly newspaper, sold between 12,000 and 16,000 copies per issue,[68] with a readership that would have been considerably higher as many more additional people read radical newspapers than their respectable counterparts. Distribution was crucial to the success of the radical press. Denied access to regular news vendors and agents such as W.H. Smith, which had outgrown the news walk to become a national distributor of newspapers,[69] radical papers had to develop their own, clandestine systems of distribution. A variety of ways were devised to send the newspaper from London to the country, including in coffins. Flagging sales would sometimes see editors submit themselves for trial, with the corresponding publicity helping circulation. Hetherington and fellow radical editors had to work hard to cultivate their readership, particularly in the wake of the passing of the Reform Act when the intensity of political feeling dissipated as concessions were seen to have been made by government. Hetherington, O'Brien and William Cleave, the editor of the *Weekly Police Gazette*, realised the importance of combining political information and analysis with some form of entertainment and local news. Hetherington encouraged his agents and readers to act as collectors of local news and often printed provincial letters instead of London ones.[70] To compete with the respectable press – as well as the magazines and papers devoted to the promotion of 'useful knowledge' – radical newspapers became more effective at combining politics and news. From 1833 the *Destructive* began to devote more space to police news at the behest of its readers, while a publication launched in 1833, the *Man*, turned over three of its pages to police news, poetry, cuttings and 'scraps of everything'.[71] Hetherington eventually turned the *Destructive* into the *Twopenny Dispatch*, promising his readers it would:

> Henceforward be a repository of all gems and treasures, and fun and frolic and 'news and occurrences' of the week. It shall abound in Police Intelligence, in Murders, Rapes, Suicides, Burnings, Maimings, Theatricals, Races, Pugilism and all manner of moving 'accidents by flood and field'. In short, it will be stuffed with every sort of devilment that will make it sell ... Our object is not to make money, but to beat the Government.[72]

Hetherington and his colleagues had to rely on other kinds of stories to attract readers, and moved a long way from the politics that dominated their earlier publications. Cleave's *Weekly Police Gazette* was most successful at combining politics and entertainment; 'shocking crime' and police court reports helped the newspaper to reach a circulation which is estimated to have been between 20,000 and 40,000.[73] Cleave – as other Radical editors – drew on the tradition of street literature, the broadsides, ballads and other ephemeral forms of literature that were popular with ordinary people. Broadsides, usually of murders and crimes, produced by the likes of James Catach had always sold well – their formula centred around bold headlines such as 'Horrid Murder' and the use of illustrations to capture the event or the likeness of the murderer.[74] They competed with the radical newspapers for the working-class reader, and Cleave and his colleagues adapted from them to maintain and enhance the appeal of their newspapers.

Unlike *The Times*, which had adopted steam-driven presses to turn out its newspaper, most of the radical newspapers were produced by hand press. However, the Stanhope iron hand press, which was patented in 1800 and could be used by anyone with a little skill and determination, had an impact on the appearance of the newspaper.[75] Wooden presses did not provide a heavy imprint, limiting the use of dense black typeface. The heavier iron presses created styles which 'seemed to shout at the reader from the page' and 'gave print some of the rhetorical devices of tone and emphasis natural to speaking'.[76] This could be seen as an aid to reading the newspaper aloud as well as leading to the expansion of the use of posters, which became 'the language of the walls' in Britain in the early nineteenth century. Pictorial representation became an essential part of print culture; books, magazines and to a lesser extent newspapers took on a visual dimension which is often neglected in discussion of the period. The developments of mechanised printing, combined with Thomas Bewick's pioneering the process of wood engraving, saw woodcuts incorporated into the newspaper.[77] These innovations could not prevent the second wave of radical newspapers petering out in 1836. The reasons for their demise can be located in the decline of political activity following the Reform Act of 1832 and the decision to reduce newspaper stamp duty in 1836. The prosecution of radical newspapers had also exacted a high price; the focus of the government attention on the hawkers had slowed down the ability of the newspapers to reach their audience. The National Union of the Working Classes collapsed in 1834 and, with the competition from reformist publications such as the *Penny Magazine* intensifying, the radical newspapers struggled to hold their own. Sales of the *Poor Man's Guardian* fell and it finally closed in 1835.

The Chartist press: the *Northern Star*

The last phase of the Radical press occurred between 1839 and 1858, which are the dates usually associated with the rise and fall of Chartism, the first political movement of working people in Britain. In this period over 120 Chartist newspapers and periodicals were established around the country; most were short lived, some were stamped, all were propaganda instruments of the movement.[78] The movement's leading newspaper was the *Northern Star*, launched in Leeds in 1837. By 1839 it was the 'most popular selling newspaper' in Britain, selling, it is estimated, 50,000 copies per week, more than most respectable newspapers. Circulation does not tell the full story, as with an estimated twenty additional readers per copy we could be talking about a readership of anything up to a million. Accounting for the newspaper's rapid success is problematic in some ways. It did not differ from most other newspapers of the period, consisting of 'six columns a page of unbroken nonpareil ... sparsely paragraphed and wholly without crossheads'.[79] For one press historian it was 'curiously out-of-date and its advertisements were strikingly reminiscent of eighteenth century newspapers'.[80] It was produced with the same printing technology, transferring its printing to London in 1844, relying on sales and advertisers, although the latter were less inclined to use the *Star*. Unlike its predecessors of the 1830s, it was a legal newspaper, taking the stamp. Feargus O'Connor in the first issue drew attention to 'that little red spot in the corner of my newspaper. That is the stamp; the Whig *beauty* spot; your *plague* spot'.[81] The *Northern Star* in 1838 commented on the state of the press in Britain, highlighting that the reduction in stamp duty had 'made the rich man's paper cheaper and the poor man's paper dearer'.[82] Yet within a couple of years the newspaper was outselling nearly all of its rivals, respectable and radical.

The reasons given to account for this rapid success are varied. Malcolm Chase[83] draws attention to the role of gifts and special offers to regular subscribers to account for the rapid rise in circulation. Illustrated items, usually specially commissioned portraits, were used to encourage subscribers in an early example of promotional culture. The quality of the writing is also singled out; the *Star* developed a network of paid correspondents around the country, often working men, and O'Connor placed great emphasis on the reporting of events abroad so that readers should be 'aware of the part that was being played by their brethren on different stages of the political world'.[84] O'Connor's style, polemical and full of jokes, was popular.[85] However, it was by acting as the champion of Chartism that the paper flourished. While most Chartist newspapers and journals acted as the mouthpiece of sectional or individual interests within the movement, the *Northern Star* established itself as the 'comprehensive and definitive voice' of Chartism.[86] It succeeded, unlike the efforts of Hetherington and his colleagues in the 1830s, to bring together local and sectional struggles across Britain into a political movement of national significance. It provided Chartism with an identity and national platform. The newspaper did this by encouraging differing views to be expressed in its pages, and complementing political commentary with news.

The economic structure of the radical press

The growth of radical newspapers was supported by the economic structure of the newspaper industry in the early nineteenth century. The cost of running a radical newspaper was relatively small. Most newspapers were printed on hand presses which were cheap to purchase, at around £10 to £15. Labour costs were low and much of the material that filled the columns of the newspapers was provided by readers, in the form of either correspondence or reports of events and meetings from their part of the country. The *Twopenny Dispatch*, founded by Hetherington in 1835, is estimated to have cost only £6 per week to run. The *Northern Star* differed from other radical newspapers in the network of correspondents it employed to provide national coverage; reportedly at a cost of just over £9 per week in 1841.[87] The main cost was the editor and he was often happy to take a basic salary in the name of the political struggle. However, gifted writers such as O'Brien were able to command high remuneration as a result of their appeal to the public. The operating costs of most radical papers were small. Distribution costs were kept low by the use of a system of volunteers and, with a high number of readers per copy, print runs could also be kept low. A limited amount of capital was needed to establish a radical paper. The *Northern Star* was launched with capital of £690 raised largely from subscriptions from the public in the main towns of the North of England.[88] Radical newspapers could cover their costs simply on sales alone. It is estimated that the *Northern Star* broke even on sales of 6,200 copies per week, while those of the *Poor Man's Guardian* were as low as 2,500.[89] Low capital and running costs had consequences for the ownership of radical newspapers. They could be owned by ordinary people. Many of the leading publishers, editors and printers came from a working-class background and ran their newspapers in the interests of their class.

They were also protected from competition from the respectable press by the very mechanism that was supposed to control them – stamp duty. Radical papers published without the stamp were much cheaper than their mainstream rivals – a radical newspaper would usually sell at 1 or 2 old pennies, while papers such as *The Times* cost 7d or 8d per issue. Advertising, not sales, was the main means by which respectable newspapers raised revenue. Such a form of finance was not available to the radical press – it is estimated that in 1817 Cobbett's *Political Register* only had three advertisements. The *Northern Star* carried fraudulent claims in its editorials for quack medical remedies in a desperate search for advertising.[90] However, radical newspapers could survive and be profitable without advertising revenue. Hetherington in 1837 is estimated as making £1,000 from his business, while the *Northern Star* made a profit of £13,000 in 1839 and £6,500 in 1840.[91] The economic circumstances that protected the Radical press began, as the paper itself noted, to slowly unravel from 1836, when the stamp tax was reduced to 1d and the competitive edge of radical newspapers declined. The disappearance of the institutional controls that had been exercised over newspapers since the early eighteenth century transformed the economic structure that had supported the radical press – and for some critics this was a conscious strategy to manage radical newspapers and publications more effectively.

Repeal of the taxes on knowledge

The struggle for the freedom of the press from regulation returned as a major political issue in the 1830s with the widespread evasion of the stamp duty. Between 1830 and 1836 nearly 800 publishers and vendors of unstamped newspapers were imprisoned for publishing or selling a newspaper without a stamp.[92] The government's campaign to break the radical press had foundered on the unlimited supply of people willing to go to jail for their rights. In an atmosphere more sympathetic to individual rights, the government found it more difficult to prosecute the press with any degree of success. The system of press control based on taxation started to collapse. Some argued for the introduction of more draconian measures to curtail the growing radical press. Others called for the repeal of the taxation system altogether. They argued that besides being unenforceable, the system restricted trade and the dissemination of knowledge, in particular useful knowledge.

The campaign to abolish press taxation involved a variety of people from different political backgrounds and from both radical and respectable newspapers. In Parliament many campaigners were primarily motivated by the desire to remove the threat that Radicalism posed to British society. James Curran[93] has argued that their main objective was to ensure that the press played an effective role in engineering consent from the lower classes for the social order being established by capitalism. A free press, unencumbered by taxation, would be a better instrument of social control than state coercion. It was no longer about whether people should be allowed to read but rather what they should read. 'Instruction rather than the strong arm of the law is the only way to put the unions down', proclaimed one of the leading parliamentary supporters of the campaign.[94] For one of his colleagues popular unrest amongst working people was a result of the lack of 'proper instruction ... caused by the restraints on a free press'.[95] Milner-Gibson, the President of the Association for the Repeal of the Taxes on Knowledge, argued that the removal of press taxes would lead to 'a cheap press in the hands of men of good moral character, of respectability and of capital'.[96] A press 'in the hands of parties who are great capitalists' could be relied on to impart 'sound doctrines' and, as the *Spectator* argued in 1835, help to dispel ignorance and put an end to trade unions, rick burning and machine breaking.[97] The campaign for the abolition of press taxes was not driven by a principled commitment to freedom of expression in the press but rather by the desire to 'ensure the press provided institutional support for the social order'.[98] As a result of the campaign's success, the duties on newspapers were relaxed. Advertising duty was reduced in 1833, while stamp duty and the excise duty on paper were cut back in 1836. It took another couple of decades and several further campaigns to finally end press taxation. Advertising duty was eventually abolished in 1853, stamp duty in 1855 and the duty on paper in 1861.

The demise of radical newspapers

Greater competition from respectable newspapers was accompanied by the increase in the costs of newspaper production from the late 1830s. Machinery started to become more expensive from the 1830s; the new steam-driven presses of the 1830s were costly. Hetherington spent 350 guineas purchasing a Napier machine in 1835.[99] Larger and more regular newspapers meant employing more staff, which resulted in rising operating costs, greater break-even circulations and longer periods of time before initial investments could be recouped. Changing economic circumstances were an important part of the decline of radical newspapers but there were also a number of social and political changes that contributed. The political struggles of the 1840s and 1850s were successful in ameliorating the conditions of work and wresting better pay for many working people. Average real wages rose by around 40 per cent between 1862 and 1875 and wealthy philanthropists provided housing, schools, orphanages, baths and drinking fountains which improved the lives of working people.[100] The consequence of these changes was a decline in working-class militancy from the 1860s onwards. Acceptance amongst working people of 'consensus ideology' emphasising that capital and labour can work together increased. The mobilisation of resources by the middle class to compete with the radical press for the hearts and minds of working people also played an important role. The mid-Victorian period saw a revival of periodicals devoted to the improvement of the working class. Publications such as *True Briton* sought to educate working people 'not only to morality and Christian principles, to truth and good conduct but also to purely patriotic feelings'.[101] God, King and Country were mobilised; the 'fulsome reporting' of royal events was emphasised.[102] Some journals, such as the *British Workman* and the *Cottager and Artisan*, had learned how to address working people in a less patronising way, emphasising heroic depictions of the working man and the nobility of labour. Much was made of how working people could better themselves. But it was perhaps new forms of popular entertainment, such as the music halls, in propagandising the values of nation and empire amongst working people, that were most significant. By showing how 'domestic "under-classes" could become imperial "over-classes"' they encouraged people in all walks of life that they 'could feel part of a national enterprise on which the majority had been persuaded to agree'.[103] Trade union organisations emerged, such as the National Union of Practical Miners, which preached consensus ideology. In its newspaper, the *Miner's and Workman's Advocate*, the union made its position clear:

> We offer no antagonisms to capital. Capital and Labour as far as interests are concerned are identical. Let the union of ALL be cemented and a brighter day will dawn on the poor pitmen of this country.[104]

Social-economic factors and ideological developments can account for the fate of radical press in the latter part of the nineteenth century. They do not fully explain why periods of political unrest and economic slumps later in the nineteenth century and in the early twentieth century did not see the return of such newspapers. The capacity of radical newspapers to attract readers in the numbers of the *Northern Star* and *Poor Man's Guardian* was never recaptured. The radical and socialist newspapers that were launched in times of trouble and strife, of renewed class conflict, for example the *Clarion* (1891) and the *Daily Citizen* (1911), did not survive very long – and repeated efforts by many on the left of British politics to establish newspapers that reflected their politics failed.

This failure is attributed to the increasing reliance of newspapers on advertising revenue. Radical newspapers could not operate in such conditions. Advertisers were not sympathetic to radical ideas and shied away from newspapers that promulgated them. A more substantial handicap was the perception that advertisers had of the readership of radical papers. In their view the kind of people who read radical newspapers lacked sufficient purchasing power to make it worthwhile for them to advertise in the pages of such publications. The head of one of the largest advertising agencies in Victorian Britain stated in 1856 that despite the large circulations of radical newspapers 'their readers are not purchasers: and any money thrown on them is so much money thrown away'.[105] By the early twentieth century advertising revenue had become integral to the economic survival of the press. radical newspapers had a number of choices: they closed down, became more 'respectable' by moving up market, condemned themselves to a political ghetto with small readerships or acquired alternative sources of finance.[106] Karl Marx's *Beehive* was taken over by a Liberal millionaire before its eventual demise, while the radical Sunday newspapers such as *Reynolds News* and *Lloyd's Weekly News* became less radical. The last decade of the nineteenth century saw the beginning of mass circulation newspapers that would attract a large number of working-class readers. They were different in both content and nature from the radical working-class press of the early years of the century.

TRIAL OF RICHARD PATCH.

Mr. BLIGHT's HOUSE.

Ground Plan of Mr. BLIGHT's House.

The Times, 7 April 1806

4

TRANSITION TO DEMOCRACY

The press as 'the fourth estate', 1850–90

Journalism is now truly an estate of the realm; more powerful than any of the other estates; more powerful than all of them combined if it could ever be brought to act as a united and concentrated whole. Nor need we wonder at its sway. It furnishes the daily reading of millions. It furnishes the exclusive reading of hundreds and thousands. Not only does it supply the nation with nearly all the information on public topics which it possesses, but it supplies it with its notions and opinions in addition ... for five pence to a penny (as the case may be) it does all the thinking of the nation; saves us the trouble of weighting and perpending, of comparing and deliberating; and presents us with ready-made opinions clearly and forcibly expressed.

William Rathbone Greg, 'The newspaper press', Edinburgh Review, October, 1855[1]

More newspaper titles, expanding circulations and a widening readership followed the demise of the 'taxes on knowledge'. Between 1856 and 1914 the number of newspapers published in Britain and Ireland increased more than eightfold, from 274 to 2,205, with London numbers tripling from 151 to 478.[2] By 1881 18 daily newspapers were appearing in the nation's capital city, 96 in the English provinces, 21 in Scotland, 17 in Ireland and only 4 in Wales.[3] In spite of the increase in the number of titles and in sales, the total circulation of British newspapers was still relatively small and confined to a relatively narrow segment of society. However, in the late nineteenth century newspapers began to extend their reach throughout Victorian society. Daily newspapers led this gradual growth, going through a period of change with the advent of the one penny newspaper. The Sunday press built up a circulation which was the envy of the modern world – the first newspaper to reach a million sales was Lloyd's Weekly News in 1896. The provincial press grew at a more rapid pace, to the extent that most major and even some minor cities in Britain had two, if not more, daily newspapers by the end of the century. The most notable casualty was the radical press, which virtually disappeared.

The fate of the radical newspapers was tied up with the changing nature of the economic structure of the newspaper industry. Advertising increased its prominence in press finances, taking up more space within the newspaper. Newspapers became more independent from politicians and political parties in the second half of the nineteenth century, although political subsidies still played a role in the financing of the press, particularly outside London, where a close connection between the Liberal Party and provincial newspapers was established. Politics still dominated the content of the newspapers but it slowly began to decline as other forms of news and information expanded. Foreign news was a crucial ingredient of the late Victorian paper, with foreign and war correspondents such as Henri de Blowitz and William Howard Russell becoming household names. The *Daily Telegraph*, founded in 1855, was one of the first newspapers to take advantage of the new environment. It reduced its price, changed its content, incorporated techniques associated with the American press and employed the most celebrated journalist of the day, George Augustus Sala, whose prose resonated with the Victorian imagination, to become the leading newspaper of the period.

The nineteenth century is often portrayed as the era of the 'sovereign editor', epitomised by John Delane at the *Times* and C.P. Scott of the *Manchester Guardian*. They are seen as partisan, opinionated and in total control of the content and direction of their newspapers. They are credited with exercising the sovereign right of the editor to edit the newspaper without any intervention from owners or financial backers or government. They asserted the independence of their newspapers and the press in general by articulating the principle of the press as the 'fourth estate' of the realm. For some critics the notion that the press operated as a 'fourth estate' is a 'political myth' promoted by the industry and profession to cement a privileged position in the political process, the 'indispensable link between public opinion and the governing institutions of the country'.[4] The extent to which the great editors of the late Victorian era were independent actors is a matter of conjecture. The tradition of sovereign editorship appears in some cases to have historical substance; but it is limited and has been exaggerated to reinforce over time the perception that newspapers are free from the control of their owners.

Technological changes such as the introduction of the telegraph and the advent of Pitman's shorthand helped to develop the practice of reporting. The speed and immediacy of the news was enhanced; eyewitness news accounts were now possible. The previous struggles of editors to find material to fill their pages were replaced by a situation in which they had to select from a stream of information that poured into their offices. News reporting, reporting what was happening, became a vital ingredient of the newspaper, although it did not usurp the key role of comment, analysis and interpreting the 'politics of the day'. 'Views rather than news' were the 'hallmark' of the late Victorian newspaper.[5] Lengthy articles laid out in narrow, heavily compacted columns made up the newspaper. 'Every reader knew ... that every word in the paper was indispensable, he worked his way through the entire solid and black print, from the first page to the last'.[6] The reader that these newspapers had in mind was a man of leisure and education who was interested in the great issues of the day, home and abroad.

Changes began to creep into the industry in the 1880s with the arrival of what was labelled the 'New Journalism'. Svennik Hoyer and Horst Pottker[7] identify five key elements to the journalism that developed: the twenty-four-hour news cycle, the focus on news values as the basis of determining the content of the press, the introduction of the 'inverted pyramid' style of writing, the invention of the news interview as a tool for gathering and presenting news and information, and the rise of objectivity as the central tenet of the profession of journalism. Editors, freed from the need to gather enough information to fill their pages, began to address presentation and display. As competition increased with the arrival of more newspapers, the specific look of a newspaper became more important to commercial success. To attract more readers, newspapers introduced a number of typographical innovations to make their product more readable.

The *Daily Telegraph*

Taxes on newspapers were gradually relaxed from the 1830s, disappearing completely by 1861. This was the culmination of several campaigns for the repeal of press taxation which had been launched in the 1830s. The motives of those involved in the campaigns, as we have seen, varied enormously (see Chapter 3). Radical newspapers and politicians, including the Chartist movement, saw the struggle in terms of freeing them of barriers which restricted the dissemination of their ideas to the broader public. Their respectable counterparts were more concerned that newspapers would instruct the people 'to read in the best manner'; that is, in a way which is 'most safe for the constitution of the country'.[8] Many of those who edited and owned the press opposed repeal. The Provincial Newspaper Society feared that it would 'lower the character of the press', create cheap competition and undermine the 'gentlemanly status' of proprietors.[9]

The Society was correct, as repeal increased competition as new newspapers flooded onto the market. The most significant was the *Daily Telegraph and Courier*, launched at what was then the extremely low price of 2 pence in June 1855 by Colonel Arthur Sleigh. Losses led to it falling into the hands of its main creditor, the printer Joesph Moses Levy, who re-launched the newspaper, dropping the *Courier* reference and giving London 'its first, double-sheet, eight-page, morning newspaper at the sensationally low price of one penny'.[10] Many believed that 'it is impossible to produce a first class newspaper at that price'.[11] London's leading newspaper in the mid-1850s, *The Times*, cost 7 pence and its main competitors around 5 pence. The *Telegraph* disagreed: 'cheapness is consistent with excellence' and 'there is no reason why a daily newspaper, conducted with a high tone, should not be produced at a price which will place it within the means of all classes of the community'.[12] The price reduction brought a sales increase, and within a short time the *Telegraph* was selling over 27,000 copies, second only to *The Times* and half its circulation.[13] Under the editorial control of Levy's son, Edward Levy-Lawson, the *Telegraph* was to acquire in 1876 what it described as the largest circulation in the world, touching on daily sales of nearly a quarter of a million, and remained the market leader until the arrival of the *Daily Mail* in the last decade of the century. It was clearly reaching readers who had not been previously able to afford to purchase a daily newspaper regularly.

Levy-Lawson changed the format of the paper, increasing the range of the topics covered – he often cautioned his staff against the 'unforgivable sin of lack of variety in the paper'[14] – and developing classified advertising through the invention of the box number.[15] He borrowed many techniques from the American press, including the use of numerous headlines on a big story. He also employed a number of talented writers, including George Augustus Sala. Sala quarrelled and fell out with nearly all the leading editors and newspaper owners of his times. Irascible, vain and with the reputation of a 'bohemian', he developed a style of descriptive writing which was to be dubbed 'Telegraphese'.[16] Highly descriptive, sometimes referred to as 'florid', 'flamboyant' and suffused with 'picturesqueness and gusto',[17] his writing style was honed to please the middle-class reader. Sala had established his reputation covering the American Civil War. The *Telegraph* spared no expense on its coverage of foreign events. Special correspondents were appointed such as John Merry Le Sage, who during the Franco-German War of 1870–1 scooped his fellow reporters to provide the first account of the German army's entry into Paris. The newspaper co-sponsored H.M. Stanley's expedition to find Dr Livingstone, his dispatches giving the *Telegraph* an 'impressive reputation for enterprise'.[18]

Sala's reporting

The Trial (and failure) of the 'Great Eastern'
George Augustus Sala,
Daily Telegraph, 12 September 1859

On Board the *Great Eastern*, Portland Harbour, Saturday, 10.30 a.m.

We had dined. It was six o'clock, and we were off Hastings, at about seven miles' distance from the shore. The majority of the passengers having finished their repast, had gone on deck ... The dining saloon was deserted, save by a small knot of joyous guests, all known to each other, who had gathered round the most popular of the directors, Mr Ingram. That gentleman, his hand on the shoulders of his young son, was listening, not apparently unpleased, to the eloquence of a friend, who was decanting on his merits while proposing his health. The glasses were charged; the orator's peroration had culminated; the revellers

---

were upstanding; when – as if the fingers of a man's hand had come out against the cabin wall, and written, as in sand, that the Medes and Persians were at the gate, the verberation of a tremendous explosion was heard. Then came – to our ears, who were in the dining room – a tremendous crash, not hollow, as of thunder, but solid, as of objects that offered resistance. Then a sweeping, rolling, swooping, rumbling sound, as of cannon balls scudding along the deck above.

Source: Fisher, J. (1960) *Eye Witness: An Anthology of British Reporting* London: Cassell, 41–5.

Such innovation should not distract from the fact that the *Daily Telegraph* was a serious newspaper, highlighted by the background of its chief leader writer, Edwin Arnold. Arnold spoke ten living and dead languages and was the author of tomes such as *Griselda, a Drama*, *The Poets of Greece* and *The History of the Administration of India under the Late Marquis of Dalhousie (1862–64)*, the latter in two volumes.[19] Arnold stressed 'the value of a classical as well as general training for editorial work' and commented that he found 'immense advantage arising from my academical studies', asserting that it was 'impossible for a newspaper man to be too widely read'.[20] Arnold typified the 'gentlemen of the press'. This was a time when journalists wore 'top hats', a sign of respectability in late Victorian society, and 'the newspapers wore top hats as well as those who produced them'.[21] They were in general 'stolidly respectable', 'clung to tradition' and 'valued dignity above enterprise'.[22] Respectability was conveyed by undisturbed columns, long articles, bookish typeface, few drawings or illustrations and a focus on politics and the great affairs of state and government.

Make-up of the pages

Politics made up much of the content of papers such as the *Morning Post*, *The Times*, *Morning Herald*, *Daily News*, *Globe*, *Morning Chronicle* and *Morning Advertiser*. Political coverage had changed from the eighteenth-century essays and commentaries on the issues and personalities of the day to long detailed sometimes verbatim accounts of debates in Parliament and speeches made at meetings up and down the country. Such reports were facilitated by the development of shorthand. Shorthand was not a new invention (see Chapter 1) but the adoption of a universal system of shorthand, perfected by Isaac Pitman in the 1840s, helped to elevate *accuracy* to a primary place in assessing the performance of journalism and provided the basis for drawing a distinction between *fact and comment* in the reproduction of knowledge in the press. Shorthand 'transformed the business of reporting into a kind of science' by promising readers for the first time 'the complete recovery of some semblance of reality'.[23] Pitman's system of note taking made it possible 'to specialise in observing or hearing and recording with precision'.[24] This enhanced the status of the reporter as the possessor of a particular skill and elevated the importance of reported speech.

Reporters established themselves as the major providers of information to the press in the late eighteenth century. Papers paid individuals to attend trials, interview criminals and provide accounts of executions.[25] Parliamentary reporting developed as a specialist area as newspapers increased their capacity and ability to cover the proceedings of the legislature. The repeal of the ban on parliamentary reporting in 1771 was not accompanied by the granting of any special facilities to enable the press to report what MPs said. Reporters had to queue like ordinary citizens to obtain entrance to Parliament and note taking was banned. Men with the capacity to remember, such as William 'Memory' Woodfall, established reputations as parliamentary reporters. Woodfall's day came to an end when James Perry substituted a team of reporters in 1783 to cover debates and proceedings.[26] Official recognition of the right of the press to report came in 1803 following the failure of any newspapers to report William Pitt's speech on the opening of hostilities in the war with Napoleon.[27] The Speaker's decision to guarantee a privileged right of access to parliamentary reporters was motivated by the desire to ensure politicians were heard. By 1810 there were twenty-three fully accredited parliamentary reporters.[28] However, it was not until a fire destroyed Parliament in 1834 that reporters were granted a particular place to sit – the Press Gallery. Setting aside this space coincided with shorthand becoming a fully established part of reporting practice.

The result was that parliamentary speeches were reported in more detail. *The Times* established itself as the newspaper that produced 'the fullest debate reports'; with a team of fifteen reporters the paper produced two pages of copy when Parliament was sitting.[29] Speeches from the Commons and Lords were given precedence but the newspaper became 'the accepted channel by which a speaker ... could speak from a platform and reach thousands of people all over the country the next day'.[30] Parliament was the primary platform but, as shorthand spread throughout the rapidly growing profession of journalism, the words of other speakers in a variety of contexts appeared. Length grew in importance and 'long, dull, closely printed paragraphs of political speeches, legal judgements, and City news, and columns of foreign correspondence began to dominate the content of the mid Victorian papers'.[31] Political journalism was nevertheless competitive and new forms of writing about parliamentary debates were created – the 'sketch' was introduced by Henry Lucy in the *Daily News* in the 1870s. It added a bit of colour to the dry and dull tones of the reports and summaries of debates.[32]

There was little room for much else. What was not made up of political, court and City reports included a little sport, primarily racing, cricket and rugby. Travel articles appeared, soon becoming popular, as well as reviews of plays and music, usually theatre, opera and concerts. Books were reviewed but in a 'haphazard' way – those interested in the latest publications would turn to weeklies devoted to literature such as the *Athenaeum* and *Academy* or book notices in publications such as the *Spectator* magazine and the *Saturday Review*.[33] The content and layout of the newspaper in the late Victorian period reflected the view that most papers of that period had of their reader. Newspapers were aimed at the educated elite, male in tone and content, and 'suitable only for those who could retire to their clubs at four o'clock and spend two or three hours in digesting [them]'.[34] According to one leading editor:

> Men were considered to be absorbed in politics, law, foreign affairs, money, stocks and shares. Women, if they were considered at all, were taken to have the sombre interests of their men-folk.[35]

The closeness between the newspaper and the world of politics was cemented in the 1880s through the Lobby system. In 1884 reporters were granted exclusive access to Westminster in return for maintaining the anonymity of their sources of information. Precipitated by the bombing of the House by Sein Fein, the Members' Lobby was sealed off from the public. Only journalists whose names were registered with the authorities could gain access. In return for their compliance with parliamentary procedures they were granted privileges at Westminster, including having their own quarters.[36] Rule breaking could see a journalist lose his or her privileges and access. This was the first formal effort by government to control the flow of political information. It was followed by legislation such as the Official Secrets Act in 1889, which restricted the passing of information between civil servants and the press. The extension of the franchise in 1832, 1867 and 1884 was followed by the introduction of new mechanisms 'to control, channel and even manufacture the political news'.[37] These mechanisms ensured that newspapers became an intimate part of the British political system.

Secrecy proliferated throughout late Victorian society and it was not only political coverage that was affected. In 1868 public execution was abolished. Long a staple feature of the newspaper, such stories usually increased circulation. Newspapers now had to negotiate with prison authorities to gain access to jails to cover such events.[38] This proved difficult as fewer sheriffs who exercised the power were willing to admit reporters. The police were also reluctant to co-operate with the press. Editors and reporters increasingly had to negotiate access to events that were established features of the news they carried. The relationship between editors and reporters and those in positions of authority had never been either comfortable or cosy. Distrust pervaded the interaction; the old feelings of newspaper men being 'spies' continued for a long time and critical comment was feared. As the press became more integrated into the corridors of power this antipathy and distrust slowly faded. The requirements of the authorities and the operational needs of newspapers necessitated some form of accommodation.

Newspapers in the second half of the nineteenth century were primarily purveyors of political news, depending on a small and educated body of readers whose political opinions they articulated and to whom they provided direction on the great political issues of the day. They had close connections with politicians and party leaders. *The Times* epitomised this world. It had attained its market leadership of the stamped press in 1839, culminating in a high point in 1855. That year the newspaper monopolised nearly three-quarters of the circulation of the London daily press. In the first six months of 1855 it sold, according to the stamp returns, more than nine million copies; its nearest rival, the *Morning Advertiser*, just one million.[39] It sold twice as many copies as the other five leading daily London papers put together.[40] Its dominance of press advertising was even more complete; packed with advertisements, estimated in the issue of 3 July 1830 to have been in excess of 600, the paper often produced special advertising supplements.[41] Advertisers were attracted not only by the paper's large number of readers but also by their quality. Everyone who was anybody or aspired to be anybody read the paper which described itself as the 'leading journal in Europe'. Its editors wined and dined at the tables of the rich, famous and powerful: as the MP Richard Cobden noted of John Delane, who edited the newspaper from 1841 to 1877, he routinely dined at tables where 'every other guest but himself was an ambassador, Cabinet Minister or a Bishop'.[42] This was the 'age of *The Times*' and from its extraordinary position of power and influence it came to articulate and embody the role of the newspaper as the 'fourth estate'.

Newspapers as the fourth estate

The concept of the 'fourth estate' had been instigated under Barnes's editorship but the classic description of the relations between the press and government which it represents was laid out by John Delane in the 1850s. The need for the clear articulation of the role of the press in politics came as a result of the newspaper's response to the British government's support for the coup d'état of Louis Napoleon in France in December 1851. The Foreign Secretary eventually resigned and within two months the whole government of Lord Russell collapsed. *The Times* was blamed and the incoming Prime Minister, Lord Derby, in a speech in Parliament admonished the paper for its outspoken criticism of the government. He stated that 'as in these days the English Press aspires to share the influence of the statesmen, so also must it share in the responsibilities of statesmen'.[43] Delane responded by instructing his editorial writer to refute Lord Derby's criticism and outline the principles that govern the conduct of the press in a free society. The editorials of 6 and 7 February are the most clear exposition of the doctrine of the 'fourth estate', stressing the independence of journalism from government and politics and identifying the role of the newspaper as a channel of communication between the people and the institutions that govern them, including the right to act as a watchdog over and check on government and those who govern.

Delane on journalism and the press

The Times, 6 February 1852

To perform its duties with entire independence, and consequently with the utmost public advantage, the Press can enter into no close or binding alliances with the statesmen of the day, nor can it surrender its permanent interests to the convenience of the ephemeral power of Government. The first duty of the Press is to obtain the earliest and most correct intelligence of the events of the time, and instantly, by disclosing them, to make them the common property of the nation.

The Times, 7 February 1852

The ends which a really patriotic and enlightened journal should have in view are, we conceive, absolutely identical with the ends of an enlightened and patriotic Minister, but the means by which the journal and the Minister work out these ends, and the conditions under which they work, are essentially and widely different. The statesman in opposition must speak as one prepared to take office; the statesman in office must speak as one prepared to act. A pledge or despatch with them is something more than an argument or essay – it is a measure. Undertaking not so much the investigation of political problems as the conduct of political affairs, they necessarily not so much seekers after truth as expediency. The Press, on the other hand, has no practical function; it works out the ends it has in view by argument and discussion alone, and, being perfectly unconnected with administrative or executive duties, may and must roam at free will over topics which men of political action dare not touch ... Government must treat other Governments with external respect, however black their origins or foul their deeds; but happily the press is under no such trammels, and, while diplomatists are exchanging courtesies, can unmask the mean heart that beats beneath a star, or point out the blood stains on the hand which grasps the spectre. The duty of the journalist is the same thing as that of the historian – to seek out truth, above all things, and to present to his readers not such things that statecraft would wish them to know but the truth as near as he can attain it ... To require, then, the journalist and the statesman to conform to the same rules is to mix up things essentially different, and is as unsound in theory as unheard of in practice.

Source: Steed, *The Press*, 75–8.

The Times played out its role as the 'fourth estate' in the 1850s, particularly during the Crimean War (1854–6). An early episode of the newspaper crossing swords with the government came over the reports of *The Times*'s man in the Crimea, William Howard Russell, the first full-time war correspondent who is held to have brought down the government of the day.[44] Russell is most famous today for his eyewitness account of the charge of the Light Brigade – and his brilliant accounts of battlefield tactics and manoeuvres – but his despatches from the Crimea often focussed on the incompetence of the generals, the lack of administration of supply lines and the plight of the ordinary soldiers, large numbers of whom died from disease. Russell, his *Times* colleague Thomas Chenery and Edwin Godkin of the *Daily News* reported the 'folly … ignorance … mistakes … blunders … oversights' that characterised the conduct of the war.[45] Realising the potential impact of such reporting Russell sought advice from Delane: 'Am I to tell these things or hold my tongue?' His editor was emphatic that he should tell: 'continue as you have done, to tell the truth, and as much of it as you can, and leave such comment as may be dangerous to us, who are out of danger'.[46] The comment was uncompromising:

> The noblest army ever sent from these shores has been sacrificed to the greatest mismanagement. Incompetency, lethargy, aristocratic hauteur, official indifference, favour, routine, perverseness and stupidity reign, revel and riot in the camp before Sebastopol, in the harbour of Balaklava, in the hospital of Scutari and how much nearer home we dare not venture to say.
>
> (*The Times* editorial, 23 December 1854)[47]

Delane's connections led him to circulate to Cabinet members material from Russell he would not print for fear of inflaming the accusations of a lack of patriotism that came thick and fast from government.[48] One critic was Prince Albert, who complained that 'the pen and ink of one miserable scribbler is despoiling the country'.[49] However, the reporting of the war led to a vote of confidence which the government lost and its fall was attributed to the enormous power of *The Times* newspaper.

For many *The Times* had exceeded its duty as the 'fourth estate' of the realm. It had abused its position of power and 'mistook privilege for duty'.[50] Concerns about the paper's influence were expressed as early as the 1820s. Cobbett denounced the paper as 'that cunning old trout', 'that ranting, trimming old *Times*' and 'that brazen old slut'.[51] The political essayist William Hazlitt described it in 1823 as 'valiant, swaggering, insolent, with 100,000 readers at its heels; but the instant the rascal rout turns round with the "whiff and whim" of some fell circumstance, *The Times*, not constant *Times*, turns with them'.[52] As the paper's sales and influence increased, most of its rivals and many politicians perceived it as becoming corrupted by its own sense of power.[53] It was accused of despotism and having contempt for the truth; according to one of its rivals, the *Manchester Guardian*, Delane's claim of independence had come to include 'the liberty to declaim and depreciate without the attestation of facts'.[54] The charge of arrogance appeared to be confirmed by the appearance of the paper's business manager, Mowbray Morris, before a Select Committee inquiry into the newspaper industry in 1852. When asked if cheaper newspapers should be made available to the general public he stated that he had 'very little opinion of the sagacity of uneducated people', agreeing that newspapers 'should be limited to a few hands' and those hands should be 'parties who are great capitalists'.[55] His view corresponded with those in authority such as the Prime Minister Lord John Russell, who, in helping to defeat a motion to repeal press taxes a few years earlier, had stated that he would 'give no countenance to any plans encouraging such abominations as popular education in Britain'.[56]

Successive governments attempted to check the power of *The Times*. They concurred with Lord John Russell, who found the 'degree of information possessed by the *Times* with regard to the most secret affairs of State ... mortifying, humiliating and incomprehensible'.[57] Efforts were sought to bolster rival newspapers. Repeated interventions were made to manage the flow of information, including some early forms of spin. The preferential leaking of information to papers supportive of the government was tried and a government press bureau to co-ordinate the supply of information to the press was envisaged as early as 1809. Croker, Secretary to the Admiralty during the Crimean War, foresaw the birth of spin when he stated that 'the day is not far distant when ... someone in the Cabinet (is) entrusted with what will be thought of as one of the most important duties of the State, the regulation of public opinion'.[58] None of these measures succeeded in shaking *The Times* from its pre-eminent position. It was the repeal of the 'taxes on knowledge' that enabled the 'powers-that-be' to take revenge on their tormentor.

The stamp had enabled *The Times* to stave off competition. Its readers were primarily well-off members of the middle and upper classes who could afford to buy the paper at the inflated cover price. It also benefited from the dispensation all stamped papers received of free postage. The sixteen-page *Times* paid as much for postage as its lighter-weight competitors – most of the rival London newspapers were between four and eight pages. In abolishing the stamp the government attached the caveat that free postage only applied to papers below four ounces in weight – *The Times* did not qualify, thereby increasing its cost of production. From the late 1850s the paper's influence began to decline; circulation fell relatively quickly from 65,000 in 1861 to 49,000 in 1883, slumping to 32,000 by 1904. It posted a deficit for the first time in 1887, following the loss of a legal case for printing a false letter slandering the Irish nationalist MP Charles Stuart Parnell.[59] Discredited by this event, the paper ceased to thunder, consigned to be an ever-diminishing voice in the British press. By 1880 the circulation of the *Telegraph* and the

Standard was approaching 300,000, with the *Daily News* and *Daily Chronicle* standing at just over 100,000[60] – the age of *The Times* had passed.

The sovereign editor

The end of press taxation is often regarded as issuing in the 'age of the sovereign editor'. Prominent amongst the great editors of the late nineteenth century are Delane and Levy-Lawson, as well as W.T. Stead of the *Pall Mall Gazette*, C.P. Scott, who was appointed editor of the *Manchester Guardian* in 1872 and served as MP for Leigh from 1895–1906, and H.G. Massingham, who edited the *Daily Chronicle* in the 1890s. Opinionated and partisan, their influence over their paper, its politics and production was seen as absolute. As newspapers in this period concentrated on politics it is not surprising that their editors should be men of strong political opinion with close connections to political parties and politicians. The close ties are highlighted by the number of editors, owners and reporters who found their way into Parliament in the late Victorian period. By 1892 there were 30 newspaper proprietors and 29 journalists in the House of Commons.[61] Some attained prominent positions in government – for example, Henry Reeve, a *Times* leader writer, became Chancellor of the Exchequer. The practice of anonymous journalism reinforced the perception of the editor's pre-eminence. The assertion by most newspapers, following the example of *The Times*, that articles should be published anonymously reflected the desire to ensure that the authority of the newspaper was paramount.[62] Barnes was a believer in the 'power of dignified anonymity' as it helped him to forge *The Times* into one of Britain's 'independent, responsible, impersonal national institutions'.[63] By-lines, the names of reporters attached to articles, did not appear until later in the century, and then only sparingly. As late as 1905 Winston Churchill could complain about the impact of anonymity on journalism: 'if more articles were signed, individual journalists would acquire a greater weight and authority in the politics of the country'.[64] The voice of the paper was associated with the editor and nothing should detract from this.

Delane is seen as the best example of the great Victorian editor. He exercised political influence in a variety of ways: his paper's extensive reporting of the proceedings of Parliament; the official and unofficial access he had to leading politicians and the attention paid to *The Times*'s leaders and editorials produced every day by a team of six writers.[65] Delane's connections ensured that exclusive, insider information appeared in the paper's leading articles. He also oversaw the letters published in the paper, usually spending three hours a day reading through the correspondence.[66] This helped him to gauge the state of public opinion as well as frame political debate in his paper. Delane regularly visited his reporters abroad and exercised ultimate control over the paper by reading through all editorial copy at the proof stage, often making detailed changes in long hand.[67] He sought to ensure that the paper had an overall tone and style and the content was consistent. This reflected his perception that he was the chief writer or author of *The Times*.

Delane at work

He insisted on being himself responsible for all the news supplied to the public; he was solely responsible for the interpretation of the news and for the comments upon them. He selected the letters addressed to the *Times* which were to be published; he chose the books which were to be reviewed, and exercised an independent judgement on the reviews that were supplied; he was scrupulous as to the way in which even small matters of social interest were announced and handled.

In short, the paper every morning was not a mere collection of pieces of news from all parts of the world, of various opinions, and of more or less valuable essays. It was Mr Delane's report to the public of the news of the day, interpreted by Mr Delane's opinions, and directed throughout by Mr Delane's principles and purpose.

Source: James, *Print and the People 1819–1851*, 81.

The authority of the editor is seen as diminishing towards the end of the nineteenth century. The demise is associated with the growing importance of business considerations to the operation of the newspaper. Delane's departure from *The Times* in 1877 is represented as a significant moment, presaging the decline of the sovereign editor. It became more common for editors to resign following disputes with the papers' owners and sponsors. Incidents such as the refusal of the *Westminster Gazette*'s editor J.A. Spender to print a letter from the paper's owner, Sir Alfred Mond, served only to reinforce the perception of editorial independence.[68] The reality was that editors held less sway than previously. Part of this reality was the re-evaluation of the extent to which the 'great editors' had exercised control over their papers. Delane's authority over *The Times* was never absolute, nor did he attain the supremacy that his predecessor, Thomas Barnes, had in the 1820s and 1830s under John Walter II.[69] Delane's power had been restricted by John Walter III, who was far more active than his father in the running of the paper. Delane also had to share power with *The Times*'s business manager, Mowbray Morris. Morris had considerable involvement in the operation of the newspaper, hiring and firing correspondents, overseeing the expenditure on news gathering and directing the advertising side of the business. Printing was left in the hands of the printer as Delane had 'a remarkable lack of interest … in the whole production area'.[70] Delane owed his position to Walter and shared it with Morris. Walter emphasised his authority on taking over by reappointing Delane only on a temporary basis. Throughout his editorship Delane's influence over the newspaper was circumscribed by the proprietor and business manager.

In the face of popular perceptions of editorial control, Jeremy Tunstall argues that the tradition of the sovereign editor has little basis in historical fact. Such editors only ever existed in 'exceptional circumstances'.[71] These circumstances usually involved the editor as part or whole owner or having a particular contractual arrangement that allowed him or her to exercise total control over the paper. C.P. Scott of the *Manchester Guardian* was able to act as a sovereign editor because he became the owner of the newspaper. Scott, famous for his aphorism that 'comment is free but facts are sacred', played a considerable role in promoting editorial freedom, willing to sacrifice commercial interests when conscience demanded.[72] He was an exception. Many owners sought to emphasise the concept of editorial sovereignty in order to perpetuate the notion that newspapers are run independently from commercial, proprietorial and political considerations.

Penny newspapers

The penny newspaper thrived in the 1870s and 1880s. The four best-selling newspapers, the ailing *Times*, the rising *Daily Telegraph*, the *Standard* and *Daily News*, were joined by a number of other newspapers which sought to make a profit by reducing their cover price. *The Times* sold at 3 pence to support the vast network of correspondents it had developed to gather news at home and abroad, thereby placing the newspaper at a competitive disadvantage. The *Daily News* dropped its cover price to one penny in 1868 to make it viable, which, with the additional input of finance from the millionaire Henry Labouchere, it did, rapidly putting on circulation. The *Standard* became a daily newspaper in 1858; a newspaper for country gentry with a close association with the Conservative Party, it bumped along in the 1860s with a circulation of around 60,000. The appointment of William Mudford as editor in 1874 changed its fortunes and circulation grew rapidly, so that by 1882 it rivalled closely that of the *Telegraph* at or about a quarter of a million readers.[73]

It was the *Daily Telegraph* that epitomised the penny newspaper. Coming into the hands of the Levy family by accident, the *Telegraph*, unlike many of its rivals, had no formal or informal political ties or links; it described itself as 'independent Liberal'.[74] The concept of the 'fourth estate' was articulated and practised in a context in which Victorian politicians were adroit at installing and controlling their friends and acquaintances in the press. Politicians served on the boards of newspapers, had a stake in the financial side of the press and regularly made contributions to newspapers in the form of loans and subsidies, informal briefings and the leaking of information.[75] This informal system of control started to break down with the expansion of newspaper titles and the increasing involvement of men who wanted to make money out of the press. The Levy family was an example of owners who appeared more interested in operating a paper as a commercial venture. They sought to make their newspaper more readable to compete with their rivals, all of whom had reduced their cover price to a penny. The exception was *The Times*, whose business manager refused to countenance a drop in price to compete with the penny papers. While never going as far as attempting to give their readers what they wanted, the *Telegraph*'s owner and editor were aware that they should try to know what people were talking about.[76] More attention was paid to the content and appearance of the newspaper. Rival newspapers responded and the nature of the British newspaper began to change. The Franco-Prussian War (1870–1) was a crucial episode in the process; it 'transformed the behaviour of the British press'.[77] Competition to provide news to a public hungry for information about a war that was taking place on the other side of the Channel led to innovations in news gathering and presentation that became permanent features of the press.

The arrival of the penny press coincided with technological changes that strongly influenced newspaper production. The rotary press – as well as developments in the quality and nature of newsprint – increased the number of copies that could be produced. Newspapers were able to go to press later, ensuring that news reports had greater immediacy. New machinery was labour saving; fewer compositors were required. But overall the savings in this area were offset by the increased cost of introducing new technology. Rotary presses were expensive. *The Times* and *Telegraph* brought in the technology in the late 1860s; an essential step to provide the public with the latest news. Another addition to the costs of production came with the electric telegraph. The telegraph had been expanding across Europe since the 1840s but two key advances were made in the 1860s; the completion of the cable to the US in 1865 and to India in 1869.[78] The speed of the transmission of news increased enormously, so much so that one commentator of the period could state:

> We are witness to a series of conversations carried out with all corners of the island, and between the metropolis of the world and every capital of northern and central Europe, as intimately as though the speakers were bending their heads over the dinner table and talking confidentially to their hosts.[79]

The service of the news agencies which were established in the 1840s further assisted the penny press in attaining the latest news. By 1858 Reuter had signed up most of the morning London dailies – and some provincial newspapers (see pp. 117–18) – to his subscription service.[80] A systematic communication of information from the Continent to Britain, the Reuters service included regular telegrams offering summaries of news that was in the public domain in the country it reported from – as well as appointments and resignations, new legislation, weather reports, crop and harvest information and disasters and accidents.[81] While this service was not a substitute for a correspondent on the spot, it did enable the London papers to compete with the sophisticated network of correspondents deployed by *The Times*.

The importance of foreign news to the London press is attributable to the dominant position of *The Times* in the immediate years after the repeal of press taxation. The supremacy of the Thunderer's foreign news service was one of the primary features of its role as market leader. A leading *Times* foreign correspondent was Paris-based Henri Stefan Opper de Blowitz, who specialised in obtaining exclusive interviews with the leading European statesmen of the day. His greatest scoop was at the Congress of Berlin in 1870, when, in addition to a rare interview with the Reich's Chancellor Bismarck, he secured a copy of the Treaty which *The Times* published as it was being signed.[82] *The Times*'s rivals struggled to compete with such coverage, but compete they had to. Not only did the readership expect foreign news coverage but it was also the case that foreign news stories could generate large boosts in circulation.

The primary mechanism by which de Blowitz and his colleagues communicated news was the long personal despatch. Correspondents produced a long letter, outlining in detail the events that they were describing and providing their interpretation of what had happened. These reports were sent by mail, and usually took up a prominent place in the newspaper when they were published. The speed of getting the news home was a matter of concern. *The Times* from the 1830s sought to develop the fastest possible routes to receive the reports from its men in the field. No matter what route and method were discovered a time lag occurred; it took some of Russell's dispatches from the Crimea nearly twenty-two days to reach London. The electric telegraph changed this; for example, reports from India were now available within hours rather than weeks. Expectations that foreign news would be available for the next morning's edition rose and, according to a *Daily Telegraph* correspondent, the demand for 'copious information' about 'alien peoples' increased sharply after 1860.[83] The Franco-Prussian war brought home to Fleet Street the increasingly competitive nature of foreign news coverage; this war was the 'beginning of the rush to get news first and to be ahead of the other newspapers'.[84]

That war is good for newspaper sales was underlined by the events of the Franco-Prussian War of 1870–1. Stories of the conflict dominated the pages of the British press and circulations increased. The *Daily News* is estimated to have trebled its sales.[85] Trying to respond to the demand for news, the press transformed news gathering techniques, placing more emphasis on the speed of processing news. Prior to the war newspapers used the electric telegraph to acquire a summary of events; the foreign correspondent's long letter would arrive by whatever available post and be published a few days after the telegraph account.[86] This practice unravelled during the Franco-Prussian

War as it failed to produce either the latest news or a coherent account of events. The long letters appeared 'stale' and the telegrams 'inadequate' to cover events that were unfolding quickly. The *Daily News* directed its correspondents to telegraph their long account directly. Other newspapers followed suit and correspondents in the field were soon developing arrangements to ensure their copy was back in the home office within twenty-four hours. This was to have a profound impact on the perception of the timeframe within which the 'newsworthiness' of events should be assessed. The twenty-four-hour time period for news deadlines emerged out of the use of wire services and other time-saving devices, such as the telephone and telex, which were developed later.

For Delane the wires and the requirement for immediate reports marked the end of the foreign correspondent. The telegraph, he believed, removed any necessity to maintain permanent correspondents aboard. 'The telegraph has superseded them as regards news and, except in extraordinary circumstances, the (foreign) papers supply all the rest. When an extraordinary case occurs, we always hear of it clearly enough to send a "special"'.[87] His early articulation of the concept of 'parachute journalism' would only become a reality in the broadcasting era. What was clear was that correspondents would have to change their style; 'they would have to be more reflective than narrative, with a wider scope and greater breadth of views'.[88] More feelings and reactions would have to be recorded. Hard news could be clearly distinguished from comment and correspondents would have to file shorter pieces more quickly to satisfy the changing news culture. Commentaries and 'think pieces' would still have a role, only now it was secondary to the primary task of providing the immediate news. Graphic and descriptive accounts became a feature of the reports from the special correspondents for the *Daily Telegraph* and *Daily News*. Archibald Forbes, Henry Lucy and G.A. Henty sent back despatches on the impact of the war on daily life. Their coverage of the siege of Paris is distinguished by reports of the trials and tribulations of ordinary people – accounts which could more easily and quickly be amassed by the man or woman on the spot.

The need that newspapers had for a regular and rapid supply of news was exploited by those in power. Unprecedented access was provided by the Prussians to the battlefield as Bismarck recognised the propaganda value of press coverage: 'Nothing will be more favourable for our political standing in England and America than the appearance in the two most influential newspapers of these countries ... of very detailed accounts of our army in the field'.[89] The war did not end the career of foreign correspondents as Delane had predicted. It did end the career of William Howard Russell, who failed to adapt to the concise, factual writing style required for the telegraph and the demands of ensuring that copy reached London promptly.[90] His passing was accompanied by that of Delane's *Times*, whose conservatism prevented the newspaper from adapting to the changes that technology and competition had brought to the industry.

New technology and increased competition in the 1870s may have changed the understanding of what was newsworthy, the nature of news writing
and how news was gathered, but it came at a price. The costs of producing
newspapers significantly increased. It is documented that there was a threefold recorded increase in the expenditure of newspapers on inland telegrams
sent by their own reporters in the six years following the takeover of the
telegraph system by the Post Office in 1870.[91] Subscriptions to the news
agencies for a regular flow of stories from around the UK and beyond and
the rise in salaries of experienced correspondents added to operational costs.
Rising costs could not be avoided; newspapers had to adopt new technolo-
gies if they were to compete. The outcome was that the capital needed to set
up a newspaper and the costs of keeping it going grew enormously in the
1870s. It became more costly and more risky to launch a newspaper. This
was most apparent with London papers, as foreign news constituted a major
component of the information they provided. In contrast the provincial newspapers appeared to improve their competitive position against their London
rivals.

Provincial expansion

Newspapers grew disproportionately outside London after 1855. That year
there was a 300 per cent increase in the consumption of newspapers across
the UK, compared to a 60 per cent improvement in London.[92] Previously
most newspapers published outside London were bi-weekly or tri-weekly
publications, heavily dependent on London newspapers for their news. These
newspapers attempted to 'target a particular locality and use a distinctive
political voice'.[93] Radical provincial papers such as the *Sheffield Register*, *Birmingham Inspector* and *Dudley Patriot* bloomed for a short time, to be replaced
by more moderate publications run by middle-class reformers such as the
Manchester Guardian. The removal of press taxation enabled many to become
dailies and soon most of Britain's major cities had their own daily newspaper. Seventy-eight new dailies were founded between 1856 and 1870,
most surviving for a substantial period of time.[94] Evening newspapers made
up a significant proportion of these new titles, the first evening provincial
paper appearing in Liverpool in 1855.[95] Many of the new dailies were located in the new urban, industrial areas of the North of England, Lancashire,
Yorkshire, Northumberland and Durham.[96] These newspapers competed
with each other within their regions or districts, and the 'chief differentiating feature between these rival titles tended to be political allegiance'.[97]
The majority of titles tended to side with the Liberal Party, fuelled in some
part by the need for many city and town newspapers to address the
problems created by urbanisation and industrialisation such as cramped
living conditions and the associated problems of health, transport and the
environment.[98]

The remarkable growth of the provincial press was facilitated by several factors in addition to the new economic climate created by the repeal of press taxation. The telegraph reduced the dependency of provincial newspapers on the London press for national and international news. Local dailies could now print such news before the London newspapers arrived. Evening editions, in particular, had a competitive edge; it is claimed the telegraph 'virtually created the evening press of the provinces'.[99] News agencies further helped regional papers to gather general and parliamentary news to equal that provided by the London press.[100] Britain's leading news agency, the Press Association (PA), was established in 1868 when, the story has it, four provincial newspaper editors in a hansom cab in a fog-bound London pondered the best way to produce a cheap, reliable and national news service for the regional press.[101] Owned by the regional press, PA produced a regular, rapid and reliable flow of news to provincial newspapers. PA was soon joined by other agencies, the result of which was the disappearance of the penny-a-liners as well as the wordiness that characterised their output. Shorter and sharper prose was required not only by the new medium of transmission but also by the rise of the news agencies.[102] If the telegraph assisted the growth of the provincial newspapers, other technological advances were to put them at a disadvantage. The most significant was the growth of the railways, which brought more competition from the London newspapers. The balance between the rapidly expanding provincial newspapers and their London counterparts was 'fairly even' up to the 1880s, but as the railways reached every region, province and nation of Britain the London papers gradually began to exert themselves.[103]

Newspapers and the electric telegraph

Relations between provincial newspapers and the electric telegraph in the nineteenth century were fraught. As provincial newspapers began to be published daily their need for up-to-date news increased. Introduced in the 1840s, the electric telegraph was seen as a means by which to obtain news from around the country and beyond. Developed by private companies such as the *Electric and International* and the *British and Irish Magnetic*, technical imperfections made the operation of the telegraph in the 1850s and 1860s inefficient and uncertain. This was not the only source of tension with the press. They were costly and newspapers were not awarded preferential rates or treatment. In the early 1850s the two telegraph companies merged to offer one supply of news, setting up its own news gathering department to supply news to the press. It offered 4000 words a day, including parliamentary summaries, court and society gossip, commercial and sporting news, law reports and weather. Newspapers had to subscribe to the service but

117

the uncertain transmission and doubts about the accuracy of the material soured relations. Lateness of transmission and mounting inaccuracies led them to complain to the telegraph company which was intransigent. Papers gathered together to establish their own companies which eventually led to the birth of the Press Association (1868). In 1869 the government bought up the telegraph companies and the Telegraph Act of that year ensured the operation of the service. However, in its early days it was the newspapers that sought to impress on the telegraph company the need for accuracy and immediacy in the delivery of news.

Source: Scott, *Reporters Anonymous*, pps. 13 – 30.

The most noticeable change in provincial newspapers was the increased coverage of local news. Local stories had from the early nineteenth century slowly begun to replace the cut-and-paste material taken from the London press. The rise of local interest reflected the way in which provincial newspapers sought to act as 'the notice board for the community covered by their hinterland'.[104] The features associated with today's local papers developed, including comprehensive accounts of local courts, council meetings, the gatherings of various social, cultural and religious bodies, creating the impression that the provincial newspaper was 'omniscient'.[105] Competition from London papers forced the local papers to concentrate on copy that provided them with an advantage. News, opinion and comment within their own areas figured more prominently. According to an editorial in the *Yorkshire Post* in 1866:

> When we consider that the population of two such counties as Lancashire and Yorkshire, to say nothing of the North of England in general, now draws its political opinions quite as much from the Press of Manchester, Liverpool and Leeds as from the Press of London, we shall understand at once the whole extent of the power which for good or for evil may be wielded by provincial journalism.[106]

The type of news stories that appeared in provincial newspapers did not differ substantially from what appeared in the London papers. Politics predominated – reflecting the interests of those who owned and edited these papers. The only divergence was the space devoted in the provincial papers to local politics as the town hall became the centre of political attention.

Sunday entertainment

Readers interested in matters other than politics would turn to the Sunday newspapers. After surviving several attempts to close these in the 1830s, the Sunday press expanded rapidly in the 1840s. The leading Sunday papers of the nineteenth century were launched during this decade. Sunday papers always sold better than their daily counterparts, mainly due to their ability to reach a wider range of readers from a variety of social backgrounds. In the 1840s three newspapers, all emerging from a radical political background, were launched: *Lloyd's Weekly News* (1842), the *News of the World* (1843) and *Reynolds News* (1850). The Sundays could not avoid politics but they mixed it with sensationalism, a combination that was highly successful in attracting readers, particularly from a working-class background. Their circulations exploded and by 1854 they were selling around 100,000 copies each, dwarfing the sales of the dailies by a ratio of nearly 5 to 1.[107] The radical Sunday newspapers sold well in the areas of the country that had most strongly supported the Chartist press, the textiles areas of Lancashire, Yorkshire and the Midlands and the industrial belts of South Wales and Scotland.

The growing popularity of the Sunday newspapers was based on their sensational reports of murder, robbery and scandal. They did not neglect serious political news, with, for example, 20 per cent of the news and editorial content of *Reynolds News* before 1880 devoted to such material, thereby retaining some commitment to its roots as a radical newspaper.[108] But as sales expanded, political analysis was increasingly watered down in favour of more sensational reporting. The importance of such material was apparent from the beginning: the first edition of the *News of the World* in 1843 carried a story entitled 'Extraordinary case of drugging and violation'. By the 1880s the bulk of the stories concentrated on murder, crime and other 'thrilling events' – which in 1886 made up over 50 per cent of the news stories in *Lloyd's Weekly News*.[109] Sensational reporting was sometimes used as part of the radical propaganda of the Sunday papers, with personal revelations and scandals often reinforcing a radical analysis of society. But as the Sunday press became more profitable, commercial gain tended to replace radical politics as the main driving force.

The Sundays provided the basis for the changes that were to take place in the daily press in the last decade of the century. The kinds of sensational stories they carried, as we have seen, had always been part of popular literature but from the middle of the century they began to become a regular feature of the British Sunday press. The radical newspapers of the 1830s acknowledged the role of entertainment in popular culture, when, in the face of declining readerships, they had responded by trying to combine political analysis with entertainment and crime. However, it was the Sunday newspapers that successfully combined the two, and in the process laid the foundations for the formula which would drive the rise of the popular press, with their emphasis on murders, executions, elopements and a miscellany of small features.

New Journalism

In the 1880s there was growing recognition that changes were taking place in the newspaper industry with the advent of what the cultural commentator and poet Matthew Arnold labelled the 'New Journalism'. Arnold is supposed to have coined the term in 1887 when writing about the *Pall Mall Gazette*, which was then edited by one of the great figures of nineteenth-century journalism, William Thomas Stead. It is often forgotten that Arnold, in his review of the newspaper and its contemporaries, complemented the 'ability, novelty, variety, sensation, sympathy, (and) generous instincts' of such publications.[110] He stated that the *Pall Mall Gazette* only had one fault: it was 'feather-brained'. Arnold's description stuck and was used to sum up the view many intellectuals and old-fashioned journalists had of the development of newspapers at the end of the nineteenth century. Arnold's battle against what he believed was the growing Philistinism in British cultural life had its roots in the 1860s, and his main target was the *Daily Telegraph* and, in particular, its correspondent George Augustus Sala.[111] His concern about the New Journalism focussed on the explosion of anxiety about the commercialisation and industrialisation of the industry and its impact on culture.

There was nothing much that was 'new' about the New Journalism. In many ways the *Pall Mall Gazette* under Stead in the 1880s and that other target of intellectual opprobrium the *Star*, launched in 1888 and edited by the Radical journalist T.P. O'Connor, were simply extending the changes introduced by the *Daily Telegraph*. Like Levy-Lawson they were conscious of the need in an increasingly commercial environment to make newspapers more readable. Unlike Levy-Lawson neither publication gained a large circulation – the *Gazette*'s circulation never exceeded 13,000. However, Stead and O'Connor were gifted journalists and self-publicists. They adapted and initiated a number of changes that were the basis of the 'Northcliffe revolution' (see Chapter 5). Stead was an advocate of campaigning journalism. Motivated by strong religious convictions, he argued that the press was an 'engine of social reform'.[112] To this end he sought to galvanise public opinion to pressurise Parliament to introduce legislation to tackle what he had identified as social problems. His exposure of the inadequate housing conditions of the urban poor led to the establishment of a Royal Commission on Housing.[113] His most famous campaign, which gained notoriety, put him in jail and attracted considerable criticism of his newspaper, concerned child prostitution. It changed the law, increasing the legal age of consent from 13 to 16, and provided the basis for an extension of the role of the press as the fourth estate and the cause of sensational reporting.

Stead's investigations into juvenile prostitution and the trafficking of young girls appeared in the *Pall Mall Gazette* in July 1885. Under the heading 'The Maiden Tribute of Modern Babylon', a series of articles exposed the ease with which young girls could be purchased in London. The evils of the trade were presented in a sensationalist way: sub-headings such as 'The Violation of Virgins', 'The Confession of a Brothel-Keeper', 'Strapping Girls Down', 'The Forcing of Unwilling Maids', 'I Order Five Virgins' and 'Delivered from Seduction' were used in a way resonant of the Sunday papers.[114] Stead had gone undercover to substantiate allegations that children could be purchased.

His exposé produced a furore of criticism from politicians and other news-papers and W.H. Smith refused to handle the *Gazette* in the week the articles were published. Many readers and advertisers were unhappy at finding 'words used and things described which had never before been used and described in a British newspaper'.[115] Subscriptions were cancelled and the new readers attracted were only temporary; the circulation of the newspaper never recovered under Stead's editorship.[116] It was as much how the stories were written as their content that alienated readers. His sensational prose was used 'to arrest the eye of the public and compel them to admit the necessity of action'.[117] Sensationalism was a means to an end, to get someone to do something about an injustice. Stead believed in the 'presentation of the facts with such vividness and graphic force' as would make an impact.

Unfortunately Stead had, in uncovering the injustice perpetrated on young girls, broken the law and he served a three-month prison sentence. This did not dampen his campaign or his crusading zeal. He used his imprisonment to attract more publicity to the rights and wrongs of the issue. On his release, he toured the country to mobilise opinion in defence of his cam-paign, in a manner reminiscent of the editors of the radical newspapers in the 1830s. However, Stead's motives were questioned; for come critics he was driven by profit, drawing on sex and sensation to bring in readers. The *Pall Mall Gazette*, as Stead pointed out, did not financially benefit from the articles. His approach had been consistent; journalism was deployed to attain the maximum effect. As editor he had introduced a number of fresh features: the use of illustrations, the introduction of crossheads and the securing of scoops.[118] He initiated the celebrity interview in 1883, compil-ing 134 of them in the following year at a time when *The Times* refused to print an interview with anyone on British soil.[119] The tone of the *Gazette* was distinctive, more vigorous and urgent, and Stead's prose style was described as 'compelling'.[120] Much of what he developed was drawn from his experience in America – he actually wrote a book in 1902 in praise of *The Americanisation of the World*. He was an adapter of the American tradition and techniques of muckraking journalism. The peculiar feature of his exposé, now accepted as one of the great moments in nineteenth-century press his-tory, was that the series of articles were 'not heralded with bold captions' and 'began only a few lines from the foot of a column'.[121] The failure of such an outstanding piece of muckraking journalism to help the *Gazette* increase sales was the result of Stead's journalism not corresponding to what his readers wanted. The *Gazette* had started as a review 'for the cultivated, well-to-do public interested in politics, social questions and the arts'.[122] They were not ready for Stead's style and methods, let alone the full and frank discussion of sex he introduced. Stead's journalism was directed more towards reaching the broader public.[123] This was beyond the confines of a small, evening, literary newspaper which appealed to the educated middle classes. He parted com-pany with the newspaper in 1890. However, the crusades of the *Pall Mall*

Gazette reinforced the notion that the newspaper should act as an organ of public opinion.

The other vehicle by which the New Journalism found its way into Fleet Street was the *Star*. Launched in January 1888 as a Radical, half-penny evening newspaper, the *Star* eschewed what it labelled the 'obsolete journalism' of the London newspapers. Its founder, T.P. O'Connor, recently returned from the United States, told his readers he would do away with verbose, long-winded and flowery writing. Many of the *Star*'s articles were less than half a column and accompanied by large headlines.[124] He pledged to provide 'plenty of entirely unpolitical literature', adding that 'our ideal is to leave no event unrecorded; to be the earliest with every item of news; to be thorough and unmistakeable in our meaning; to be animated, readable and stirring'.[125] The *Star* was true to its word in reporting politics – for example, it referred to 'the few dozen lines of drivel known as the Queen's Speech' in an early edition (9 February 1888).[126] It produced a regular gossip column – 'Mainly About People' – a sports section and the first Stop Press.[127] Racing tips appeared in what is described as a 'crisp, cheerful, humorous and commonsensical as a Cockney bus conductor' newspaper.[128] Crime stories were to the fore, with the paper enjoying great success in recording the gruesome details of the Jack the Ripper murders.[129] The paper had some success in attracting readers – reaching a circulation of over 140,000 within a couple of years.[130] However, O'Connor was not a competent or committed businessman. Many of his financial backers had political motives; they withdrew support when they believed O'Connor could not be relied on. He was forced out of the editorship in 1890, signing a severance agreement that he would not launch a rival publication to the *Star*. In the short time he edited the *Star* O'Connor showed how the principles of cheap newspaper journalism could be applied to the daily newspaper. The *Star* and *Gazette* reported the serious in an entertaining form and paved the way for journalistic entrepreneurs who would be less inhibited in their application of popular journalism to the daily press.

Daily Mail, 6 May 1896

5

THE NORTHCLIFFE REVOLUTION

The rise of the commercial newspaper, 1890–1922

There is one kind of journalism which directs the affairs of nations: it makes and unmakes cabinets; it upsets governments, builds up Navies and does many other great things. It is magnificent ... There is another kind of journalism which has no such great ambitions. It is content to plod on, year after year, giving wholesome and harmless entertainment to crowds of hardworking people, craving for a little fun and amusement. It is quite humble and unpretentious. This is my journalism.

George Newnes, founder of *Tit-Bits*[1]

The 1890s are often seen as a period in which the British newspaper underwent 'historic change'. The press is described as moving from a situation in which newspapers 'were limited by their own traditions and the modest demands of their readers to one whose capacity for change was seemingly without end'.[2] There was a transformation in the content and layout as well as the economic structure of the newspaper industry[3] which is usually associated with one man, Alfred Harmsworth, later ennobled as Lord Northcliffe. His innovations, according to traditional histories of the British press, 'created a revolution that transformed the nation ... perhaps he did more than anyone to create the modern British democracy of the next hundred years – for better or worse'.[4] Northcliffe casts a long shadow over the times in which he lived. The archetypal press baron, he exerted total control over his newspapers, issuing a constant stream of instructions to his editors. Amassing an ever greater number of titles, he involved himself in the minutiae of newspaper production, altering layout and design and conducting interviews, usually relating to death and torture, a lifelong obsession of his. Running his newspapers as if they were his personal fiefdom, Northoleon or the Chief, as he was nicknamed, used his papers to promote his political views and messages. His newspapers, the most important of which was the *Daily Mail*, launched in 1896, intimidated his rivals as well as government ministers. By the beginning of the 1920s Northcliffe and his brother Harold, later Viscount Rothermere, controlled newspapers that had a total circulation of six million – probably the newspaper group with the largest circulation in the world at that time.[5] The extent of his press empire and the claims he made about the power his papers exercised over the public – 'we can cause the whole country to think with us overnight whenever we say the word'[6] – shaped the perception of many of his contemporaries and subsequent historians that he profoundly changed the nature of the British newspaper.

While Northcliffe was a dominant figure in the rise of the popular press at the start of the twentieth century when the newspaper underwent a considerable makeover, it is possible to exaggerate the part he and his fellow newspaper owners played. Many of the innovations associated with Northcliffe and his newspapers had been pioneered and developed by others. Northcliffe imported ideas and practices from the United States, where mass circulation newspapers had started nearly fifty years earlier, and also from the continent, particularly France. His focus on short, sharp and snappy stories and use of headings and sub-headings had been part of the 'New Journalism' which entered the daily press from the 1880s onwards. Northcliffe adopted and adapted these techniques to his newspapers, which he positioned to take advantage of the social changes that were taking place around him. The most significant was the emergence of a new reading public brought about by the 1870 Education Act. Northcliffe's talent was that he was in tune with what these readers wanted and his papers made greater efforts to understand and respond to their readers. He was highly critical of the late Victorian newspaper, which he believed had failed to provide the things that interested the 'new sort of newspaper reader',[7] and stated that prior to the *Mail* 'newspapers dealt with only a few aspects of life'. He complained that 'highly educated men … have no sense of news … and they are woefully ignorant of anything that has happened since BC 42'.[8] Northcliffe's colleagues believed he had the ability to engage the public at their level of comprehension as he 'possessed the common mind to an uncommon degree'.[9]

More than developing a product that appealed to the millions, Northcliffe's revolution speeded up the process by which newspapers became a fully fledged branch of commerce. The rise of personal disposable income, increased leisure time brought about by a shortening of the average working week and the growing educational aspirations of working people enlarged the demand for newspapers. Northcliffe organised his newspapers to exploit this demand by 'giving the public what they want'. In the process British newspapers changed as sales and profitability rather than political and cultural influence became their primary goals. As Northcliffe's editor at the *Daily Mail*, Kennedy Jones, told one of his predecessors: 'You left journalism a profession and we have made it a branch of commerce'.[10]

The market leader – the *Daily Mail*

Alfred Harmsworth[11] had always wanted to be a journalist. At the first opportunity he left for Fleet Street to take up whatever freelance work he could find.[12] He found his way to George Newnes's publication *Tit-Bits*, 'a miscellany of little known facts assembled for amusement'.[13] Launched in 1881 as a weekly magazine selling at one penny, *Tit-Bits* soon attained a circulation of around 700,000.[14] Newnes's scraps of information culled from a variety of sources, including 'from all the Most Interesting Books, periodicals and Newspapers of the World', was 'to modify in the most profound degree the intellectual, social and political tone of the press'.[15] It was not Newnes who was to do this – but Northcliffe. He realised the potential of what *Tit-Bits* was doing:

> The Board Schools are turning out hundreds and thousands of boys and girls annually who are anxious to read. They do not care for the ordinary newspaper. They have no interest in Society, but they will read anything which is simple and is sufficiently interesting. The man who produced this *Tit Bits* has got hold of a bigger thing than he imagines. He is only at the beginning of a development which is going to change the whole face of journalism. I shall try to get in with him.[16]

The ultimate objective was to apply the *Tit-Bits* formula to the daily newspaper market. Before he embarked on this project, Northcliffe launched his own magazine, *Answers to Correspondents*, in 1888. (See Figure 5.1) It was not an immediate success. A direct copy of *Tit-Bits*, Northcliffe added his own features: publicity stunts and competitions. These included sending his colleagues out to report on a ride in a locomotive engine, a postal railway van, a diver's bell and a climb up a steeple.[17] Copies of the first issue were given away free to advertise the new magazine but within weeks circulation started to fall and the situation looked precarious.[18] It was saved by a device that was to become a feature of the promotional activities of the press. He came up with a competition which offered the prize of £1 a week for life for guessing how much gold there would be in the Bank of England on 4 December 1889.[19] We are told that 700,000 people entered and nearly 250,000 copies of the edition which announced the result were sold. *Answers* was saved, and with the addition of competitions, short stories and interviews with famous people the magazine went from strength to strength, attaining a circulation of just under 718,000.

Joined by his brother Harold, who oversaw the financial side of the press empire, Northcliffe followed up *Answers* with a variety of titles: *Comic Cuts*, *Chips*, which included for the first time the strip cartoon, *Forget-Me-Not* and *Home Sweet Home*. By 1892 their publications were selling over one million copies every week.[20] The profits enabled them to enter the daily newspaper market with the purchase in 1894 of the *Evening News*, one of nine evening papers in London at the time, all of which were losing money.[21] Northcliffe applied his formula, short paragraphs, snappy sentences and bold headlines, to the ailing paper and his brother made considerable savings in the purchase of newsprint and by overhauling the system of distribution. Northcliffe

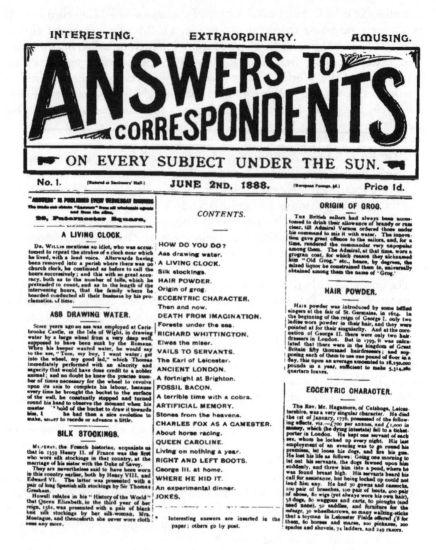

Figure 5.1 Answers to Correspondents, 2 June 1888

adopted a newer and more modern typeface, emboldened the headlines, placed features in the same place every day and reduced the number of political stories.[22] Besides making his newspaper an easier read and more navigable, he introduced football pools and maps to illustrate foreign stories. Snippets resembling what appeared in *Answers* crept in and a women's page made its appearance. This was not to the liking of his journalistic partner,

Kennedy Jones, who had been a long-serving news editor in Fleet Street and held to the view that the newspaper reader was male. Northcliffe's brother, ennobled as Lord Rothermere, contributed by developing the distribution system that ensured the paper appeared at various points throughout London where people congregated in large numbers. These changes turned the *Evening News* around, and soon it was making a profit and it was not long before its circulation passed one million. However, the experience was a dry run for the launch of a new daily morning newspaper.

The *Daily Mail* appeared on 4 May 1896 as an eight-page paper which advertised itself as 'A Penny Newspaper for a Halfpenny' and described itself as 'The Busy Man's Daily Journal'.[23] In many ways it was not very different from the other Fleet Street dailies of the period. It had advertisements on the front page and many of the features on the inside pages would have been found in other newspapers. It looked like all its rivals: a broadsheet with Old English typeface. However, there were noticeable differences. There were shorter articles which were 'crisply written and lavishly headlined' in keeping with Northcliffe's view that his readers should be able to gather a summary of the day's events by simply scanning the headings.[24] Illustrated feature articles appeared inside the paper – although it is noticeable that compared with the *Evening News* there were fewer illustrations. 'The Daily Magazine' appeared on page 7, catering for women readers, and the paper also included a serial, which Northcliffe believed essential in building circulation. The *Daily Mail* sought variety and universality in appeal and, as it stated in a short leader in its inaugural issue, 'the note of the *Daily Mail* is not so much economy of price as conciseness and compactness'.[25]

While it was not as innovative as expected – and certainly adopting a more conservative approach to daily newspaper journalism than the *Evening News* – the attractiveness of the new paper appealed to readers. Short, one-paragraph items, usually columns of political, society and sports gossip, proved popular.[26] The contrast with the rival daily newspapers was spelled out by Northcliffe in a signed editorial on the *Mail*'s first anniversary:

> The warmth of the reception of the new methods of the *Daily Mail* brought about a number of much needed changes in the working arrangements of other journals. American news had hitherto been almost neglected ... India rarely mentioned ... And apart from the local nature of the unimproved London daily, there was the drawback of its verbosity. The press had not kept pace with the people in quickness and movement, in the desire to obtain the largest result with the smallest loss of time ... the Master, had in fact, learned a good deal from the Pupil.[27]

The brevity of the *Mail* contrasted with the long-windedness of rival newspapers, still happy to run articles of 6,000 words in length, such as that on the coronation of Czar Nicholas II in 1895 which reproduced a list of those who attended and the order of the procession.[28] The *Mail*'s 'clear and complete' content and its focus on 'news out of the ordinary' was a refreshing antidote to the dryness and dullness of the late Victorian newspaper.[29] Dismissed as 'a newspaper for office boys written by office boys' and disliked for its 'triviality' by politicians and established journalists, the newspaper's circulation started to grow steadily.[30] By 1897 it attained sales of 400,000, justifying the claim to be 'the largest circulation in the world' and hit the million mark during the Boer War, finally settling down at around 700,000 for most of the years leading up to the First World War.[31] Britain's most popular newspaper prior to the war, the *Daily Mail*, presented a 'world fit for the middle classes to live in'.[32] Its jingoism, imperialism, nationalism and patriotism – as well as the emotional tone of the copy – captured the feelings of the Edwardian middle classes during a period of relative political and social stability.

The crusading newspaper – the *Daily Express*

The success of the *Daily Mail* paved the way for the rise of other mass circulation daily newspapers. Northcliffe's paper was joined by the *Daily Express* (1900) and the *Daily Mirror* (1903) in achieving mass appeal. The *Daily Express* was started by Arthur Pearson as a rival to the *Daily Mail*. Pearson had, like Northcliffe, worked on *Tit-Bits*; in fact he had won a competition to join the staff at a salary of £100 per year.[33] His career profile resembled that of Northcliffe, leaving *Tit-Bits* to found his own publication, *Pearson's Weekly*, which aimed to 'To Interest, to Elevate and to Amuse'. Pearson was more innovative with his daily newspaper than his rival and did not shy away from making changes that might not be accepted by Britain's newspaper reading public. The *Express* was the first daily newspaper to regularly appear with only news stories on the front page. Readers were attracted to the *Express* but high launch costs ensured that for its first two years it lost money. The decision to put news instead of advertisements on the front page added to the newspaper's financial problems by depriving it of the large revenue advertisers paid for that position.[34] In 1902 Pearson recruited R.D. Blumenfeld to take over as foreign editor. An American who had made his way to London in the late 1880s to pursue a career in Fleet Street, Blumenfeld on his arrival found the British press populated with 'great heavy sided blanket sheets full of dull advertisements and duller news announcements'.[35] A believer in newspaper modernisation, he was soon elevated to the editor's chair and for the next couple of decades kept the *Express* going as Pearson's interest declined. Loans from financiers and the Tory party, which the newspaper supported, were necessary. When Pearson's ill health forced him to withdraw from the business Blumenfeld was instrumental in engineering the sale of the paper to Max Aitken, Lord Beaverbrook, who turned the newspaper's fortunes around.

Beaverbrook's involvement with the *Daily Express* began in 1912 when he loaned the newspaper money to bail it out of its difficulties. A Canadian entrepreneur who had come to Britain and bought Rolls-Royce, he had little interest in the newspaper business. His aspirations focussed on a career in politics and in 1910 he became the Tory MP for Ashton-under-Lyne. His involvement with the *Express* was initially motivated by his interest in maintaining the newspaper's support for his party. A man of almost unparalleled energy, the world of politics proved too sedentary for him and he soon lost interest. His recompense was to become more engaged in journalism and in 1916, with the newspaper estimated to be losing £3,000 a day, he bought the *Express*. It was not until 1922 that the newspaper first showed a profit; its circulation was then 793,000 per day.[36] He did little to change the newspaper. Blumenfeld produced a paper which drew heavily on the *Daily Mail*, with news, a woman's section, money matters and sports figuring prominently. Leisure pages with stories such as 'Popular Phrases: What do they mean?' were clearly inspired by the *Daily Mail*.[37] However, Blumenfeld combined entertainment with long political leaders and comment, indicating that his understanding of what pleased a mass audience was still steeped in the late Victorian newspaper world. He acknowledged in 1933 that 'mass thinking is a strange and unaccountable thing'.[38]

It is not clear that Beaverbrook had any greater insight into 'mass thinking'; his biographers state that he 'never had a conscious marketing strategy' and 'produced a newspaper that would interest him and discovered his interests were those of the masses'.[39] What he brought to the newspaper was strong political opinions, certainty about what should be included and an edge generated from his passionately held but iconoclastic views. This made the *Express* look 'sharp and confident', with considerable bite to its leading articles. Beaverbrook was happy to tell his readers what to think – and he did not confine this to the editorials. There were no major innovations in the layout and content until the 1930s when the brilliant technical editor, Arthur Christansen, took over (see Chapter 6). Beaverbrook in the initial years increased the number of photographs in the paper and introduced the crossword, which he believed was 'a great educational force'. Martin Conboy[40] argues that what distinguished the *Express* was its 'unbounded enthusiasm and confidence', differentiating it from the 'individualistic bent' of the *Daily Mail*. Its dynamism, a reflection of its new owner, was in tune with the spirit of the age and the basis of its appeal. Biographers Anne Chisholm and Michael Davie[41] believe the *Daily Express* under Beaverbrook presented itself 'more than ever as the tribune of the people', questioning, criticising, denouncing and attacking the performance of the authorities across a range of everyday activities. This contrasted with the *Daily Mail*, which provided amusement, entertainment and diversion for its readers, a set of values the *Express* aspired to when it was launched, only to be set aside when Beaverbrook took charge. Another biographer emphasises that the *Daily Express* was 'a paper for everyone the moment Beaverbrook took hold of it'.[42] The historian A.J.P. Taylor described the *Daily Express* as 'the only classless and ageless newspaper in the world' as a result of its ability to draw 'readers in equal proportions ... from every social group'.[43]

The *Daily Express* increasingly became the voice of its owner. Beaverbrook had no hesitation in using his newspapers as vehicles for political propaganda, admitting so to the Royal Commission on the Press in 1948. He believed in the 'efficacy of the weapon of the Press' and that 'when skilfully employed at the psychological moment no politician of any party can resist it. It is a flaming sword that can cut through any political armour'.[44] His campaigning style became part of the newspaper's remit. Beaverbrook believed in crusading journalism so much that he placed the 'Red Crusader' at the top of the front page of the *Daily Express* as a symbol of the paper's core value. The crusade was also a feature of the *Daily Mail* but in this case campaigning was more commercial than political, as with the drive in 1911 to support wholemeal bread, or 'standard bread' as it was described. The cause of this campaign was notionally a concern about the nourishment of young children and the lower nutritional value of white bread; 202 articles were run by the newspaper on the topic in that year, with free offers of brown loaves and prizes for the best school essay on brown bread. Support was marshalled for legislation banning white bread. The net result was limited but the publicity generated for the *Mail* was enormous.[45]

The picture paper – the *Daily Mirror*

The *Daily Mirror*'s appeal to a mass readership was not based on political crusades. The paper has a special place in history as the first – and only – daily newspaper designed to appeal exclusively to women. Founded in 1903 by Northcliffe, it was run by a woman editor, Mary Howarth, who had edited the *Mail*'s women's page, and an all-women editorial team. The paper was aimed at the 'New Woman', that is, the woman who wanted to work and vote.[46] Its circulation plummeted, from a starting point of around 276,000 to below 25,000, over three months.[47] The blame for this calamitous development was laid at the door of the staff. Hamilton Fyfe, who was sent in to rescue the paper, attributed the situation to the opinion that 'women can't write and don't want to read'.[48] Fyfe's prejudices hid Northcliffe's and his senior managers' complete misunderstanding of the intended audience. They produced a newspaper for 'gentlewomen', focussing on 'Fashionable Announcements', 'Our Birthday List', 'Where Notable People Spent the Weekend', 'Yesterday in Town' and 'Dishes of the Day'. While this formula may have proven successful with women's magazines, it was inappropriate for a daily newspaper, particularly at a time of major political agitation surrounding rights for women. Not only did the New Woman not read it but it failed to attract readers from the sixpenny women's magazines, who saw its content as way out of their reach. 'It had the air of superior culture which those lacking in culture despised, and features designed to satisfy the latter, at which the woman of taste and intellect shuddered'.[49]

In January 1904 the *Daily Mirror* was re-launched, according to its own marketing blurb, as 'the first daily illustrated publication in the history of journalism'.[50] (See Figure 5.2) The re-launch was an instant success; the failure of a newspaper for women fortuitously enabled Northcliffe to discover the public's demand for pictorial newspapers. Within a year the paper was selling 300,000 copies daily, attaining its highest sales point of 800,000 the year before the Great War broke out.[51] The *Mirror*'s success as an illustrated paper spawned several competitors: *Daily Sketch* (1908), *Daily Picture Paper* (1911), a Sheffield-based morning newspaper, and the *Bulletin*, a Scottish picture paper.[52] The *Daily Graphic* (1890) had been the first pictorial paper but technology allowed it only occasionally to produce half-tone pictures. It is claimed that technological innovation pioneered by the *Mirror* allowed the printing of better-quality pictures more quickly on established presses, but Wright[53] contests the view that the newspaper had such an impact on the development of press photography. He argues that the paper simply applied more rigorously a development that had been spreading throughout the British press since the 1880s. What cannot be denied was that the *Mirror*'s emphasis on the visual satisfied the new reading public's demand for photographs. *Mirror* photographers went to great lengths, and at great personal risk, to produce eye-catching photographs, including photographing the interior of Vesuvius, climbing Mont Blanc and crossing the Alps in a balloon.[54]

Photographs, however, were not the only feature that helped the *Mirror* to increase circulation. Hamilton Fyfe, in his autobiography *My Seven Selves*, identified the layout and presentation of the *Mirror* as crucial to its success:

> The shape and content of the *Daily Mirror* recommended it strongly to those who needed something to help them through their half-hour's journey to work in the morning. Packed in tram, train, or omnibus, standing up perhaps and holding on to a strap with one hand, they required in the other, not a journal to stir thought or supply serious information, but one to entertain them, occupy their minds pleasantly, prevent them from thinking. It was easier to look at pictures than to read print. The news was displayed and worded in a manner that made assimilation simple. Everything in the *Daily Mirror* was calculated to be easy of absorption by the most ordinary intelligence.[55]

The Northcliffe formula of publicity stunts, competitions and innovative journalism played its part in building circulation. Readers were invited to spot the *Daily Mirror* bicycle in the streets of London, buskers were encouraged to participate in a competition at the Apollo Theatre, the winner

Figure 5.2 The *Daily Illustrated Mirror*, 25 January 1904

obtaining a music hall contract, and a journalist travelled steerage class across the Atlantic to share the experience of emigrants.[56] There is no doubt that the *Mirror* provided an impetus to the development of photojournalism.[57] One Fleet Street photographer noted that 'Northcliffe ... raised all branches of journalism, and made Press photography a respectable and well paid job'.[58]

The *Mirror*'s influence waned in the immediate post-war period, gradually declining from 1917 onwards.[59] The emphasis on pictures and the limited news the newspaper carried made it seem tangential to the great events of the day – politicians did not take picture newspapers seriously. Northcliffe took little interest in the paper after he purchased *The Times* in 1908, which he believed would enable him to be taken more seriously in political circles. In spite of rising sales, Northcliffe sold his interest in the *Mirror* to his brother Rothermere and had nothing more to do with the paper. Rothermere's purchase of the *Mirror* coincided with the outbreak of the First World War, which temporarily increased demand for newspapers specialising in photographs, drawings and cartoons.[60] The *Mirror* outsold the *Mail* in the early war years and Rothermere's launch of the *Sunday Pictorial* in 1915 added to his brother's chagrin. By its third issue the illustrated Sunday paper was selling just below two million copies, a record for the time. A twenty-four-page penny newspaper combining patriotic commentaries with gossip and six pages of pictures, its success confirmed that the million-selling newspaper had arrived.

Newspapers for the millions

The *Express* and *Mirror* took longer to establish themselves than the *Daily Mail* but these papers dominated the newspaper market in Britain prior to the First World War. By 1918 the total circulation of the national daily press stood at 3.1 million a day.[61] The *Mail* had replaced the *Daily Telegraph* as the market leader and at the time of Northcliffe's death in 1922 its circulation is estimated to have been 1.75 million.[62] The new popular newspapers were selling in quantities previously considered impossible. *The Times* in its heyday dominated the newspaper market with a circulation of around 50,000 and the *Daily Telegraph* had extended circulation during its period of ascendancy to around 300,000. The circulations of the *Mail*, *Mirror* and *Express* ran at around a million, establishing the British newspaper as a medium of mass communication. This achievement was not simply due to better quality and more accessible newspapers and the rise of a mass reading public. Larger circulations were also a product of several technological developments that occurred in the early twentieth century. Faster presses, quick-drying ink and a railway service dedicated to the distribution of newspapers played their part. By the eve of the 1914–18 War most newspapers were sent by train and distributed by van to newsagents. The Post Office's monopoly of newspaper distribution had declined as the railways reached even the most distant outposts of the British Isles. The rapidity of the service meant that newspapers could now reach many of the larger conurbations in time for breakfast. Northcliffe ensured that a week after the outbreak of the Boer War the *Daily Mail* was being delivered by express train to reach the breakfast tables of people in the Midlands and the North of England.[63] He started printing a northern edition in Manchester in 1902, reducing his costs of distribution. Soon afterwards the *Mail* was printing editions simultaneously in London and Manchester, serving the South and North of the country, respectively.[64] The *Mail* extended the reach of London newspapers to a larger number of readers across the country than ever before, providing the platform for the 'nationalisation' of the London press.

The process of urbanisation further assisted London newspapers to extend their national reach. By 1890 nearly two out of three people in the British Isles lived in conurbations of over 100,000 people and the population of Britain's seven largest cities grew by 150 per cent between 1890 and 1930.[65] The extent of the urban market in Britain 'offered press magnates the opportunity to expand both the circulation of their newspapers and their press empire at a relatively low cost'.[66] The number of provincial daily newspapers peaked in 1900 with an estimated 171 titles on the market.[67] Decline started to set in prior to the war. Competition, particularly from the expanding London papers, had reduced their number by 1921 to 41 provincial morning and 89 evening newspapers.[68] The general expansion of circulation was accompanied by a slow but steady decline in the number of newspapers. It was not necessary to lose circulation to fall behind your competitors. More money had to be found to keep newspapers going, although the amount required in the provinces was lower than in London. Catering to the new reading public was often the only way to increase circulation. Provincial newspapers began to introduce many of the features of the mass circulation London press. The advance of the half-penny London newspapers into the provinces was at the expense of the penny morning papers, of which most large British cities had a couple. These papers were as a group politically aligned with the Liberal Party and had been able to survive on circulations between 40,000 and 50,000. Competition from the cheaper London papers meant they became the first victims of the Northcliffe revolution.[69] Financial gain encouraged London newspaper proprietors 'to dabble' in the provincial press. Pearson, George Riddell, owner of the *News of the World*, and the Cadbury family bought up metropolitan and provincial titles. The involvement of the Cadburys was a desperate attempt to save the Liberal press.[70] The decline of the Liberal Party was presaged by a collapse of the papers in London and the provinces that supported the Liberal cause. The final factor that undermined the provincial press was the passing of legislation towards the end of the nineteenth century that reduced the powers of local government, making local politics less newsworthy and thereby undermining the staple feature of the provincial press.[71]

The arrival of mass circulation newspapers coincided with a momentous event in British imperial history, the Boer War (1899–1902). The war was ultimately an immense blow to the Empire, with the British Army suffering considerable losses and reversals. It has been described as a 'seminal and crucial period in the evolution of the British Press'.[72] Wars have always been good for selling newspapers.[73] The Boer War was the first war fought in the age of mass literacy, and instead of the 'traditional, relatively restrained reporting' of the established newspapers, it was subject to the vibrant and colourful coverage of the new popular newspapers, led by the *Daily Mail*.[74] The *Mail* and the rest of the British press sought to 'arouse public demand for news',[75] devoting considerable resources and effort to their war coverage. Many of the leading writers and reporters of the day were sent to South Africa – such as Kipling and Conan Doyle – and others established their reputations during the war, including a reporter for the *Morning Post*, Winston Churchill. The leading war correspondent of the day, the *Daily Mail*'s G.W. Steevens, died at the siege of Ladysmith and correspondents such as Edgar Wallace wrote with considerable sympathy of the sufferings of the ordinary soldier, the British Tommy, on the South African plains. A distinctive feature of the reporting of the war was the use of photography. The invention of the lightweight camera, which could be hand held, enabled reporters to send back a greater variety of pictures of the battlefield. Photographs of war were also taken by soldiers and ordinary men and women caught up in the fighting. British military triumphs and setbacks could now be brought home to readers in greater numbers and more graphic details.[76] Magazines such as *Pearson's War Pictures* attained large sales and the arrival of moving pictures further forced newspapers and magazines to provide more vivid pictures of the battlefield.

Adopting a strongly pro-war stance in favour of 'our boys' helped the *Mail*'s circulation to soar.[77] Newspapers also played their role in rousing anti-war sentiments later in the conflict. The *Manchester Guardian*'s reporting of Emily Hobhouse's graphic description of mass death amongst Boer families in the concentration camps set up by the British Army had a powerful impact on the public.[78] Greater publicity changed the nature of the interaction between reporters and the senior army figures. Some of the latter realised the importance of good publicity to career advancement. They sought to ensure heavy press coverage of military triumphs. Media-conscious soldiers such as Baden Powell and Lord Roberts were able to enhance their reputations through the press coverage they engineered of their doubtful successes.

Improvements in print technology, the development of more effective, quicker and cheaper means of distribution, the growth of the urban population congregated in large conurbations, and a war which mobilised British public opinion and increased demand for news facilitated the expansion of the press. Without these changes the large circulations attained by the *Mail*,

Mirror and *Express* would not have occurred. However, the character of the newspaper was more profoundly affected by the new economic realities of newspaper production. Many newspapers remained 'old fashioned' up to and well beyond the First World War but the freshness of the mass circulation newspapers reflected the increasing economic pressure to chase more readers. The need to make newspapers profitable forced them to find content and a mode of presentation which appealed to a wider range of readers; they had to cater to the interests of the mass of people.

The changing economics of newspaper production

Newspapers during the Edwardian era were transformed from 'marginal commercial ventures' into 'highly lucrative businesses'.[79] They ceased to be small-scale operations. By the beginning of the 1930s the net output of the newspaper industry was greater than that of shipbuilding and chemicals.[80] The perceived motive of nineteenth-century newspaper proprietors, editors and journalists – to guide public opinion – was pushed into the background as the opportunities to make money increased. Critics argue it was Northcliffe's desire for financial profit that led him to initiate radical changes in the content, layout and presentation of the newspaper. The motives of the press owners have been the subject of much debate and conjecture. This debate seems slightly redundant, as to survive in the changing economic circumstances that faced the Edwardian press, proprietors had to find a way of selling the cheapest conceivable newspaper to the greatest possible number of people'.[81]

Politics and press ownership

Fears of the political intentions of the owners of the mass circulation newspapers were fuelled by the pronouncements and actions of Beaverbrook and Northcliffe. While eschewing the inclusion of too much politics in their newspapers, the founders of the mass circulation press often declaimed their purpose of influencing the political process. In 1903 Northcliffe wrote that 'every extension of the franchise renders more powerful the newspaper and less powerful the politician'.[82] Perceptions of their power were reinforced by the part they played in bringing down the Asquith government in 1916[83] and the appointment of Beaverbrook and Northcliffe as ministers in the wartime coalition the following year. For Northcliffe the war was 'almost a personal crusade' and his style of launching 'a harassing, loud, merciless public barrage against all those members of the government' deemed to have failed in their duty to the nation reinforced perceptions of the power of newspaper owners to direct government and determine policy.[84]

Members of the emerging Labour Party and trade union movement argued that the press was 'gradually passing out of the control of the reader and ... becoming the organ of advertisers and the convenience of the capitalist'.[85] The National Union of Journalists (NUJ), set up in 1906, was critical of newspaper chains and the insecurity they created amongst their members.[86] J.A. Spender, editor of the liberal political weekly the *Westminster Gazette*, regretted that 'politics had lost its pre-eminence in the Press'.[87] Writing in 1925, Spender complained that Parliament 'was reduced to half a column of small type' and 'the claim of the great, wise and eminent to occupy space urgently required for crime and football was openly derided'. Spender had witnessed what he believed was the unravelling of the fourth estate role of the newspaper as the 'old machinery of politics' was thrown 'out of gear' and the atmosphere of public life had been considerably changed. Reason and argument were replaced by emotion and prejudice as catchphrases and screaming headlines dominated the output of the mass circulation press. Sloganeering was seen as the preferred mode of political debate; a 'degradation of political discourse' according to Spender.[88] Disillusion-ment with the performance of the press spread after the war, to the extent that press ownership was regarded as much as a threat to press freedom as State control (see Chapter 6). The fear of Northcliffe and Beaverbrook led some to advocate public control of newspapers.

The cost of launching and running a newspaper had increased enormously. It has been estimated that it cost around £25,000 to set up a London daily newspaper in 1850, rising to £100,000 by 1870, and Northcliffe's launch of the *Daily Mail* cost £500,000. Rising costs, particularly in relation to new printing technology, distribution and the larger staff needed to compile bigger newspapers, made it more difficult for newcomers to enter the industry. The failed attempt to set up a 'Great Liberal Daily Paper', the *Tribune*, in the wake of the party's 1906 electoral victory cost its owner Franklin Tho-masson more than £300,000.[89] Rising costs of production changed the nature of newspaper ownership. The traditional unit of newspaper ownership during the nineteenth century had been a single owner or family business, usually based on the printing trade. Following the repeal of the press taxes, news-paper companies started to be formed in large numbers. It is estimated that 4,000 newspaper companies were founded in the second half of the nine-teenth century.[90] From 1870 most newspapers became limited companies, with family businesses adopting the status in order to preserve their com-mercial interests. Northcliffe was the first to offer shares in a newspaper company, which made more capital available to plough into his ventures and cover the rising costs of newspaper production. Share ownership not only widened the range of those who had an interest in the newspaper industry but also incorporated the profit motive more fully into newspaper production. The pressure to provide strong dividend payments to the investing public ensured that maximising circulation and advertising revenue would be the driving force behind the newspaper – pleasing the reader became an economic necessity.[91] Amusement and thrills were essential to the economic model that Northcliffe adopted for the newspaper.

Newspaper chains were a feature of the period between 1890 and 1920. By 1910 Northcliffe's Amalgamated Press controlled 39 per cent of the circulation of London morning daily newspapers, just over 31 per cent of the evening papers and nearly 12 per cent of the Sundays.[92] Four newspaper chains controlled over 80 per cent of the circulation of Sunday newspapers, while three companies accounted for more than two-thirds of London's morning newspapers and four-fifths of the evening newspapers.[93] Chains had existed prior to the Northcliffe revolution,[94] most commonly amongst the provincial weekly press, but changing economic circumstances provided an impetus to the growth of national newspaper chains. Such enterprises could take advantage of the economies of large-scale production, more easily affording the latest and most efficient technology, spreading financial risk, enjoying a more sophisticated division of labour and as a result producing newspapers at a lower unit cost.[95]

Northcliffe's model tied the newspaper more firmly to the ability to maximise advertising revenue. The commercial success of the *Daily Mail* owed a lot to the way in which it was promoted to advertisers. The innovation of audited circulation figures was used to attract advertisers. The second issue of the newspaper contained an announcement, signed by a Fellow of the Institute of Chartered Accountants, that the circulation of the *Daily Mail* was 397,215, 'a world record for a first number'.[96] Advertising, as we have seen, became important in determining the economic structure of the press in the late nineteenth century. Who was reading, what they were reading and how many readers could be attracted were key determinants in drawing advertisers to particular publications. However, up to the 1920s accurate circulation figures, as well as accurate details of the kind of readers, were difficult to obtain.[97] Newspapers were either highly circumspect about revealing circulation and readership statistics or went to great efforts to manipulate these figures. The accuracy of the *Mail*'s published circulation figure for its first issue is questionable. Talking up or 'booming' the success of his newspapers was a feature of Northcliffe's way of doing business.[98]

The introduction of audited circulation figures, however, allowed Northcliffe to charge advertisers on the basis of circulation, per 1,000 readers, thereby linking advertising and sales. Previously advertising rates had been based on space, per column inch. Creditable and supposedly reliable 'net sales certificates' were to become an integral part of the commercial operation of the press. By 1914 Northcliffe had joined with other newspaper owners to call for the publication of honest circulation figures. Advertisers started to campaign in 1921 for the publication of reliable data and in 1931 the Audit Bureau of Circulation (ABC) was established.[99] It took many years for all newspaper owners to co-operate and disputes over figures have continued until the present day, but by the late 1930s reliable circulation data existed. This was accompanied by readership research, including surveys of reading habits, likes and dislikes, and by the Second World War the quantity and quality of information available to advertisers about newspapers, their circulation and readers was far reaching. This enabled advertisers to improve the ways in which they targeted their audiences, and media planning became a feature of their work. The influence advertisers exercised over the content and form of the newspaper correspondingly increased. Newspapers unable to attract large readerships or enough readers of sufficient purchasing power faced more problems in maintaining their position in the market.

There are three main areas in which the impact of the new economic circumstances of newspaper production can be identified: the nature of news; the presentation, layout and language of newspapers; and the way in which they were organised. The success of the *Mail*, *Mirror* and *Express* forced the industry to re-evaluate what it did and ultimately compelled other newspapers to follow suit. Some resisted, violently attacking the new methods and techniques deployed, and the new environment allowed a few of them to reject the 'popularisation' of the press and survive economically. The result was that a wedge was driven between small and 'serious' newspapers and mass circulation and 'popular' newspapers.

The nature of news

Newspapers were better written, presented and organised following Northcliffe's arrival in Fleet Street. Many of the innovations, such as clarity, brevity, simplicity and narrative, attributed to the press barons had long been part of the newspaper industry. They were now just embraced with more commitment and energy, a necessary response to the requirements of the market. Northcliffe, Pearson and Beaverbrook were responding to the new set of readers who had an appetite for cheap reading matter. They did not overestimate what their readers wanted. According to Dibblee,[100] the 1870 Education Act brought into existence 'an enormous number of immature minds ready for the simplest information and oldest stories, as yet quite unsophisticated and disinclined to raffishness or vice'. Newnes first tapped into these new readers with his weekly magazine *Tit-Bits* but his desire for social acceptability prevented him from applying his formula to the daily newspaper. He sought respectability, buying up established newspapers and running them in the time-honoured way. Northcliffe, Beaverbrook and Pearson were less inhibited. They adapted many of the basic techniques of selling and marketing to ensure their newspapers reached as many people as possible. Giving the public what it wanted in the days before market research was not straightforward; intuition, luck and happenstance played their part. But packaging a newspaper that was widely accessible was crucial to their attempt to survive and prosper.

Mass circulation newspapers increased the range and variety of their content, combining news and comment with a number of innovations borrowed primarily from fiction and magazines. As Northcliffe said about *Answers*, 'anyone who reads our paper will be able to converse on many subjects on which he was entirely ignorant'.[101] The *Mail*, *Mirror* and *Express* tapped into people's desire to know, to be informed as well as entertained – in fact entertainment and information were synonymous to the new reading public. The mass circulation newspaper had to be 'a coalition of tastes, interests and political positions'; there had to be something for everyone.[102] However, the central component of Northcliffe's formula for success was news.

Northcliffe emphasised news as the main selling point for his newspapers and, above all, being first with the news. His insistence on 'scoops' and exclusives turned a 'singular aversion to being beaten by competitors in the field of news' into a key component of modern journalism, the necessity of beating the competition in the daily hunt for news.[103] It is 'hard news that captures readers ... and it is features that hold them'.[104] The *Daily Mail* offered more news to its readers, about a broader range of subject matter, than ever before. He was especially keen on news from abroad, reflecting his enthusiasm for the British Empire. The paper became the 'embodiment of the imperial idea' as Northcliffe committed his editors to bringing 'the Empire, the world to the cottage door'.[105] Readers were provided with 'frequent, lengthy and well-informed' accounts by a number of travelling correspondents; within a short period of its launch the *Mail* had developed an international news gathering organisation which rivalled that of *The Times* and Reuters.[106] He regularly cajoled his staff to produce more foreign news stories: 'We have not enough authoritative foreign or empire news in the paper ... we do not get sufficiently in touch with big men visiting London from our great overseas Dominions ... Dig them out. They have wonderful news stories to tell, and are most interesting and refreshing personalities'. He launched an *Overseas Daily Mail* edition in 1904, connecting the British people scattered across the world. The *Mail* depicted itself as the 'Voice of Empire'.[107]

Northcliffe attempted to 'avoid politics in the papers he launched and depoliticised those he acquired'.[108] The *Mail* kept parliamentary reports to a minimum; during the first month of its existence the average size of parliamentary columns was seven lines from the House of Lords and eight from the Commons.[109] Politics lost its privileged position and he insisted on it being treated like all other stories – 'on its merits. It has no "divine right" on newspaper space'.[110] When Northcliffe took over *The Times* he told its editorial staff he wanted more topicality, readability, lighter content and 'fewer and shorter articles on politics', and similarly he warned the *Observer*'s editor,

James Garvin, to avoid 'heavy politics' since it 'will prevent you getting cir-culation'.[111] Garvin ignored him: 'I mean to give the public what they don't want'; and under Astor, to whom Northcliffe sold the paper in 1911, he eschewed news in favour of the expression of 'independent ideas'.[112] Garvin's *Observer* employed few reporters, taking news from the wire services, and instead built up a formidable 'galaxy of contributors' who aired their views weekly on a variety of subjects.[113] Garvin provided a 'views' paper, pro-nouncing on the important issues of the day, judging success not in sales but in terms of political influence and cultural reputation.[114] Garvin's elitist agenda contrasted with Northcliffe's efforts to reach the man-in-the-street. The press baron believed that a newspaper should 'take pains to touch his life and interests at every conceivable point'.[115] News was expanded to cover a broader range of topics; snippets on a wide variety of events uncovered in the past, many of little importance, featured as the 'press magnate's news-papers explored new territories and reported aspects of personal and social life previously unrecorded in the daily press'.[116]

It was not simply what news was about but also how it was reported. Northcliffe wanted his news pages to be full of short items that would sur-prise the reader and to this end prominence was given to sensational copy. Sensational copy in popular newspapers before the First World War is not the kind of material we associate with the tabloids today – Page 3 girls and salacious accounts of people's private lives were not in keeping with the social mores of Edwardian Britain. Sensational news focussed on crime and news of the unusual, bizarre and abnormal. Northcliffe defined news as 'anything out of the ordinary' and believed that this was the 'only thing that will sell a newspaper'.[117] The *Evening News*, *Mail* and *Mirror* specialised in such stories. Analysis[118] of the *Mail*, the least sensational of the three papers, in its early years illustrates the nature of sensational copy. Examples of the stories found in the edition of 11 May 1896 included:

- 'A Spanish Lady's Death in Pimlico'
- 'Death from Excitement'
- 'Murder near Matlock'
- 'An Unaccountable Crime'
- 'Extraordinary Scare at Forest Hill'
- 'Corpse in a Burning House'
- 'Ghastly Scene in Camberwell'

It was not only domestic stories that focussed on the sensational; the 18 May 1896 edition carried the following stories on the foreign news page:

- 'Texas Tornado: Two Hundred Lives Lost: Enormous Damage'
- 'At Bida: Terrible Explosion: Two Hundred People Killed'
- 'Rioting in Paris'

- 'Brigandage in Italy'
- 'Distress in Italy'
- 'The Cholera in Egypt'
- 'Tribal Fighting at Berbier'
- 'The Transvaal: Suicide of Prisoner'

Sensational stories were written up with an emphasis on their emotion and drama. A breathless quality in much of the writing was noticeable. Jean Chalaby's examination[119] of the stories notes the intention of stirring the readers' emotions in a story of a mine accident reported on 31 March 1906. Trapped for several days below ground, the miners' experience is described as 'terrible', their 'fight for life' 'desperate', their narrative 'thrilling', their meeting with the rescue team 'dramatic', their escape 'miraculous', their emotions 'indescribable' and the suspense 'dreadful'. The emotion and sensation of the *Mail* and other mass circulation newspapers contrasted with the dry tones of the established newspapers.

House rules of the *Daily Express*

R.D. Blumenfeld defined the house style of the *Daily Express* which he edited from 1904 to 1932. He instructed his reporters that 'the newspaper-reading public appreciate good, clear English. *Simplicity, accuracy, conciseness*, and *purity of style* are the surest signposts of success'. Articles ought to 'keep to the POINT' and sentences should be 'short, sharp, clear-cut ... Give the gist of the story in the first paragraph and build upon that foundation'. Diction should be familiar, concrete and lively. A 'BRIGHT STYLE' meant 'SHORT WORDS in preference to long ones' and the frequent use of EMPHATIC words like MUST, WILL'. Since headlines 'should leave the reader with a desire to read the story itself', writers should try to employ words such as 'MYSTERY, SECRET, TRAGEDY, DRAMA, COMEDY, SCANDAL and HUMAN'. Verbs were usually more 'newsy' than adjectives.

Source: LeMahieu, *A Culture for Democracy*, 27.

Presentation

How the news and other content of the newspaper were packaged and presented was also crucial. Relatively little attention was paid by Victorian newspapers to the layout of material. Newspapers such as *The Times* 'couldn't be scanned quickly' and 'demanded leisure time, concentration and formal education' to be read.[120] Few allowances were made for the reader, who was expected to plough through the tightly packaged columns 'word by word, paragraph by paragraph, absorbing information and entertainment in a sequential, linear pattern'.[121] As newspapers began to think about their readers, and acknowledge the minimal levels of literacy and time they may be deploying to read their newspaper, presentation and layout began to change.

Headlines had been the first feature to be used to change the way newspapers looked. Bolder headlines and crossheads were increasing deployed in the late Victorian period to break up columns. The *Evening News* in 1895 was one of the first British newspapers to use banner headlines which stretched across the whole width of the page.[122] This helped readers to navigate the newspaper, selecting the stories they wanted to read. Visual readjusting was also embarked on as 'it was easier to look at pictures than to read print'.[123] Typeface was altered and developed to make newspapers more readable; the use of upper and lower case as well as typefaces that appeared more modern increased the appeal of newspapers. It also helped to differentiate newspapers from one another. Developments in printing technology such as stereotyped plates enabled greater use of headlines and helped to break up the columns that had dominated newspaper design. It is hardly surprising that the claim is made that typography was the means by which the struggle between tradition and modernity took place in Fleet Street in the early twentieth century.[124]

Greater emphasis on the look of the newspaper encouraged the use of photographs, illustrations and cartoons. The pioneering work of the *Mirror* was soon aped by the rest of Fleet Street. Photographs and picture pages found their way into other newspapers, with *The Times* succumbing in 1922. This is what ordinary men and women increasingly wanted; their expectation amplified by regularly attending the cinema in large numbers from the 1900s. 'Their literacy was one of pictures, not words.'[125] They wanted to see things and newspapers responded. The extent of this response is reflected in the establishment of a number of small agencies in the 1890s providing photographs for the national press.[126] Cartoons were another means to do this. The first staff cartoonist on a daily newspaper was hired by the *Pall Mall Gazette*, a few years prior to the launch of the *Daily Mail*.[127] Caricatures had been a feature of the domestic magazine industry throughout the late nineteenth century – *Punch* was the most celebrated example – as well as appearing irregularly in the early unstamped newspapers.[128] Cartoons and illustrations fitted Northcliffe's notions of a 'picture news book' and he recruited a cartoonist for the *Mirror* soon after it became an illustrated newspaper.[129]

This emphasis on display and design was also manifest in newspaper advertising. Display advertising made its entrance into Fleet Street in the 1880s. Prior to this press ads were classified and easily fitted into the narrow columns of the Victorian newspaper. The *Daily News* allowed ads to spread across columns but it was the *Mail* that ran the first full-page advertisements, on its back page in 1896.[130] Between 1900 and 1910 display advertising established itself as the primary form of advertising in the mass circulation newspapers. It is estimated that it accounted for 75 per cent of the advertising space available in the *Daily Express*. It also increased its presence in established newspapers, becoming the 'most prominent daily visual feature of many daily newspapers'.[131] Large display ads took space away from news and editorials and Northcliffe was one of many in Fleet Street who worried about their intrusiveness.[132] By this time display advertising had become vital to the state of newspaper finances and their visual boldness and minimal copy had reshaped the presentation of the page.

The organisation of newspapers

Prior to the beginning of the twentieth century newspaper production had been 'casual' and 'unorganised', and what emerged during the Northcliffe revolution was 'systematized, carefully planned, with a routine that leaves nothing to chance, with an organisation designed to meet every possible contingency'.[133] The central point of the new system was the daily news conference. Editors no longer looked after the whole newspaper, but delegated specific tasks to various assistants and sub-editors. The news and sports editors emerged as the most powerful figures; what space they demanded was usually granted. The foreign editor gained a higher profile but had to compete with features, the women's page, social news, art, literary news as well as the crossword compiler for space. According to newspaper editor Hamilton Fyfe, it seemed 'as if the whole office consists of editors'.[134] The newspaper ceased to be a vehicle to record and interpret events and became more concerned with 'the art of structuring reality'.[135] What was happening in the world was now fitted into designated pages – home, overseas, women's interest, City, sport, etc. – as the 'skilful filling of pre-defined genres' became the basic practice of the newspaper. These genres partly reflected what the newspaper believed its audience wanted but they also exhibited the needs of efficient and speedy news gathering and processing. The 'bureaucratisation' of the newspaper impacted on the role of the editor, who was becoming a backstop in the struggle for space that was central to the internal dynamics of the organisation. He or she dictated the tone and style of the newspaper, looked after the editorial page and chaired the daily conference. However, the character of a newspaper was influenced more by the 'chief sub' than by any other member of staff; 'upon his taste and interests, then, the nature of the news must largely depend – also upon his conception of what the public like to read'.[136]

The notion of the 'sovereign editor' was undermined by interventionist proprietors. The extent of editorial sovereignty in the nineteenth century is a matter of dispute (see Chapter 4). Journalism continued to pay lip-service to the notion that the editor acted independently of his employers and was the dominant voice in determining the direction and content of the newspaper. The owners of the *Mail*, *Express* and *Mirror* were 'no ordinary newspaper owners'; they were more involved in the day-to-day running of their papers than their nineteenth-century predecessors. Motivated not only by their political and personal objectives but also by their journalistic knowledge and expertise, Northcliffe, Beaverbrook and Rothermere had strong opinions based on years of experience of running newspapers and magazines which they sought to communicate to their staff. Their editors were forced to work under regimes that consigned them to the role of minor functionaries in a marketing and editorial plan decided and executed by proprietors. Editors who did not do as they were told left or were fired. Mostly editors were appointed not to run a newspaper but to execute their owners' policies; these editors usually saw the world through the same eyes as their employers.

The bureaucratic needs of the newspaper created specialist reporting to provide the regular flow of news and information to the predefined genres. The generalist reporter dispatched to cover events anywhere and everywhere across the country gradually declined. The arrival of telegraph meant that reports could be sent directly to the news desk and the sub-editors. The news gathering operation was reorganised to ensure that news flowed from specific 'beats' policed by particular correspondents. More crucially, the supply of routine general news became the function of the news agencies. With increasing importance attached to the regularity of news supply PA and other such agencies became better organised and more central to the operation of the press. Competitors such as Central News (1871), Exchange Telegraph (1872) and Dalziel (1890) – and much later the British United Press (1922) – emerged. In the 1900s these news services thrived. Such agencies supplied a variety of newspapers and as a result had to keep their stories 'matter-of-fact and colourless' so that the individual newspapers could put their own personality into the despatches.[137] The growing dependency on the agencies held the potential for the standardisation of news. Selling news that pleased a range of newspapers of differing political persuasions placed more emphasis on accuracy and impartiality.

Perhaps the most significant shift took place between the reporter and sub-editor. If the latter part of the nineteenth century had witnessed the rise of the reporter, the early twentieth century 'tilted the balance in the sub-editor's favour'.[138] Reporters were increasingly relegated to the role of gatherers of material, 'news hounds', while the masters of the news hunt were the sub-editors or 'rewrite' men and women who put the stories into shape as they organised the layout of the newspaper. Copy painstakingly put together by reporters could be completely changed, or 'cut, sliced and slaughtered' in the reporter's view, to fit the requirements of that day's newspaper.[139] Space and simple to-the-point copy was managed by the sub-editing department, which grew stronger at the expense of reporters.

Northcliffe's impact

Northcliffe's revolution was not greeted with much enthusiasm by many in Fleet Street who were highly critical of mass circulation papers, dismissing their readers, in the words of the editor of the *Daily News*, as the 'mobocracy'. Northcliffe's account of the launch of the *Daily Mail* emphasised the failings of the established newspaper: 'the instant success of the *Daily Mail* was due to the combination of good luck and careful preparation. The good luck was the inertia of the London newspapers, none of which seemed to observe the writing on the wall in the reduction of French morning newspapers from ten to five centimetres and the great public demand for more cable news'.[140] Newspapers such as *The Times*, *Daily Telegraph*, *Morning Post* and *Daily News* were wary of the appeal to the masses launched by Northcliffe's papers. Their 'old journalists' attempted to resist what they saw as the harmful consequences of the Northcliffe press. This was not easy. For example, A.G. Gardiner of the *Daily News* struggled against the efforts of his owners, the Cadbury family, to reduce the amount of space devoted to parliamentary and religious material.[141] Suggestions from the owners that pictures be included fell on deaf ears; Gardiner eventually resigned in 1921, with the *News* adopting many of the techniques associated with the Northcliffe press. Gardiner was a longstanding critic of Northcliffe, accusing him of being 'the most sinister influence who has ever corrupted the soul of English journalism'.[142] He was particularly scathing about the role of the *Mail* in whipping up anti-German hysteria prior to the First World War, a war he believed Northcliffe's scaremongering had brought about.[143]

The attempt of Gardiner, Garvin and others to maintain serious news and serious newspapers was assisted by the economic structure of the newspaper industry that emerged in the early twentieth century. A newspaper with small sales could maintain profitability if its readers were deemed worthy of the attention of advertisers. Professionals with high disposable income helped a newspaper to draw in advertising revenue which more than compensated for small circulations. Northcliffe's revolution did not end serious, highbrow, political journalism – but it did lay down the foundations for the division of the British press between 'serious' and 'popular' newspapers.

Daily Express

TO-DAY'S WEATHER: Showers ; Cold.

NO. 9517.   MONDAY, NOVEMBER 3, 1930.   ONE PENNY.

THUNDERSTORM FREAKS ON SEA AND LAND.

GIANT WAVE STRIKES CHANNEL BOATS.

FOUR PASSENGERS INJURED.

RAIN, HAIL, SNOW AND LIGHTNING.

TWO MEN KILLED.

LONDON REFLECTING in the rain near the Law Courts after yesterday's heavy rain.

MOTOR-CARS BLOWN OVER.

SOUTHERN ENGLAND and a large part of the midlands were swept yesterday morning by one of the most violent and sudden thunderstorms on record for this time of the year.

It lasted only about half an hour, but during its brief passage several people were struck by lightning, two men being killed, torrential rain fell, and pedestrians and cats were blown over and shop windows smashed.

SHATTERED WINDOWS.

DRIVE THROUGH THE STORM.

FAMOUS BRITISH CAVALRY COMMANDER DEAD.

"BETHUNE'S HORSE."

MARQUIS OF WINCHESTER INTERVIEWED.

His Home In An Old French Chateau.

"I AM HERE."

By C. J. KETCHUM,
"Daily Express" Special
Correspondent.

ABBEVILLE, Sunday, Nov. 2.

A quaint little sixteenth-century chateau, with red-tiled roof and latticed French windows, lying in a deep green valley at the foot of the Quesnoy Mountains, on the southern banks of the Somme — such was the picturesque background in which, late yesterday afternoon, I succeeded in securing a brief interview with the Marquis of Winchester, England's premier marquis, whose position as chairman of various City companies a year ago brought him before the public.

"HIS OWN BUSINESS."

ENGLISH BUTLER.

LOVELY GARDENS.

INDIGNATION.

IN SPLENDOUR ENTHRONED in the courtyard of his small palace at Addis Ababa, Ras Tafari, who was solemnly crowned king of kings and Emperor of Ethiopia, the Lion of Judah. The leopard-skin adds to the Arabian Nights appearance of the scene.

ABYSSINIA'S EMPEROR CROWNED AT DAWN.

SCENE OF BARBARIC SPLENDOUR.

CRIMSON ROBE.

PRIESTS IN VELVET AND GOLD.

ADDIS ABABA, Sunday, Nov. 2.

AT 7.30 this morning, in a setting of barbaric splendour that far sheer magnificence of colouring it would be difficult to surpass, Ras Tafari Makonnen was crowned King of Kings and Emperor of Ethiopia in the specially constructed church within the grounds of the Cathedral of St. George here.

THE EMPRESS OF ABYSSINIA.

NEW SEARCH FOR LOST VICAR.

WOMAN'S STATEMENT TO POLICE.

"Daily Express" Special
Correspondent.

SOCIALIST DEFEATS IN ELECTIONS.

92 SEATS LOST : 78 WINS
FOR CONSERVATIVES.

CORONATION COACH.

CATHEDRAL CEREMONY.

Ras Tafari.

SECRET KINGS OF DRUG TRAFFIC.

TRAITORS DOOMED TO TORTURE AND DEATH.

HUGE FACTORIES.

"Daily Express" Correspondent.
PARIS, Sunday, Nov. 2.

Behind the startling announcement recently made by the French Customs authorities at Marseilles that they have in four months—June to September—seized 27cwt. of smuggled drugs from incoming and outgoing ships, compared with roughly 5cwt. during 1929, lies a thrilling romance of a ceaseless struggle against one of the greatest curses of our time.

MYSTERY JAPANESE.

Pilot Knocks Out A Woman In The Air.

"Daily Express" Correspondent.
SYDNEY, Sunday, Nov. 2.

LATE NEWS.

FAMOUS SOLDIER DEAD.

Broadcasting Programmes on Page 15

ADMIRAL TAYLOR IN THE HOUSE TO-DAY.

PAGE TWO, COL. ONE.

PAGE TWO, COL. THREE.

6

NEWSPAPER WARS

The press in the inter-war years, 1922–39

It is the duty of newspapers to advocate a policy of optimism in the broadest sense and to declare almost daily their belief in the future of England. Optimism is a frail and tender flower springing from the crevice in the barren rock of depression. Expose it to the east wind of analysis, or the cold sleet of criticism and it will surely die. Sustain it with the hot breath of confidence and the glowing warmth of courage and it will flourish.

Lord Beaverbrook, owner of the *Daily Express*, 1922[1]

The years between the two great wars, especially the 'Thirties', have a particular place in popular memory. Labour politician Hugh Dalton labelled them the 'The Thoughtless Thirties and the Workless Thirties'.[2] The common images of the decade are of hunger marches, dole queues, idleness, poverty, slums, ill health and the rise of fascism. Revisionist historians challenge this recollection. John Stevenson and Chris Cook claim the decade was not a period of absolute misery and depression.[3] Unemployment and hardship, they point out, were unevenly spread, concentrated mainly in the old industrial areas of the North, Scotland and Wales, where the jobless rates were particularly high. For those in work the 1930s were not 'wasted years' but years of prosperity. Some people were 'enjoying a richer life than any previously known in the history of the world: longer holidays, shorter hours, higher real wages'.[4] Stevenson and Cook argue that British society was not as divided by social conflict as the popular recollection would have us believe. They suggest that Britain was relatively stable and comparatively unified, arguing that a consensus of values existed between the wars.

The role of the newspapers is seen by many scholars as providing a 'feel good factor' in the face of rising tensions at home and abroad. Brian Whitaker[5] refers to pressures from advertisers and business to remain cheerful, citing as one example the *Daily Express* front-page headline of 30 September 1938, which screamed 'There Will Be No War This Year Nor Next Year'. The decline of the space devoted to public affairs stories in the 1930s is seen as another example of the desire to escape from the realities of politics and current affairs to a more comfortable world of gossip, entertainment and human interest stories.[6] The British press is criticised for deliberately downplaying the threat of war.[7] The editor of *The Times*, Geoffrey Dawson, wrote in 1937 that he did his 'utmost, night after night, to keep out of the paper anything that might hurt their (the German Government) susceptibilities'.[8] The newspapers are accused of painting a rosy picture of unemployment and its attendant problems, and like the newsreels concentrating more on 'successes, at sport, in economic terms and in both domestic and international politics'.[9] Peddling optimism is partly attributed to the competition that pervaded Fleet Street between 1922 and 1939. The 'circulation wars' were an outcome of the changes wrought by Northcliffe and mass circulation papers, with popular journalism extending its influence throughout Fleet Street, through the skills of brilliant technical editors such as Arthur Christiansen at the *Express* and Guy Bartholomew at the *Mirror*, who eschewed politics for entertainment.

Newspapers for the first time faced competition from other forms of mass media, particularly cinema, which in the 1930s had established itself as the 'essential social habit of the age'.[10] The competition from other media led newspapers to place more emphasis on their visual appeal. The visual reorientation of the press gathered pace as audiences became more accustomed to increasingly sophisticated forms of visual representation on screen and on the page.[11] There was a transformation in newspaper typography, with a significant reform of layout and presentation. The wireless and cinema newsreel posed a threat to newspapers' monopoly of news provision. Newspaper proprietors struggled with the newly formed British Broadcasting Company (BBC) to prevent it setting up a radio news service. The BBC's news coverage, it is argued, helped to keep newspapers honest.[12] Stephen Tallents, the BBC's Public Relations Director, believed the radio made it more difficult for 'a newspaper with a private axe to grind' to 'invent or suppress news'.[13] Broadcasters' focus on impartiality also had the effect of making the press more careful in its gathering and reporting of the facts; newspapers between the wars began to place more emphasis on the distinction between fact and comment. The immediacy of radio forced them to re-evaluate their news coverage, further extending what was defined as news.[14]

Competition in the newspaper industry in the 1920s and 1930s was 'fierce', leading to a reduction in the number of newspaper titles as circulation mushroomed.[15] The newspapers that closed completed a shift in the balance between provincial and national newspapers and between serious and popular newspapers that had begun prior to the First World War. The national daily newspapers were strengthened. The competition between newspapers should be seen in the light of the changing pattern of ownership in Fleet Street. Attention is usually drawn to the concerns about the influence of press owners expressed by politicians of both the left and right. Prime Minister Stanley Baldwin articulated these anxieties when he declared, 'what proprietorship of these papers is aiming at is power, power without responsibility – the prerogative of the harlot throughout the ages'.[16] Concerns about the influence newspapers and their owners exerted over public opinion and parliamentary politics, particularly given the social unrest and instability that prevailed, were justified. However, they mask the co-operation that existed between press owners and newspaper groups and the accommodation that developed between politicians and the press. Political and commercial collaboration between newspapers, newspaper groups and their proprietors was a feature of the 1930s. Beaverbrook and Rothermere encouraged their newspapers to compete for readers but they also collaborated in political campaigns such as that in support of Empire free trade and were happy to take part ownership in each other's companies. Competition and co-operation went side by side in the process of building newspaper chains.

Accommodation between the press and politics is most clearly seen in the rise of news management in the 1930s. The coming of mass democracy in 1918 with the extension of the vote to all men and to women over 30 posed new challenges to the political process. The British State had to adjust to new problems of political, social and cultural management in the era of mass democracy. Newspapers – and other forms of mass communication – presented both an opportunity and threat. They could be seen as a potentially danger-ous catalyst for growing political tension and a threat to the authority of the State as well as a means to manage public discourse and mould popular taste. Mechanisms to manage the press were developed in this period which cemented newspapers into a particular relationship with government when it came to gathering news. Most newspapers were happy to co-operate with the system of news management developed by the State.

Circulation wars

The million-selling daily newspaper was a common feature of the 1930s; several newspapers regularly sold in their millions. It was the 'defining decade for the direction of popular daily newspapers in Britain', with their 'greatest expansion in terms of sales and readers'.[17] Sales increased rapidly, 'mushrooming' from an estimated total circulation of 4.7 million in 1926 to 10.6 million in 1939.[18] The impetus for this boom was an intense circula-tion war, particularly at the popular end of the market that dominated the period; the *Mail* and *Express* were joined by a new rival, the *Daily Herald*, whose entry into the newspaper market dramatically transformed the nature of the competition. The origins of the *Daily Herald* were completely at odds with those of most of its rivals. It started life in 1912 as a socialist news-paper. Founded by a group of trade union activists, it became a daily news-paper in 1919 under George Lansbury, who was to become the leader of the Labour Party. Dwindling finances and enthusiasm led to its takeover by the Trade Union Congress (TUC) in 1922 and it was then run as the official organ of the movement until 1929, when it entered into a deal with the publishers, Odhams Press.[19] The arrangement was that the paper would

remain editorially committed to Labour politics but commercially the operation would be run by Odhams and its boss, Julias Elias, Lord Southwood.
Elias, a self-made businessman with little or no political interests, was keen
to make a commercial success of the *Herald*. To this end he resorted to what
has been described as 'buying readers'.[20]

The use of gimmicks and gifts to sell newspapers had been part of
Northcliffe's contribution to the economics of the industry. Odhams took
things one step further, re-launching the *Herald* in 1929 with a substantial
number of sales offers, including a variety of free gifts such as pens, tea-sets,
clothes, kitchen equipment, cut-glass vases and complete bound sets of Dickens
for subscribers to the paper.[21] His competitors responded, substantially increasing the costs of newspaper production. It is estimated that Fleet Street's four
leading papers were spending £3 million per year showering offerings on the
British newspaper reading public.[22] Alarm at such costs led the Newspaper
Proprietors Association (NPA) to ban free gifts. Odhams responded by offering
products at 'bargain prices'. A vast number of door-to-door canvassers were
hired to sell newspapers; it is estimated that the staff of the national press
increased by 72 per cent between 1924 and 1935, most of whom were canvassers, calculated to be 40 per cent of new staff by 1934. By the mid-1930s
more than 50,000 canvassers, employed at £3 a week, were knocking at the
doors of British households.[23]

The *Herald*'s campaign realised its intended objective; it became the first
newspaper to reach the two million circulation mark in 1933. Most of its
competitors fell by the wayside, unable to keep up with Elias's marketing
blitz. The circulation of the *Mail* fell from 1.85 million in 1930 to 1.58
million by 1937; that of the *News Chronicle* (formed by a merger of the *Daily
News* and *Daily Chronicle* in 1930) dropped from around 1.6 million to just
over 1.3 million over the same period.[24] The *Daily Mirror*'s circulation
declined steadily from the end of the First World War. The only paper that
was able to compete – and eventually overtake the *Herald* – was Beaverbrook's
Daily Express, which in 1937 reached a circulation high of 2.37 million.[25]
Beaverbrook had been so incensed by what he labelled Odhams's 'mad campaign'
that he had vowed to fight on to the death.[26] He realised that the increased
circulation of the *Herald* had been bought at a high price and that it would
be difficult for Odhams to maintain the loyalty of his new readers. The
weakness of the commitment of readers had been brought home to Beaverbrook when the *Daily Express* suspended canvassing, to find that its circulation dropped by nearly a quarter of a million overnight.[27] Odhams had to
spend £5,000 a week to maintain its circulation levels. Beaverbrook decided
to spend more money on the editorial content and presentation of his newspapers. The *Herald* was paying its readers to keep reading, while the *Express*
stimulated its readers by expanding its news service and brightened up its
presentation. The *Express* was relentlessly cheerful and optimistic in its
reporting at a time when economic and political storm clouds were

gathering over Europe. This contrasted with the editorial content of the *Herald*, which maintained a commitment to serious news and warned of the dangers of what was happening. If ordinary people objected to the *Daily Mail* and *Daily Express* as 'all blinkin lies!', they complained the *Herald* was 'all blinkin trouble!'[28] Some innovations were introduced but the *Herald*'s staff refused to co-operate in any effort to 'lighten up' the newspaper: it was the only popular paper not to publish horoscopes and carry comic strips.[29] Advertisers were not seduced by Elias's numbers, preferring in the long run the *Express*'s attempts to build up a loyal readership and encourage people to 'look on the bright side of life and go out and buy things'.[30]

The circulation wars eventually came to an end in 1938 when the NPA opened informal talks to suspend hostilities. It was not motivated by exhaustion of the struggle but by the impending arrival of the Second World War. Odhams had considerable resources to draw on to pursue its circulation drive. Whether it could have continued much longer is debatable but the promotional activities of Odhams and its owner, Julias Elias, were responsible for a huge surge in the circulation of British newspapers. For someone not allegedly interested in the content of newspapers this was a major achievement. Much of this circulation increase might have been 'fictitious',[31] but it brought into the market many readers who had never before read a newspaper. The circulation wars, as the *News Chronicle*'s editor A.J. Cummings wrote at the outset of his book *The Press and a Changing Civilisation*, made newspapers 'almost as much a part of our lives as the houses we live in'.[32] On the eve of the Second World War 69 per cent of the British people regularly read a national daily newspaper and 82 per cent a Sunday newspaper; taking into account literacy rates at the time, this meant that nearly every literate person read a Sunday newspaper.[33] This extension of newspaper readership was achieved at the expense of the loss of titles, the provincial newspapers being the major victims of the Odhams-inspired circulation wars.

As more people read or at least subscribed to newspapers, the number of papers they could buy diminished. Rising costs of production forced the closure of 30 daily and Sunday national newspaper titles between 1921 and 1937.[34] Provincial morning newspapers suffered the most. In 1921 there were 41 such titles in the United Kingdom; by 1937 there were only 28.[35] This was the start of a trend – with a temporary respite during the war – which has continued to the present day. The number of towns and cities outside London with competing daily titles has plummeted. Provincial newspaper readers experienced a sharp decline in the choice of political perspectives they had on social and civic affairs. Increased competition from the London press was the main reason. Eight national newspapers followed the example set by the *Daily Mail* at the beginning of the century in setting up regional production centres in Glasgow, Manchester and Leeds in the 1920s and 1930s.[36] Evening and weekly papers in the provinces also decreased in number as the trend to more people reading fewer papers characterised the 1930s.

The display mind

The circulation wars had an impact on the content, market orientation and presentation of British newspapers, particularly popular papers. The most significant advance occurred in the visual dimension of newspaper layout and design. Competition provided some of the incentive that changed the appearance and content of newspapers but the rising prominence of other forms of mass communication, such as the cinema and wireless, was a significant factor. Newspapers also became more aware of their readers, who they were and what they liked as a result of the advent of market research. The ability to respond to readers' likes and the introduction of technical innovations is attributed to the skills of a 'new breed, the production journalist – the editorial man concerned with the typographic design of his paper'.[37] One such editor was Arthur Christiansen, known as 'Chris' to his colleagues, at the *Daily Express*, who strongly believed that layout and design were fundamental to the success of a newspaper. His objective was to produce a paper that people enjoyed reading; what one critic described as 'sophisticated escapism with the bright romantic treatment of news'.[38]

Unlike most of his predecessors in Fleet Street 'Chris' was not interested in politics. He wrote: 'I was not a political animal ... The politics were Lord Beaverbrook's, the presentation was mine'.[39] He was fascinated with the technical side of newspaper production as befits his early background as a typographer, illustrator and writer of headlines. Previously editors had left such matters to their printers or compositors. Christiansen started his editorial career running the *Express*'s Manchester edition, where he introduced an eight-page children's comic supplement, a pull-out racing section and some colour reproduction.[40] He took over at the *Daily Express* in 1933, running it until 1957, a quarter-century of experimentation in the layout, design and production of the newspaper which was emulated by most of his competitors in Fleet Street. His design was dictated by what he believed the 'Common Man' wanted. Maintaining the common touch was vital and to this end he devised two characters, the Man on the Rhyl Promenade and the Man in the Back Street of Derby, who staff should bear in mind when writing their stories and laying out the newspaper.[41] Christiansen's readers wanted news that was 'simple, immediate, personal and visually astonishing'.[42] As a result the *Express* had to be lively, exciting, direct, eye-catching, pithy and fun.

To achieve his goals Christiansen introduced several features. The *Daily Express* became a sub-editor's newspaper; the sub-editorial team at the paper was the largest in Fleet Street at the time and it was responsible for basically rewriting the whole newspaper to produce a slick, synthetic product that conformed to Christiansen's formula.[43] That formula was communicated daily to staff in an editorial bulletin that bestowed praise and criticism of the day's paper, transmitting Christiansen's general principles of what constituted a good, popular newspaper. To make the newspaper more readable he enlarged the print size, increased banner headlines, changed the font to make it more appealing to the eye, and used headlines on the lower half of the page, what is called 'below the fold'.[44] Fewer words were used but they were deployed to gain maximum attention. Headlines became crucial; shorter, bigger, bolder and more dramatic, they drew on the language of advertising to grab the reader's attention.[45] Bold illustrations were incorporated in a variety of ways and text was indented to break up the columns and introduce other decorative devices.[46]

The general principles of Arthur Christiansen

- There is no subject, no abstract thing that cannot be translated in terms of people.
- Avoid words of Latin or French derivation and try to find the Anglo-Saxon word that does the job.
- The last paragraph of a story should be as punchy as the first.
- One good home story is worth two foreign stories.
- Always in every story, even stories of high international significance, the warm human element will attract attention.
- Always, always, tell the news through people.
- Good stories flow like honey. Bad stories stick in the craw. What is a bad story? It is a story that cannot be absorbed on the first time of reading. It is a story that leaves questions unanswered. It is a story that has to be read two or three times to be comprehended. And a good story can be turned into a bad story by just one obscure sentence.
- Make the news exciting, even when it (is) dull ... make the news palatable by lavish presentation ... the viewpoint that is optimistic.

Source: Williams, *Dangerous Estate*, 190–2;
Baistow, *Fourth Rate Estate*, 42.

The revolutionary quality of Christiansen's design and layout ended the dominance that the column had exercised over the composition of the newspaper page for the previous two hundred years or more. Readers were made to read horizontally across the page rather than vertically, up and down. The densely crammed columns that had characterised the nineteenth-century newspaper vanished as Christiansen and his contemporaries emphasised the use of white spaces on the page. The whole newspaper was woven together to ensure that the pages of the *Express* were not simply 'a space in which print conveyed information, but an image that engaged the eye'.[47] The visual appeal of reading a newspaper 'might not stimulate the brain but was pleasing to the palate'.[48]

157

The emphasis on imagery is attributed to the advent of the cinema, which was blamed by some contemporary critics for the 'atrophy of public intelligence'.[49] Cinematography was held responsible for the expansion of illustrations and pictures in newspapers as well as the focus on a more accessible display of material. The shortening of articles is associated with people 'growing accustomed to ... impressions that could be received through the eye without mental effort'.[50] The 'modern mind', according to one commentator in the 1930s, 'has become a cinema mind'.[51] Advertising contributed to enhancement of the visual environment; display ads sought to capture the 'ephemeral glance of the popular reader' by producing images that conveyed information quickly, without too many words, and triggered a broad range of responses.[52] Newspapers recognised they had to operate in an environment in which their readers were increasingly bombarded by visual imagery. The success of the *Mirror* and the *Daily Sketch*, launched in 1909 as an illustrated paper, indicated that since the early days of the silent film newspaper readers were increasingly familiar with and fond of visual imagery. By the 1930s their familiarity was breeding a demand for more photographs, pictures, illustrations and other forms of pictorial representation – the amount of written newspaper copy was in retreat.

The design revolution spread across Fleet Street, like an infection. Typographical freedom was realised in its own peculiar way in other popular daily newspapers. The so-called serious newspapers also caught the disease and in 1932 the bastion of newspaper tradition, *The Times*, went through a radical makeover. Changing Britain's best-known newspaper was not easy. Attempts to modify the layout began in 1929 and were only accepted after they had been approved by a specially established committee. Even then change was only agreed to if a series of typographical experiments were conducted to test the suitability of a variety of fonts and font sizes. The committee set the goal of a new typography which must be 'masculine, English, direct, simple ... and absolutely free from faddishness and frivolity'.[53] The font 'Times New Roman' was born and brought to an end 130 years of a particular style. The new *Times* was not only easier to read but also included articles on fashion, broadcasting and cinema, as well as carrying a crossword for the first time and putting news photographs on an entire page.[54] The changes could not, however, go as far as shifting ads from the front page; that was only allowed in 1966. Christiansen's effect on Fleet Street meant that no newspaper, not even *The Times*, could avoid rethinking its layout, presentation and content.

Not everyone was in favour of such changes. New techniques were resisted inside newspapers; Christiansen, for example, had a bitter struggle with some of his colleagues over his decision to remove full stops from headlines. Some observers worried about the 'dictatorship of the layout man'.[55] A pamphlet published under this title argued that the typographical pictorialisation of the popular newspaper undermined its capacity to inform the reader in any meaningful way, claiming photographs and illustrations 'disintegrated the text until consecutive reading of more than five hundred words is becoming impossible'.[56] Some writers associated the typographical changes with the devaluation of words; others blamed readers, especially women readers, for the demand for pictures. Henry Wickham Steed, who had edited Northcliffe's *Times*, believed women 'preferred "pictures" to verbal statements and either subscribed to "picture papers" or kept the "picture pages" of more serious journals in their homes'.[57] A relatively untapped pool of new readers, women had begun to again attract the attention of newspapers and in the competitive environment of the 1930s a variety of changes were made to bring in more of them.

The abbreviation of journalism, whether in the form of shorter articles or more pictures, was seen as a product of the weakened power of attention among the reading public.[58] The state of what was commonly referred to as 'the public mind' was a matter of much consideration in the first half of the twentieth century. Many intellectuals were concerned about the capacity of the public mind to engage with the political issues of the day. The philosopher Graham Wallas[59] argued that men and women are governed by emotion as much as they are by reason, and they often act on impulses and instincts which can be shaped and channelled by skilful manipulators. This concern was reinforced by the experience of First World War propaganda and the rise of fascism in the 1920s and 1930s. People were seen as being persuaded into paths of action – against their better judgement – by the skilful use of the mass media, particularly the new media of radio and cinema, by propagandists. Contemporary readers were described as 'busy, pre-occupied folk, reading "catchy headlines" in underground trains, offices and tea rooms', who no longer had the time to consider carefully and reflect on what they read.[60] The *Daily Mail*'s description of itself as 'The Busy Man's Newspaper' highlighted the changing reading habits that worried intellectuals. They appeared to believe that newspapers were conditioning their readers to accept loudly shouted slogans and words of command.[61] Newspapers appeared to affirm their readers as 'a complacent, prejudiced and unthinking mass'.[62] The decline of the 'soundness of public judgement' was also attributed to the growth of personal journalism and the decline of political coverage in the press in this period.

The rise of the human interest story

The informality that Christiansen encouraged in newspapers was accompanied by a decline in the space devoted to public affairs coverage. A content analysis found that 'the *Daily Mail* and the *Daily Mirror* ... reduced coverage of political, social and economic affairs during the inter war period. Most strikingly the *Daily Mirror* halved its public affairs coverage'.[63] This was contrasted with *The Times*, in which there was 'no comparable change'. This analysis bears out the anecdotal impression provided by commentators at the

time who found 'think stuff unwanted' in the press.[64] This examination of
the political content of the press has been contested.[65] Dispute over the
interpretation of data, however, cannot hide the fact that stories of human
interest with universal appeal were given more prominence in the 1920s and
1930s than they had been previously. It did not apply uniformly across Fleet
Street – as we have seen, the *Daily Herald* was less receptive to the innovation. Human interest stories were nevertheless part of the process of attracting new readers in an era of increasing competition; according to the writer
Aldous Huxley, 'most people choose their daily paper, not for its opinions,
but for its entertainingness, its capacity to amuse and fill the vacancies of
leisure'.[66]

Complaints were made by commentators at the time about the rise of
commercial journalism which was responding to readers' appetite for 'pictures, "snippets", "human stories", the antics of film stars, football competitions and the profits of professional bruisers'.[67] The gradual replacement of
politics in the newspapers reflected the growing capacity and need of the
industry to know and respond to what its readers wanted. The growth of
market research in the 1930s produced considerable data on the consumption habits and wants of the newspaper reader. Much indicated that readers
were less and less interested in 'serious' news. A review of the press by Mass
Observation (M-O) at the end of the war found that in the case of most
newspapers less than a quarter of readers had a 'genuine interest' in 'serious
news'.[68] Readers of the Sunday newspapers had the least interest, while the
readers of newspapers with strong political lines such as the *Daily Herald* had
more interest in political affairs and news. The rise of the human interest
story is connected with the fall in public interest in news. That's if it can be
called a 'fall'; knowledge of readers' likes and dislikes was limited prior to
the First World War. The novelist and journalist George Orwell was highly
pessimistic about the public's desire for serious news, believing Britain was a
'low brow country ... [where] it is felt that the printed word doesn't matter
greatly'.[69]

Like many of his contemporaries Orwell believed the commercialisation of
newspapers was the problem; he complained that 'a large circulation, got by
fair means or foul, is a newspaper's one and only aim'.[70] To please their
readers, newspapers in the 1930s were seen as willing to do anything, from
showering them with gifts to satisfying their whims, prejudices, likes and
dislikes. Surveys found that many people were happy to escape from the
problems of their age. Matthew Engel[71] is reluctant to criticise them: 'people
who lived through the most ghastly war in history to so little purpose were
understandably reluctant to rush towards another'. While intellectuals and
the politically active complained that they were not getting factual information on political matters (see pp. 162–64), the mass of the people sought
reassurance in an age of fear, doubt and uncertainty. Newspapers remained
upbeat to provide escapism for a country weighed down by difficulty.

Gossip, entertainment and human interest stories provided far more comfortable reading than the realities of politics and current affairs. As with the news-reels, which 'were basically trivial in content and offered nothing to trouble the conscience',[72] the British press in the 1930s sought to avoid challenging matters and provide images of the nation as stable, harmonious and happy.

One indication of the public's need for reassurance was the inclusion of the horoscopes in the pages of newspapers. By the end of the 1930s virtually all the popular newspapers carried a horoscope.[73] The horoscope had first appeared in the *Sunday Express* in 1930 when R.H. Naylor, the doyen of prediction in this period, published an examination of what the future held for the recently born Princess Margaret.[74] Their popularity amongst people of all walks of life and class was a testament, according to the *Spectator*, of the fear and doubt that gripped British society and which 'made even educated men and women seek to lift the veil off the future and find guidance and reassurance concerning things to come'.[75]

Objective news

Newspapers have throughout their history claimed to provide factual accounts, truthful reporting and faithful coverage. Their ability to deliver a true and faithful account of an event or an issue has always been stymied in practice. From the middle of the nineteenth century onwards several devel-opments have improved the capacity of newspapers to fulfil their claims. Changes in technology, professional practice and economic circumstances and the rise of democracy came together to enhance the opportunity and desire to practice objective reporting. Newspapers have never been able to fully live up to their claim in this area – unlike broadcasting, where legal requirements have reinforced professional and organisational intentions. Certain kinds of newspapers have also had less incentive to be objective. The detachment of the 'objective reporter' in producing non-biased, factual accounts has to be set alongside the commitment of popular journalists to entertain, attract and hold the attention of their readers. Journalism as a profession – particularly as practised in the broadsheet newspapers – became more committed to the principle of objectivity to help to distinguish it from other kinds of writers and authors. Prior to the beginning of the twentieth century journalists were part of an 'undifferentiated' literary system, members of a 'loose and infor-mal' collection of writers who plied their trade through a variety of pub-lications.[76] The expansion of newspapers and other forms of mass media had by the 1930s transformed the cultural professions. Those describing them-selves as 'authors, editors and journalists' increased threefold between 1891 and 1931; a rate of increase six times that of the whole population.[77] The attempt by journalism to distinguish itself elevated the principle of objec-tivity to the centre of the profession, and in particular in the gathering and processing of news.

The pressure for newspapers to pay more attention to the tenets of objectivity in their reporting came from the advent of other media. The initial response of the NPA and newspaper industry to the wireless was to 'undermine radio's innate competitive advantage of immediacy'[78] by attempting to prevent the BBC becoming an 'independent provider of news'. Their pressures, however, gave BBC news a distinct brand in an already overcrowded marketplace for news and helped the Corporation to establish a reputation for authority and integrity. Sian Nicholas documents how restrictions on news gathering and processing determined BBC news.[79] BBC news was limited, with a ban in the early years on broadcasting news before 7 p.m. The Corporation was also not allowed to transmit football and racing results.[80] As a result, bulletins were short and sharp. Their brevity and clarity were accompanied by an impersonal style of news reading. Obliged to rewrite raw material supplied by the news agencies, the Corporation excluded sensational copy, presenting news in a factual, impersonal and accurate way.[81] By distancing itself from the sensationalism of the press, the BBC enhanced its 'air of authority' as a news provider,[82] and by the end of the 1930s 'all but a small minority gave more credence to the political objectivity of the broadcast news when compared with the coverage of the press'.[83]

Assessing the impact of the wireless on newspapers is far from straightforward. Like the cinema, it can be argued that the new medium altered how popular newspapers were written and presented. The brevity of radio news bulletins is linked to the adoption of a lower density of print and shorter sentences in newspapers and the introduction of 'the rhythms, clichés and slang terms of ordinary speech'.[84] Competition from the wireless and the newsreels which had become established viewing on any visit to the cinema forced the newspapers to reassess their role. News of breaking events became the domain of radio and the press had to 'concentrate on recapitulation, amplification, interpretation and comment'.[85] Human interest stories and other forms of entertainment were another way of adjusting to the loss of the press's monopoly of news reporting. Whether the wireless helped to make newspapers more 'honest' in their reporting is more dubious.

Reporting the 1930s

British newspapers of nearly all shades of opinion failed in their efforts to fully, frankly and fairly report the events of the inter-war years, in particular the conditions of poverty and unemployment, the rise of fascism and the crises in British institutions such as the abdication in 1936. The failure of newspapers to do their basic job of reporting the news is illustrated by the return of the personal newsletter, the most famous of which was the weekly bulletin *K-H News Letter*, which was first published in 1938.[86] Like their seventeenth- and eighteenth-century counterparts these newsletters attempted to provide facts that were 'overlooked or suppressed' by the newspapers.

Personal accounts of events, they were written by a variety of people, including newspaper correspondents who believed they were prevented from writing the 'truth'. Suspicions that newspapers did not always tell the truth – and even sometimes told lies – had increased during the First World War. The publication of casualty lists was often at odds with the reports of success and progress that dominated the news columns.[87] The credibility of the newspapers was severely damaged, resurfacing in the midst of politically sensitive issues such as the 1926 General Strike. However, newspapers' willingness to censor the news of controversial political topics was seen as attaining new heights in the 1930s.

The 'hush-hush' surrounding the events leading up to the abdication of King Edward VIII in 1936 was a noticeable example of the secrecy and censoriousness of newspapers. Details of the king's relationship with an American divorcee went largely unreported up until a couple of weeks prior to the radio announcement by the king that he was quitting his throne to marry the woman he loved. This feat of 'collective' and 'almost complete silence' was all the more remarkable given that the looming crisis was fully reported in foreign newspapers.[88] Wholesalers censored overseas newspapers and *Time* magazine even appeared in Britain with pages ripped or cut out.[89] The conspiracy of silence around the marital affairs of the monarch should be seen in the context of the adulation of the monarchy in the press at this time, which was described by one then Fleet Street editor as having 'no precedent in our history'.[90] The reverence shown to even minor royalty is seen as part of the efforts of many newspapers to draw attention away from everyday realities. The abdication story was eventually broken by a provincial newspaper, the *Yorkshire Post*, whose editor Arthur Mann was highly critical of editors' close relationships with Ministers of the Crown.[91]

A more significant example of the failure of the press in the 1930s was the support the majority of British newspapers gave to Neville Chamberlain and his policy of appeasement between 1937 and 1940. The rise of fascism in Germany and Italy had been reported by newspapers – and other mass media – with great circumspection. Papers of all political persuasions and opinions supported the government's policy of 'appeasement', keeping much criticism of the Nazi regime out of their pages and trying to minimise any talk of war. *The Times*, under the editorship of Geoffrey Dawson, led the efforts of the British press in backing the appeasement policy, attempting to keep anti-German comment out of his paper.[92] Outspoken critics of appeasement, including Winston Churchill, were denied or given restricted access to newspaper columns. Even Liberal and Labour-leaning papers, such as the *Daily Herald* and the *News Chronicle*, often co-operated with this policy. Vernon Bartlett, foreign correspondent of the *News Chronicle* and a vigorous critic of fascism, found his newspaper refused to print his report on the Munich Agreement.[93] The disregard editors and owners had for the reports of their own correspondents is one of the 'remarkable features' of the conduct of the British press at this time.[94] By 1938, the year of the Munich Crisis, most of the press was either muted in its criticisms of Germany and its allies or enthusiastic about the possibilities of a resolution of tensions.[95] The reporting of the Munich Agreement was the low point in one of the sorriest chapters in British newspaper history. Partiality was also found in the coverage of unemployment and poverty. The Great National Hunger March of 1932 was reported in many newspapers as part of the efforts of the Soviet Union to destabilise British society. The *Daily Mail*, *Manchester Guardian*, *Daily Telegraph* and *The Times* all reiterated the government's view that the marchers were 'Moscow dupes' or 'pawns in a Communist game' and that the marchers threatened 'incalculable damage' and 'violence'.[96]

Putting the principle of objectivity into practice in the newspaper business of the 1930s was seen as highly problematic. Many journalists spoke of the ways in which commercial pressures and the concentration of press ownership restricted their freedom not only to report what they saw and heard but also to critically comment. They acknowledged that the individual reporter and writer could not escape the conditions he or she worked in any more than the corner shopkeeper could 'preserve his independence in the teeth of the chain-stores'.[97] Deference, commercial advantage, personal reward and political leverage were held responsible for the restriction placed on what could be covered.[98] Claud Cockburn resigned from *The Times* in 1932 to found his own six-page cyclostyled weekly paper, the *Week*, offering 'inside information' on international political machinations because of what he believed was the press's cosy relationship with the Establishment.[99] The root cause of the suppression of information and news was the small number of men who owned and controlled British newspapers. Labour MP Norman Angell in 1922 drew attention to the influence of press owners when he wrote:

> What England (sic) thinks is largely controlled by a very few men, not by virtue of the direct expression of any opinion of their own but by controlling the distribution of emphasis in the telling of facts: so stressing one group of them and keeping another group in the background as to make a given conclusion inevitable.[100]

The era of the press barons

Press ownership had been an issue prior to the First World War. By 1914 one man, Lord Northcliffe, had become a leading political and journalistic force in the country by owning and controlling 40 per cent of the national morning, 45 per cent of the evening and 15 per cent of the Sunday total newspaper circulations.[101] Northcliffe's pre-eminence in the newspaper market has never been surpassed.[102] His political influence was due to his ability to exercise 'the power of suggestion to millions'.[103] The extension of newspaper readership appeared to provide proprietors with more power. The press empires that began to emerge prior to the First World War extended their reach in the 1920s and 1930s. As the smaller, independent titles were forced out of business, gobbled up by newspaper chains, the market domination of the leading companies was extended. The owners changed but the pattern of ownership remained the same – a small number of large newspaper chains controlled the market. Lord Rothermere assumed control of Associated Newspapers on his brother's death in 1922. Associated Newspapers controlled more than 100 weeklies and monthlies, four national dailies (the *Evening Mail*, *Daily Mail*, *Daily Mirror* and *The Times*) and several Sunday papers in addition to a large number of magazines.[104] Rothermere sold *The Times* to the Astor family, who had already bought the *Observer* from Northcliffe. Lord Beaverbrook's empire was much smaller; besides the *Express* newspapers he owned only two other papers, one of which was the *Evening Standard*. However, their combined circulation of 4.1 million provided Beaverbrook with a substantial influence over the market. The new major newspaper owners were the Berry brothers from South Wales, who, as Lords Camrose and Kemsley, established themselves as the owners of the largest newspaper chain in the country. Like Northcliffe, Newnes and Pearson they started their careers in magazines. Their success with *Advertising World* and *Boxing* indicates their astuteness in identifying trends in the publishing industry. The money they accrued from these two publications and other magazines, such as *Health and Strength* and the *Penny Illustrated Paper*, enabled the Berrys to buy up other newspaper titles.[105] In 1915 they bought the *Sunday Times* and it was not long before they had amassed 20 daily newspapers, 3 nationals – the *Daily Telegraph*, the *Financial Times* and the *Daily Sketch* – 6 Sundays, 6 weeklies and over 80 magazines, as well as numerous provincial and local papers.[106] The Berry brothers' consortium broke up in 1937. Between them these four Lords of Fleet Street owned nearly one out of two national and local daily newspapers sold in Britain and one in three Sunday papers; the total circulation of their newspapers was over 13 million by the eve of the war.[107]

The ownership of so many newspapers equated with extensive political influence, and was a matter of public and political debate in the 1930s. The 'era of the press barons' is identified by the interventionist nature of proprietors motivated by political considerations. Beaverbrook and his colleagues certainly sent a continuous stream of instructions to editors about the layout of their newspapers and provided comments, observations and instruction on how matters should be covered, including the possibility of war and criticism of the German government. Their intervention is seen as having played an important part in the misreporting of key events of the 1920s and 1930s. Their fascist sympathies are highlighted by Rothermere's flirtation with the British Union of Fascists (BUF). In January 1934 the *Mirror* ran a story entitled 'Give the Blackshirts a Helping Hand' and a headline in the *Daily Mail* trumpeted 'Hurrah for the Blackshirts'. The *Evening News* ran a

letter competition called 'Why I Like the Blackshirts'.[108] Beaverbrook's intervention in party politics was a regular feature of the 1920s. He sought 'to
bully politicians' by setting up his own political party, the United Empire
Party (UEP), in 1930 – in collaboration with Rothermere.[109] The party
campaigned for 'Empire Free Trade' and candidates ran against the official
government candidates at by-elections supported by the full weight of the
Mail and *Express* groups. Two by-election victories were won, trumpeted in
the *Express* by headlines such as 'The Empire Wins South Paddington'.[110]
When Prime Minister Baldwin put his personal leadership on the line in
another by-election, threatening to resign if the UEP won, the press barons
lost the test of strength and withdrew. Lord Kemsley was a close personal friend
and confidant of Neville Chamberlain, actually meeting Hitler in Berlin in
1939 and setting the Führer's mind at rest that Britain did not have any
aggressive intentions and disparaging Churchill's bellicose comments.[111]

To portray the inter-war years as an era in which a specific form of ownership
and control of the press was exercised to exert unprecedented influence over
politics and its reporting is slightly misleading. The political involvement of
Beaverbook, Rothermere, Kemsley and Camrose was not typical. Many of
their fellow newspaper owners – for example Lord Riddell, owner of Britain's
best-selling paper the *News of the World*, and paradoxically Lord Southwood,
of the Labour Party-supporting *Daily Herald*, had no interest in the politics
of their newspapers. Not all proprietors had the desire to exercise political
power and influence. They were more interested in making money, 'obliged
to work hard at the undignified business of maintaining commercial solvency;
closures, mergers and take-overs were a far from solid foundation for a press
lord constituency'.[112] There was no consistency or uniformity in the way in
which the press barons attempted to intervene in politics. They tended to pay
attention to certain of their newspapers, ignoring the others they controlled
or had interests in. Beaverbrook's desire for cheerful and upbeat news in the
Daily Express was to some extent contradicted by the *Evening Standard* advocating a popular front against fascism and the *Sunday Express* warning about
the dangers of German militarisation.[113] They did not appear to follow a
consistent line. Baldwin noted that their 'engines of propaganda' were used
to push 'constantly changing policies, desires, personal wishes, personal likes and
dislikes'.[114] Northcliffe used his papers to support a series of idiosyncratic
campaigns in favour of wholemeal bread, the sweet pea and the Homburg hat.
The 'press barons' were outsiders; they were not clubbable members of the
Establishment. They did not have the same kind of access to the inner workings
of power that some of their nineteenth-century predecessors had. They were
too independent, too unreliable and not from the right background – usually
self-made men from the margins of the United Kingdom or her colonies.

There is limited evidence to show that the press barons were successful in
exerting any significant sway over British politics. Northcliffe and Beaverbrook
did appear to exercise some influence during the Great War[115] but this was

a time of crisis when government and society had to mobilise to fight a total war. Outside this abnormal set of circumstances the influence of the press barons was more restricted. Few of the campaigns their newspapers ran had any success in shifting public opinion – not many people heeded calls to wear a Homburg hat. Personal political goals were never attained; for example, Northcliffe failed in his effort to be elected as MP for Portsmouth in 1895 despite buying up the local press to support his venture. Rothermere and Beaverbrook's efforts to promote an Empire Free Trade Zone came to nothing and Rothermere's endeavour to gain support for the BUF led to his newspapers actually losing readers. The press barons also had to balance political aspirations against commercial considerations. When political objectives cut into profits they backed down. Northcliffe, for example, suspended his campaign against Kitchener's command of the British Army during the First World War when his newspapers lost circulation. The press barons could not get too much out of step with their readers.

To assess the power of the press barons in terms of their ability to persuade people to vote for new parties or candidates or to buy new products or take up new causes is to misunderstand their influence. Rather, this lay in the way in which their newspapers 'selectively represented the world' and 'tended to strengthen the mainly conservative prejudices of their readers and reinforce opposition, particularly among the middle class, to progressive change'.[116] They provided support for the status quo and the dominant culture, selecting certain issues for discussion while marginalising or ignoring others, in particular those voices calling for progressive change. It was their ability to help shape the whole environment in which politics was conducted that was significant. They helped to create a climate of opinion between the wars which emphasised optimism and discouraged politicians and the public from facing up to some of the most momentous issues of the day. Paul Ferris, one of Northcliffe's biographers, describes the press lord's papers as lacking a social conscience.[117] The reluctance to look for social evils characterised most of the newspapers owned by the press barons in the 1930s.

In their style, methods and background the press barons may have differed from their contemporaries and many of their predecessors. The extent to which they issued instructions and intervened in the layout, design and content of their papers may have exceeded what had gone before. But 'the reign of the press barons did not constitute an exceptional pathology in the evolution of the press, but merely a continuation of tendencies already present before'.[118] The press barons did not usurp the sovereign role of their editors in conducting the affairs of newspapers. Using newspapers as tools of propaganda was nothing new and the era of the 'sovereign editor', if it ever existed, had started to melt away well before the advent of mass circulation popular newspapers. However, as these 'press barons' built vast newspaper empires, swallowing up many independent newspapers, their influence came to be seen as a threat to press freedom and the newly emerging mass democracy.

Commercial accommodations

Concentration of ownership in the newspaper industry in the 1930s was developed by a series of acquisitions and accommodations between newspaper owners. Mergers and take-overs figured prominently as newspaper empires were built across the country. Chain ownership was not new; multiple ownership of weekly newspapers had started in the eighteenth century. Local chains existed in the 1880s but their proprietors did not seem 'very co-operative' and were 'not much interested in building empires'.[119] In many ways the empires of the press barons were simply the continuation of an already established trend.[120] What was different was the extent to which national newspapers' owners penetrated the provincial market and the concentration of ownership of the provincial and local press. Local competition was diminished as the press barons extended their commercial hold over the newspaper industry. Many chains acquired monopoly positions in certain parts of the country. Between 1921 and 1939 the share of provincial evening titles owned by the five big chains grew from 8 per cent to 40 per cent, while morning titles saw an increase from 12 per cent to 44 per cent.[121] Consolidation of ownership occurred across the industry and this was done primarily by a process of co-operation rather than competition.

Connections between the press chains and newspaper owners existed at a number of levels. Titles were exchanged or sold between the barons. Business collaboration between Beaverbrook and Rothermere was extensive. In 1919 an agreement was made that the *Mirror* would produce the *Express* in case of breakdown or fire or accident.[122] In 1922 Rothermere bought a 49 per cent holding in the Express Group, which he only relinquished ten years later, and in 1924 they joined forces to buy out the Manchester-based newspaper chain of Sir Edward Hulton.[123] Beaverbrook held total control of only one title, the London *Evening Standard*. Co-operation broke out between Rothermere and the Berrys after a long drawn-out battle in the provinces. They ended their local circulation wars by agreeing a series of treaties which simply divided the country up between them.[124] The circulation wars of the 1930s were accompanied by business collaboration between the newspaper owners. This reflected the oligopolistic nature of the newspaper market that had developed in the years between the wars. The costs of setting up and operating a newspaper were more prohibitive and the barrier to entry into the market was raised. It was in the interests of the press barons to maintain this state of affairs and hence competition was managed; much of the intensity of the circulation wars of the 1930s can be attributed to the effort to resist what was seen as an interloper – Southwood's *Daily Herald*. The extent of the commercial control exercised over the newspapers by a small number of newspaper chains is regarded by some economists as leading to an increase in conformity in the style and substance in the press.[125] It also made newspapers vulnerable to pressure from outside interests.

Press and news management

Explanations of the nature of the coverage of the 1930s focus on the attempts of newspaper owners and their advertisers to maintain a stable environment conducive to business. A deepening trade depression in the summer of 1938 adds weight to the argument that newspapers avoided a 'war scare mentality' so as not to lose readers, advertisers and revenue.[126] Anecdotal evidence to support this contention abounds. Francis Williams, who at this time edited the *Herald*, stated that Southwood's 'No Gloom' slogan was translated into commercial directors intervening to tone down editorial copy.[127] Close relations between editors and owners and the politicians also played their part in shaping the reporting. These connections, described as 'incestuous', were governed by intimate, personal and informal contacts sometimes dating back to shared schooldays which allowed the Chamberlain government to prevent critical reporting of British foreign policy. The interventionist approach and political stances of the press barons are also considered as a compelling account of what happened. However, it is also the case that the government in the 1930s became more effective at managing and controlling the flow of news.

The dissemination of political news was institutionalised by the government in the 1930s. Newspapers gave up some of their freedom in return for a regular and reliable supply of news and access to the thinking that was going on in the corridors of power – off the record. The desire for privileged information was a feature of these years, with popular newspapers carrying columns with names such as 'Insider Information' to convey what was going on inside Whitehall.[128] Gaining access to official thinking was important if the newspapers were to provide informed conjecture. Political reporting in Britain was conducted under the Lobby system which had been established in the 1880s to replace the informal system of cronyism and influence that pervaded the press prior to this date. By 1910 there were thirty correspondents, each writing for around six newspapers.[129] In the 1920s in response to requests from correspondents the system was formalised.[130] A news cartel was created by setting up a formal mechanism for the flow of information from government to the press. Political reporting was conducted through this cartel. A system of weekly unattributable briefings, usually given by the Prime Minister's Press Secretary, a post created in 1931, was established, and in return for the regular supply of information members of the press accepted restrictions on what they could and could not report.[131] The institutionalisation of 'the peculiarly English customs and habits that had governed the relationship between the government and press' was 'to the permanent advantage of the incumbent government'.[132] It created a group of insiders who were susceptible to the planting of stories or the government's interpretation of events.[133] Politicians and civil servants had come to realise following the First World War that they could not simply depend on crude mechanisms such as censorship to effectively manage the press and public opinion. They set about creating an apparatus that would 'sell' information the government wanted released. Press officers, official spokespersons, public relations advisors and information officers became a feature of Westminster and Whitehall. The first ministry to set up a unit to perform this function was the News Department of the Foreign and Commonwealth Office, founded in 1916. The Air Ministry was the first government department to appoint a press officer in 1919, with the Ministry of Health and War Office soon following its example. Until 1926 the peacetime press and publicity work undertaken by the government was modest in scope, but the establishment of the Empire Marketing Board (EMB) in that year marked the advent of a large-scale government propaganda and publicity machine.

The EMB was primarily established to promote trade with the Empire but was also seen by some government ministers as a means to counter the expansion of socialism in Britain. Under the direction of Stephen Tallents, it was highly innovative in the area of publicity. Tallents appreciated the importance of advertising and 'translated the message of the advertising profession into a language of government service'.[134] The EMB took out advertisements in the British press and employed a press officer to regularly inform the newspapers of its activities. Tallents moved to the General Post Office in 1934, which up to the outbreak of the Second World War spent more money on publicity than any other government department.[135]

Many of the techniques of modern political propaganda and campaigning were pioneered by the Conservative Party under Baldwin, who emphasised the importance of 'unceasing propaganda' to maintain an educated democracy.[136] The National Publicity Bureau spearheaded the publicity efforts of the government in the late 1930s. Set up in 1935 by the national government, the Bureau 'carried through the first modern, large scale propaganda campaign on a national basis in the history of British politics, yet it worked so unobtrusively and anonymously that few outside the ranks of the professional politician and organization men had any appreciation of its potency'.[137] The Bureau, as a 'non-political' organisation, was designed to bring about national unity on a non-partisan basis.[138] However, working closely with the Conservative Party, the main partner in the national government, the Bureau utilised modern forms of mass communication to pioneer many innovative techniques of propaganda. The combination of effective propaganda and sophisticated news management helped the government to convey a message of optimism through the press to the people of Britain. The feel good disposition of the press was carefully managed and directed by those in positions of authority, helped by the relative naiveté with which newspapers reacted to the attempts to 'spin' them, the highly competitive market in which newspapers had to operate, the public mood, which was in favour of peace, and the general deference of the age, in which newspapers and their editors tended to defer to what government said.

Daily Mirror, 8 May 1945

7

WAR, SOCIAL CHANGE AND RECONSTRUCTION

Newspapers at war and peace, 1939–67

We are forced to the conclusion – which we regret because of our clear realisation of the dangers which exist – that there is no acceptable legislative or fiscal way of regulating the competitive and economic forces so as to ensure a sufficient diversity of newspapers. The only hope of weaker newspapers is to secure – as some have done in the past – managers and editors of such enterprise and originality as will enable these publications to overcome the economic forces affecting them.

Royal Commission of the Press, 1962

The Second World War and its aftermath had a considerable impact on the British media and society. For the press it represented the end of its ascendancy over the process of mass communication in this country. This was relinquished to the wireless: radio and the BBC had a good war. Auntie, as the BBC affectionately came to be known, emerged 'from the war as both a symbol and an agent of the victory'.[1] The press was under public regulation from 1939 to 1945 and the issue of censorship and news management was even more sensitive than during the First World War due to the greater threat posed to national survival. What was peculiar about the system of censorship adopted in Britain was its basis in the tacit assumptions shared by newspaper proprietors and editors, civil servants and politicians, senior military personnel and ministers that coming from the same social background they would co-operate in the prosecution of the war.[2] Considerable unity underpinned Britain's war effort and newspapers that criticised or put forward alternatives to the government strategy were closed or threatened with closure – most notably the *Daily Worker* and the *Daily Mirror*. Tension between parts of the press and the government over the conduct of the conflict was a feature of the Second World War. The 'British way of censorship' conducted during the war[3] laid down the framework within which relations between newspapers – and the rest of the mass media – and the State have developed since 1945. A system of nods and winks determined what the public should and should not be told.

The functioning of newspapers changed significantly on the outbreak of war. Shortage of newsprint meant that newspapers had to shrink in size. The typical daily newspaper between 1939 and 1945 had just four pages. Distribution was disrupted by the dislocation of people and production was affected as many newspaper men and women went into the armed forces or domestic wartime service. Demand for news increased, producing a radical readjustment in the content of the press which saw news stories reassert themselves against other kinds of content. Efforts to understand the public improved as the government propaganda machine sought to gauge as accurately as possible the state of public opinion and adjust policy to ensure morale was maintained. Mass Observation gathered valuable information about newspaper consumption habits. Newspapers increasingly emphasised the importance of knowing their readers, and employed more sophisticated means of investigating their tastes and values.

The most noteworthy occurrence in press history during the Second World War was the success of the *Daily Mirror*. Struggling on the eve of the war, the newspaper emerged from the combat to speak for a wide cross-section of society. The *Mirror* articulated the views of the British people more consistently and clearly than any of its rivals. The close relationship it forged with its readers was in spite of the troubled relationship the newspaper had with Prime Minister Winston Churchill and the wartime coalition government. By 1945 it was Britain's most widely read newspaper, with a reputation for serious popular journalism which has never been surpassed. The *Mirror* played a crucial role in the post-war reconstruction, representing the opinion of many working people about the kind of society that should be rebuilt following the decimation wreaked by the war. Its support for the welfare state and the pursuit of a more just society was a major factor in shaping its reporting.

The adjustment of the newspaper industry to the economic and social circumstances in post-war Britain proved painful. The lifting of the restrictions on newsprint in the mid-1950s exposed the vulnerabilities of many newspapers which had been hidden by the special circumstances of the war. Many in Fleet Street called for the restrictions to be lifted more slowly.[4] Rising costs and increased competition resulted in the demise of many famous and longstanding titles. Most of the newspapers that disappeared were mid-market papers, dailies, Sundays and provincial titles, which further widened the gap between the popular and serious press. Their death was attributed to the arrival of commercial television in 1955, which heightened competition to attract advertisers. There is a debate about the extent to which television was responsible for the demise of these newspapers but by 1958 ITV's advertising revenue had exceeded that of the combined total of national newspapers.[5] Advertising agencies were also more discerning in their choice of newspapers as a result of the increasing amount of market research available to them. The closure of newspapers raised questions about the diversity of opinion represented in the press; the 1961 Royal Commission on the Press was charged with the task of examining how diversity could be maintained in the changing economic circumstances. Its conclusions were pessimistic, reinforced by growing tensions in industrial relations in Fleet Street.

Much of the pessimism about the future of newspapers in the 1950s and 1960s was due to the rapid rise of television as a medium of mass communication. Television had resumed as a service in 1947, limited primarily to the London area. By the end of the 1950s most households in the country had a television set. As television established itself as the dominant media, newspapers had to change their content to maintain their readers.[6] Competing with the immediacy of TV news forced newspapers to emphasise other kinds of content. The shift inside newspapers from hard to soft news was one response. The expansion of specialist reporters and beats was another. The year 1957 was the high point for newspaper sales. The next three decades would witness a steady decline in the number of people reading newspapers. This decline was hidden by the high profits and high reputation of the newspapers which survived in this period.

The day war broke out

The declaration of war in 1939 had a profound impact on the way in which the British press operated. The establishment of the Ministry of Information and the imposition of censorship created the basic wartime conditions within which the newspapers operated. Under Defence Regulation 3 British citizens were prohibited from 'obtaining, recording, communicating to any other person or publishing information which might be useful to the enemy'.[7] In addition, it was an offence 'in any manner likely to prejudice the efficient prosecution of the war to obtain, possess or publish information on military matters'. The Ministry scrutinised all copy and photographs and any material likely to be militarily sensitive had to be submitted for clearance. Failure to comply could cause a publication to be closed down.

This happened to the *Daily Worker*, which was closed down in January 1941 on the basis of a unanimous decision by the War Cabinet. The Communist Party newspaper had a small circulation, less than 1 per cent of the total daily national circulation, which was partly due to the breadth of its sports coverage and a very successful horse racing tipster.[8] Its offence was to turn people against the war – according to the government. The evidence for this is minimal, even though the paper's anti-fascist stance which characterised its coverage during the inter-war years changed due to the Nazi–Soviet pact in 1939. Criticism of the government was a feature of the paper's reporting between 1939 and 1941, including personal attacks such as a cartoon portraying Labour and trade union leader Ernest Bevin as in the pay of the capitalist bosses, which caused great offence.[9] The banning of the *Daily Worker* was part of what has been described as a wider policy of curtailing criticism in the press – left-leaning papers such as *Reynolds News*, the *Sunday Pictorial* and the *Daily Mirror* were also subject to pressure. Such pressure led newspapers to tread warily in their reporting – even so, there was criticism of war policy and the War Cabinet. Newspapers were not completely gagged in what they could report. Papers such as the *Mirror* and the *Sunday Pictorial* within the confines of supporting the war effort were willing to raise questions about the competence of the officer class, the civil service and the plans for post-war reconstruction. The negative impact on morale of the 'old school tie' in the army and War Office was a recurring theme which brought newspapers into conflict with government.[10] Censorship did play a part in shaping the way in which the press reported the war – particularly episodes such as Dunkirk, when the severity of the defeat went unreported and, at the behest of the government, the newspapers focussed on the 'good news' of the evacuation. Stories such as men deserting and throwing their guns away on the railway lines into London never made it into print.[11] Of greater significance in restricting what the press could say was the lack of the basic material required to produce a newspaper – paper and print.

Newsprint rationing

One of the main problems that confronted the press during and after the war was the shortage of newsprint. Before the war, the newspapers were using approximately 22,000 tons of newsprint every week – this plummeted to 4,300 by 1942 and newsprint had become 'rarer than gold' by 1940.[12] The shortage continued after the war and rationing was not phased out until 1956. The absence of one of the basic ingredients required to print a newspaper had a dramatic impact on content and form. From 1939 the size of the British newspaper shrank, so that by 1941 the number of pages had fallen to four. Newspapers were to remain in this shrivelled state for the next decade. The consequence of this shortage was to relieve the economic pressures on the newspaper industry. Fewer pages meant that there was less space for advertisements. In 1942 the government placed formal restrictions on how much advertising could be carried: the maximum advertising space for dailies and Sunday newspapers was limited to 40 per cent and for the evenings to 45 per cent of the paper.[13] Display advertising was virtually displaced by small ads, with newspapers beginning to resemble the eighteenth-century press. Income from advertising dropped from an overall figure of 60 per cent of the earnings of the press in 1938 to 30 per cent in 1943.[14] There was a redistribution of advertising revenue between newspapers. The shortage of space forced advertisers to go to papers which had had difficulties in attracting their interest prior to the war. Papers that had been commercially less well off benefited. Advertisers were now the 'wooers' rather than the 'wooed' and the rates that could be charged soared.[15] The reduction in cover price also assisted these papers; people now would buy two or even three newspapers.

James Curran argues that public regulation and the changed economic circumstances of the war 'helped rather than hindered the growth of radical journalism'.[16] Freed from the economic restraint that advertising had placed on the press, newspapers such as the *Daily Mirror* and *Sunday Pictorial* moved further to the left and engaged in a more critical approach to public affairs. They reflected the growing calls for social change. Newspaper rationing also helped to reduce the polarisation of the press; popular papers no longer had to compete as vigorously for readers, and in the context of the demand for war news, the space devoted to serious journalism doubled in most British newspapers.[17] The increased seriousness and radicalisation of the British press are seen most acutely in the case of the *Daily Mirror*, which entered the war with a readership representing a cross-section of British society, and emerged with an overwhelmingly working-class audience. This was facilitated by the economic environment in which the press had to operate.

Post-war Fleet Street

During the first decade after the war little change took place in the newspaper industry because of the profusion of advertising revenue and the continued restrictions on newsprint. The balance of payments crisis and a worldwide paper shortage meant that newspapers remained one-third of their pre-war size, usually twelve pages or so, and people still held on to the wartime habit of purchasing more than one paper. The year 1955 ushered in significant change: newsprint restrictions were lifted and a new commercial television channel funded by advertising was born. Papers increased in size and cover price, and newspaper reading habits returned to normal. The protection rationing gave to weaker newspapers disappeared at the same time as ITV began to compete for advertising revenue. The consequence was the demise of some of Britain's best-known papers. The first major casualty was the *News Chronicle*, which was abruptly amalgamated with the *Daily Mail* in 1960. Readers of the liberal-leaning *Chronicle* woke up one morning in October to find the *Daily Mail* on their doorstep. The demise of the *Chronicle* was followed four years later by the closure of the *Daily Herald*. One of the market leaders of the 1930s, the newspaper did not survive the post-war world. The final national casualty was the *Daily Sketch*, which limped on until 1971 when it was merged into a new tabloid *Daily Mail*. Bought from Kemsley in 1953, the *Sketch* had been turned by the Mail Group into a downmarket popular newspaper aimed at working-class Tory readers.[18] The contraction in the national daily press was not as pronounced as in other sectors of the industry.

The sectors that suffered most from the removal of newsprint restrictions were the Sunday papers and the evening press.[19] Several Sunday papers bowed out: *Sunday Dispatch* (1961), *Sunday Graphic* (1960), *Empire News* (1961) and finally the long-established *Reynolds News*, which had been renamed the *Sunday Citizen* in 1962 and closed in 1967. The London evening press almost vanished. In 1920 there had been six titles, and this figure was halved by the start of the post-war period. The Cadbury family closed their London evening paper, the *Star*, in the same year as they sold the *News Chronicle*, and by 1989 there was only one evening newspaper left in London – the *Standard*. In 1963 the wave of closures reached a peak in the regional evening press; papers with total sales of more than 650,000 were shut down in Birmingham, Nottingham, Manchester, Leicester, Leeds and Edinburgh, leaving these cities with only one evening newspaper.[20] Five provincial morning newspapers closed between 1948 and 1961, in Nottingham, Brighton, Manchester, Birmingham and Glasgow.[21] While there was a significant decline in the number of newspapers, the total circulation of the national press only experienced a small drop between 1948 and 1968.[22] During this period the fate of the national dailies compared favourably to that of the Sundays, whose circulation dropped by nearly one-sixth, and the provincial morning papers which lost one-third of their sales.

The newspapers that disappeared in these twilight years of the British press had several features in common. The *News Chronicle*, the *Daily Herald* and the *Daily Sketch* had relatively healthy circulations when they were closed. The *News Chronicle* was selling 1.16 million copies, the *Daily Sketch* 1.3 million and the *Daily Herald* 1.26 million, nearly 8 per cent of Fleet Street's total circulation at the time and five times that of *The Times*.[23] While large, these circulation figures represented a significant fall from their pre-war numbers. This does not, however, explain their inability to keep on trading. The major problem faced by so-called mid-market, centre-left newspapers was their failure to attract sufficient advertising revenue and to attain a sufficiently high level of circulation to compensate. The *Daily Herald* by the time of its closure had a 3.5 per cent share of newspaper advertising revenue. The overwhelming majority of its readers were working class, which did not appeal to advertisers attempting to reach readers with a high disposable income and purchasing power. Advertising revenue had been resurrected as the driving force of the industry and a newspaper could only survive by having a high proportion of its readers drawn from the upper strata of society or a vast number of working-class readers, measured in their millions. Anything in between threatened viability.

Regulating newspapers

In 1947 the Labour government appointed a Royal Commission to assess the role of the press as part of post-war reconstruction – it was also motivated by the hostility of the majority of newspapers to their policies. Few titles in Fleet Street had any sympathy for the new government. They were critical of the continuation of rationing and opposed the nationalisation of major industries and utilities. Leaks of sensitive information to the press were a theme of Cabinet discussion[24] and ministers were concerned about what they perceived were efforts to 'sabotage' their endeavours. Decisions to suspend newsprint supplies during the fuel crisis in 1947, to establish a Central Office of Information (COI) and to allow greater control over the flow of information from government generated charges from Fleet Street that the Atlee government was interfering in the exercise of free speech. Many in the Labour Party accused press owners and controllers of sabotaging national recovery.[25] It was not surprising, then, that the setting up of an inquiry into the operation of the press was seen by many in Fleet Street as motivated by a 'desire to muzzle' newspapers.[26]

Supporters of the Commission sought to draw attention to the real problems that faced the newspaper industry in the wake of the war. They wanted to discuss the increasing concentration of ownership in the newspaper market, the influence of advertising on the performance of the industry and the growing centralisation of the press in London. These trends had been apparent prior to the war and contributed to the concerns expressed by the Labour movement. The view that a small number of 'hard faced men' controlled the press and used newspapers to make profits rather than inform people and transform attitudes through education had been a continual theme in Labour's analysis of the industry.[27] Despite the relatively benign conditions in the industry following the war, Labour supporters were troubled by what they believed was the bias to 'Big Business' in Fleet Street and the monopoly owners had over the press in certain cities and towns across the United Kingdom. The Labour MP Michael Foot wrote of his worries over centralised control of local newspapers: 'London ownership has invaded the provinces and there is a steady growth of the syndicated leading article'.[28] The war had assisted the press by allowing newspaper owners to make huge profits and increase their editorial control, and, he believed, once the wartime controls were loosened the situation would worsen. Newspaper chains would advance across the country, he said, and the Commission should examine ways in which the law could be used to restrict concentration of ownership and increase diversity of the press.

The Commission examined how the economic structure of the industry impacted on freedom of expression and shaped newspaper coverage of the issues of the day. It concluded that there was nothing that could be described as a monopoly in the press. There were local monopolies in certain areas – something which the Commission saw as regrettable but inevitable – and dangers were inherent in concentrated ownership. However, the Commission did not accept that these were matters of urgency at the time. It found that 'excessive bias' did exist in the popular and some quality newspapers and this was the fault of nobody but those 'who own and conduct the Press'.[29] The Commission reinforced that traditional view of the 'fourth estate', concluding that 'free enterprise is a pre-requisite of a free press'.[30] Such an analysis – described by the left-leaning weekly newspaper *Tribune* as 'tepid and unimaginative' – produced recommendations that were mild in their nature. The emphasis was on voluntary reform, of which the most important example was the establishment of the Press Council, a means by which the industry would police the activities of newspapers and journalists.

Self-regulation has been the primary means by which the newspaper industry has been supervised in the post-war period. The Press Council was finally established in 1953 in a much watered-down form and only after the threat of legislation from government. It was never the broad protector of the public interest that the Commission envisaged. Its terms of reference were vague and it was treated by the press with 'defensive resignation'.[31] Its members were appointed from the industry and it was financed by the industry. It had no means to enforce any decision it made and it soon became a mere bystander in the affairs of the press. In spite of hopes it would monitor the monopoly tendencies in the industry, the Council came to focus primarily on complaints. Any complaint from a member of the public about their treatment by a newspaper had to first be directed to the newspaper before coming to the Council, and if the Council found in favour of the complainant, then its only weapons against the offender was public criticism. It soon became apparent that the newspapers paid no attention to the Council. Newspapers in most cases published adjudications against them but were content to do nothing further. Codification of written rules by the Council on matters such as the payment of criminals for their stories – chequebook journalism – made no difference. The newspapers continued to ignore the Council – competition and the pursuit of sensational copy almost compelled the press to take this position. Complaints rose regularly, from a dozen or so in the first place to over 1,500 in 1989,[32] and as they increased attempts were made to give the Council more clout. Following the 1962 Commission on the Press lay members were appointed, and their number increased in 1974.[33] Under the chairmanship of a lay person, the former judge Lord Devlin, the Council won some respect amongst newspaper editors – the decision of key Fleet Street owners in the 1960s to support the Council assisted. But it proved a relatively anonymous and toothless body in controlling what and how newspapers reported.

Renewed competition

The reluctance of the press to accede to the authority of the Council can be explained by the return of the newspaper industry to fierce competition following the ending of newsprint rationing. The nature of this period of competition was very different from the circulation wars of the 1930s – the newspapers' advertising base was now threatened by other, more powerful means of mass communication. Newspapers have had a 'continuing love–hate relationship' with television since its arrival in 1936.[34] Television and the stars of the small screen have been a source of good newspaper copy. The first show business correspondents in the 1950s did not cover television, concentrating instead on film and theatre stars.[35] The mass circulation papers started to provide the gossip and scandal behind programmes when TV established itself in the nation's homes at the end of the 1950s. Reviewers exerted a powerful influence over what people should see and how programmes were received. In later years parts of the newspaper industry ran effective campaigns critical of television as part of attempts to deregulate the medium. But it was the challenge that ITV posed to newspapers' main source of revenue that had a long-lasting impact. Between 1948 and 1968 the press share of advertising fell from 83 per cent to 70 per cent[36] – but the decline was disproportionate. The national newspapers actually saw their share increase; it was the provincial press that was hit hardest. ITV, as a regional commercial company, was considered more effective at directing advertising to regional markets. Advertising revenue expanded during a period of economic growth in the 1950s and 1960s – the total advertising expenditure doubled between 1945 and 1995.[37] Only now newspapers had to compete with a medium the advertisers believed was better able to reach their target audiences. The broadsheet papers were least threatened. Their readers tended to be 'light ITV viewers' and television struggled to compete with the broadsheets for the expanding classified advertising.[38] It was the mid-market paper that fared the worst: their readers tended to be the highest consumers of television.

Competition brought about a rationalisation of provincial newspaper ownership. The decline of titles and the increasingly competitive market led to the consolidation of local chains in regions of the country. Regional newspaper groups concentrated their ownership in particular areas: Associated Newspapers developed their strength in the South West, Iliffe in the West Midlands, United in Lancashire and Westminster in the North and parts of the South East.[39] This was driven by several economic factors. Economies could be generated through joint production of evening and weekly newspapers and to that effect seventy-nine printing centres closed between 1961 and 1979.[40] Series publications with local editions for different regions provided editorial economies of scale and more compact market-assisted advertising sales. Such concentration of provincial ownership reduced competition in many areas of the United Kingdom but also made it easier for national newspaper groups to expand into the regions.

The degree of competition in the 1960s was relatively benign compared to what was to follow but the shifts that would lead to fundamental changes from the 1970s onwards were apparent. Total newspaper circulation remained fairly steady. However, the papers had to adjust to significant social changes that were happening in Britain. The newspapers in the 1950s and 1960s reflected the changing pattern of life of post-war Britain. The initial years of austerity that accompanied the efforts to rebuild Britain gave way to renewed affluence. The late 1950s ushered in a period in which British people were told they had 'never had it so good'. The Welfare State, the building of new and better housing, the growth of white-collar and semi-skilled jobs, the advent of full employment and increased educational opportunities convinced many working people that times were going to be better. The clouds of the depression years had been blown away as Britain started to enjoy itself and working people participated in this more than ever before. The *Daily Mirror* established a rapport with working people during the late 1950s and early 1960s which saw it becoming Britain's best-selling daily newspaper – ever.

The rise of the *Daily Mirror*

The *Daily Mirror*'s special relationship with British working people began during the Second World War. The seeds of the social change that swept through British society in the 1950s and 1960s were planted during the war years and the *Mirror* was at the forefront of articulating these changes. The newspaper had been re-launched in 1935 as Britain's first mass-market tabloid.[41] Under Rothermere's control the newspaper, despite gaining a reputation for picture journalism, declined throughout the 1920s. By 1934 it was dying, its reputation shattered by Rothermere's use of the paper as a propaganda tool in favour of fascism, home and abroad.[42] With its circulation down to 700,000 it came under the editorial control of Harry 'Guy' Bartholomew. The tabloid appearance distinguished the *Mirror* from its competitors, but it had to find an authentic voice to accompany the presentational and stylistic changes. Bartholomew – who later enjoyed the epithet the 'godfather of the British tabloids'[43] – carefully set about realigning the tone of the newspaper, to match the sensational approach his newspaper took to presentation. He sought to find a way of expressing the feelings of millions of ordinary British people.[44] To this end he appointed William Connor, a copywriter for the American advertising agency J. Walter Thompson on the Harpic account, who became Britain's most famous columnist under the name Cassandra.[45] Cassandra was adopted as a *nom de plume* as she was the figure in Greek mythology destined to utter true prophecies that would never be believed.[46] Labelled a master of invective, his 'rough, violent style expressed the rebellious mood of the submerged classes of the 1930s'.[47] His columns 'railed against unemployment and appeasement and the complacency of the ruling classes in a language able to provoke debate and stir up passions'.[48] Bartholomew also brought in the cartoonist Phillip Zec, who matched Connor's style in visual terms and came to be known as the 'people's cartoonist'.[49] The non-conformism of Connor and Zec reinforced the 'conscious radicalism' of Cudlipp and the 'spontaneous anti-Establishment attitude' of Bartholomew, which helped the *Mirror* to exploit technical and editorial innovations to acquire what the newspaper's historian Maurice Edelman labels the 'common touch'.[50] The *Mirror* began to pick up readership in the late 1930s but it was not until the war that it established itself as the spokesperson of the ordinary British man and woman.

182

Cassandra's columns

According to Hugh Cudlipp Cassandra could 'make his column purr or bark, nuzzle or bite, canter or gallop, soothe or repel'. Peppered with adjectives, the columns were famous for provoking readers to take sides. One of his most famous columns, 'The Woman Who Hangs Today' (13 July 1955) was a plea for clemency for the last women to be executed in Britain. It began:

It's a fine day for hay-making. A fine day for fishing. A fine day for lolling around in the sunshine. And if you feel that way – a fine day for a hanging. If you read this before four o'clock this morning, the last dreadful and obscene preparations for hanging her are about to start.

If you are reading this column at 6am, they are waking her up to have her last breakfast (if she was able to sleep at all).

If you are reading this column and the time is showing 6.45am she is most probably taking her last shower.

If you are reading this at 7.30am she is brushing her teeth before taking a final look in the mirror.

If you are reading this at 7.45am, the gaolers are now leading her towards the platform of death.

If you are reading this at 7.55am they are putting the hanging rope around her neck and a hood over her head.

If you are reading this at 8am the stroke of eight, a stroke of fate, as Oscar Wilde said in 'The Ballad of Reading Gaol', has sounded. One minute later her body is dancing the dance of death. And if you read this at midday she is buried and her book of life has been folded for good.

Cassandra concluded his column with the plea:

In human nature where passion is involved, love and hate walk hand in hand and side by side ... Ruth Ellis does not matter. But what we do to her – you and I – matters very much. And if we do it, and we continue to do it to her successors, then we all bear the guilt of savagery, untinged with mercy.

Source: Connor, *Cassandra: Reflections in a Mirror*;
Cudlipp, *Publish and Be Damned*.

On 11 May 1945 the *Daily Mirror* adopted the slogan 'Forward with the People'. The *Mirror* is credited with a large amount of responsibility for Labour's unpredicted landslide victory in the 1945 general election. This was the result of the consistent effort the newspaper put behind the campaign for a better, fairer and more just Britain when the war was over. The paper attained huge popularity amongst servicemen and women, as well as factory workers and those working in key industries on the home front and housewives struggling to keep the home fires burning. The *Mirror* was particularly popular amongst women readers; a survey of women readers during the war found that twice as many women read the newspaper – one in four of all women readers – than its nearest rival.[51] The *Mirror's* popularity reflected its ability to tap into and develop the public mood of the 'People's War'. Evidence of this is found in the space devoted to letters and stories derived from the experience of readers.[52] The paper published letters from men and women in the armed forces, expressing their concerns about bureaucratic inefficiencies and other kinds of obstacles that hampered the war effort. The letters page also encouraged readers to share their personal problems, with the newspaper providing advice and reassurance which was described as 'cathartic'.[53] Advice was dispensed in brusque terms, combining reproach and praise in equal measure. For a nation at war seeking urgent and clear advice on sex, survival and relationships, the *Mirror* provided a confessional outlet. But it was above all the *Mirror's* defence of the ordinary soldier, sailor and airman that struck a chord.

Throughout the Second World War the *Mirror's* relations with the government and those in charge of prosecuting the war were characterised by tension and discord. On several occasions the government came close to closing the newspaper down. The most famous controversy was over a Zec cartoon in 1942. The cartoon showed a torpedoed sailor clinging onto a piece of debris adrift at sea and the caption read: 'The price of petrol has just been increased by one penny – official'. The government and the Prime Minister in particular interpreted this as an attack on government for endorsing oil company profiteering while service people sacrificed their lives. The cartoon appeared at the nadir of British fortunes during the war when the government was overly sensitive to criticism – Zec stated that his intention was to shock the nation by highlighting that the black marketeering of petrol at home was built on the hardship and sacrifice of the fighting forces.[54] Herbert Morrison, a member of the War Cabinet, described the cartoon as 'a particularly evil example, of the policy and methods of a newspaper which, intent on exploiting an appetite for sensation ... had repeatedly published scurrilous misrepresentations, distorted and exaggerated statements and irresponsible generalisations'.[55] An inquiry was held into whether the newspaper should be closed down for impeding the successful prosecution of the war. The attempt to ban the paper foundered on the strength of opposition within the House of Commons and from the overwhelming majority of the British press. The extent of the opposition ensured the *Mirror* was not proscribed but following the dispute the newspaper tempered its criticisms of the government, helped by Cassandra joining the army. The *Mirror*'s fractious relationship with the government gained high levels of public approval for what many people saw as its principled support for the armed forces and the heroic sacrifices they were making.

The *Mirror* was a strong champion of radical social change. Making preparations for post-war reconstruction, the government had commissioned Sir William Beveridge to report on social welfare provision. The report became the basis for the introduction of the Welfare State and most of the press supported the report when it was published in 1942. Some advocated the rapid implementation of its main recommendations. However, it was the *Mirror* that became most associated with Beveridge's plan for post-war Britain.[56] Its direct style of address singled it out from competitors, particularly those papers such as the *Herald* on the left of British politics who shared the same commitment to Beveridge's notion of social equality. The *Daily Mirror* popularised the phrase 'from cradle to grave' and outlined the impact of the proposals on people's everyday lives in punchy articles with headlines such as 'How to Be Born, Bred and Buried by Beveridge'.[57] Its adoption of the language and topics of 'four-ale bars, works canteens, shopping queues, fish-and-chip saloons, dance halls and the jug and bottle departments' was the basis of its appeal to ordinary readers.[58] This contrasted with what Orwell, slightly unfairly, labelled the 'bombastic style' of the mainstream newspapers of the Left.[59] Comparison of the *Herald* and *Mirror*'s coverage of the Allied military debacle in Crete highlights that while both newspapers were critical of policy the *Herald* lacked the aggressive 'Us and Them' tone that characterised the *Mirror*, which located itself 'among the people, a tribune loyal to its readers and owning no obligation of respectfulness to the government it criticises'.[60] Its sense of solidarity with its readers was indicated by the adoption of by-lines such as 'Your Political Correspondent' or 'Your Own Special Correspondent'.[61] The paper's party affiliations were understated and its lack of a single directing proprietor as a result of Rothermere's divestiture in 1931, which had distributed shares in the newspaper to a wide number of shareholders, can also be seen as an advantage in a period in which the British press was able to 'escape' from the press barons. The historian A.J.P. Taylor argues that the *Daily Mirror* was popular in a 'special sense': 'previous popular newspapers, the *Daily Mail* and *Daily Express*, were created by their proprietors, Northcliffe and Beaverbrook – men not at all ordinary. The *Mirror* had no proprietor. It was created by the ordinary people on its staff'.[62]

The *Mirror*'s capacity to provide a voice for ordinary people came at a time when the size, layout and distribution of newspapers were severely curtailed. It was the paper's ability to identify with the concerns of ordinary people and speak to them in their own language, a more conversational style of writing, that enhanced its reach.[63] Campaigns about the price of a cup of tea in cafes and cruelty to greyhounds and bureaucratic inefficiencies which hampered the everyday lives of soldiers, factory workers and housewives also helped.[64] This culminated in its reporting of the 1945 general election. Zec's cartoon of a wounded soldier holding out a laurel with the label 'Victory and Peace in Europe' above a caption which stated, 'Here you are – don't lose it again!' resonated with many voters who were determined that the sacrifices of the war would not be forgotten as they had been in 1918. The *Mirror* adopted the slogan 'Vote for Them' on the eve of polling: 'The man who would fill that chair in your home. The mate you miss at work. The pal you like to meet in the pub, the boy friend – Vote for Them'.[65] At no point did the *Mirror* advocate voting for Labour, which distinguished it from other papers calling for change, such as the *Herald*. The traditional left-wing rhetoric of the *Herald*, with headlines such as 'A Vote for Churchill is a Vote for Franco', contrasted with the more contemplative and sober tone of the *Mirror*.[66] Many voters were not keen on the class-based politics of the 1930s which Churchill and his supporters in the right-wing newspapers and the *Herald* seemed to be resurrecting.[67] The *Mirror* represented the public desire for change better than its rivals, and Atlee benefited.

Following the 1945 election the newspaper continued to campaign for a better Britain, articulating the people's aspirations for change and their determination to attain it. Within five years it had overtaken the *Daily Express* as Britain's best-selling newspaper and consolidated its position as market leader throughout the 1950s with sustained attacks on petty bureaucracy and promoting a sense of fun which people craved following years of war and austerity. 'Wholly frivolous, a little bit naughty, but charmingly innocent – it was what people wanted.'[68] Fun came in many forms; usually 'good clean fun' but focussed on sex and sensation. Building on the success of Jane, the strip – or some would say striptease – cartoon of the war years, the paper in the post-war period started to carry stories such as 'The Girl with the Most Shapely Shoulders in the World' and 'The Girl with the Perfect Legs'. As editor of the *Sunday Pictorial* (renamed the *Sunday Mirror* in 1962) Hugh Cudlipp had produced the first picture of a topless model as sex and sensation combined to push the paper's circulation upwards more quickly than the *Mirror*.[69] However, it was the *Mirror*'s reports that were the centrepiece of its success, described as 'masterpieces of exposition and magnificently displayed'.[70] Cudlipp, who took over as editorial director of the Mirror Group in 1951, and Jack Nener, who became editor of the *Mirror* in 1953, perfected the tone and style of the newspaper. Sylvester Bolam, who edited the paper between 1948 and 1953, most clearly articulated the *Mirror*'s approach. He defended the ideal of sensational reporting in a manner reminiscent of Stead in the 1880s:

> The *Mirror* is a sensational paper. We make no apology for that. We believe in the sensational presentation of news and views, especially important news and views, as a necessary and valuable service in these days of mass readership and democratic responsibility. We shall go on being sensational to the best of our ability. Sensationalism

186

does not mean distorting the truth. It means the vivid and dramatic picture of presentation of events so as to impact on the mind of the reader. It means big headlines, vigorous writing, simplification into everyday language and the wide use of illustrations by cartoon and photograph. Every great problem facing us. ... will only be understood by the ordinary man busy with his daily tasks if he is hit hard, and hit often with the facts. Sensational treatment is the answer, whatever sober and 'superior' readers of some other journals may prefer. No doubt we shall make mistakes, but we are at least alive.[71]

The *Mirror* in the late 1940s and early 1950s came close to living up to the ideal. This was not easy in practice, as Bolam found out when he served a three-month jail sentence for publishing a story that prejudiced a fair trial. Like most of its rivals, the *Mirror* did not always resist pressure to step over the mark for a good story. The paper's special relationship with working people had begun to wane prior to a decline in circulation. Labour's slippage in the polls was not reflected in the paper's circulation – its circulation peaked in 1967 at 5.82 million. However, the rapport of the war years started to slip with affluence, rising living standards and the growth of consumerism. 'Forward with the People' was no longer a slogan that captured the feelings of British working people. The slogan was dropped in 1959, after the Conservative Party's third successive election victory, together with the Jane cartoon. The conditions of working people had improved and progress had been made. Young people were more assertive in putting across their views and less deferential. With greater personal disposable income they exerted more influence in the newspaper market. The *Mirror* struggled to come to terms with the changing conditions and in particular the attitudes of young working people. Its language became increasingly proletarian and self-consciously constructed for the masses.[72] Younger people found it paternalistic and representative of 'Old Codgers'. Struggling to embrace the world of 'youth', it appeared coy and prudish about what young people were up to. The *Mirror* seemed not to be able to take off its cloth cap. Henry Fairlie, in the heyday of the paper's success in 1957, wrote a prophetic critique. He described the paper as

a clean and healthy extrovert; it understands the qualities which make the British working class decent and civilised. It does the job of catering for its class of readers far better than any other British newspaper has ever done. But if it reflects the good features of the proletarian personality, it reflects the bad ones as well. It is mentally lazy, emotionally sloppy and incurably insular ... it gets under the skin of its readers and stays there. But why be satisfied with being skin deep.[73]

While difficulties could be hidden during the years of Tory rule by playing the class card, defending working people against the 'Toffs' who ran the country, it became more complicated under the Wilson government, which the *Mirror* had strongly supported at the 1964 election. Benefits did accrue with greater access to the government but the newspaper also became associated with government failures, which stacked up at a time of economic recession.[74] Many of the paper's executives and leading writers were now close to the corridors of power, having benefited from the prosperity of the 1950s. They were part of the 'Establishment' they had been knocking for most of their careers. This was reflected in the paper, which, as Matthew Engel notes, increasingly had the 'whiff of the lecture theatre'.[75]

New owners

The personal hand of press owners continued to direct the British press in the immediate post-war years. There might have been a new generation but the names Rothermere, Beaverbrook, Kemsley and Camrose still loudly echoed through the passages and alleyways of Fleet Street. The passing away of the old guard – Beaverbrook died in 1964 – brought about a shift in the way in which owners ran their newspapers. Newspaper owners kept a lower profile in the 1950s and early 1960s. Public debate around newspaper ownership initiated by the Royal Commissions in 1947 and 1962 encouraged proprietors to avoid overt interventions in the politics of the nation. Two men came to epitomise the kind of owners that emerged: the Canadian Roy Thomson (Lord Thomson) and Cecil King, a descendant of the Harmsworth family and the chairman of IPC, owners of the *Mirror* and its sister newspapers.

Lord Thomson had amassed a newspaper and radio conglomerate in Canada before moving to Britain in 1953, following his failure to build a political career in his own country. He bought the *Scotsman* newspaper as well as the Edinburgh *Evening Dispatch*, which furnished him with the basis for a bid to run the new ITV licence for Scottish television, which he later described as a 'licence to print money'.[76] In 1959 he acquired the *Sunday Times* when he bought out Kemsley's newspaper group – dispensing with Kemsley's other Sunday newspapers, closing the *Sunday Graphic* and selling *Empire News* to the News of the World Group.[77] *The Times* fell into his hands a few years later; Thomson informed the paper's dwindling band of readers that the paper's 'special position will now be safeguarded for all times'.[78] He also owned a chain of regional newspapers, Thomson Regional News, and a number of magazines. Thomson was seen as a 'new owner' in that he ran his newspapers purely as a business. His appearance before the Royal Commission on the Press in 1961 is seen as highlighting his position as an 'entrepreneurial proprietor'. He told the Commission that his purpose 'is to run newspapers as a business' and 'to make money'.[79] This is often contrasted with Beaverbrook's assertion to the 1947 Commission that his purpose 'was to set up a propaganda paper'. Thomson emphasised the principle of non-intervention in the editorial side of the business; when he took over *The Times* he stated that the editor would be 'guaranteed absolute freedom from interference. He will direct the paper in the best interests of the country'.[80] It is stated that he did not care what stances his papers took as long as they were profitable. Simon Jenkins notes that 'whatever recklessness might be perpetuated on the editorial floor, he appeared to smile indulgently and sign another cheque'.[81]

The one exception to the commercial success Thomson accomplished was *The Times*, which continued to lose money under him. He had foreseen this, admitting that his purchase of the paper was 'something beyond the limits of normal business'.[82] He made strenuous efforts to increase the newspaper's circulation; the cover price was reduced, by-lines were introduced, the running order of the pages was reconfigured and new sections were launched.[83] Advertisements disappeared from the front page in 1966 just prior to Thomson's purchase, with a beneficial impact on sales. Staff complained and resignations ensued as the 'old guard' objected to what they believed was an assault on tradition. The new editor, William Rees Mogg, had to face down a revolt from senior staff who argued the new changes were diminishing the paper's authority.[84] Circulation rose but profits did not, as increased costs absorbed the revenue brought in by new readers. It is estimated that Thomson spent £8 million of his own personal fortune in keeping the newspaper afloat.[85] His philanthropy in supporting the ailing newspaper was offset by the profitability of his other media interests.

The other character whose career is seen as illustrating the changes that were taking place in newspaper ownership was Cecil King. On the surface King appears not to have been very different from the great press barons of the pre-war years. A member of the Harmsworth family – Northcliffe was his uncle – he was interested in politics and intervened in the government of the country in a way in which Northcliffe, Beaverbrook and Rothermere may never have done. He is actually accused of participating in an attempt to organise a coup to bring down the Labour government in 1968. In May that year he wrote a signed editorial headlined 'Enough Is Enough', which appeared in the *Daily Mirror* and was copiously quoted in IPC's other newspapers, in which he called for a new Prime Minister and for a new leader of the Labour Party.[86] His disillusionment with Labour had grown steadily since 1964 when he believed he was snubbed by not being offered a Cabinet post. The *Mirror* – like many other Fleet Street papers – had become increasingly critical of the government, fearing the country was run by the trade unions and, with a financial crisis looming, King acted. His actions resulted in his downfall – other newspapers referred to 'government by the *Daily Mirror*' and King was seen as keeping up the family trait of the 'Harmsworths – megalomania'.[87] Unlike his uncle, King did not exercise total control over the newspaper empire he managed – he was a salaried member of IPC and could be sacked by the board. This duly happened and King was fired as chairman. The attack on the Labour government was not the only factor in King's downfall. IPC had been experiencing commercial problems prior to King's editorial. The firm's expansion was slowing down; the *Mirror* lost circulation as a result of its opposition to Suez in 1956 and costs were rising due to what Graham Cleverley, a former manager at IPC in the 1960s, described as 'serious mismanagement'.[88]

King's dismissal by the IPC board is seen as reinforcing the waning of the political influence and managerial control of newspaper owners. Ownership was becoming a collective enterprise, directed to ensuring financial and commercial success. Absolute control lapsed as the newspaper business moved to a more delegated pattern of decision-making. This shift was apparent even amongst the sons who had replaced their fathers as newspaper owners, such as Max Aitken, the inheritor of Beaverbrook's *Express* titles. Less dictatorial, they 'kept their minds on money rather than policy', ceasing to attend editorial conferences.[89] They were increasingly happy to let others manage their newspapers. Powerful managing directors and chief executives emerged, such as Jocelyn Stevens at the *Express* and Michael Shealds at Associated Newspapers. Some of these could act like press barons but their power was curtailed by greater managerial accountability, the requirements of managing more complicated businesses and the increasing strength of journalists and unions. Ownership in these circumstances could be – and was – described as more benign and less hierarchical than in previous times. The waning of the power of owners was reinforced by the growing perception of the power of print unions in Fleet Street in the 1960s and 1970s.

Industrial relations

New types of owners did not make Fleet Street management structures and style less idiosyncratic. A 1966 report on the industry by the Economist Intelligence Unit (EIU) concluded that 'the most striking feature, and possibly its greatest problem, is its dominance by a small number of highly individualistic proprietors with their own personal interests and philosophy of management'.[90] King and his deputy chairman, Hugh Cudlipp, highlighted this in their appearance together before the 1962 Royal Commission when King acknowledged that the editorial strategy of the group was not decided by a committee but by 'Cudlipp and myself'.[91] However, as newspaper empires diversified their commercial activities into other industries and businesses in the 1960s (see Chapter 8) they had to operate closer to the norms of British business practice. One area which Fleet Street had to address was the state of industrial relations. The power of the print unions is illustrated by a story often told about Lord Thomson's visit to the *Sunday Times* after he bought it in 1959. He introduced himself to a union representative by stating that he was 'the new owner of the paper', to which the representative replied, 'you may own it but I run it'.[92] This story highlights the perception many owners, editors, advertisers and journalists had of the 'power of the printers'.[93] They could hold newspapers to ransom. Most print unions could trace their lineage back to the guilds and statutes of the Elizabethan period. They were organised as 'societies' and 'associations' rather than traditional trade unions and carefully protected entry into their trade. Every newspaper was organised as a closed shop, where only those who belonged to the chapel – a term specific to the newspaper industry, used to describe the groupings of those who worked on the shop floor – could work. Often membership was confined to family, friends and acceptable acquaintances. These chapels had existed since the early eighteenth century and enforced strict boundaries between the wide variety of tasks associated with the production of a newspaper, from composing type, setting lines, inking rollers and loading paper.[94] Throughout their history the chapels and societies had struggled in the wake of considerable technological changes to protect these individual tasks from infringement or eradication. Their success in defending their practices skewed the economics of newspaper production as much as the idiosyncratic nature of press ownership, the distorting influence of advertising revenue and the damaging impact of circulation wars.

High rates of remuneration and high manning levels in the industry were the product of the chapel system. Negotiations over the decades, indeed centuries, had paid print workers on the basis of what they did when they were at work and how long it took them to do it – a combination of piece and time rates. Those printers working in the newspaper industry earned much more than their counterparts in other parts of the publishing and printing world. The growth in the size of newspapers in the 1960s increased the activities of printers and therefore brought about a considerable rise in their wages. The EIU reported that 'the general level of pay in the newspaper industry is out of all proportion to the effort expended and the skill employed compared with most other industries'.[95] Over-manning was a product of the system and by the early 1980s was estimated by newspaper proprietors to be running at 40 per cent across the industry.[96] Savings of between £25 and £30 million could have been made on some papers if manning levels were reduced to those actually needed to operate the presses. This position had been created by legally drawn-up agreements rather than through union militancy. Newspapers, as a perishable commodity, were subject to the exertion of industrial muscle and the threat of strike action could force employers to accede to demands. Objections by printers to what appeared on the page could halt the production line and had to be taken seriously. However, management was more often happy enough to agree to such arrangements. This was as much a product of the maverick nature of newspaper ownership and the profitability of newspapers as it was of management weakness.

New technology, changes in the kind of people who owned and ran newspapers and the introduction of an incomes policy by the Labour government in the mid-1960s led to a more concerted attempt to rationalise the payments system, reduce over-manning and introduce technical change. On the union side the chapels and societies came together into larger groups – the

National Graphic Association (NGA) was formed in the 1960s when an array of craft societies amalgamated.[97] This facilitated negotiations; previously management had to negotiate agreements with anything up to sixty-five different 'fathers of chapel'. Comprehensive agreements were concluded, resulting in a reduction in staff in the late 1960s,[98] but the 'new realism' did not tackle the fundamental issues of pay, rigid demarcation lines and the introduction of new technology. Union leaders were aware of the need to negotiate, fearful that unless they co-operated they would be 'engulfed in a tidal wave of technology which we will not be able to control'.[99] However, the chapels would not listen to arguments for changes in their working practices to accommodate new technology. A policy document adopted by the six leading unions in 1975 that acknowledged the more effective use of manpower and more appropriate demarcation lines, amongst other things, was rejected by the chapels. Unlike their brothers in Europe, British print workers failed to negotiate the changes that technical advances brought and it was the use of industrial and commercial force in the Wapping dispute that decided matters and in the process wiped out the print unions (see Chapter 8).

Standardising the news

Gathering news was becoming an increasingly complex and costly process. The stereotype of the general reporter as a man with a nose for news dressed in a dirty raincoat was becoming obsolete. The 1950s and 1960s witnessed a huge growth in the number of specialist news reporters or correspondents, usually better educated than the ordinary news reporter. Specialist political and foreign reporters had existed in the nineteenth century, and sports and crime reporting as a specialist area developed in the 1930s.[100] After the war they were joined by fashion, aviation, motoring, defence, labour, health, education, travel and finance. The expansion was fuelled by a number of factors. Crime and sport, particularly football, sold a lot of newspapers, and in order to provide more stories to satisfy public interest specialist reporters were hired or assigned. Motoring and fashion, however, were crucial to attracting advertising revenue. Reports of the latest car or dress coming onto the market helped to promote products. Fashion coverage was assisted by developments in colour printing. The specialist areas covered by newspapers varied; most noticeably between upmarket and downmarket papers. A popular paper was more likely to employ a royal correspondent and less likely to retain foreign correspondent, an area which was seen as 'losing money'.[101] Specialisation was also more apparent in the broadsheet newspapers, whose readers required in certain areas more specialist knowledge.

The growth of specialist news gatherers had the effect of changing the balance of power between the reporter and the news desk. Jeremy Tunstall, in his study[102] of specialist reporters in the 1960s, found that they tended to collaborate, sharing the legwork required to stand up a story. The extent to which specialist reporting has group allegiances is seen in the number of associations that have been established. The Labour and Industrial Correspondents' Group was founded in 1937; the Education Correspondents' Group (1962), the Football Writers' Association (1947), the Crime Reporters' Association (1945) and Guild of Motoring Writers (1968). These associations did not always represent everyone and divisions within them were apparent; however, they signified a growing group identity amongst specialist correspondents. Hunting in packs, regularly exchanging information and ideas helped them to build up a kind of camaraderie which enabled them to resist pressure from their own news desks. Specialist journalism also 'migrated out of the news pages' into special sections with specialist subs, further increasing the autonomy of the reporter. They also appeared to some to bring a greater consensus to what was newsworthy and what should be reported.

The nature of news has by and large changed very little since the early days of the newspaper. Sex, crime, politics and sports have been a constant feature of the output. Newspapers may 'change shape, order news differently and target different groups of people ... but the hard news agenda itself seems ... unalterable'.[103] What is striking, as Colin Seymour-Ure points out, is 'not the contrasting contents but the remarkably similar ones'.[104] Scoops and exclusives are a strong element in the rhetoric of newspapers – but the number of exclusive stories is limited and often the term is used to promote a story as part of the marketing of the newspaper. Few scoops are genuine and they are usually a presentational device. Editors stick to the same basic ingredients in compiling their newspapers and are more concerned that their reporters provide the stories their competitors have. Competition for specialist reporters has more of an internal dimension; with a finite space available they are seeking to beat out their fellow specialist reporters. The arrival of radio and television had an impact on the presentation of news but it did little to change what was considered newsworthy. If the kinds of news stories did not change, there was a shift between the amount of news devoted to certain types of stories – this is most apparent from the 1970s (see Chapter 8), but one area that had started to decline in the immediate post-war years was political coverage.

The de-politicisation of popular newspapers has been a theme of academic research. The changing economic circumstances that began to sweep through Fleet Street following the end of rationing gradually – and then more briskly – began to change the content and nature of British newspapers. Rising costs of production combined with declining advertising revenue caused them to concentrate on maximising sales. The number of pages in national newspapers increased fourfold between 1945 and 1974, staff size and salaries escalated, and overall the annual costs of running the average national daily grew fourteenfold.[105] The editorial space devoted to stories that readers liked least – that is, politics and current affairs – declined noticeably in the popular press. Front-page leads on public affairs stories fell off between 1936 and

1976 as the rise of the 'human interest' story proceeded inexorably.[106] This was accompanied by a polarisation between broadsheet and popular newspapers, as the amount of political coverage in the broadsheet newspapers remained steady or rose slightly. However, several authors draw attention to 'the increasing conformity of the British quality press, in style and substance' in the 1960s, which is attributed to the 'fundamental tendency of oligopolistic competition to serve the centre of the market at the expense of minority tastes' and the erosion of the close informal connections between newspapers and political parties.[107] The convergence of style and substance within each sector of an increasingly polarised newspaper market, the accommodation between employers and unions in Fleet Street, the decline in political reporting in parts of the press and the emergence of more benign forms of ownership reflect the stability, complacency and conformity of the immediate post-war world, in which reconstruction and consensus determined the public mood.

NEW POULSON CASE SHOCK

MINISTER AND THE '£500 COFFEE POT'

FORWARD WITH THE PEOPLE 3p

Tuesday, January 30, 1973

PAY AND PRICES—VIC FEATHER HITS BACK

The TUC is not a rubber stamp!

THE TRADE UNIONS believe that there must be a policy against inflation. We have been saying this for years, and not just yesterday.

What the trade union movement does not accept is that wages and salaries are the only factor affecting prices.

The freeze on wages has not brought about a freeze on prices. There were hundreds of price rises during the freeze and there will be thousands during Phase Two.

It is not wages—of farm workers or shop assistants—that pushed up the price of beef or that are now pushing up the price of chicken.

And you can't blame today's pay packets for the soaring cost of houses built 40, 50, and 60 years ago.

If British goods are not selling well enough in the world's markets, it is not because our competitors are paying lower wages. Wages here are only at about the average for industrial countries, and in the past 10 years our rate of increase has been below the average.

VIC FEATHER replies in yesterday's Sun leader.

It is not true to say that new moves have been suggested by the Government and the TUC said "we cannot talk about them."

We went on talking, at Downing Street and Chequers, as long as there was a point in it. But there is not much point in talking about shaping Phase Two, when decisions have already been made by the Government. We want a better choice from the Government than "any policy you like—so long as it's ours."

Positively, we want direct action as we talk about them.

Continued on Page Two

All I want to do is to get rid of the bloody thing, says Crosland

By MICHAEL McDONOUGH and GORDON BROOME

A TOP Minister in the last Labour Government was named yesterday in the Poulson bankruptcy case.

The Minister, Anthony Crosland, received a silver coffee pot after he opened a school designed by architect John Poulson.

Labour's former deputy leader, Lord George-Brown, was also mentioned during the hearing.

It was suggested that he had a holiday at Mr Poulson's expense. But he and the architect denied this.

'KARATE CHOP'

Last night Mr Crosland said he was sending his gift back.

"All I want to do is to get rid of the bloody thing," he said.

He added: "I feel like somebody innocently walking through Hyde Park and somebody gives him a karate chop."

He said he would return the coffee pot to Mr Poulson's bankruptcy trustees.

"I don't care twopence about the pot and, if that is stirring up trouble somewhere, the trustees can have it," he said.

"I don't care. It is of no interest to me in the slightest degree, this damned pot.

Asked if the pot would harm his political reputation, he replied: "I would think it would be treated as a storm in a teacup, which it is."

During yesterday's court hearing, at Wakefield,

Continued on Page 5

Ex-striptease star Rusty Humphreys with her husband

STRIPPER IN PLOT CASE

By ROBERT TRAINI

FORMER Soho stripper "Rusty" Humphreys will appear in court with 10 men today following the massive porn swoops by Scotland Yard.

Mrs Humphreys was charged last night with offering £2,000 to the victim of an attempted murder not to give evidence.

She was also accused of conspiracy to cause grievous bodily harm.

Mrs Humphreys, whose husband, James, is believed to be in Spain, will face magistrates at Old Street Court, Mrs Humphreys.

Turn to Page Two

16 BRITONS KILLED AS PLANE HITS MOUNTAIN

SIXTEEN Britons on a package holiday died last night when an airliner crashed on a mountainside in Cyprus.

They were among 37 people aboard the plane—a Soviet-built Ilyushin 18—operated by the Egyptian airline Misrair. There were no survivors.

The Britons—15 holidaymakers and a tour company representative—were off a scheduled flight from Cairo to Nicosia, the capital of Cyprus. They were to have spent two days there before returning home.

The jet crashed on a 1,000ft-high ridge on the heavily wooded slopes of the Kyrenian Mountains in North Cyprus.

After the crash, flames burst from the plane. A rescue team found bodies scattered among the wreckage.

Nicosia airport officials said the plane crashed as it was making its way to land.

—Page Back

NORWICH ARE MASSACRED!—See Back Page

8

THE LAND OF THE RISING SUN

The emergence of the tabloid newspaper, 1967–89

The Sun's greatest offence was to start publishing scandalous and sometimes untrue stories about well-known people, whereas the *News of the World*, which was a scandal sheet in the old days, only reported the goings on of vicars and other relatively unimportant people.

Lord Rothermere, former owner of the *Daily Mail*[1]

The tabloid newspaper became an established feature of the British press in the 1970s. Most of Fleet Street's best-selling newspapers went tabloid, incorporating changes in the size, values and production methods associated with 'tabloidisation' which many associate with the 'dumbing down' of the British press. In the process the industry vacated Fleet Street en masse, relocating to other parts of London, primarily Wapping. The event that led to the move was the sale of the *Sun* newspaper to Australian entrepreneur Rupert Murdoch in November 1969. Within a relatively short period of time the *Sun* became Britain's best-selling newspaper, overtaking the *Mirror* in circulation terms in 1978. The newspaper dominated the market for the next twenty years. It achieved this by pushing the newspaper's content relentlessly downmarket and by a combination of brilliant marketing and innovative layout. It was assisted by several other factors: changes in the ownership of its major competitors which made them less responsive to the market; the economic problems of the 1970s, which had a profound impact on the newspaper business and social changes which emphasised individualism and self-interest. The capacity of the *Sun* to tune into the changes in British society that brought Margaret Thatcher to power was significant to its success.

The increased competition the *Sun* brought to Fleet Street in the 1980s intensified the pace of change in the popular and mid-market newspapers. The *Daily Mail* went tabloid in 1971, followed by the *Express* in 1977. The *Daily Star* was launched by the Express Group from its Manchester office to compete with the *Sun* in 1978 and by the beginning of the 1980s Britain had five tabloid newspapers pursuing a circulation war more savage than anything that had gone before. Promotions, gimmicks and gifts made their return when the *Star* introduced 'bingo' with major cash giveaways to lure more readers. Huge amounts were spent on television advertising, particularly by the *Sun*, which targeted slots on Sunday night to tell its readers what was coming up in the following week.[2] Murdoch even bought a large stake in the ITV company London Weekend Television to sustain this operation. The *Sun*'s formula for tabloidisation set the agenda for Fleet Street as a whole – and broadsheet newspapers were not averse to publishing 'a species of nonsense and trivia which in better times a gentleman would have only discerned by rummaging through the drawers of a valet'.[3] Broadsheets did not adopt the tabloid size until later – but it can be argued that tabloid values started to permeate these papers in the 1980s. Other media such as radio and television were also seen as 'dumbing down' their content as the influence of the 'soaraway *Sun*' stretched beyond the boundaries of the newspaper business.

The tabloid revolution coincided with the 'end of the Street'. In 1986 a dispute with the trade unions was the excuse Murdoch was looking for to move his newspapers – which now included *The Times* and *Sunday Times*, which he had acquired five years earlier – from Fleet Street to Wapping. The opportunity for Murdoch to select the time and place of his final battle with the print unions was made possible by the rapid pace of change in print technology. The new technology facilitated a fundamental shift in the balance of power in the newspaper industry – between management and unions, editors and owners, journalists and news desks. Several new newspapers were launched in the midst of the new climate created post-Wapping – including *Today*, the *Post*, the *Sunday Correspondent*, *News on Sunday*, the *Independent* and the *Daily Sport*. Some came and went very quickly. Others stayed. All attested to the volatility in the national newspaper market in the 1980s when most of the major newspaper titles changed hands. The British newspaper was increasingly integrated into the world of big business. Many of the new owners were large conglomerates better known for producing other kinds of products. The subsidiary role of newspapers was seen by many editors as a handicap; owners were criticised for showing little interest in their newspapers, their inability to act swiftly or decisively in a highly competitive environment and their lack of comprehension of what was required to run a successful newspaper. The return of more interventionist proprietors around and after the Wapping episode – men such as Robert Maxwell and Conrad Black – was welcomed by some in the industry. There were several newspaper editors who believed strong management would make the decisions that would help to compete more effectively with the Murdoch press, which by 1986 dominated the national newspaper scene. This did not happen.

News was further marginalized in the columns of British newspapers. The success of the *Sun* was based on soft news such as sport, celebrities and royal stories, which increasingly found their way into the columns of popular and broadsheet newspapers. Travel, lifestyle as well as a variety of other forms of entertainment-related copy burgeoned. The cult of personality swamped the pages of the press as celebrities of all shapes, sizes and status had their lives exposed through the lens of the paparazzi and the pens of the gossip columnists. The growth of space created by more newspapers and more pages was more easily filled by features than news stories. A drop occurred in the proportion of general news carried by newspapers. Politics continued to recede as a newsworthy topic but serious news of all kinds suffered.

The most fundamental change in the industry took place in the provincial newspaper market. Provincial newspapers started to decline again following a fairly prosperous decade in the 1970s when their share of advertising increased considerably. The relatively buoyant advertising masked the steady drop in the number of people reading local papers. In 1970 42 per cent of adults read an evening provincial paper, compared to 32 per cent in 1981/2.[4] In the 1980s provincial papers underwent what has been dramatically described as a 'meltdown' as advertising and sales plummeted. Robust competition came from changes in the regulation of local radio and the advent of a new kind of newspaper – the 'free sheet'. This newspaper represented the logical development of a press financed primarily by advertising – it was distributed free of charge. Their growth was 'breath taking', mushrooming from 185 titles in 1975 to nearly 900 in 1986,[5] and at the expense of provincial titles – with the exception of Sunday papers, whose numbers and circulation increased in the provinces and nations of Britain.

Let the games begin

In 1969 IPC sold the *Sun* newspaper to Rupert Murdoch, the owner of the *News of the World*. Hugh Cudlipp, who had taken over as the IPC Chairman, believed this was good business. The efforts to re-launch the *Daily Herald* under the new name of the *Sun* had failed miserably. By 1968 the newspaper was losing £1.75 million a year; after selling around 3.5 million copies on its first day it slumped within a week to 1.75 million, never to recover.[6] It became a greater liability than the newspaper it had replaced, with losses at the beginning of 1968 estimated to be running at just under £2 million a year.[7] Cudlipp had tried to market the *Sun* as a modern newspaper in touch with the new, post-war generation of readers. Drawing on the latest audience research, the newspaper identified the post-war generation as better off, better educated and keen to enjoy their growing leisure time. Living standards were rising; more people owned their own home and the consumer society had arrived, with people revelling in the consumption of hi-tech goods such as television sets, washing machines and refrigerators which had previously been confined to the rich. A readers' survey designated the younger generation as 'pace setters' and the extent to which they valued their leisure time was captured by the less than felicitous description of Britain as a 'nation of steak eating weekenders'.[8]

Cudlipp targeted these aspirational readers, incorporating Harold Wilson's vision of a new age of white-hot technology into his 'new paper, born of the age we live in'.[9] The steak eaters did not bite; the paper was an 'ad man's fantasy of what readers wanted, not a real, living, breathing newspaper'.[10] Even if they had bitten it was not clear there were enough of these 'pace setters' to replace the 'cloth-cap' readers of the *Daily Herald*. Money drained away and Cudlipp decided to dispose of the *Sun*, eventually selling it at a knock-down price with no strings attached. Given the commercial success Murdoch had with the *Sun* it is often argued that IPC should have closed the paper. Closure was not an option according to Cudlipp, as the unions would have shut down the whole of IPC's operations in response to the level of redundancies that would have resulted. The costs of such a stoppage militated against the possible benefit of closure.[11] The original sale to IPC in 1961 was on the condition that it would continue to support the Labour Party. This condition was shelved in Cudlipp's desperation to rid IPC of the ailing paper, which Murdoch acquired at an 'astonishingly low' price.

Cudlipp had expected the *Sun* to disappear in a very short time. The first editions of the newspaper appeared to confirm the prognosis; the paper was 'full of spelling errors, layout problems, blotchy pictures and badly fitting headlines, some of which did not make sense'.[12] There was 'no original journalistic magic' that transformed the paper; the formula of 'crumpet, crime and cricket' which was used in the *News of the World* – then nicknamed 'Screws of the World' – was applied, with a beefing up of stories about sex.[13] Sex, sex and more sex was the basis of the *Sun*'s recipe for success. The front page advertised the delights that awaited the reader inside, which for the first edition included 'Beautiful Women – *Sun* exclusive' and 'The Love Machine – *Sun* exclusive', a serialisation of Jacqueline Susann's sequel to *The Valley of the Dolls*. On page 3 there appeared a half-dressed 'Swedish charmer', as well as a news story about a man described as a 'walking lust automat'. The page soon became synonymous with topless models. Murdoch insisted that the words 'win', 'free' and 'sex' had to appear on the front pages as much as possible.[14] While not original, this was effective, as within eighteen months of its re-launch the *Sun* was selling 2.5 million copies – while its main rival, the *Mirror*, had lost a million readers.[15] The rise of the *Sun* was to profoundly influence the development of popular journalism in Britain – and for many in and out of Fleet Street, for the worse. The hold the newspaper exercised over the market brought about what one critic described as the 'metamorphosis of relatively healthy popular journalism into the junk food of the mass mind market'.[16]

The success of Murdoch's *Sun* was as much to do with the failure of its competitors, especially the *Daily Mirror*, as it was with the introduction of a winning formula. A high degree of complacency characterised the *Mirror*'s response to its brash and vulgar rival. IPC and its Chairman underestimated Murdoch's drive and commitment to making the *Sun* a success. Larry Lamb, a former chief sub-editor on the *Mirror*, hired to edit the paper, believed the *Sun* would have struggled to survive if the *Mirror* had deployed the full weight of its resources to battle it out.[17] That it did not is attributable to two factors. The *Mirror* had made a serious mistake with its launch of a glossy, giveaway magazine weeks before the *Sun*'s re-launch. Based on the successful colour supplements developed by the quality Sunday broadsheets, the *Mirror*'s magazine came out every Wednesday. The objective was to boost weekday circulation and increase revenue by attracting upmarket colour advertising.[18] Neither transpired and within weeks the magazine was making huge losses, forecast to reach £5 million a year; people were throwing the magazine away and advertisers were unimpressed. It was 'a catastrophe to rank with North-cliffe's miscalculation in launching the original *Daily Mirror* as a paper for gentlewomen'.[19] Putting an immediate stop to the magazine was tricky due to agreements with the unions. With losses mounting the *Mirror* and IPC were forced to make economies. Murdoch was provided with some breathing space and given an opportunity to gain the favour of the newsagents. Newsagents were hostile to the *Mirror* magazine; it had forced them to get up earlier to insert the magazine into the paper, only for it to be discarded by many of their customers. Murdoch exploited their dissatisfaction, promising them a greater return on sales of his newspaper than the *Mirror*, as well as not charging for unsold copies – in these circumstances newsagents became more sympathetic to the *Sun*.[20]

The immediate problems of the loss-making magazine reinforced the lethargy which years of a virtual monopoly of the popular newspaper market had created within IPC. The 1961 Royal Commission had identified considerable overstaffing on the paper, the result of years of growth and success when management had agreed to generous settlements with the print unions.[21] Corners were cut in producing the paper, which would rebound on the *Mirror* when the competition got tougher. One example was the quality of the paper used. IPC had been using substandard paper for many years as part of off-loading material from its Canadian mills.[22] When the *Sun* appeared on higher calibre paper it immediately felt like a better quality product. It was also recognised by Murdoch and Lamb that the *Mirror* was losing its radical edge.[23] The close relations with the government of the day strengthened this perception. The newspaper was described by one of its editors as 'middle aged' and 'too frightened or unable to change the formula'.[24] It struggled to embrace or adapt to the emerging youth culture, let alone understand it.[25] This was the so-called permissive revolution and the *Mirror*'s tentativeness on the subject of sex contrasted to that of the *Sun*'s breaking down of the barriers of taste.

The *Mirror*'s failure to compete was also due to Cudlipp's reluctance to take the newspaper downmarket. He 'did not wish ... to compete with the tit and bum policy'.[26] He had become interested in moving the tabloid newspaper in the opposite direction, combining more serious news with the usual material that appeared in popular newspapers. He wanted to produce a 'quality tabloid'. A move in this direction was apparent in the *Mirror* prior to the *Sun*'s success. Cudlipp wanted more current affairs coverage as well as more stories on the arts and science. Younger journalists such as John Pilger and Paul Foot were appointed to produce more investigative and critical reporting. The vehicle for their stories was the *Mirrorscope*, a newspaper within a newspaper, launched in 1969 with a focus on a more serious news agenda. Shock issues were produced on the pressing social, international and political stories of the day.

The *Sun*'s success was the *Mirror*'s failure. As circulation continued to slip, IPC merged in 1970 with the paper company Reed to form Reed International. As the ramshackle and unwieldy business empire that Cecil King had built started to crumble, Reed International reorganised the company to create a separate division, Mirror Group Newspapers (MGN), which Cudlipp oversaw. Cudlipp departed in 1974 to become a member of the House of Lords as a Labour peer; declining circulation had pushed the *Mirror* closer to the Labour Party. Even after Cudlipp's departure the *Mirror* was reticent in its efforts to go downmarket – the first nude appeared in the *Mirror* in 1975 but an internal staff revolt in which agony aunt Marge Proops had a high profile brought the experiment to a rapid conclusion. Spasmodic efforts to reintroduce naked women were met by opposition from within. As MGN struggled, Reed International showed little enthusiasm for keeping the paper going; profits were only maintained by cutting back on marketing, newsprint quality and selling at a cover price higher than the *Sun* – all of which assisted its main competitor. It was the antipathy that the Reed board and its chairman Alex Jarratt showed to the paper's editorial support for the Labour Party that finally led them to decide to sell MGN. Robert Maxwell, after nearly fifteen years of trying to get into Fleet Street, won the battle, gaining control of the newspaper in 1984 in the face of opposition from the print unions, the National Union of Journalists (NUJ) and many in the Labour Party. A pledge by Reed not to sell it to one single owner was not honoured. Maxwell – described as 'not a person who can be relied upon to exercise proper stewardship of a publicly quoted company' following a Department of Trade inquiry into his business affairs at Pergamon Press – could not halt the slide.[27] Cap'n Bob – as Maxwell was nicknamed – used the paper to promote himself and ventures in which he was involved, turning the newspaper 'into a family album'.[28]

The rise of the tabloids

When the *Sun* succeeded the *Mirror* as Britain's best-selling newspaper there were five daily tabloids. The rise of the tabloids took place against a deteriorating economic climate. The British economy was buffeted by a series of shocks, starting with the first major hike in oil prices, which occurred in 1973. Rapid inflation meant that the cost of newsprint rose almost 100 per cent and press advertising – the first thing to be cut back in an economic downturn – experienced a sharp fall in 1974. The cover price of newspapers rose to meet rising costs. Competition intensified, and as the *Sun* and *Mirror* slugged it out the *Mail* and *Express* slowly lost ground. Following the death of Lord Beaverbrook the circulation of the *Express* declined rapidly. At his death in 1964 it was selling 4.2 million, more than holding its own in a market dominated by the *Mirror*. Between 1970 and 1983 the newspaper went though seven editors, eleven increases in its cover price, a 1,440 per cent rise in the running costs of the newspaper and a drop in circulation to just below two million.[29] The readership profile did not hold out much hope for the future; by 1976 58 per cent of *Express* readers were over 45 and 22 per cent were drawing their pension.[30] With advertising still in the doldrums Beaverbrook's newspapers, with the exception of the *Sunday Express*, were ailing. The printing machinery was old and urgently required investment; costs were higher than any in other newspaper groups and the Beaverbrook press was borrowing more and more just to stand still. Problems had risen to a 'spectacular order' by the beginning of 1977 and, faced with more trials and tribulations, Beaverbrook's son, Sir Max Aitken, himself struggling with ill health, sold up.

Beaverbrook's main rival throughout the first half of the twentieth century, Associated Press, fared only slightly better. The *Daily Mail* also experienced several image changes, editors and re-launches in order to find 'an elixir to recapture past glory'.[31] New readers continued to elude them; sales slowly declined from 2.46 million in 1965 to 1.76 million in 1975.[32] Weakening financial fortunes resulted in the closure of the *Sketch* and the *Mail*'s conversion into a tabloid. It sought to become a middle of the road, middle-brow tabloid aimed at a middle-class readership – similar to the efforts Cudlipp had made with the *Sun* in its initial days. Concerns about the appeal of a tabloid to such an audience led Associated Newspapers to refer to the new *Mail* as a 'compact'.[33] Over 400 jobs were lost in the reorganisation and the new *Mail*, under the editorship of David English, started off as a 'very small' and 'rather unsophisticated' newspaper; it was never more than twelve or sixteen pages.[34] However, the new format helped to stem the newspaper's losses and sales remained on an even keel for the rest of the decade. Competition took on an additional edge in 1978 when the new owners of the *Express* newspaper launched the *Daily Star*, which drowned Fleet Street in a deluge of bingo and jingo.

Eyes down

The *Daily Star* emerged from the troubles the new management of the *Express* papers had with the print unions when they first took over the business. Confrontation occurred over the replacement of ageing plant and the underutilisation of the printing presses, particularly in Manchester. Trafalgar House's boss, Victor Matthews, believed 'Fleet Street is not over manned; it is under worked'.[35] Profligate agreements with the unions had brought about this state of affairs. In 1978 it was decided to use the spare capacity in Manchester to print a brand new newspaper – the first in Britain for seventy-five years. Its managing editor was Derek Jameson, former Northern Editor of the *Daily Mirror*, and the only member of the *Mirror* stable to have made an effort to compete with the *Sun*. The *Sun* was printed in South East England and Jameson, from his base in Manchester, had taken advantage of the additional time he had to print his paper by adapting material from his rivals. His efforts were successful as sales of the Northern edition of the *Mirror* held up well – setting a pattern for the 1980s whereby the *Mirror* sold well in the North and the *Sun* in the South. His sleazy stories and pictures were not appreciated by the *Mirror*'s London management and he was finally told to stop. His success showed it was propitious for someone to launch a 'clone' of the *Sun*. The *Star* was virtually identical to the *Sun*, with the exception that its nudes appeared on page 7 and it was less censorious of the unions and Labour.[36] The objective was to woo readers away from the *Mirror* and do battle with the *Sun*. Editorial content was not its primary weapon, but rather a new gimmick – bingo.

By equating his newspaper with a scratch card, Jameson increased circulation of the *Star* to just over a million in a relatively short time – his rivals underestimating the pulling power of bingo. Jameson later described bingo as 'the biggest and best circulation builder in history, far outstripping anything a newspaper could do editorially'.[37] The *Sun* and *Mirror* followed suit; the *Express* launched the Millionaires' Club and the *Mail* 'Casino', and soon the jackpot had risen to a £1 million. The *Daily Star* could not compete with the size of the prizes offered by its rivals but by stealing a march it was able to hit 1.7 million sales by the end of 1984. This was the pinnacle of its sales success, circulation eventually settling down to a respectable 1.4 million copies during the 1980s.[38] It was never able to compete with the *Sun* and *Mirror*, proving more of an irritant than a challenger to the market leaders. The shelving of its commitment to Labour may also have hindered its progress. Matthews, now ennobled, had always been uncomfortable with the political position of the new newspaper; his firm Trafalgar House was a major contributor to Tory party funds. Overruling his editor, the paper urged its readers at the 1983 general election to vote for Mrs Thatcher, despite market research showing most of them supported Labour.[39]

On quality street

The first crisis in the newspaper industry as a result of the worsening economic circumstances of the 1970s occurred in the quality press. In 1981 the Thomson organisation put *The Times* and *Sunday Times* newspapers up for sale. *The Times* was not like other newspapers; it had become part of 'the Establishment' and could be seen as institutionalised through the presence on its board of 'national' directors such as the Governor of the Bank of England and the President of the Royal Society. As a 'newspaper of record' it carried law reports, the daily Court Circular, parliamentary coverage and various official announcements that most other newspaper no longer justified in terms of everyday news values.[40] It prided itself on a letters page which provided a 'nationally unique forum'[41] and did not see itself as solely accountable to the market – and it never made money. Various owners, Northcliffe, the Astor family and Thomson, were happy to enjoy the kudos of owning the paper while supporting it financially from the profits of their other newspapers. Under Thomson it was the *Sunday Times* that made the profits that kept *The Times* in business.

In 1979 both newspapers ceased publishing for most of the year as a result of a management lockout following a dispute with the print unions over the introduction of new technology. The stoppage is estimated to have cost Thomson anything between £35 and £46 million.[42] The *Sunday Times* was hit particularly hard. Much to the surprise of most commentators, when the newspapers resumed publication they regained the circulation and readership levels they had enjoyed several months earlier. However, a strike by journalists in 1980 added to their woes and, with a projected loss of £13 million for that year, Lord Thomson's son, who had taken over in 1976, decided to sell. After a protracted and controversial process Rupert Murdoch acquired the papers. One of the conditions of the buyout was that he would maintain the special character of *The Times* – he didn't.

The crisis at *The Times* did not reflect the general position of the quality press in the late 1970s and early 1980s. The total circulation of national daily broadsheet newspapers rose – slightly – between 1965 and 1985.[43] The market leader in the late 1960s was the *Daily Telegraph*, whose circulation accounted for nearly two-thirds of the sales of quality papers. From its heyday in the late nineteenth century the circulation of the *Daily Telegraph* had slowly started to slide away. Under the stewardship of Harry Lawson (Viscount Burnham), who ran the paper from 1902 to 1928, sales plunged to around 84,000.[44] Sold to the Berry Brothers, a combination of investment in new plant, cuts in the cover price and an editorial emphasis on news rather than features turned the newspaper around so that by the end of the 1930s it was selling around 750,000 copies.[45] The boost the war gave to newspaper circulation helped the *Telegraph* to exceed the one million mark. A strongly Conservative paper but independent in its thinking, the *Telegraph*'s support for Churchill against Chamberlain assisted its growth. Taken over by Lord Camrose when the Berry Brothers split up their empire in 1937, the paper was left to his eldest son, Michael Berry (Lord Hartwell), who succeeded in 1954. As sole proprietor and editor-in-chief Lord Hartwell ran his paper as a private company. Few innovations were made – although a Sunday version was launched 1961 and a colour supplement introduced in 1965.[46] Circulation remained fairly steady, dropping slightly in the mid-1970s, but with the worsening economic climate and growing competition from the *Guardian*, which had relocated its operation to London in 1960, the newspaper started to struggle financially. Wildcat strikes in 1978 and a hasty and ill-prepared decision to move the operation out of Fleet Street forced the *Telegraph* to raise capital. The way was paved for Canadian entrepreneur Conrad Black to gradually increase his holding in the company until he became the majority shareholder in 1985.

The trajectory of the *Guardian* and the *Financial Times* was in the opposite direction. The *Guardian* struggled to make a profit for most of the years between 1965 and 1985; it was supported initially by the profitability of its sister paper, the *Manchester Evening News*. Hit by the downturn in the provincial market, the ability of the *Evening News* to subsidise the *Guardian* declined from the mid-1970s. On the eve of Wapping the paper's sales had almost doubled over the previous two decades. Its readership appealed to advertisers; it had developed a strong niche market of left-of-centre professionals and had the youngest readership profile of all the quality broadsheet newspapers.[47] A different but equally appealing niche market had been developed by the *Financial Times*, which had cornered high-priced financial advertising. While the quality press faced a number of economic problems, its share of circulation had grown strongly in the thirty years following the end of newsprint rationing.[48]

Sunday shrinkage

Quality newspapers prior to the decision by most of Britain's press to move out of Fleet Street in 1986 experienced a healthy improvement in sales; Sunday papers, however, suffered a considerable dip in their circulations. Total circulation of the Sundays dropped from 23.6 million in 1965 to 17.7 million in 1985.[49] The British love affair with the Sunday newspaper had begun to wane. The segment of the Sunday market which suffered most was the popular newspapers – the *News of the World*, the *Sunday People* and the *Sunday Mirror* lost a substantial slice of their sales. The sales of the world's best-selling newspaper of the 1950s were reduced by half, touching 4.1 million in 1985. The decline of the mass Sunday newspaper is attributed to the incorporation of its values into the mainstream daily papers. The reader did not have to wait for the sleaze, scandals and sex that up until the 1960s had only been available on Sundays. The Sunday newspapers also placed a lot of emphasis on sports coverage, especially football and horse racing, which was more heavily hit by television than other parts of the newspaper market. It was at this time that the specialist football papers, the pink evening sheets published around the country, started to close.

It was the quality end of the Sunday market that stood up best. The major success was the *Sunday Times*, which, having emerged from the moribund and disintegrating Kemsley press empire, entered into a period of rapid

growth following the appointment of Dennis Hamilton as editor. He is credited with 'the most important innovation in quality journalism' in the post-
war period – the introduction of the colour supplement in 1962. The fortunes
of the *Sunday Times* began to change in 1957. Immediately after the war the
paper had lost ground to the *Observer*, which briefly in 1956 was Britain's
best-selling quality Sunday paper. Circulation increased as a result of the *Observer*
losing readers over its opposition to the invasion of Suez and the introduction of the 'Big Read' – the serialisation of best-selling books.[50] The *Sunday
Times* passed the million sales mark in 1960 and gradually increased circulation
up to the mid-1970s under the direction of Harold Evans, who refreshed the
newspaper editorially. He used the 'Insight' team, who specialised in investigative journalism, to promote the paper. Evans gave the 'Insight' team considerable time to dig up stories, selecting those that could be turned into
best-selling books. The most famous investigation was in the early 1970s
into the supply of the Thalidomide drug by the Distillers' Company, which
became a long-running campaign.[51] 'Insight' became a by-word for quality
journalism in the British press and the paper attracted the best and most
gifted journalists, who considered the *Sunday Times* under Evans as 'the only
paper which took its craft seriously'.[52] Changing economic circumstances
returned the *Sunday Times* by 1985 to roughly the same circulation level as it
had in 1965.[53]

The *Sunday Times* Insight team and investigative journalism

The 'Insight' section had started in 1963, pioneering a new investigative form of journalism. The first issue, 'INSIGHT: the news in a new
dimension' was spread across two pages, carried a mixture of 13 stories
treated to a 'soft news' approach which attempted to interpret rather
than report the news. The stories covered ranged from religion and
insurance to shipping and sociology. The multiple story format was
referred to by *Sunday Times* staff as 'the ologies'. The layout of the
pages was revolutionary; divided into squares and rectangles with each
story self contained and separated by heavy ruled borders. The stories
got away 'from the "24-hours fashion" of treating news and by looking
at it more deeply could give it deeper interest'. With the expansion
of the page numbers from 42 to 72 as a result of the expansion of
advertising in 1963 the Insight team could write longer stories to
support their in-depth coverage. The first major story on the Profumo
Affair in June, 1963 was 6,000 words long, an exceptionally long read
at that time.

Source: Hobson, Knightley and Russell, *The Pearl of Days*, 380–3.

Concentration of ownership

Radical changes in the nature of newspaper ownership accompanied the return of competition to Fleet Street in the 1970s. The old-style press lords and their heirs apparent finally withered away. The sons of the press lords either sold up or sold out. The new faces of ownership were the media moguls or the hired chief executives. Rupert Murdoch, Robert Maxwell and Conrad Black epitomised the mogul, whereas Lord Stevens at United Newspapers and Lord Matthews at *Express* newspapers typified the chief executive. These owners were not specifically interested in newspapers. Rupert Murdoch had a background in the industry; his father was a famous Australian journalist and he worked for a short period of time as a journalist, including as a sub on the *Daily Express*.[54] He is credited with showing a strong interest in his papers, their content, design and layout. However, as with fellow moguls, his interest rests in the business of newspapers. The main *modus operandi* is acquisitions, take-overs and mergers. The moguls borrow to build up their media and business empires, of which newspapers are only one element. In many ways the media moguls of the 1970s represented a return to what many would describe as the 'bad old days' of the press barons. They were more autocratic in the way in which they ran their businesses, intervening more than their predecessors of the 1950s and 1960s. Lord Matthews's view of editorial independence accords with that of the press barons: 'By and large the editor will have complete freedom as long as they agree with the policy I have laid down'.[55] Their newspapers were highly partisan, particularly in the coverage of dissenting opinions and their support for Mrs Thatcher's radical, right-wing government which came to office in 1979. They differed from the press barons in that their primary motivation was financial rather than political.

The new breed of owner was first and foremost an entrepreneur who took risks building up the business through the financing and refinancing of its assets. Ownership of newspapers was 'one strategy by which large business organisations sought to influence the environment in which they operated'.[56] Newspapers figured as part of conglomerates which owned and controlled a range of media and other business enterprises. These conglomerates used their press holdings to support the expansion of their media interests elsewhere – for example, Murdoch invested the profits from his British newspapers to finance his expansion into the more lucrative US television market with his establishment of the Fox TV network. Newspaper support for political parties was another way of securing political influence in the battle to improve the opportunities for business. Murdoch's newspapers were happy to switch support from the Conservatives to Tony Blair at the 1997 general election, believing he was better for Murdoch's business. Continued expansion was a necessary component of the acquisitions strategy. Without expansion and profits the enterprise could collapse. The risks were enormous and the consequences of failure could be catastrophic. Robert Maxwell's over-commitments led him to engage in financial illegality and finally apparently take his own life in 1991.

Media moguls

The label 'media moguls' was coined by Jeremy Tunstall and Michael Palmer to describe the qualitative changes that took place in media ownership in the post-war period. Moguls not only acted as owners but operated as chief executives, building financial empires through mergers and acquisitions as part of a risk-taking strategy. Their media empires, which extended across a variety of media forms, were dependent on the financial ties and commercial connections and arrangements they made. Sometimes they indulged in political machinations but this was secondary to the commercial interests that motivated them and their companies. This means they could switch their political allegiance and that of their newspapers from parties, as they did in Britain when in 1997 Murdoch and his papers shifted their support from the Conservatives to Tony Blair's New Labour, which they believed would better serve their commercial interests. Newspaper ownership enables them to maintain connections with politicians and high-level businessmen and women. Their operations are run by a series of managers with whom they maintain close contact in their operations which stretch across the world. Murdoch has interests in Europe, North America, Asia and Australia.

Source: Tunstall and Palmer, *Media Moguls*;
Tunstall, *Newspaper Power*, Chapter 5.

The trend to the conglomeration of press ownership was a feature of the late 1960s and 1970s. IPC and the Thomson organisation were perhaps the first examples of this development. Increased competition led to newspaper groups diversifying into other media operations such as television and other industries. Newspaper publishers have always held interests in related areas such as periodicals, journals and magazines as well as those industries which are intimately tied to the production of newspaper – for example newsprint and paper manufacture. However, in the 1960s they diversified into book publishing, television, music, film, as well as other media interests. Financial involvement in other media had been apparent in the 1930s – for example, Camrose had shares in Britain's leading film company, Gaumont British, and Rothermere was joint owner of the newsreel company British Movietone News.[57] This was the exception rather than the rule. In post-war Britain it became 'a useful counterweight to falling newspaper revenue'.[58] The development of the Thomson organisation is typical. In 1961 it bought the

Edinburgh-based educational publisher Thomas Nelson and launched Sphere Books in 1966; it owned 55 per cent of the voting shares of Scottish Television; and bought into radio stations when local commercial radio began in the late 1960s. Acquisitions were not only a feature of the newspaper industry – they were part of a trend within the capitalist societies as the era of the single product company was disappearing, to be replaced by the rise of highly diversified conglomerates.[59]

The economic problems of the 1970s led to a further change in the way in which companies such as Thomson operated. They branched out into non-media activities; Thomson acquired a major holiday and leisure business as well as a major stake in an oil exploration company. The high dependence of Thomson's media interests on advertising revenue was a major factor behind this diversification.[60] Thomson also took on a more international character with further acquisitions of media and non-media holdings in Canada and North America. Newspaper organisations prior to the end of newsprint rationing in 1956 had tended to be single product businesses with limited investments in subsidiary industries; by the 1960s they had started to turn into large conglomerates with investments in a wide range of diverse and often unrelated businesses. The process of conglomeration and diversification was also facilitated by the entry of non-newspaper companies into the market. Companies such as Atlantic Richfield, Trafalgar House and Lonhro became newspaper owners. Some remained in the newspaper industry, building their interests into large media conglomerates. Others left the business as quickly as they had acquired an interest. Trafalgar House was a property company with hotel, travel and civil engineering interests which bought Beaverbrook's papers in 1978, only to sell them on in 1985 to United Newspapers. The American oil company Atlantic Richfield purchased the *Observer* from the Astors in 1975, then sold it to another non-media conglomerate, Lonhro, six years later.[61] By the 1980s British newspapers were owned and controlled by large media conglomerations that were characterised by the complexities and the intricacies of their links with other businesses in Britain and abroad. The nature of the newspaper was subject to the requirements of these conglomerates, above all the chopping and changing that is a feature of the world of acquisitions and mergers which had created them.

The integration of the newspaper further into the world of business had consequences for performance. Between 1969 and 1986 nine multinational conglomerates bought more than 200 newspapers and magazines, with a total circulation of 46 million.[62] The concentration of the British newspaper industry intensified. Confronted by the risks inherent in the process of conglomeration the media moguls reasserted a more hierarchical managerial regime in their newspapers. Editors such as Andrew Neil at the *Sunday Times* (1983–94) were appointed to ensure that newspapers would make money and toe the line in relation to political and corporate interests. Business and commercial criteria became more central to the running of the paper, often outweighing editorial considerations. The embedding of the press in a variety of commercial, financial and corporate enterprises led to the growth of an increasing number of no-go areas for newspaper investigations. The ability and capacity of some parts of the press to scrutinise and criticise business activities was made more difficult. Some editorial battles were made public; such as the attempts by Tiny Rowlands to prevent the *Observer* in 1984 reporting the murder of citizens by the armed forces in Zimbabwe, where his company Lonhro had considerable commercial interests.[63] Others remained behind closed doors. Newspapers were also used to promote corporate objectives in take-over bids.[64] Rupert Murdoch has used his newspapers to promote the commercial interests of his satellite television station, Sky.[65]

Murdochvision

By 1987 one in three newspapers sold daily and on Sundays was a Murdoch paper. Within a decade the *Sun* had usurped the role of the *Mirror* and as market leader had not only changed popular newspaper culture but also had a crucial impact on the rest of the newspaper industry. If the *Sun* had started out by copying the *Mirror*, by the mid-1980s Fleet Street's finest were drawing on the *Sun*. Tabloid values permeated the newspaper business as the broadsheet newspapers started to incorporate tabloid-size sections into their pages. According to the *Sun*'s owner his newspaper 'stands for opportunities for working people, and for change in this society. It is a real catalyst for change; it's a very radical newspaper'.[66] Many commentators do not share Rupert Murdoch's vision of the *Sun*, preferring to emphasise the deleterious impact the paper has had on the press, society and social discourse. They accuse Murdoch and his newspapers of leading a descent into declining standards. Competition brought about an increase in the sales of popular newspapers between 1968 and the 1980s; 2.5 million additional readers entered the market.[67] Survival as a business depended on the popular press attracting large circulations and the *Sun*'s formula of fun, frivolity and fornication captured the market. In 1981 Larry Lamb was sacked by Murdoch; he resisted introducing 'bingo' and his replacement, Kelvin MacKenzie, embarked on a more aggressive strategy in pursuit of readers. 'Dumbing down', 'tabloidisation', 'infotaintment' and 'newszak' are a variety of labels used to describe what was happening to the British popular press.

The debate about the drift away from substance in the popular press has to be treated with some care; previous chapters of this book have drawn attention to entertainment, gossip and fun as a consistent feature of the content of newspapers since their earliest days. There has never been a 'golden age' in which newspapers have focussed on serving up serious, weighty news on the great issues of the day to produce an informed citizenry to drive the wheels of democracy. Even in the late Victorian period, when newspapers were perhaps at their most serious, entertainment was dished up in healthy proportions, particularly in the best-selling papers of that era, the Sundays. Balancing the serious and entertaining is an essential part of what newspapers do. However, many commentators argue that in the 1980s there was an 'unprecedented and significant' shift in the balance.[68] This is attributed to a number of features, the first of which was the unparalleled nature of competition in the industry. Newspapers were competing not only with each other to provide news but also with a proliferating number of other news outlets. Second, increasing costs of production meant it was easier to fill the mushrooming number of pages with non-news material, which was cheaper to gather. Increased pagination has resulted in more attention devoted to sport, television, entertainment, lifestyle and leisure.[69] Third, and related to this, less attention was paid to news, particularly politics, foreign news and investigative journalism. And, finally, changes in the law, in industrial relations, financial regulations and media policy, such as that relating to cross-media ownership, all part of the Thatcher drive to 'deregulate' the British economy and liberalise British business, increased the commercial imperative in the industry and the ability of owners to pursue it. These factors helped to empower proprietors, exposing the myth in the eyes of some scholars and commentators that newspaper ownership had become more benign.[70] The empires of the media moguls were larger operations, more geographically diverse and more culturally and politically influential than the kingdoms that Northcliffe, Beaverbrook and Rothermere presided over. The extent of their influence is illustrated by the unwillingness of government to regulate their operations and the willingness of prime ministers to pay court to them. Tony Blair's flying out to Australia within months of being elected leader of the Labour Party in 1995 to address a Murdoch News Corporation conference helped to gain the media mogul's support – as well as a commitment to opening up media markets.[71]

Murdoch's vision was encapsulated in the shift from editorial to marketing as the driving force in the newspaper industry.[72] At the time many were more concerned about Fleet Street's political shift to the right. The disappearance of left-leaning newspapers such as the *Daily Herald* and the *News Chronicle* and the declining circulation of the *Daily Mirror* had resulted in Fleet Street becoming less representative of the range of views within British politics. The triumph of the *Sun*, with its loyalty to Mrs Thatcher's government and radical populism, accentuated the feeling of many in the Labour Party and on the centre-left of politics that they could not get a fair hearing in the press.[73] The *Sun* provided a particular impetus to the partisan belligerence in the 1980s with its highly personalised support of Mrs Thatcher, but most of Fleet Street was skewed to backing the Conservative Party.[74] By the 1992 general election, won by John Major's Conservatives, the press was divided in terms of circulation as follows: 70 per cent for the Tories and 27 per cent for the Labour Party.[75] The electoral success of the Tories during the 1980s is attributed to the stream of anti-Labour stories that appeared in the newspapers. Visions of the 'loony left' appeared regularly in the early 1980s and helped to undermine Michael Foot's attempts to win the 1983 general election.[76] The political role of the press in the 1980s might have been extreme in its support of Mrs Thatcher and its anti-Labour bias. However, the extent to which it was able to sway voters and determine the outcome of elections is questionable. Some in the press attributed to themselves 'fabulous powers'; the *Sun* trumpeted after the 1992 election that 'It's the *Sun* Wot Won It' (11 April 1992). Labour leader Neil Kinnock also blamed the press for his party's defeat. The knighthoods handed out in large number to Fleet Street editors by Mrs Thatcher suggest that she believed that their support was invaluable. Yet throughout the 1980s there was not a strong correlation between the editorial positions taken by the press and the voting preferences of their readers. The slavish loyalty of the press did not result in overwhelming electoral support or opinion poll standings. Many of the *Sun*'s readers remained loyal to the Labour Party. Nevertheless the tone and style of press reporting of British politics changed. The decline in the amount of politics was accompanied by a more belligerent, aggressive and highly personalised political journalism. Deliberate partisanship had dissipated in the thirty years following the end of the war.[77] Reconstruction, consensus politics and the dominance that the political parties exerted over the newspapers that supported them in an 'age of deference' encouraged this development. The return of partisan politics in the press can be attributed to the growth in competition. Quiet elections do not sell newspapers. Restrained politics does not help sales. Scandal, sleaze and direct confrontation do. Driven by competition the *Sun* and its tabloid colleagues commercialised the reporting of politics. Murdoch's support for the Thatcher government may have coincided with his personal political convictions but it was motivated by the need to sell more papers and gain legislative support for his business. His shift to supporting Tony Blair's New Labour in 1996 is consistent with these objectives. The clearest example of how government policy assisted his commercial goals was the decision to move his newspaper operations to Wapping in 1986.

Fortress Wapping[78]

In 1986 Rupert Murdoch relocated the production of his newspapers from Fleet Street to Wapping. This shift fundamentally changed the balance of power between the unions and management in the newspaper industry. An executive of the *Financial Times* reflecting on the move a year later stated:

> Sunday, January 26, 1986 was the day on which Fleet Street, as we have known it for all our working lives ceased to exist. That was the day on which Rupert Murdoch proved that it was possible to produce two mass circulation newspapers without a single member of

his existing print workforce; without using railways and with roughly one fifth of the numbers that he had been employing before.[79]

The unions had resisted the introduction of new technology throughout the 1970s, resulting in major stoppages in production such as the year-long lockout at *The Times* and *Sunday Times* in 1979. The closed shop and the ability to halt the production of a perishable product had made it possible for them to resist technical changes. Newspaper production prior to Wapping was labour intensive; labour costs are estimated to have run at about 40–50 per cent.[80] This was partly due to management having negotiated generous wage settlements in the 1950s. High pay and high manning levels characterised the position of print workers. Unions sought to ensure their privileges would be maintained. Equipment such as computer typesetting – which allowed journalists and advertising staff to set their own copy – threatened the power of the unions. New technology promised employers a massive reduction in labour costs and higher productivity. The new owners and managers of Fleet Street decided to act.

The first step on the road to change was not taken in London but in Stockport, Lancashire, when a local newspaper owner, Eddie Shah, used non-union labour to print and distribute his *Messenger* newspapers. This led to a six-month dispute in 1983, during which Shah invoked the new Employment Act, which prevented secondary picketing. The print unions were fined over £700,000 for being in contempt of the law on picketing and lost the dispute.[81] Shah's triumph emboldened Fleet Street newspaper owners, knowing they had the support of the law and the government of the day, to act. A macho management style was the flavour of the day; as exemplified by Ian Macgregor, Chairman of the National Coal Board, in the 1984–5 miners' strike. Maxwell, on taking over MGN, had initiated redundancies; 240 members of the National Graphical Union (NGA) lost their jobs at the horse racing daily *Sporting Life*. Further redundancies came at the *Mirror* papers but in the process collective bargaining established agreed procedures for the job cuts. This was not easy for the unions but some agreement was found to proceed. Rupert Murdoch took another option; he made over 5,000 print workers redundant overnight in his move to Wapping, which brought what Mrs Thatcher described as 'sanity to Fleet Street'.[82]

Murdoch's move to Wapping was cloaked in secrecy. Planning took place well in advance of the move; equipment was brought into the plant at Wapping under cover of darkness and executives met in different venues with little or no paperwork to avoid anything leaking out. Members of the electricians union (the EEPTU) were hired and bussed in from Southampton daily to familiarise themselves with the new technology.[83] Preparations were also made for the response of the print unions. Murdoch registered his new operations as separate companies in order that he could most effectively use the law on picketing against the unions. Murdoch was not alone in his plans to switch operations from Fleet Street; most of his rivals also had plans to redeploy to Docklands. Murdoch went first and, in a dispute that lasted more than a year, mass picketing took place outside the barbed wire compound at Wapping. For the first 300 days it is estimated that 1,000 policemen were present; violence occurred, including a mounted police charge on 12,000 demonstrators who gathered outside the plant on the first anniversary of the dispute.[84] To keep the plant operating Murdoch had to have the compliance of his journalists. Many members of the profession and its union the NUJ crossed the picket line. It is estimated the 90 per cent of the journalists working on the *Sun*, *News of the World*, *The Times* and *Sunday Times* went to work at Wapping, now 'a newspaper factory fenced by twelve foot high spiked steel railings, topped by coils of razor wire and monitored by closed-circuit television'.[85] Financial incentives helped, as did the animus some held against the printers and the cajoling and pressures put on individuals by management. One 'refusenik' complained of the 'ruthless and bullying management which regards all employees as cattle'.[86] Many of the journalists who refused to go came from the *Sunday Times*, a newspaper which was to see a considerable shift in its politics and character post-Wapping.

A hundred papers may bloom

Murdoch's triumph was primarily built on Mrs Thatcher's industrial relations legislation. Fines and the sequestration of their assets for being in contempt of the law left the unions powerless in their efforts to resist change. With the Wapping plant established, other newspapers followed. The workforce of most newspapers was considerably reduced. The Express Group cut one-third of its 6,000 staff, while the *Guardian* lost 200 jobs and the *Daily* and *Sunday Telegraph* newspapers under new owner Conrad Black axed 2,000 jobs from a total staff of 3,300.[87] Profits rose. Murdoch's move to Wapping had reduced his costs by almost £80 million and by the year ending June 1987 News International's profits had risen to £111.5 million.[88]

The reduction in the costs of newspaper production also brought about the launch of many more newspapers. Eddie Shah in 1986 launched a new daily national, *Today*, and within three years of Wapping a variety of other titles appeared. They included the *Independent* as well as the *North West Times* and the *Post*; eight Sundays emerged, including *News on Sunday*, *Sunday Correspondent*, *Scotland on Sunday* and *Wales on Sunday*. This was supposed to represent the blossoming of the newspaper industry. However, many of these newspapers were short lived and the promise of the entry of new and different kinds of newspapers into the market, which many had expected the Wapping revolution to facilitate, never materialised. The British newspaper market was a brutally competitive arena and the fate of many of these newspaper showed that it required more than capital to succeed. However, many of these launches were undercapitalised. The *Correspondent* and *News on Sunday* struggled to raise funds. The latter was conceived of as a workers' cooperative with a left-wing editorial stance. It employed the services of John Pilger and sought to attract funds from trade unions and local government.[89] The £6.5 million secured was not enough to keep the newspaper going as it failed to reach its circulation targets at the outset. It lasted for eight months. Internal divisions fuelled by marketing slogans such as 'No tits, but a lot of balls', combined with higher running costs as a result of using NGA members to paste up, also contributed to the paper's failure.[90]

The *Correspondent* did not last much longer; it folded just over a year after its launch in 1989. Started by journalists, the paper took longer to raise funds due to the 1987 stock market crash and the delay allowed another group of journalists to launch a rival paper to spoil the *Correspondent*'s chances. The rival was the *Independent on Sunday*, the sister paper of the *Independent*, which had been launched as a daily paper by Andreas Whittam Smith and several fellow journalists in 1986. Unlike many of the other new newspapers the *Independent* was able to establish a niche in the market. It gained a reputation for 'doing things differently' such as championing photographic design and pioneering a comprehensive arts and leisure listings service.[91] It also cast itself in the role of defender of press freedom, serialising the banned autobiography of MI5 operative Peter Wright, which brought a writ from the government, and under its extremely combative political editor Anthony Bevins the *Independent* withdrew from the Lobby system. The paper's decision not to support any political party in the 1987 general election reinforced its reputation for independence and helped it to sustain a readership. It did this by taking readers off other broadsheets, in particular the *Guardian*, which is estimated in these years to have lost 80,000 readers to its new rival.[92] Many of these were younger readers, who attracted advertisers to the paper; however, a lapse in appointing sufficient classified-sales staff meant they could not fully capitalise on this. The decision to launch a Sunday version of the paper was more reminiscent of old press barons' practices; the main beneficiary was Murdoch, who could watch rival Sunday newspapers slug it out with one another while the *Sunday Times* consolidated its hold over the Sunday quality market.

The collapse of *Today* in 1995 marked the end of the Wapping promise of a proliferation of new newspapers. The fate of *Today* reveals the reality of the changes brought about by Wapping. Shah, unable to keep the paper going, sold a controlling interest to Lonhro before it was acquired by Murdoch. Under David Montgomery the newspaper put on circulation as a mid-market daily. However, without tradition, secure finances, solid advertising and sufficient staff it petered out, losing circulation gradually from 1990. The new climate was not as advantageous to newspaper production as many Wappingistas believed. Costs rose in the post-Wapping years; distribution costs and newsprint prices increased, colour printing added additional expense and competition for advertising became more cut-throat.[93] Start-up costs were still prohibitive and newspapers, whatever the economic climate, still required a unique selling point which reached readers – many of the new newspapers never made this connection. As Hugh Stephenson and Mike Bromley[94] state, 'Wapping was to open the eyes of national newspaper managements to the potential for profitability of already well-established titles, if they were managed and marketed aggressively with the aim of maximising revenues and minimising costs'. With few exceptions, Wapping benefited established newspapers.

Provincial meltdown

The pace at which provincial newspapers contracted had increased in the early 1960s. Local monopolies increasingly became a feature of the press outside London as major conurbations experienced a loss of titles. Fewer local newspapers were published and sold, and those that remained printed less news, especially local news, leaving the 'local rag in tatters'.[95] Changing social structures accounted for the decline in readership. Evening newspapers in particular were affected by the changing pattern of work; they had depended on a 'world where workers left a factory and bought a newspaper to read while they caught the bus or tram home'.[96] Closely associated with large factories and offices with regular shift work and short commuting distances, the evening newspaper suffered with the introduction of flexible work hours, changing shift patterns and the arrival of the motor car.[97] With advertising as the driving force, the local press continued to make profits and within the context of overall decline nearly 200 new titles were born between 1961 and 1974.[98] Many of these were new editions of pre-existing weekly newspapers. As newspapers consolidated their monopolies they produced several locally based editions within their region.[99] New technology and the high dependence of the local newspaper on classified advertising led to the emergence of a revolutionary new type of newspaper, the free sheet. The decline of the weekly paid-for local newspaper was complemented in the 1970s by the rise of the local free sheet. Between 1977 and 1986 the number of titles is estimated to have increased from 201 to 882, with the rate of expansion hitting its highest point in 1981; distribution figures were also rising significantly, from 15 million copies in 1981 to 42 million by 1989.[100] The success of the free sheet is most apparent in the increased share of local advertising it acquired; in 1970 free sheets only attracted 1.4 per cent of advertising in the regional press but by 1990 this had risen to 35 per cent.[101] By Wapping there were almost as many free newspaper titles as paid for; local newspaper chains realising the competitive threat of the free sheets added to their expansion by starting their own. They eventually bought up many of those launched by small proprietors.[102] However, in the 1980s there was a radical shift in the local newspaper market from the paid-for newspaper to the free sheet.

The free newspaper revolution had a significant impact on the nature of the local newspaper. Free sheets are delivered to people's homes, changing the relationship between the newspaper and the reader. Readers are no longer purchasers of the newspaper; they are the 'product' which is for sale to advertisers.[103] It is the advertisers who have become the primary audience for the newspaper. Editorial content is no longer central to the process of newspaper production, as free distribution ensures the newspaper reaches them. Quality reporting of local issues has declined, much of what appears is assembled from already available sources such as commercial and public sector press releases and other news media.[104] What is required in editorial terms is that there is 'just enough to cause the householder to pick it up and read it'.[105] In the early days of the free newspaper revolution a number of the free sheets attempted to provide substantial editorial content. Some free newspapers still maintain a commitment to local news but the economic realities of producing these newspapers means that there is minimal space for such copy. Most free newspapers are primarily local only in the sense of their title and place of publication; local content consists of listings and the classified ads. Much of the content, usually more than 75 per cent, is devoted to advertising and much of the editorial content is bland, descriptive and 'consumer led'.[106] The result is that staffing levels and news gathering resources in the local press declined in the 1980s and the costs of production dropped. For some, free newspapers had 'more to do with business than journalism'.[107]

The advent of the free newspaper meant that the provincial press became less local. The stories that distinguished the local newspaper, the detailed reports of local council meetings, weddings and funerals, clubs and sports days, ceased to be an important component of the free sheets which had come to constitute nearly 50 per cent of the provincial press in the 1980s. The distinctive characteristic of the provincial newspaper's mode of address to its audience was changing. The commitment to locality, community and local democracy wavered as local newspapers ceased to 'flag up' local identity in the ways and to the extent they used to. With perhaps the exception of local newspapers in the nations of the United Kingdom (see Chapter 9), the bond between the local newspaper and the local community started to weaken in the 1980s. It is also the case that the free sheets paved the way for the introduction of new technology and the challenge to the unions which was the basis of the move to Wapping. The free newspapers propelled paid-for dailies and weeklies to change; Eddie Shah's march to Fleet Street began in Warrington and Stockport.

mediaguardian.co.uk

🔊 Webfeed

Latest news

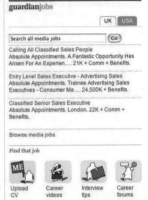

Lebedev lines up Geordie Greig for Evening Standard role

12.20pm: Tatler editor Geordie Greig is being tipped as the new editor of the Standard after it is sold to Alexander Lebedev. By **Stephen Brook** and **Mark Sweney**

- ◄» Luke Harding and Mark Sweney on the deal 🖃
- Greenslade: Will Lebedev go for the Indy too?
- Can the Standard survive under Lebedev?
- Dave Hill: What will happen to the Standard?

Mullins tipped for Standard promotion

1pm: London Evening Standard managing director Andrew Mullins is in line to become the paper's chief executive after it is sold to Alexander Lebedev. By **Mark Sweney**

- Evening Standard prepares for new owner
- A history of the London Evening Standard

Lebedev to buy London Evening Standard

Exclusive: The billionaire and former KGB agent will today meet Lord Rothermere to clinch the deal. By **Luke Harding** in Moscow and **Mark Sweney**
🖃 83 comments

- How we first broke the story
- Profile: Alexander Lebedev
- Who are the Russians in 'Londongrad'?
- 📷 In pictures: the key players

All stories from the last 24 hours

Duncan dismisses merger of C4 with Five

The Channel 4 chief executive has said a tie-up with Five would be like trying to 'mix oil and water'. By **Mark Sweney**
🖃 6 comments

- Read Andy Duncan's full speech (pdf)
- Thompson backs merger of C4 and Five
- TV licence 'could become cheaper'
- Lord Carter drops hint on broadband
- BBC deal offers hope for ITV local news
- Grade makes final plea on regulation

OFT recommends easing of ITV's CRR

The Office of Fair Trading has recommended that CRR, the mechanism that protects advertisers from ITV1 abusing its dominant position in the ad market, be eased. By **Mark Sweney**
🖃 Post your comment

- Grade makes final plea on PSB
- BBC deal could secure ITV local news until 2016
- More on ITV

Sharon Osbourne wins Sun payout

Sharon Osbourne has won substantial libel damages from News International after the Sun claimed she was risking her husband's life by overworking him. By **Oliver Luft**

Facebook: a place for flirting

One in five users of MySpace and Facebook have admitted they use them to flirt, says a report on US social networking trends. By **Jemima Kiss**
🖃 2 comments

More media news

Google axes 100 jobs in cost-cutting

Shrimsley moves up at FT.com

Independent in al-Jazeera video tie-up

Radio
Alive and kicking

Mark Lawson
Reggie Perrin RIP

Gaza conflict
Media strategy

On this site

- Media Monkey
- Organ Grinder
- Greenslade
- PDA
- TV ratings
- Media Talk podcast
- More audio
- Video
- Photo galleries
- Columnists
- Media quiz
- Today in media
- Media 100 2008
- Media briefing
- Text alerts
- Contact us
- A-Z index

Latest from our blogs

What the commentators say today ...
Roy Greenslade, 15 Jan 2009, 12.06pm
🖃 Post your comment

PDA's Newsbucket
Jemima Kiss, 14 Jan 2009, 10.44pm
🖃 Post your comment

Web page from *mediaguardian.co.uk*, the *Guardian*, 15 January 2009.
Source: © Guardian News & Media Ltd 2009

9

THE LONG GOODBYE

The newspaper and technological change, 1989 to the present

Power is moving away from those who own and manage the media to a new and demanding generation of consumers – consumers who are better educated, unwilling to be led, and who know that in a competitive world they can get what they want, when they want it. The challenge for us in the traditional media is how to engage with this new audience.

There is only one way. That is by using our skills to create and distribute dynamic, exciting content. King Content, The Economist called it recently. But – and this is a very big but – newspapers will have to adapt as their readers demand news and sport on a variety of platforms: websites, iPods, mobile phones or laptops.

Rupert Murdoch, proprietor of the *Sun*, *News of the World*,
The Times and *Sunday Times*[1]

The 1990s brought 'super competition' to Fleet Street.[2] The evaporation of the promise of the Wapping revolution was followed by the sustained decline of the British press. Most newspapers have in recent times experienced a fall in sales, a drop in readership and a cut in staff. Titles have closed, especially in the local and provincial newspaper market. This state of affairs has led some to speculate about the imminent end of the newspaper. They believe the newspaper might soon outlive its usefulness as a vehicle for the communication of news, information and entertainment: the *Economist* magazine in 2006 asked the question 'who killed the newspaper?'[3] Newspapers are facing more competition than ever before – from the twenty-four-hour TV news networks and new forms of mass communication such as the internet. A large proportion of younger people have ceased to read a newspaper and if they do it is on the screens of their VDUs or the pocket computers they carry around or their mobile phones. According to Rupert Murdoch,

[a] new generation of media consumers has risen demanding content delivered when they want it, how they want it, and very much as they want it. This new media audience – and we are talking here of tens of millions of young people around the world – is already using technology, especially the web, to inform, entertain and above all to educate itself.[4]

Britain's leading newspaper owner recognises that his industry is going through a fundamental transformation which might end up with the demise of the old printed newspaper. Lord Fowler, who chaired a parliamentary inquiry in 2008 on media ownership, concluded that 'the newspaper industry is facing severe problems as readership levels fall; young people turn to other sources of news; and advertising moves to the internet'.[5] He believes that the change is 'unprecedented' and there is 'considerable uncertainty about the future'.

Announcements of the death of the printed newspaper seem somewhat premature given the enormous expansion in its size since the end of the 1980s. Newspapers today have more pages than ever. Colour printing has been perfected and papers are packaged in new ways. Supplements and sections have been added and expanded to cover a broader range of topics. Most broadsheet newspapers have introduced two, three and four or more sections to fatten up their daily output. Edited with some autonomy, they allow papers to increase editorial space, boost circulation on certain days by targeting particular readers and encourage more niche advertising. Features have extended their scope to incorporate subject matter such as work, media, pop music, parenthood, technology, childhood and other kinds of 'soft news' that traditionally has not featured. The style, tone and layout of the broadsheet newspaper are beginning to resemble the tabloid. Their front pages are full of bold, colourful blurb drawing the reader's attention to stories on the inside pages that they would never have previously given space to. Many have adopted a smaller size, whether tabloid or 'compact' or 'Berliner', as in the case of the *Guardian*. Opinion, comment and advice of all kinds are prevalent, centred on the 'proliferation of columnists'[6] who nowadays do not have to be journalists or follow the news agenda. Celebrity columnists writing about their own lives – the 'me' column – are more common and the tabloid obsession with celebrities epitomised by the *Daily Mirror*'s 3 a.m. girls, a celebrity gossip team who appear to stalk celebs in the early hours of the morning, has become part of the broadsheet agenda. Opinion journalism is turning newspapers back into 'views papers', furthered by online editions which encourage readers to post their views and reporters to blog their attitudes on a variety of topics in and out of the news of the day.

As newspapers have become bigger and launched online editions, the number of people employed to fill them has not kept pace. Longer hours, lower wages, more space and shorter deadlines within which to turn copy around have transformed the working environment. This has made newspapers more dependent on their sources of information. News agencies, public relations professionals and official sources have increased their involvement in the supply of news stories. It is claimed that PA has become the 'prime artery of the news on this island' and the 'UK's monopoly reporter'.[7] Dubbed the 'fifth estate', the PR industry has become a vital part of the everyday operation of newspapers. The ability of press officers, public relations officials and spin doctors to plug, promote and push stories is far-reaching. For one critic of modern journalism[8] this dependence has led to an increase in the falsehoods and fabrications in British newspapers; many stories are simply 'pseudo-events', manufactured by the PR industry. The lack of time and resources to check the facts and dig up stories, it is claimed, has contributed to the corruption of the profession.

Such criticism taps into growing public distrust of the press and the media more generally. Fewer people attribute much credibility to what they read in their newspapers. This lack of trust used to be confined to the red-top tabloids but has spread in recent years to the quality newspapers. In 2003 a poll found that only 20 per cent of the British public surveyed trusted their newspapers to tell them the truth – this compared with an average for EU countries of 46 per cent.[9] Despite rising levels of distrust more people in Britain continue to read their newspapers than in most other EU countries. There is not necessarily a correlation between growing distrust and declining circulation. What is clear is that falling sales, declining readership, fewer titles, relatively smaller staff and growing distrust have not hit the financial bottom line. Profitability characterises the contemporary newspaper. This is most apparent at the local level but profits for newspapers 'are exceptionally high compared to other industries'.[10]

Super competition

Since 1985 the sales of national daily and Sunday newspapers have fallen by 41 per cent, a drop of nearly 16 million copies.[11] This has been most noticeable in the popular or tabloid market, which lost well over 3.5 million readers between 1985 and 2006.[12] This considerable decline is most acute in the cases of the *Daily Mirror*, *Daily Express* and *Daily Star*, whose sales have more than halved. The *Sun* has lost nearly one-quarter of its readers. The only daily newspaper to have increased circulation over the last couple of decades is the *Daily Mail*, whose sales have risen by just over 470,000.[13] In 1998 the *Mail* overtook the *Mirror* to become Britain's second best-selling newspaper. The success of the *Mail* is attributed to its capacity to take advantage of 'the increase in female-buyers, the blurring of class divisions and unashamed growth of free-market individualism'.[14] Strongly identified with the Thatcherite, share-owning, home-owning new middle classes, its editor David English's decision to emphasise the values of 'Middle England' in the early 1970s appeared to reap dividends in the mid-1990s. The *Mail* remained steadfast in its commitment to defend these values against what it saw as the politically correct and morally bankrupt society emerging from the 1960s. Readers responded over time. The closure of *Today* in 1995 benefited the *Mail* as it attracted many of the readers of the former Murdoch paper. It was in that year that the *Daily Mail* regained a circulation of more than two million, for the first time since the late 1970s.[15]

The *Daily Mail*'s success was mirrored by its Sunday paper, the *Mail on Sunday*. Launched in May 1982 the paper increased sales from 1.6 to 2.27

million between 1985 and 2007 in stark contrast with other Sunday newspapers, which have suffered huge losses – overall a 36 per cent fall in total sales.[16] The collapse of the *Sunday Express* and *Sunday People* has been spectacular. The *People*'s circulation hit a high point of over 5.3 million in the 1960s, only to plummet to 729,000 by 2007. Quality Sunday newspapers have suffered a modest drop in circulation, around 5 per cent between 1965 and 2007. Decline has occurred in spite of the launch of new newspapers such as the *Independent on Sunday* and several efforts to boost sales, some of which have been dubious. The use of multiple selling, known as bulk sales, which saw thousands of copies sold at a reduced price to airlines, hotels, fast-food chains and other such outlets, to be handed out free to customers, was particularly problematic.[17] Newspapers were accused of dumping bulk copies to boost sales; advertisers were concerned and the newspaper circulation auditors alarmed. In 1995 the system was changed to list multiple copies separately but the use of bulk sales indicated the extent of the competitive pressures that act on the press.

Declining circulation also hit the most successful part of the newspaper business in the 1980s, free sheets. The number of free titles peaked in 1986 and has fallen rapidly ever since; the numbers of copies of free newspapers distributed weekly dropped from 42 to 29 million between 1989 and 2004.[18] Today there are over 200 fewer free titles. In 1999 Associated Newspapers started to give away a free newspaper at tube stations across London. The *Metro* was soon being handed out in ten cities across Britain, a regular feature of the morning commuter train ride. The total circulation is estimated to be 1.9 million, which according to its owners makes *Metro* Britain's fourth largest newspaper.[19] In London the *Metro* was joined by other free sheets. Associated launched the *Standard Lite*, a slimmed-down version of the evening newspaper, only available from *Standard* vendors in the lunch hour, when it is estimated 600,000 people leave their offices in Central London. A free daily business newspaper, City A.M., made it onto the streets in 2005 and News International launched the *London Paper* in 2006.[20] While these papers have reshaped the newspaper market they do not detract from the overall picture of decline.

Reading a newspaper in 2008 is more than ever an unpopular activity. The most recent British Social Attitudes report shows that newspaper readership is collapsing. A smaller proportion of each age group reads a paper than the generation before. In 2006, 42 per cent of 18- to 27-year-olds read a daily paper at least three days a week, compared with 72 per cent in 1986. As older readers die off, they are not being replaced. Newspaper readers in the immediate post-war period exhibited an almost die-hard loyalty to their paper; readers today are more casual and less committed in their reading habits. An attitude change to news is found amongst younger readers, who are less interested in news and only likely to pick up a newspaper when they already know there is something they want to read.[21] The Social Attitudes survey also found that among those who do not read a paper regularly, only 3 per cent regularly consult a newspaper website.

Price war

Declining sales were triggered by a serious economic downturn in the 1990s. In the first three years of the decade every major national daily newspaper suffered a drop in sales, including the *Sun*, which experienced the worst slump since its launch.[22] Murdoch, now a major global media magnate with interests in film and television from America to Asia, was under intense financial pressure. News Corporation, his global company, was in difficulties and, with huge debts of around 13 billion Australian dollars, on the brink of bankruptcy.[23] A renegotiation of his debt – which involved selling some of his Australian publications – staved off bankruptcy. To protect his profits and respond to new competitors Murdoch launched a price war. In July 1993 the price of the *Sun* was cut by one-fifth.[24] The effect was immediate: the paper's sales began to climb back up to the four million figure. The decline of the *Sun*'s competitors quickened. If the decision to cut the price of the *Sun* surprised the industry, the cut in the price of *The Times* in September was a profound shock. Using the success of the *Sun*, Murdoch was able to subsidise the price of the loss-making *Times*, an action deemed illegal in many other countries. The *Independent* complained to the Office of Fair Trading to no avail and one of the bitterest price wars in British newspaper history began.

The decision to cut the price of *The Times* was calculated to attract readers from the *Daily Telegraph*, Britain's best-selling quality paper. The reduction from 45 to 30 pence doubled the sales of *The Times*; a further drop to 20 pence, with Monday's copy of the newspaper selling at 10 pence, resulted in sales rising to 880,000 per day.[25] The newspaper had increased its circulation by more than half a million within a short period of time. The *Telegraph*'s owner, Conrad Black, at first resisted the temptation to compete on price, assuming that Murdoch could not operate at a substantial loss for very long. He also assumed that any readers who switched to *The Times* on the basis of price would soon return when they discovered the 'inferior' nature of the product. However, when the *Telegraph*'s circulation dropped below one million in May 1994 he had to follow suit and cut the price of his newspapers. The price war was an element of the newspaper market until 2005, when Murdoch put the price of *The Times* back up to 60 pence. It is estimated to have cost News International £175 million but when the war was over the circulation of *The Times* had almost doubled. In the process there were a number of casualties.

The major casualty in the quality press was the *Independent*. Already overstretched by its decision to launch a Sunday version to compete with the *Correspondent*, the paper lost an estimated 20 per cent of its sales.[26] Falling circulation and advertising revenue led the newspaper to fall into the joint ownership of MGN and Tony O'Reilly's Independent Newspapers, which owned titles in the Irish Republic. Losses continued to mount and in 1998 O'Reilly became the sole proprietor and the *Independent* limped on. A similar change of ownership took place with the Telegraph papers; two months before Murdoch called a halt to his war, Conrad Black sold the *Telegraph* and its sister publications to the Barclay brothers, owners of the *Scotsman* newspaper, for £665 million.[27] The resources of Black's Hollinger Company were simply not deep enough to compete with the News Corporation.

At the tabloid end of the market the immediate casualty was *Today*, which closed in 1995. Bought by Murdoch in 1988, the newspaper was used to cream off readers from the *Mirror* in its battle with the *Sun*. Murdoch positioned *Today* to attract *Mirror* readers who were becoming increasingly fed up with Maxwell's descent into girlie pictures, celebrity stories and bingo.[28] With a slightly more serious news agenda and aimed at the 'classless' and 'aspirational ... children of Thatcher's generation', the newspaper increased circulation. With the threat of the *Mirror* dissipated, and the failure in circulation terms of several attempts to re-launch, *Today* closed. The paper's circulation, at 560,000, was satisfactory, rising to 650,000 on the three days its cover price was dropped to 10 pence.[29] According to the paper's political editor, Alastair Campbell, 'journalistically the newspaper was the success of the decade' but rising costs and static advertising meant it was still losing money when it was closed.[30]

The *Mirror* and *Express* struggled during Murdoch's price war. Maxwell's death saw the *Mirror* stumble into the hands of a variety of new owners when the extent of the debt, mismanagement and double dealing was revealed. MGN went into administration and David Montgomery, the former *Today* editor and Murdoch protégé, took the helm as chief executive in 1992. Deeply disliked by journalists – the staff of the *Daily Mirror* voted overwhelmingly not to co-operate with him – Montgomery set about introducing efficiency savings and ensuring MGN ran a tighter ship. Sales, however, of all the MGN newspapers continued to decline; even bringing in Kelvin MacKenzie, who had resigned from the *Sun*'s editorship in the wake of its circulation dip in the early 1990s, could not turn the situation around. Montgomery had stabilised matters in the wake of the Maxwell fiasco, putting the group on a sound financial footing and gaining the confidence of the banks. Doubts arose when a foray into cable TV, with topless darts and naked weather forecasters, failed; as did purchases of regional newspaper groups such as the Midland Independent Newspapers. The arrival of a new chairman, a falling share price and the growth of negative perceptions of Montgomery in the City led to change. Montgomery departed and in 1999 MGN merged with the regional newspaper chain Trinity to become Britain largest newspaper publisher, Trinity Mirror plc.

The fate of the *Daily Express* and its sister newspapers was to become part of a pornography empire. Richard Desmond was the owner of magazines such as *Nude Wives*, *Asian Babes* and *40 Plus*, as well as the celebrity gossip magazine *OK!* Under United News & Media (UNM) circulation was allowed to 'dwindle away'.[31] UNM was an amalgamation of United Newspapers and the Communications company MAI, whose interests lay in a variety of financial services as well as media and communications interests, including television. The left-of-centre-ish politics of MAI chairman Lord Hollick and United's boss Lord Stevens' Toryism made the life of the group's newspaper editors complicated. Hollick prevailed and persuaded the editor-in-chief, Rosie Boycott, to support the new leader of the Labour Party, Tony Blair. Revamping the crusading spirit of Beaverbrook, she positioned the *Express* to fight against injustice, employing like-minded journalists to support her. Traditional right-wing columnists such as Peter Hitchens remained but the paper was divided. Operating with a small staff – since the 1980s the numbers employed by Express newspapers had fallen from 7,000 to 1,700[32] – the *Daily Express* struggled to compete with its main competitor, the *Daily Mail*, and the *Mail on Sunday*.[33] Hollick's interest in the newspaper side of UNM operation faded; it was only a small part of his company's operation. Resources were less and less forthcoming and in 1999 UMN sold the business to Desmond.

Going compact

The early 1990s witnessed the 'greatest turnaround in editors' in the history of national newspapers.[34] The majority of titles went through three or more in a short five-year period. This was a response to the severe difficulties that faced the industry; little time was given to editors by proprietors to make the necessary changes they believed were required. Major changes took place in appearance and content, most noticeably amongst the broadsheets which converted to the tabloid format and, some would argue, tabloid values. Murdoch's price war had forced broadsheet newspapers to find alternative ways to boost circulation. Giveaways such as CDs and DVDs – and more recently wallcharts – attracted readers, but at a cost. As with the 1930s circulation wars, gimmicks could only bring in readers in the short run. Faced with the desperate need to hold onto more readers, newspapers looked to sections of the community that 'under-read' such as young people and women. Many broadsheet editors believed that going tabloid was the best way to achieve this. The first broadsheet newspaper to downsize was the one that suffered the greatest dip in sales, the *Independent*.

Under David Montgomery, who had taken over the reins of the newspaper in 1994, resources, morale and sales declined. Cost cutting was the flavour of the day as the *Independent* limped from one circulation low to another. Successive editors struggled to re-launch the newspaper on restricted resources.[35] Andrew Marr,[36] who edited the newspaper in the late 1990s, suggested a complete redesign of the newspaper as a 'qualoid' – an intermediate size between broadsheet and quality, and the size of many of the more successful

European newspapers. Marr was stymied by the lack of availability of European presses to print the newspaper on and 'we could not afford to tinker with someone else's presses or buy second hand ones'. The possibility of a tabloid format was rejected by management. By 2003 they were no longer able to be so choosy. New editor Simon Kelner turned the paper into a tabloid. Doubts remained about the decision and the *Independent* was distributed in a broadsheet and tabloid format for several months. The term 'compact' was used to describe the new size. Secure in readers' preference for the 'compact' version, the decision was made to cease production of the broadsheet *Independent* in 2004. The redesign was accompanied by a rise in sales, with the paper gaining a quarter of a million extra readers.[37]

The *Independent*'s conversion was followed by other broadsheets. *The Times* adopted a dual-track approach for slightly longer before it became a 'compact' in 2005. The *Guardian* decided against becoming a tabloid, adopting what was the inelegantly named 'Berliner' format the same year. An intermediate size, which, according to the editor Alan Rusbridger, combines 'the convenience of the tabloid and the sensibility of a broadsheet',[38] required new printing presses to be installed in Manchester and London. The smaller-sized quality newspaper is now an accepted part of the newspaper industry. The only quality to resist the conversion was the *Telegraph*, which decided, in the words of its then editor Martin Newland, 'to stay quality and milk everything we can out of being the last broadsheet in the market'.[39] Costs were cut but emphasis was also placed on more pages, more news, more colour and a sports tabloid nestling amongst its broadsheet pages.

The *Telegraph*'s decision to emphasise news could also be seen as a conscious reaction to the increasing space given to opinion and comment in the broadsheet press. Opinion and comment have always constituted an important ingredient of the British newspaper, incorporated in a variety of forms, from leader and editorial columns to advice and analysis pieces. During the 1990s the personal column grew in importance. As the immediacy of news became the work of the electronic media, newspapers fell back on providing the background, context and analysis of the news events of the day. Columnists came to perform a crucial commercial role for newspapers.[40] According to *Guardian* columnist Christina Odone, 'in an age when news no longer sells newspapers, columnists are the miracle ingredient that can win you readers'.[41] Columnists command high fees for their services and are highly wooed by editors. Matthew Parris, it is rumoured, was offered £300,000 a year to transfer his column to the *Independent*.[42] The argument that columnists help to draw in readers is somewhat tendentious. Columnists who have shifted newspapers, such as Richard Littlejohn and Keith Waterhouse, have not brought additional readers to their new papers, nor have their old employers suffered. Opinion is, however, less costly, and as papers grow in size it is a 'safe space-filler'.[43]

The history of the column

The column is a feature of the post-1945 newspaper world. Its specific roots, however, rest in the nineteenth century. The *Telegraph*'s Peterborough column, which consisted of a collection of short stories, primarily about politics and the arts, was a revival of a feature that was conceived in the 1880s. Peterborough first appeared in 1929 and over the years gained a reputation for trenchant criticism, particularly of those who it perceived had broken the bounds of traditional morality. Radcyffe Hall's 'lesbian novel' *The Well of Loneliness* was banned in 1929 as a result of a furore whipped up by Peterborough. As with editorial leaders, Peterborough was anonymous and edited by an unnamed individual. Anonymity was not necessarily a barrier to ascertaining the views of a commentator. In the 1930s, according to Harold Macmillan, British Prime Minister from 1959 to 1963, 'we read the *Observer*, not really for anything in it, but to see what Garvin had written ... Everybody wanted to know what Garvin's views were'. Garvin's articles were unsigned and it was the ultimate irony that he was sacked by the *Observer* in 1942 for writing signed columns for the *Express* and *Telegraph*. Another successful column in the 1930s was the *Mirror*'s 'Talk of the Town', which spawned the William Hickey column, anonymously produced by Tom Driberg, later to be a Labour MP and Party Chairman, and which brought together social gossip, long a feature of newspapers, with commentary on political issues. Named columnists appeared in the 1950s, one of the most famous being Henry Fairlie. Now almost forgotten, Fairlie, with Hugh Massingham of the *Observer*, is credited as the founder of the modern political column. Never a member of the parliamentary Lobby he did not show up very often at Westminster, confining his activities, according to the political commentator Alan Watkins, to 'the topping and tailing of agency reports'.[44] With the intensification of competition in the late 1960s columnists attained more space and greater prominence; Peter Jenkins, William Rees Mogg and Bernard Levin are but a few examples of writers whose opinion was apparently valued by readers. Many had been leader writers before emerging into the light of personal publicity. Until the late 1970s most of these columns were about politics, public affairs and arts and culture. However, the personality of the writer became as important as the subject matter and the birth of supplements spawned a whole new species of columnist who broadened their subject matter to include lifestyle, leisure and ultimately their own lives. In the 1990s the personal, totally subjective 'me column' proliferated. Whether it was Bridget Jones's Diary in the *Independent*, John Diamond documenting the progress of his illness in *The Times* or

Suzanne Moore in the *Guardian*, personal narratives constituted a substantial amount of column writing. Today newspaper columns include the views not only of journalists but also of a range of celebrities, public figures, leading politicians and academic or expert commentators of one form or another. In the age of the pundit and 'views papers' it is estimated that there are over 220 regular columns carried in national newspapers.

Source: Hart-Davies, *The House the Berry's Built*, 68–9;
Glover, *Secrets of the Press*; McNair, 'I, columnist' in
Franklin, *Pulling Newspapers Apart*.

Sections and supplements

The rise of the 'me column' coincided with the increased attention paid to soft news and feature stories. The introduction of the colour supplement in 1962 was an important step in the development of a more magazine-like approach to newspaper content and presentation. The supplements until 1981 were confined to the quality Sunday market and the *Daily Telegraph* on Fridays. The launch of the *Mail on Sunday* in 1982 brought *You* magazine to join the *Sunday Express* magazine in the popular market. Post-Wapping there was an expansion in 'non-news' – more feature stories and regular sections devoted to particular specialist and consumer themes.[45] This had been facilitated by several factors. Technological change made it easier to put together, print and publish newspapers. Prior to the introduction of new print technology glossy colour supplements were produced and printed in advance.[46] The material they covered was prone to be dated when it appeared. Colour printing within the normal newspaper deadlines accelerated the use of the supplement, causing the expansion in the size of newspapers. The number of news and editorial pages tripled between 1985 and 2006.[47] New sections and supplements flourished, spreading from national newspapers into the provincial press. This reflected a shift in weekend newspaper reading habits. Saturday newspapers turned from 'the thinnest into the fattest newspapers' of the week,[48] exhibiting the changing leisure and consumption patterns of the 1990s.[49] Sunday shopping and the emergence of what approximates to a 'café culture' in Britain undermined Sunday as a newspaper reading day. Saturdays were transformed into the day of the week on which people could indulge themselves – and consuming a newspaper was part of their Saturday leisure activities. Sales of Saturday papers, particularly quality newspapers, rose rapidly throughout the 1990s, corresponding with the decline of the Sunday readership.

Supplements and sections flourished with the attempts to reach different niche audiences. They played an increasingly important role in the economics of newspaper production, enabling advertisers to have access to specific kinds of readers. Money, health, living and lifestyle, sport, education, food, fashion, music, media, technology, business, travel and society are amongst the 'cornucopia' of supplements and sections that have appeared. Regular appearance on particular days facilitated the interaction between advertiser and reader. More soft news in the quality newspapers also indicated the growing influence of advertisers over editorial content, the extent of which has led some commentators to bemoan the power of advertisers to 'determine the allocation of space – the pages devoted to consumers, travel, entertainment – which look more and more alike'.[50] The growth of 'advertorials', material written and designed by the newspaper to promote a product and paid for by advertisers, is a further indication of their influence.

The increase of sections and supplements altered newspapers; 'in appearance, intention and content newspapers have gone through a dramatic transformation, abandoning to a certain degree their hard news rationale'.[51] Greater autonomy was ceded to those responsible for running and editing sections and supplements. With more pages, the capacity of the editor to manage the product diminished. Delegating to section and supplement editors was the outcome. Not only are these editors concerned with content, but they also oversee layout and design, and the general visual presentation of their part of the newspaper. Colour printing accentuated the importance of design and layout. The section and supplement editor hires freelance writers to produce copy, reviews and features. According to Jeremy Tunstall, they have come to exercise considerable cultural power, defining much of what makes up modern popular culture, the parameters within which it is discussed and who discusses and comments on it.[52] Newspaper columnists and supplement editors today fulfil the role that used to be performed by the 'weekly journals of opinion' such as the *Spectator*, *New Statesman* and *New Society*.[53]

The 'tabloidising' of the quality press

The growth of supplements and sections, the increased focus on comment and opinion and the physical shrinkage in the size of the newspaper page are amongst several developments that have convinced many that the 'frontier between qualities and popular newspapers has disappeared'.[54] Broadsheet newspapers now report stories that years ago they dismissed as only 'fit for the tabloids'.[55] Editor Max Hastings expressed fear of what he referred to as the 'Hurleyization' of the *Telegraph*.[56] The over-reporting of the British actress Liz Hurley was not a common feature of the quality newspapers. But what was noticeable was that the layout and style of the broadsheets came to resemble those of the popular press: screaming, bold headlines with shorter words, more and bigger colour pictures, and less text and more white space.[57] Today's *Guardian* carries fewer stories on its front page than the *Mirror* did in the 1960s.[58] Newspaper pagination has expanded again in the last decade, with sport, television, entertainment and lifestyle used to fill the additional space.[59] More pages in quality newspapers have produced more trivial and unimportant journalism.

'Tabloid' values spread into the provincial press. Veteran observers of the local press Bob Franklin and David Murphy describe the 'remarkable rate' at which the typographical, content and presentational characteristics associated with tabloidisation have entered local newspaper markets.[60] The shift away from the 'municipal and the political' has been influenced by commercial considerations and the need to please advertisers.[61] The changing economics of local newspaper production was accompanied by a consolidation of the ownership of provincial newspapers. Mergers and acquisitions resulted in four companies, Trinity–Mirror, Johnston, Newsquest and Northcliffe, owning the bulk of regional newspapers, daily and weekly, paid-for and free.[62] The total number of companies owning local newspapers declined from 200 to 91 between 1992 and 2005.[63] Declining sales[64] have not dented profits as advertising accounts for the majority of the turnover of these papers. It made up 77 per cent of the turnover of Trinity–Mirror's regional newspapers in 2005.[65] The dependency has led to changes in content; sport and consumerism have increasingly replaced the local stories that characterised the provincial newspaper's commitment to the community. The role of 'local watchdog' became more difficult as investigative reporting waned; newspapers are today more wary of rocking the citadels of economic and political power in case they disrupt the profit-making process.[66] Caution has been further facilitated by many local newspapers having a monopoly in their circulation area, making them less sensitive to local needs. Competition from free sheets has further distracted the efforts of paid-for local papers to run political and municipal stories. Cutbacks in staffing and resource following a decline in advertising revenue in 2005 further impaired the ability of local newspapers to serve their community.[67]

If the broadsheets and provincial press have succumbed to tabloidisation, then the *Sun* and *Mirror*, in the view of some commentators, have ceased to be newspapers. They are simply peddlers of entertainment and triviality.[68] The small amount of space devoted to serious news about politics and current affairs has been swamped by an 'entertainment driven agenda'. According to one executive on a popular newspaper 'our main job, about 10:1, is to entertain, rather than educate. Our policy is to "editorialise" – we don't do the bald presentation of objective facts, everything is slanted and opinionated'.[69] Cut-throat competition means that the 'red-tops' give their readers what they want, even if it is news that confirms their prejudices. What counts as 'political stories' is more often than not a 'scandal' or personal or political disputes between frontbench politicians. These can contribute to the public domain but in most cases are covered only because they sell papers. Investigative journalism, which had been a feature of the *Daily Mirror* in the 1970s, disappeared when Paul Foot left the paper in 1993, his last unpublished column distributed by hand on the steps of the *Mirror* building. The final effort to run a political campaign was perhaps the paper's stand against the invasion of Iraq in 2003. Headlines such as 'Shock and Awful' (22 March 2003) and 'UNlawful, UNethical and UNstoppable' (18 March 2003) and trenchant prose criticising the way the West went to war in Iraq recaptured the heyday of crusading journalism. The failure to attract readers for this highly praised piece of campaigning journalism – the newspaper's anti-war stance lost it a large number of readers, with circulation dropping below the two million mark for the first time in nearly seventy-five years – put an end to the attempt to revive crusading journalism.[70] The failure was reinforced by the *Sun*'s jingoistic coverage helping it to add readers. The serious news agenda seemed beyond the reach of the popular press after this episode, condemning the 'red-tops' to a more frantic and frenetic pursuit of readers.

Declining trust

Changes in the content of newspapers have been accompanied by declining public trust in the press. Faith in newspapers has never been high but since the late 1980s it has rapidly eroded. The press has become one of Britain's least trusted institutions. Fewer than one in five people believe what their newspapers tell them. The crisis of confidence is reflected in fewer people reading newspapers; even amongst better educated and higher-income groups newspaper readership is collapsing. Only 20 per cent of graduates today regularly read a quality newspaper, compared with 50 per cent in 1986.[71] There has also been a fall in the number of people who identify the newspaper, national or local, as their primary source of information about what is happening.

The performance of the tabloids played a crucial role in undermining public trust. In 1987 the owner of United Newspapers, Lord Stevens, increasingly worried about declining circulation, made a decision that would ultimately move the popular press further downmarket – he signed an agreement with David Sullivan, the owner of the *Sunday Sport*.[72] The *Sunday Sport* was printed on United's regional presses and its print runs had been expanding, encouraging speculation about a possible launch as a daily newspaper. Stevens, fearful of the possible threat posed to the *Daily Star*, appointed Mike Gabbert, the editorial advisor of the *Sport*, to run the *Star*. Gabbert brought the 'yuk' factor to 'bonk journalism'. He launched an attack on the *Sun* and *Mirror* by emphasising sex, sex and more sex. 'STARSTUNNAS' replaced 'STARBIRDS' as women started to be sprawled across the pages of the paper. Bonking stories proliferated and readers were encouraged to contact a new advice column, 'Nothing Shocks Shirl!', which Gabbert is alleged to have told a journalist should act as a 'masturbatory device for readers'.[73] Readers were also sent a T-shirt with a picture of a *Star* model announcing 'I Get It Every Day'. The *Star* put the 'Street of Shame' to shame and Gabbert's reign lasted only a few months. Advertisers were not happy, most notably

Tesco, which cancelled a £400,000 advertising contract.[74] Stevens' credibility as a newspaper owner suffered and the *Star*'s capacity to compete with its tabloid rivals was irretrievably damaged – and a new age of hysterical newspaper journalism was in full swing.

Concerns about falling standards had come to the fore in the 1980s. By the end of the decade scrutiny of how the tabloid press worked reached an unprecedented level.[75] Much of what was perceived as declining reporting standards centred on the pumping out of false information and the extensive invasion of individual privacy. In 1988 the *Sun* paid out £1 million in damages to the rock star Elton John for a false report that he had paid for sex with a rent boy.[76] In 1989 Kelvin MacKenzie's *Sun* attracted the wrath of many on Merseyside, as well as condemnation across the UK, for its 'reporting' of the deaths of Liverpool FC fans in the Hillsborough disaster. Under the headline 'The Truth', the newspaper printed a variety of unattributed claims, about the allegedly abusive behaviour of drunken Liverpool supporters. Other papers carried the story but in a less stark and more qualified way. The *Sun*'s story was damned by the Press Council with words such as 'insensitive, provocative, unwarranted … unbalanced and misleading'.[77] Overnight the paper lost circulation in Liverpool; sales fell by nearly 40 per cent as copies of the paper piled up across the city.[78] The *Sun*'s excesses, previously accepted with tolerated amusement, were now losing the paper circulation. Public distaste was also fuelled by the increasingly intrusive way in which the tabloid press operated. The word 'paparazzi' entered the vocabulary as celebrities, politicians and individuals with a story to tell were snapped in a series of compromising and sometimes personally offensive photographs. The royal family, in particular Princess Diana, were the subject of many of the most notorious examples of invasive reporting and photography. Pictures of a pregnant Princess Diana, sunbathing on a remote beach during her holidays in the Bahamas, were published by the *Sun* and *Star* in 1982. Pictures of the Duchess of York topless next to a swimming pool in the South of France with a man who was not her husband, gossip about the state of the Wales's marriage and speculation about Diana's eating disorder followed.[79] Coverage of the royals had been prurient in the 1950s but this kind of coverage, in the words of the *Daily Telegraph*, 'plumbed new depths'.[80] Another badly misreported story was the 1990 Strangeways prison riot – claims made that up to twenty people had been killed in a variety of horrible ways were proven totally incorrect. No one lost their life but the reporting reinforced the view expressed by an editorial in the *Daily Telegraph* that 'blatant exaggerations on sensitive public issues are published and stand uncorrected'.[81] Within political and public circles the view that something should be done to curb the tabloid press became more prevalent.

Several attempts were made in the late 1980s by backbench MPs to introduce legislation to 'clean up' the performance of the tabloids. The introduction of a right of reply and a law to protect individual privacy failed to win government support but the Home Office warned newspapers that if they did not improve their performance statutory legislation might be introduced to force them to do so. With no tangible shift in tabloid behaviour, the government set up a committee in 1989 under David Calcutt to explore the possibility of introducing legislation to protect individual privacy. The inquiry was recognition that the system of self-regulation established under the Press Council was not working. Following Devlin's departure in 1969 and the arrival of more ruthless and ambitious owners such as Rupert Murdoch at the *News of the World*, the flimsy nature of the body was again exposed.[82] The nadir of the Council's relationship with the press came with the case of the Yorkshire Ripper in the early 1980s. Denounced by the Council as 'lynch mob journalism', the uninhibited press coverage of the case was subjected to an 80,000 word report which condemned the collective behaviour of newspapers – and some of the broadcast media.[83] Yet the Council was unable to do anything about excesses which were seen as an all-time low in the history of Fleet Street reporting. The Council was criticised for its failure to draw up a formal code of newspaper behaviour, the slowness of its decision-making and the lack of means by which to enforce its decisions. Editors ignored the body and most people were unaware of its existence – a poll found that only one in five people had ever heard of the Council.[84] Calcutt recommended the replacement of the Council by a Press Complaints Commission (PCC) and the drawing up of a formal code of practice. He supported the strengthening of the system of self-regulation rather than its replacement. In 1991 the PCC came into existence, with the editors of the *News of the World* and the *Star* amongst its members. A code was drawn up and the PCC started to police the British press – but Calcutt laid down a condition, that there would be an eighteen-month probationary period to assess how well self-regulation was working. If things did not improve, then it was anticipated that the PCC would be given the powers to enable it to force the newspapers to publish retractions and pay compensation to injured parties.[85] The minister responsible, David Mellor, stated that the press was 'drinking in the last chance saloon'.[86]

The press for a short time seemed to improve its behaviour. However, towards the end of the period of scrutiny the *Sunday Times* serialised in 1992 Andrew Morton's approved biography of Princess Diana, which laid out a range of allegations and revelations about the princess's private life, and in particular her relationship with the royal family. Serialisation of the book increased the paper's circulation by more than 200,000 copies.[87] The newspapers were soon full of stories which the PCC described as 'an odious exhibition of journalists dabbling their fingers into the stuff of other people's souls in a manner which adds nothing to legitimate public interest in the situation of the heir to the throne'.[88] Calcutt's review in January 1993 was undertaken in the midst of a frenzy of royal stories – Di and Charles had separated in December 1992. It was no surprise that the review recommended that self-regulation was not working and statutory measures such as a protection of privacy law, the appointment of a press ombudsman and strengthening of the PCC's powers should be introduced. Support came from a report from MPs on the National Heritage Committee but the government did not act.[89] More than sixteen ministers had been forced to resign due to newspaper reports of their sexual peccadilloes, including the minister responsible for the PCC, and their financial indiscretions. Government inaction is also explained by the hostility of the broadsheet press, which believed such legislation would impede its ability to expose serious wrongdoing.[90] The tabloid press had shown that, despite its excesses in reporting the royals, it was correct about the state of the Wales's marriage.[91] John Major's government was highly unpopular and legislation to change the way in which newspapers functioned could have further weakened the government's support in Fleet Street. Nothing was done.

Driven by Murdoch's price war, newspapers continued to indulge in unrestrained behaviour in their search for the stories that would draw in readers. However, their excesses were more and more confined to 'big stories' of the day. Kelvin MacKenzie's departure from the *Sun* in 1994 signalled some restraint entering tabloid competition. The newspaper had been losing circulation since 1990 and MacKenzie's relationship with Murdoch deteriorated as a series of individual stories, such as the paper's publication of the Queen's Christmas message before it was broadcast, brought criticism.[92] The appointment of the former Chief Whip, Lord Wakeham, to head up the PCC in 1995 signalled the government's intention to take the issue of press regulation more seriously, and the incorporation into English and Welsh law of the European Convention on Human Rights Act in 1998 gave individuals more legal recourse to defend their privacy. However, it was the death of Princess Diana the previous year that led to the shift to a more subdued reporting environment. The outpouring of public grief in which the Queen was subjected to hostile comment in the press was cathartic. The PCC's Code of Practice was strengthened following a public outcry about the role of the paparazzi in Di's death. Rules about intruding into individual privacy, especially of children, were tightened and the intensity appeared to have been taken out of the issue. Many of the key debates about ethics and press regulation had centred on Diana.[93] Stories about Diana, 'the first glamorous and media friendly British royal', boosted newspaper circulation when they appeared; she was dubbed the 'princess of sales'.[94] She became the most pictured and reported celebrity in the world. The press coverage of royalty pre- and-post Diana had fundamentally changed. The continuous parade of headlines such as 'Di Found Knickers in Charles' Pocket' contrasts with the circumspect approach that had previously existed. Such tabloid reporting helped to remove the aura that had surrounded the royal family. Newspapers no longer exercised any deference in reporting royal events. However, the excesses to which they went for such stories put the matter of individual privacy into the public domain and several cases since 1997 have seen the courts extend further protection to the individual.

Efforts to establish legislation to protect the privacy of the individual were successfully resisted by the British press during the twentieth century. However, the incorporation of the European Convention on Human Rights into British law as part of the 1998 Human Rights Act guaranteed a 'right to privacy'. This allowed the courts greater involvement in defining the boundaries beyond which the press should not intrude into people's personal lives. The first test case was in 2001 when the *Daily Mirror* published pictures of supermodel Naomi Campbell leaving a Narcotics Anonymous meeting. A long court battle ended with a House of Lords ruling in her favour. Campbell only received £3,500 in damages but her case established that newspapers could be sued for 'misuse of private information'. A number of other cases followed using this right. Michael Douglas and Catherine Zeta Jones sued over the publication of unauthorised pictures of their wedding in *Hello!* magazine and the Jamie Bulger killers obtained an order protecting their anonymity after release from prison.[95] These cases helped to develop a privacy law which was extended with Max Mosley's case against the *News of the World* in 2008 for publishing pictures and a story about sadomasochistic sex sessions.[96] The ruling in favour of Mosley rejected the *News of the World's* public interest defence, drawing a clear distinction between matters which may be of interest to the public and matters which are in the public interest.

The amount awarded to Mosley for the invasion of his privacy, £60,000 plus costs, was a rejection of his claim for exemplary damages and cannot be seen as a deterrent to newspapers indulging in such activity. The cost of the legal action for the newspaper was offset by the additional revenue generated by the story.[97] It is estimated that the Mosley scoop could have added as many as 200,000 sales in the first week and £1 million to the bottom line in terms of increased sales and advertising revenues. The video of the Mosley sex sessions was more successful than the printed story, helping to establish the *News of the World* as a global brand on the internet. It brought the paper its greatest ever number of hits. Claims that 'the press is less free today' after the Mosley judgment came from many sections of the newspaper industry and there is some substance to the view that it erected a higher hurdle for the press to get over to prove that publishing details of someone's private life is in the public interest. The development of the law regarding privacy under the European Convention on Human Rights has not brought about an end to press intrusion into people's lives but it has made that intrusion more expensive and problematic.

Disappearing journalists

The growth of newspapers with more sections and more space to fill occurred at a time when Murdoch's 'price war' was leading to a reduction in resources and encouraging cost cutting. New technology added to the workload as most of the press were launching online editions (see pp. 239–41). Considerable pressure was placed on those responsible for producing the newspaper as the number of journalists employed did not keep pace with the expansion and in some cases actually fell. The average size of editorial staff decreased immediately after Wapping but rose again in the late 1990s as profits rose. However, the manning levels were only what prevailed in Fleet Street twenty years earlier.[98] A 20 per cent drop in staffing levels in the local press between 2000 and 2005 accompanied the low wages that many in local journalism received.[99] To fill the burgeoning number of pages, sections and supplements, newspapers depended more and more on news agencies and the public relations industry. Today PA is the 'central heart of the media industry'; it is the main conveyor of news and information going into newsrooms around Britain.[100] The growing reliance on PA, and other smaller news agencies up and down the country, is highlighted by recent research that indicates that almost half of the stories in the sample of newspaper material surveyed replicated PA material in one form or another.[101] National newspapers cannot fill their pages because of the lack of full-time, frontline staff; they rely on Britain's main wire agency, which is itself severely limited.[102] The number of staff deployed by PA to cover key news beats such as the courts, Parliament and local has steadily declined since the 1990s.[103] Fewer reporters means reporting is concentrated on a smaller number of sources and the time and opportunity to check information are reduced. The combination of dwindling resources and relentless pressure to produce more copy in an ever more competitive marketplace has consequences for editorial quality.

PA and smaller agencies by themselves are not sufficient to satisfy the increasingly voracious news hole. Newspapers – and other media organisations – have come to depend on another conveyor belt of news which has developed since the Second World War. The PR industry has grown exponentially as the news gathering resources of newspapers have remained constant or shrivelled. Governments, corporations, voluntary bodies, social agencies, political parties, trade unions and football clubs are amongst the wide array of institutions and groups that employ PR advisors and agents. David Miller and William Dinan[104] have documented how the PR sector grew by eleven times in real terms between 1979 and 1998. At the end of the 1990s there were an estimated 2,700 PR companies and 6,500 in-house PR departments employing around 25,000 people.[105] The rise of the profession is a response to the gaps that have emerged in the capacity of the news media to collect information. There is a growing convergence between journalism and PR, to the extent that 'much of current journalism ... is public relations in the sense that stories, ideas, features and interviews are either suggested, or in the extreme actually written by public relations people'.[106] Research found that the PR industry accounts for more than half of news stories in Britain's five most prestigious newspapers in two sample periods examined in 2005; 41 per cent were initiated by PR or contained material supplied by PR and 13 per cent showed signs of PR activity.[107] A single press release with Tony Blair's by-line was reproduced word for word by a 100 local newspapers, with only the name of the town in which the newspaper circulated changed.[108]

The impact of PR on the news gathering process has been assisted by a fundamental shift in the culture of newspaper reporting. Newspaper reporting is progressively more of an office-based activity. Technology, more space to fill and tighter and tighter deadlines mean that journalists no longer get out as much as they used to. The specialist newspaper reporter can cover the world through the screen of his or her VDU, tying him or her more and more to the office than previously. The division of labour between subs, news desks and reporters is breaking down, further discouraging reporters from finding their own stories. News flows into newsrooms at an unprecedented rate and amount; it is manufactured on an industrial scale.[109] The manufacturers are the PR and publicity machines which provide 'information subsidies'[110] to the hard-pressed press. News gathering is more than ever dominated by 'pseudo-events' such as press releases and press conferences, which are treated as newsworthy items in themselves today. Desk bound, desperate to fill more space and driven by shorter deadlines, newspaper reporters are more dependent on their sources. Not everyone sees this as an unwelcome development that undermines standards of reporting,[111] but it cannot be denied that newspapers are more dependent on PR material than ever before.

Online newspapers

National newspapers started to develop online editions in the 1990s and by 2006 there were over 800 regional newspaper websites in addition to those of the national newspapers.[112] The press was slow to get online, impeded by the advertising slump that occurred in the late 1990s when the technology became available. Newspaper groups also lacked an incentive to be online. The initial motivation was the need to keep up with growing public interest in the new technology. Most newspapers saw their online version as secondary to or separate from their printed versions. This was most crudely illustrated by the online site of the *Daily* and *Sunday Express*, which simply reproduced a copy of the papers' front pages, urging readers to go out and purchase the papers.[113] The modern-day Luddism of the Express group was atypical, as most other newspapers started to develop two versions of the newspaper to complement and reinforce each other. Guardian Unlimited, launched in 1999, became the largest and most widely read newspaper website and in 2006 became the first paper to publish stories first on the website, thereby ending the pre-eminence of the printed edition.[114] The decision to be online was propelled by the ability to seek remuneration for services – the *Financial Times* charges for the majority of its content online, while other newspapers have introduced a subscription service for particular aspects of their web content – for example, *The Times* charges for its crossword, while the *Independent* charges for articles and analysis by its internationally renowned Middle East correspondent, Robert Fisk.[115] However, the ability of newspapers to make a profit from their online editions remains doubtful. Each of the three possible business models identified – subscription, advertising and 'ad hoc' sales – has its own problems and limitations.[116] While web-based advertising revenue has grown, it is still relatively small and for most newspapers their online edition is a 'financial drain'.[117]

The major impetus to online development was the threat posed to newspaper advertising revenue by the new medium of mass communication. Spending on UK internet advertising surged in 2006, challenging newspaper ads for the first time, according to a report by the Internet Advertising Bureau and PricewaterhouseCoopers.[118] The upward momentum of net advertising contrasted with the decline of advertising in traditional media. Regional newspaper advertising fell for the first time in fourteen years in 2004–5, and in response to the threat posed by web-based classified sites such as Craigslist and online auction sites such as eBay, as well as public bodies advertising posts on their own websites, local newspapers established their own online advertising activity.[119] Classified ads, entertainment listings and personal notices are now all found online and in 2006 the four main regional newspaper groups established a searchable data base, Fish4, to provide readers with access to job, real-estate and car advertisements. The extent to which the internet poses a challenge to regional newspapers is highlighted by the amount that advertising now contributes to the overall revenue of these publications: 80 per cent of regional newspaper revenue is drawn from advertising, compared to 46 per cent for national newspapers. The growing importance of online advertising is reflected in the debate around the accuracy of the audited figures for electronic circulation. Newspapers, as they have always done, are keen to spin the statistics in their favour. Examination of the data generated by the Audit Bureau of Circulations Electronic reveals that the figures don't always compare like for like.[120]

Online developments are encouraging the growth of opinion journalism. Blogging is an increasingly popular activity.[121] Most bloggers remain known only to a small circle, mainly friends, family and like-minded individuals; a few attain greater prominence, such as the Baghdad Blogger. Attention is drawn to the interactivity of the world of blogging, with newspaper websites encouraging readers to engage in online discussion, vote in online polls and respond to particular stories or content in the paper.[122] Comparison is drawn between the old pundits of the press and the 'new commentariat' of the blogs, which is described as an 'alternative wing of the opinion industry'.[123] Whether it is the blogs of the regular columnists or the new wave of commentators, the growth of newspapers online can be seen as part of the shift from news to opinion and comment that has characterised the development of the newspaper in the twenty-first century. Contemporary newspapers, online and traditional versions, are reverting to the world of political and social comment that distinguished the newspaper in the eighteenth century. The growing concerns about the quality, veracity and accuracy of what appears online echo the criticisms made of newspaper journalism since the days of Defoe, Addison, Swift and Steele.

The end of the newspaper?

Declining readership, the near-universal reliance on television for news, free giveaway papers and the growth of the internet are seen as some of the factors that are sending the traditional newspaper to its grave. Social changes have reduced 'the time to sit down and read the paper'.[124] It is no coincidence that the only growth that can be detected within the newspaper market over the last decade or so is in the local, Saturday and regional Sunday press. The disappearing world of titles, circulations, readers and reporters is happening in an environment which has seen until recently the profitability of newspapers increase. Since 1986 the skewed nature of newspaper economics, with the high dependence on advertising, has ensured with certain exceptions healthy profits and high turnovers.[125] The paradox of declining sales and increasing profits has been accentuated by the increasing commercialisation of the industry. The commercial imperatives that weigh on the press are responsible for a greater concentration of ownership than ever before, with national and provincial newspapers now owned by a small number of owners who do not share the sense of civic or social responsibility of their predecessors. Tabloidisation, a consequence of commercialisation, is driving down standards, diminishing the divide between broadsheet and tabloid newspapers and forcing out serious news. This is compounded by the lack of regulation of newspapers, which has encouraged cheque book journalism, kiss and tell stories, and widespread intrusion into people's private lives. Newspapers have less control over what they report; content is increasingly manipulated by government and corporate news management and a rapidly expanding PR industry which is part of the burgeoning promotional culture in which celebrities thrive. Such factors present the newspaper as an increasingly marginal, more irrelevant and less powerful agent in our society.

The view that newspapers are in decline is not in accord with what many politicians, members of the press and public believe. They regard the modern newspaper as out of control, all powerful and as 'damaging the national psyche'.[126] Prime Minister Tony Blair in his last days in office described the press and other news media as 'a feral beast, just tearing people and reputations to bits', adding that the distinction between comment and news had become so blurred that it was rare to find newspapers reporting precisely what a politician said.[127] Soon after he left Downing Street in 2003, Blair's

Press Secretary Alastair Campbell blamed the press for 'turning people's natural and healthy scepticism into a near phobia of politics driven by ... relentless negativity'.[128] His words echo those of former *Financial Times* journalist John Lloyd, who argues that a 'culture of cynicism' pervades British journalism and poses a threat to democracy.[129] He singles out the mendacious, tendentious and superficial way in which the press reports the major issues of the day as the central problem. In this respect the declining readership of British newspapers can be seen as 'healthy for Britain's democracy', as fewer people are exposed to the partisan and cynical press coverage of politics.[130] Such views resound down the years, indicating that what the papers say is as controversial today as it was three hundred years ago.

FURTHER READING

There is a vast amount of material on the history of the newspapers in Britain. The list that follows recommends some further reading on particular periods, publications and topics that have only been touched on in this overview of the development of newspapers since their first, embryonic appearance in the early seventeenth century. For a discussion of the *approaches to newspaper history*, see, Boyce, D.G. 'The Fourth Estate: a reappraisal of a concept' *and* Curran, J. 'The press as an agency of social control: an historical perspective', both of which are in the collection of essays by Boyce, D.G., Curran, J. and Wingate, P. (eds) *Newspaper History: From the 17th Century to the Present Day* (Constable, 1978); Williams, R. *The Long Revolution* (Penguin, 1980); Habermas, J. *The Structural Transformation of the Public Sphere* (Polity Press, 1989) and Harrison, B. 'Press and pressure groups in modern Britain', in Shattock, J. and Wolff, M. (eds) *The Victorian Periodical Press: Samplings and Soundings* (Leicester University Press, 1982). A useful introduction to ways of thinking about newspapers is found in the opening chapters of O'Malley, T. and Soley, C. *Regulating the Press* (Pluto Press, 2000).

There are several fine *historical overviews* of the key facts, figures, personalities and events in the newspaper's development. For an encyclopaedic tour of the key moments in the growth of the press there is Derek Griffiths's *Fleet Street: Five Hundred Years of the British Press* (The British Library, 2006). This is the most up-to-date description of British newspaper history. A more authoritative account is Francis Williams's *Dangerous Estate: The Anatomy of Newspapers* (Arrow Books, 1959), but this ends in the late 1950s. A post-war history that takes on Williams's account is by another former Fleet Street editor, Roy Greenslade: *Press Gang: How Newspapers Make Profits from Propaganda* (Macmillan, 2003). A shorter and more succinct history is found in the first part of James Curran and Jean Seaton's *Power without Responsibility: A History of Press and Broadcasting in Britain* (Routledge, 2003), which is now in its sixth edition. The essays in D.G. Boyce, J. Curran and P. Wingate's *Newspaper History: From the 17th Century to the Present Day* (Constable, 1978) cover a variety of aspects of the historical development of the press. An excellent account of the newspaper's development up to the end of the nineteenth century is found in Clarke, B. *From Grub Street to Fleet Street: An Illustrated History of English Newspapers to 1899* (Ashgate, 2004). Herd, H. *The March of Journalism* (Allen & Unwin, 1952) traces press history up to the Second World War.

For specific *histories of journalism*, see Martin Conboy's account of the profession of journalism, *Journalism: A Critical History* (Sage, 2004). Phillip Knightley provides a fascinating description of the history of war reporting in *The First Casualty: The War Correspondent as Hero, Propagandist and Myth Maker from Crimea to Iraq* (Andre Deutsch, 2003), while Andrew Sparrow's *Obscure Scribblers: A History of Parliamentary Journalism* (Politico's, 2003) is an interesting account of political reporting. The most engaging text on this topic is Andrew Marr's *My Trade: A Short History of British Journalism* (Macmillan, 2004).

Keith Williams, *The English Newspaper: An Illustrated History to 1900* (Springwood, 1977) and Allen Hutt, *The Changing Newspaper: Typographical Trends in Britain and America 1622–1972* (Gordon Fraser Ltd, 1982) provide the only substantial accounts of the *changing layout and design* of newspapers. An excellent discussion on layout and design in the inter-war years is found in LeMahieu, D.L. *A Culture for Democracy: Mass Communication and the Cultivated Mind in Britain Between the Wars* (Clarendon Press, 1988).

For a discussion of the *forerunners of the newspaper*, see Frank, J. *The Beginnings of the English Newspaper* (Harvard University Press, 1961) and Shaaber, M. *Some Forerunners of the Newspaper in Britain 1476–1622* (Frank Cass, 1966). Two excellent accounts of the seventeenth-century press are: Raymond, J. *The Invention of the Newspaper: English Newsbooks 1640–49* (Clarendon Press, 1996) and Sutherland, J. *The Restoration Newspaper and Its Development* (Cambridge University Press, 2004, 2nd edition).

There are several first-class examinations of *newspapers in the eighteenth century*: Barker, H. *Newspaper, Politics and English Society 1695–1855* (Longman, 2001); Black, J. *The English Press 1621–1861* (Sutton Publishing, 2001); Cranfield, G. *The Press and Society* (Longman, 1978); Harris, B. *Politics and the Rise of the Press: Britain and France, 1620–1800* (Routledge, 1996) and Harris, M. *London Newspapers in the Age of Walpole* (Associated University Presses, 1988).

The *radical newspapers* of the early nineteenth century are discussed in Hollis, P. *The Pauper Press* (Oxford University Press, 1970); Harrison, S. *Poor Men's Guardians: A Survey of the Struggle for a Democratic Newspaper Press, 1763–1973* (Lawrence & Wishart, 1974) and Gilmartin, K. *Print Politics: The Press and Radical Opposition in Early Nineteenth Century England* (Cambridge University Press, 1996). A shorter and more analytical account is found in James Curran's essay 'Capitalism and control of the press, 1800–1975', in Curran, J., Gurevitch, M. and Woollacott, J. (eds) *Mass Communication and Society* (Edward Arnold, 1977). Joel Weiner provides a blow-by-blow account of the campaign to repeal press taxation in his book *The War of the Unstamped: The Movement to Repeal the British Newspaper Tax, 1830–36* (Cornell University Press, 1969).

For an understanding of the *role of the press in nineteenth-century society*, see Jones, A. *Powers of the Press: Newspapers, Power and the Public in Nineteenth-Century England* (Scolar Press, 1996) and Hampton, M. *Visions of the Press in Britain, 1850–1950* (University of Illinois Press, 2004). Lucy Brown provides an analysis of the development of news and news gathering in *Victorian News and Newspapers* (Clarendon Press, 1985). A feel for the style, tone and content of the debate about the press in the nineteenth century is found in King, A. and Plunkett, J. *Victorian Print Media: A Reader* (Oxford University Press, 2005).

The *rise of the popular press* in the twentieth century is well covered by Lee, A. *The Origins of the Popular Press 1855–1914* (Croom Helm, 1976); Catterall, P., Seymour-Ure, C. and Smith, A. (eds) *Northcliffe's Legacy: Aspects of the British Popular Press, 1896–1996* (Macmillan, 2000), in particular the essay by Chalaby, J. 'Northcliffe: proprietor as journalist'. Chalaby's book *The Invention of Journalism* (Macmillan, 1998) is an influential account of the rise of the mass commerical popular press. Journalist Matthew Engel's fine account of the development of the popular press in the twentieth century, *Tickle the Public: One Hundred Years of the Popular Press* (Victor Gollancz, 1996), is supplemented by several of the essays on the British tabloids in a more analytical book, Sparks, C. and Tulloch, J. (eds) *Tabloid Tales: Global Debates over Media Standards* (Rowman & Littlefield, 1999).

On the *press barons and ownership* in the twentieth century, see Brendon, P. *The Life & Death of the Press Barons* (Secker & Warburg, 1982); Boyce, D. 'Crusaders without chains: power and the press barons', in Curran, J., Smith, A. and Wingate, P. (eds) *Impacts and Influences* (Methuen, 1982); and Jenkins, S. (1986) *The Market for Glory: Fleet Street Ownership in the 20th Century* (Faber & Faber, 1986).

On the *economic history of the press*, see Cleverley, G. *The Great Fleet Street Disaster* (Constable, 1976); Curran, J., Douglas, A. and Whannel, G. 'The political economy of the human interest story', in Smith, A. (ed) *Newspapers and Democracy* (MIT Press, 1980); and Curran, J. 'Advertising as a patronage system', in Christian, H. (ed.) *The Sociology of Journalism and the Press* (Keele University Monograph, 1980). An opposing view on the role of advertising is found in Whale, J. *The Politics of the Media*, 2nd edition (Fontana, 1980).

The development of the *newspaper in the post-war period* is covered by Tunstall, J. *Newspaper Power: The New National Press in Britain* (Oxford University Press, 1996); Seymour-Ure, C. *The British Press and Broadcasting since 1945*, 2nd edition (Blackwell, 1995); and McNair, B. *News and Journalism in the UK* (Routledge, 2003). The most up-to-date discussion is to be found in Temple, M. *The British Press* (McGraw Hill, 2009) and the excellent collection of essays in Franklin, B. (ed.) *Pulling Newspapers Apart* (Routledge, 2008). Stephenson, H. and Bromley, M. *Sex, Lies and Democracy: The Press and the Public* (Longman, 1999) and Anderson, P. and Ward, G. (eds) *The Future of Journalism in Advanced Democracies* (Ashgate, 2008) also contain useful material. For a critical purchase on the modern press, see Whitaker, B. *News Ltd.: Why You Can't Read All About It* (Comedia, 1981) and Davies, N. *Flat Earth News* (Chatto & Windus, 2008).

Regional newspapers and their history are covered by Franklin, B. (ed.) *Local Journalism and Local Media: Making the local news* (Routledge, 2006); Aldridge, M. *Understanding the Local Media* (Open University Press, 2007); Cranfield, G. *The Development of the Provincial Press, 1700–60* (Clarendon Press, 1962); Walker, A. 'The development of the provincial press in England c1780–1914', *Journalism Studies*, 2006, 7(3): 373–86; Gliddon, P. (2003) 'The political importance of provincial newspapers 1903–45: the Rowntrees and the liberal press', *Twentieth Century British History*, 2003, 14(1): 24–42. Two broad accounts of the Scottish press are Hutcheson, D. (2008) 'The history of the press', in Blain, N. and Hutcheson, D. (eds) *The Media in Scotland* (Edinburgh University Press, 2008), and Smith, M. *Paper Lions: The Scottish Press and National Identity* (Polygon, 1994). For Wales, see relevant chapters in Barlow, D., Mitchell, P. and O'Malley, T. *The Media in Wales: Voices of a Small Nation* (University of Wales Press, 2005).

On the history of *censorship and news management*, see Cockerell, M., Hennessy, P. and Walker, D. (1986) *Sources Close to the Prime Minister* (Macmillan, 1986); Taylor, P. *British Propaganda in the Twentieth Century: Selling Democracy* (Edinburgh University Press, 1999); and Franklin, B. *Packaging Politics: Political Communications in Britain's Media Democracy*, 2nd edition (Arnold, 2004). For an overview of the evolution of the PR industry, see Miller, D. and Dinan, W. 'The rise of the PR industry in Britain, 1979–98', *European Journal of Communication*, 2000, 15(1): 5–35; the origins of 'spin' in government are explored in Moore, M. *The Origins of Modern Spin: Democratic Government and the Media in Britain, 1945–51* (Palgrave, 2006).

The history of *writing, reading and literacy* is covered by several key texts, perhaps the most accessible of which are Webb, R. *The British Working Class Reader 1790–1848* (Allen & Unwin, 1955); Altick, R. *The English Common Reader: A Social History of the Mass Reading Public 1800–1900* (University of Chicago Press, 1957); and Vincent, D. *Literacy and Popular Culture 1790– 1840* (Cambridge University Press, 1989). The two classic texts about the growth of mass culture in Britain are Swingewood, A. *The Myth of Mass Culture* (Macmillan, 1977) and Thompson, E.P. *The Making of the English Working Class* (Pelican, 1968), with Carey, J. *Intellectuals and the Masses: Pride and Prejudice among the Literary Intelligentsia, 1880–1939* (Faber & Faber, 1992) relating middle-class concerns about the rise of the mass newspaper and mass culture. A fascinating account of the changing nature of language used in the press is Matheson, D. 'The birth of news discourse: changes in news language in British newspapers, 1880–1930', *Media, Culture & Society*, 2000, 22: 557–73. An excellent discussion of visual literacy in the nineteenth century is Anderson, P. *The Printed Image and the Transformation of Popular Culture 1790–1860* (Clarendon Press, 1994).

There are numerous accounts of the *lives and times of owners, editors and newspapers*. The most comprehensive and lively are Bourne, R. *Lords of Fleet Street: The Harmsworth Dynasty* (Unwin & Hyman, 1990); Chippindale, P. and Horrie, C. *Stick It up Your Punter: The Rise and Fall of the Sun* (Mandarin, 1992); Evans, H. *Good Times, Bad Times* (Weidenfeld & Nicholson, 1982); Fyfe, H. *Sixty Years of Fleet Street* (W.H. Allen, 1949); Taylor, S. *The Great Outsiders: Northcliffe, Rothermere and the Daily Mail* (Weidenfeld & Nicholson, 1996); and Richards, H. *The Bloody Circus: the Daily Herald and the Left* (Pluto Press, 1997). Of the numerous accounts of Rupert Murdoch, see Leapman, M. *Barefaced Cheek: The Apotheosis of Rupert Murdoch* (Hodder & Stoughton, 1983); Shawcross, W. *Murdoch* (Chatto & Windus, 1992); and Wolff, M. *The Man Who Owns the News: Inside the Secret World of Rupert Murdoch* (Bodley Head, 2008).

On the *impact of new technology* on the press, see Hall, J. 'Online editions: the newspapers and the "new" news', in Franklin, B. (ed.) *Pulling Newspapers Apart* (Routledge, 2008), as well as his book *Online Journalism: A Critical Primer* (Pluto Press, 2001); Allan, S. (2006) *Online News* (Open University Press, 2006); Herbert, J. and Thurman, N. 'Paid content strategies for news websites: an empirical study of British newspapers', *Journalism Practice*, 2007, 1(2): 208–26; Crosbie, V. 'What newspapers and their web sites must do to survive', *Online Journalism Review*, 4 March, www.ojr.org/ojr/business/1078349998.php.

NOTES

INTRODUCTION

1 Williams, F. (1969) *The Right to Know* London: Longman, 1.
2 O'Malley, T. and Soley, C. (2000) *Regulating the Press* London: Pluto Press, 1.
3 Curran, J. and Tunstall, J. (1973) 'The mass media and leisure' in Smith, M., Parker, S. and Smith, C. (eds) *Leisure and Society in Britain* London: Allen Lane.
4 Curran and Tunstall, 'The mass media and leisure', 206.
5 Raymond, J. (1996) *The Invention of the Newspaper: English Newsbooks 1640–49* Oxford: Clarendon Press; Sutherland, J. (2004) *The Restoration Newspaper and Its Development* Cambridge: Cambridge University Press; Harris, M. (1987) *London Newspapers in the Age of Walpole: A Study in the Origins of the Modern English Press* London: Associated Universities Presses; Black, J. (1987) *The English Press in the Eighteenth Century* Beckenham: Croom Helm; Lee, A. (1976) *The Origins of the Popular Press* London: Croom Helm; Koss, S. (1990) *The Rise and Fall of the Political Press in Britain* London: Fontana; Greenslade, R. (2003) *Press Gang: How Newspapers Make Profits from Propaganda* London: Macmillan; and Tunstall, J. (1996) *Newspaper Power: The New National Press in Britain* Oxford: Oxford University Press.
6 Hunt, F. (1850/1998) *The Fourth Estate* London: Routledge/Thoemmes Press, 2 vols; Andrews, A (1859/1998) *The History of British Journalism* London: Routledge/Thoemmes Press, 2 vols; Fox Bourne, H. (1887/1998) *English Newspapers* London: Routledge/Thoemmes Press, 2 vols. Traditional historical overviews of the development of the newspaper also appeared in the twentieth century, for example the work of Francis Williams (1959) *Dangerous Estate: the Anatomy of Newspapers* London: Arrow Books.
7 Dahl, H.F. (1994) 'The pursuit of media history' *Media, Culture & Society* 16: 551–63.
8 Boyce, D.G., Curran, J. and Wingate, P. (1978) *Newspaper History: From the 17th Century to the Present Day* London: Constable.
9 Williams, R. (1970) 'Radical and/or respectable' in Boston, R. (ed.) *The Press We Deserve* London: RUP, 16.
10 Williams, 'Radical and/or respectable', 16.
11 Curran, J. (1978) 'The press as an agency of social control: an historical perspective' in Boyce, Curran and Wingate, *Newspaper History*.
12 Williams, 'Radical and/or respectable', 21.
13 Curran, J. and Seaton, J. (1988) *Power Without Responsibility: The Press and Broadcasting in Britain* London: Routledge, Third edition, 34. All reference from third edition unless stated.
14 O'Malley, P. (1981) 'Capital accumulation and press freedom 1800–850' *Media, Culture & Society* 3: 82.
15 Berridge, V. (1978) 'Popular Sunday newspapers and mid Victorian society' in Boyce, Curran and Wingate, *Newspaper History*.

16 Hutt, A. (1973) *The Changing Newspaper: Typographical Trends in Britain and America 1622–1972* London: Gordon Fraser Ltd; and Williams, K. (1977) *The English Newspaper: An Illustrated History to 1900* London: Springwood Books.

17 Matheson, D. (2000) 'The birth of news discourse: changes in news language in British newspapers, 1880–1930' *Media, Culture & Society* 22 (5): 557–68.

18 Jones, A. (1996) *Powers of the Press: Newspapers, Power and the Public in Nineteenth-Century England* Aldershot: Scolar Press, 2.

19 Tunstall, *Newspaper Power*, 9.

20 Greenslade, *Press Gang*, 112.

21 Ireland should also figure as part of a discussion about the way in which newspapers in other parts of the United Kingdom resisted the expansion of the London press. However, due to lack of space this is not examined in this book.

22 Smith, M. (1994) *Paper Lions: the Scottish Press and National Identity* Edinburgh: Polygon.

23 Hutcheson, D. (2008) 'The history of the press' in Blain, N. and Hutcheson, D. (eds) *The Media in Scotland* Edinburgh: Edinburgh University Press.

24 Walker A. (2006) 'The Development of the Provincial Press in England c1780–1914' *Journalism Studies* 7(3): 373–84.

25 Quoted in Boston, R. (1977) 'Fleet Street 100 Years Ago' *Journalism Studies Review* 1(2): 16.

26 Greenwood, F. (1897) 'The Newspaper Press' *Blackwood's Magazine*, quoted in Boston, 'Fleet Street 100 Years Ago', 16.

27 Tunstall, *Newspaper Power*, 13.

28 Tunstall, *Newspaper Power*, 44.

29 Tunstall, *Newspaper Power*, 39.

30 Berridge, 'Popular Sunday newspapers and mid Victorian society', 247.

31 Pierce, R. (1977) 'How the tabloid was born' *Journalism Studies Review*: 26–32.

32 Tulloch, J. (2000) 'The eternal recurrence of new journalism' in Sparks, C. and Tulloch, J. (eds) *Tabloid Tales: Global Debates over Media Standards* Lanham, MD: Rowman & Littlefield, 131.

33 Sparks, C. (1991) 'Goodbye, Hildy Johnson: the vanishing "serious" press' in Dahlgren, P. and Sparks, C. (eds) *Communication and Citizenship: Journalism and the Public Sphere* London: Routledge.

34 Tulloch, 'The eternal recurrence of new journalism', 137.

35 See Muggli, M. (1992) 'Ben Jonson and the business of news' *Studies in English Literature 1500–1900* 32(2): 326. For a discussion of Jonson's play *A Staple of News*, see Sherman, S. (2001) 'Eyes and ears, news and plays: the argument of Ben Jonson's *Staple*' in Dooley, B. and Baron, S. (eds) *The Politics of Information in Early Modern Europe* London: Routledge.

36 Carey, J. (1989) *Communication as Culture: Essays on Media and Society* London: Allen and Unwin.

37 Diblee, G. (1913) *The Newspaper* New York: Harold Holt, 13.

38 O'Malley and Soley, *Regulating the Press*, 12.

39 Innis, H. (1942) 'The newspaper in economic development' *Journal of Economic History* 2, Supplement: 1–33.

40 For a discussion of the definition of a newspaper and the media in general, see McQuail, D. (1994) *Mass Communication Theory* London: Sage.

41 Smith, A. (1979) *The Newspaper: An International History* London: Thames & Hudson, 10.

42 Richards, H. (1997) *The Bloody Circus: The Daily Herald and the Left* London: Pluto Press.

43 Hampton, M. (2004) *Visions of the Press in Britain, 1850–1950* Chicago: University of Illinois Press.

44 Carey, *Communication as Culture*, 21.

45 The reference to the 'British' newspaper in the title of this book is an acknowledgement of the role that the newspaper has played in fostering of a sense of British national identity and citizenship. Since the Acts of Union between Scotland and England (1707) and Ireland and England (1801) the metropolitan newspapers distributed from London have

sought to bring together the peoples and nations of Britain around a set of cultural values and practices that promote a common British national identity. The 'nationalisation' of the press, that is, the increasing dominance of the London newspapers across the UK, represented the inculcation of these values and practices into readers in the regions and other nations of Britain. For many commentators this identity has been constructed around religious bigotry, imperial superiority, racial supremacy, English nationalism and rural continuity. What it means to be British, however, has changed and has been interpreted differently in parts of the press. It is beyond the reach of this short book to trace how the press has constructed British identity, mapping out the continuities and changes that have taken place. It is nevertheless important to note that the content, form and appearance of newspapers was shaped by notions of Britishness.

46 Anderson, B. (2006 [1983]) *Imagined Communities: Reflections of the Origins and Spread of Nationalism* London: Verso.

47 Billig, M. (1995) *Banal Nationalism* London: Sage.

48 Conboy, M. (2006) *Tabloid Britain: Constructing a Community through Language* London: Routledge.

49 See several of the essays in Boyce, Curran and Wingate, *Newspaper History*.

50 Brake, L., Bell, B. and Finkelstein, D. (2000) *Nineteenth Century Media and the Construction of Identities* London: Palgrave.

51 Curran and Seaton, *Power Without Responsibility*, 9.

52 Habermas, J. (1989) *The Structural Transformation of the Public Sphere: An Inquiry into a Category of Bourgeois Society* Cambridge: Polity Press.

53 Curran, *Media and the Making of British Society*, 149.

54 Curran, J. (2002) 'Media and the making of British society c1700–2000' *Media History* 8(2): 135–54; and O'Malley, T. (2002) 'Media history and media studies: aspects of the development of the study of media history in the UK 1945–2000' *Media History* 8(2): 155–73.

55 For a discussion, see Stober, R. (2004) 'What media evolution is: a theoretical approach to the history of new media' *European Journal of Communication* 19(4): 483–505.

56 Stober, 'What media evolution is', 484.

57 For example, Winston, B. (1998) *Media, Technology and Society: A History from the Telegraph to the Internet* London: Routledge; Briggs, A. and Burke, P. (2005) *A Social History of the Media: From Gutenberg to the Internet* London: Polity, 2nd edition.

58 Nerone, J. and Barnhurst, K. (2003) 'News form and the media environment: a network of represented relationships' *Media, Culture & Society* 25: 111–24.

59 Black, J. (2002) 'The press and politics in the eighteenth century' *Media History* 8(2): 175–82.

60 Mansfield, F. (1944) *The Complete Journalist* London: Isaac Pitman & Sons, 4.

61 Barker, H. (2000) *Newspapers, Politics and English Society 1695–1855* London: Pearson Education, 216.

62 Blumenfeld, R. (1933) *The Press in My Time* London: Rich and Cowan, 33 quoted in Tunstall, J. (1977) '"Editorial sovereignty" in the British press: its past and present' *Studies on the Press*, Royal Commission on the Press London: HMSO, 264.

63 Tunstall, 'Editorial sovereignty', 261.

64 Mansfield, *The Complete Journalist*, 131.

65 Quoted in Mansfield, *The Complete Journalist*, 130.

66 For a discussion of the organisation of journalism and changing conceptions of the role of journalists in the late nineteenth, early twentieth centuries, see Hampton, M. (2005) 'Defining journalism in late nineteenth century Britain' *Critical Studies in Media Communication* 22(2): 138–55; Hampton, M. (1999) 'Journalists and the "professional ideal" in Britain: the Institute of Journalists, 1884–1907' *Historical Research* 72(178): 183–201.

67 See Hampton, M. (2008) 'The "objectivity" ideal and its limitations in 20th-century British journalism' *Journalism Studies* 9(4): 477–93.

68 Nerone and Barnhurst, 'News forms and media environment', 122–23.
69 Ibid.
70 For example Hodgson, G. (2000) 'The end of the grand narrative and the death of news' *Historical Journal of Film, Radio and Television* 20(1): 23–31.
71 Herbert, J. and Thurman, N. (2007) 'Paid content strategies for news websites' *Journalism Practice* 1(2): 208–26.

1 SPREADING THE WORD

1 Shaaber, M. (1966) *Some Forerunners of the Newspaper in Britain 1476–1622* London: Frank Cass, 3.
2 Sommerville, C.J. (1996) *The News Revolution in England: Cultural Dynamics of Daily Information* Oxford: Oxford University Press, 17.
3 Lévi Strauss, C. (1968) *Structural Anthropology*, vol. 1, trans. Jackson, C. and Brooke, G. London: Allen & Unwin, 296.
4 See Stephens, M. (1997) *A History of News* Forth Worth, TX: Harcourt Brace, Chapter 3.
5 See Hargreaves, I. and Thomas, J. (2002) *New News, Old News* London: ITC and BSC, 5; Harrison, J. (2005) *News* London: Routledge, 41.
6 Ong, W. (1982) *Orality and Literacy: The Technologizing of the Word* London: Methuen.
7 McLuhan, M. (1962) *The Gutenberg Galaxy* Toronto: University of Toronto Press.
8 Stephens, *A History of News*, 30.
9 Andrews, *The History of British Journalism*, 10
10 Stephens, *A History of News*, 55.
11 Stephens, *A History of News*, 58.
12 Stephens, *A History of News*, 62.
13 Burke, J. (2003) 'Communications in the Middle Ages' in Crowley, D. and Heyer, P. .(eds) *Communication in History: Technology, Culture and Society* New York: Pearson Education, 74.
14 Curran, J. (1982) 'Communications, power and social order' in Gurevitch, M., Bennett, T., Curran, J. and Woollacott, J. (eds) *Culture, Society and the Media* London: Methuen, 209.
15 Arblaster, P. (2005) 'Posts, newsletters, newspapers: England in a European system of communications' *Media History*, 11(1/2): 21–36.
16 Burke, P. (2000) *The Social History of Knowledge* London, Polity Press, 33.
17 Burke, P. *The Social History of Knowledge*, 2.
18 Eisenstein, E. (1983) *The Printing Revolution in Early Modern Europe* Cambridge: Cambridge University Press, 10.
19 Curran, J. (1977) 'Mass communications as a social force in history' *Mass Communications and Society*, Open University Course Unit 2 Milton Keynes: Open University Press.
20 Briggs and Burke, *A Social History of the Media*, 9.
21 Jones, W.R. (1979) 'The English Church and royal propaganda during the Hundred Years War' *Journal of British Studies* 19(1): 18.
22 Jones, 'The English Church and royal propaganda'.
23 Quoted in Levy, F. (1999) 'The decorum of news' in Raymond, J. (ed.) *News, Newspapers and Society in Early Modern Britain* London: Frank Cass, 14.
24 See Burke, *The Social History of Knowledge*.
25 Thompson, J. (1995) *The Media and Modernity* London: Polity Press, Chapter 2.
26 Burke, *The Social History of Knowledge*, Chapter 7.
27 Winston, B. (2005) *Messages: Free Expression, Media and the West from Gutenberg to Google* London: Routledge, 37; Stephens, *A History of News*, 66–8.
28 Arblaster, 'Posts, newsletters, newspapers'.
29 Stephens, *A History of News*, 66.
30 Sommerville, *The News Revolution in England*, 19.
31 Stephens, *A History of News*, 62

32 Andrews, *The History of British Journalism*, 14

33 Arblaster, 'Posts, newsletters, newspapers'.

34 Whyman, S. 'Postal censorship in England, 1635–1844', http://www.psc.gov.uk/postcomm/live/about-the-mail-market/uk-market-reviews/postalcensorship.pdf.

35 Curran, 'Mass communications as a social force in history'.

36 Ibid.

37 Stephens, *A History of News*, 76.

38 Taylor, P. (1995) *Munitions of the Mind* Manchester: Manchester University Press, 97.

39 Taylor, *Munitions of the Mind*, 98.

40 Curran, 'Communications, power and social order', 217.

41 Lebvre, L. and Martin, H.-J. (1976) *The Coming of the Book* London: Verso, 28.

42 Curran, 'Communications, power and social order', 220

43 See Eisenstein, *The Printing Press and Early Modern Europe*; Lebvre and Martin, *The Coming of the Book*; Steinberg, S.H. (1955) *Five Hundred Years of Printing* Harmondsworth: Penguin.

44 Briggs and Burke, *A Social History of the Media*, 29.

45 Lebvre and Martin, *The Coming of the Book*, 319.

46 Curran, 'Mass communications as a social force in history', 30.

47 Lebvre and Martin, *The Coming of the Book*, 323.

48 Hartley, J., Goulden, H. and O'Sullivan, T. (1985) 'The development of printing', Block Two, Unit Three 'Media Institutions' in *Making Sense of the Media* London: Comedia, 7.

49 Ibid.

50 Curran, 'Mass communications as a social force in history', 29.

51 McLuhan, *The Gutenberg Galaxy*.

52 Altick, R. (1957) *The English Common Reader*, Chicago: Chicago University Press, 26.

53 Hartley *et al.*, 'The development of printing', 7.

54 Williams, R. (1980) *The Long Revolution* Harmondsworth: Penguin, 178.

55 Price, S. (1993) *Media Studies* London: Pitman, 364.

56 Eisenstein, E. (1979) *The Printing Press as an Agent of Social Change* Cambridge: Cambridge University Press, 94.

57 Shaaber, *Some Forerunners of the Newspaper in Britain*, 11.

58 Shaaber, *Some Forerunners of the Newspaper in Britain*, 37.

59 Skeaping, L. (2005) *Broadsheet Ballads* London: Faber Music, 6.

60 Ibid.

61 Shaaber, *Some Forerunners of the Newspaper in Britain*, 194.

62 Shaaber, *Some Forerunners of the Newspaper in Britain*, 195.

63 Shaaber, *Some Forerunners of the Newspaper in Britain*, 192.

64 Stephens, *A History of News*, Chapter 7.

65 Quoted in Stephens, *A History of News*, 116.

66 Shaaber, quoted in Stephens, *A History of News*, 121.

67 Stephens, M. (n.d.) *History of Newspapers*, www.nyu.edu/classes/stephens/Collier%27s%20page.htm.

68 Shaaber, *Some Forerunners of the Newspaper in Britain*, 203.

69 Sommerville, *The News Revolution in England*, 18.

70 Sommerville, *The News Revolution in England*, 19.

71 Clarke, B. (2004) *From Grub Street to Fleet Street*, Aldershot: Ashgate, 14.

72 Cranfield, G. (1978) *The Press and Society* London: Longman, 1.

73 Williams, K. (1998) *Get Me a Murder a Day: A History of Mass Communication in Britain* London: Arnold, 16.

74 Bruce, B. (1992) *Images of Power* London: Kogan Page, 10.

75 Siebert, F. (1965) *Freedom of the Press in England 1476–1776: The Rise and Decline of Government Control* Urbana, IL: University of Illinois Press, 70.

76 Stephens, *A History of News*, 84.

77 Atherton, I. (1999) 'The itch grown a disease: manuscript transmission of news in the seventeenth century' in Raymond, *News, Newspapers and Society in Early Modern Britain*, 40.

78 Winston, *Messages*, 37.

79 Atherton, 'The itch grown a disease', 51.

80 Stephens, *A History of News*, 139.

81 Andrews, *The History of British Journalism*, 12

82 Atherton, 'The itch grown a disease', 53.

83 Steed, H.W. (1938) *The Press* Harmondsworth: Penguin, 108.

84 Ibid.

85 Black, J. (2001) *The English Press 1621–1861* Stroud: Sutton Publishing, 4.

86 Stephens, M. (n.d.) *Highlights of Journalism*, www.nyu.edu/classes/stephens/Parliament%20page.htm.

87 van Sas, N. (2002) 'The Netherlands 1750–1813' in Barker, H. and Burrows, S. (eds) *Press, Politics and the Public Sphere in Europe and North America, 1760–1820* Cambridge University Press, 49.

88 Brownlees, N. (2005) 'Spoken discourse in early English newspapers' *Media History* 11(1/2): 69–85; Lambert, S. (1992) 'Coranto printing in England: the first newsbooks' *Journal of Newspaper and Periodical History* 8(1): 3–19.

89 Lambert, 'Coranto printing in England'.

90 Brownlees, 'Spoken discourse in early English newspapers'.

91 Quoted in Arblaster, 'Posts, newsletters, newspapers', 29.

92 Williams, *The English Newspaper*, 9.

93 Gerard, D. (1982) 'The impact of the first newsmen on Jacobean London' *Journalism Studies Review* 7, July; Snoddy, R. (1993) *The Good, the Bad and the Unacceptable: The Hard News about the British Press* London: Faber & Faber, 21.

94 Smith, 'The long road', 155.

95 Stephens, *A History of News*, 149.

96 Raymond, *The Invention of the Newspaper*, 9.

97 Sommerville, *The News Revolution in England*, 25.

98 Brownlees, 'Spoken discourse in early English newspapers', 75.

99 Quoted in Sommerville, *The News Revolution in England*, 26.

100 Raymond, *The Invention of the Newspaper*, 8.

101 Brownlees, 'Spoken discourse in early English newspapers', 76.

102 Williams, *The English Newspaper*, 9.

103 Sommerville, *The News Revolution in England*, 27.

104 Lambert, 'Coranto printing in England', 12; Sommerville, *The News Revolution in England*, 27.

105 The development of news and its impact on politics is well described and discussed by Richard Cust (1986) 'News and politics in early seventeenth century England' *Past & Present* 112: 60–90.

106 Brownlees, 'Spoken discourse in early English newspapers', 76.

107 Raymond, *The Invention of the Newspaper*, 80.

108 Clarke, *From Grub Street to Fleet Street*, 17.

109 Stephens, *A History of News*, 153.

110 Raymond, *The Invention of the Newspaper*, 20; Clarke, *From Grub Street to Fleet Street*, 17.

111 Harris, 'The structure, ownership and control of the press 1620–1780', 83.

112 This debate is laid out in Raymond, *The Invention of the Newspaper*, Chapter 2.

113 Raymond, *The Invention of the Newspaper*, 20; Stephens, *A History of News*, 153.

114 Mendle, M. (2001) 'News and pamphlet culture of mid-seventeenth century England' in Dooley and Baron, *The Politics of Information*, 63.

115 Quoted in Smith, 'The long road', 155.

116 Clarke, *From Grub Street to Fleet Street*, 20.

117 The publication was misspelled throughout its first run.

118 Briggs and Burke, *A Social History of the Media*, 73–4.
119 Hunt, *The Fourth Estate*, 111.
120 Black, *The English Press*, 5.
121 Quoted in Clarke, *From Grub Street to Fleet Street*, 21.
122 Clarke, *From Grub Street to Fleet Street*, 23.
123 Cranfield, *The Press and Society*, 6, 223.
124 Briggs and Burke, *A Social History of the Media*, 74.
125 Steed, *The Press*, 110.
126 Clarke, *From Grub Street to Fleet Street*, 24.
127 Frank, J. (1961) *The Beginnings of the English Newspaper* Boston, MA: Harvard University Press.
128 Raymond, *The Invention of the Newspaper*, 46.
129 Peachey, J. (2005) 'The struggle for *Mercurius Britanicus*: factional politics and the parliamentarian press, 1643–46' *Huntington Library Quarterly* 68(3): 517–43.
130 Peachey, 'The struggle for *Mercurius Britanicus*', 519.
131 Peachey, 'The struggle for *Mercurius Britanicus*', 541.
132 See Stephens, *A History of News*, Chapter 3.

2 NEWSPAPERS FOR THE FEW

1 Williams, *The English Newspaper*, 19.
2 The statistics in this paragraph are drawn from Harris, M. (1978) 'The structure, ownership and control of the press 1620–1780' in Boyce, Curran and Wingate, *Newspaper History*, 88; circulation estimates are based on stamp returns, which have only survived spasmodically. Hence this is only a rough estimate of the total sales of newspapers in the eighteenth century.
3 Quoted in Barker, *Newspaper, Politics and English Society*, 29.
4 Harris, 'The structure, ownership and control of the press 1620–1780', 97.
5 Black, *The English Press*, 10.
6 Quoted in Barker, *Newspaper, Politics and English Society*, 97.
7 Sutherland, J. (2004) *The Restoration Newspaper and Its Development* Cambridge: Cambridge University Press, 2nd edition.
8 Quoted in Sutherland, *The Restoration Newspaper*, 2
9 Clarke, *From Grub Street to Fleet Street*, 26; Sutherland, *The Restoration Newspaper*, 2.
10 Sutherland, *The Restoration Newspaper*, 3.
11 Williams, J. (1908) *A History of English Journalism to the Foundation of the Gazette* London: Longmans, Green & Co, 187.
12 Clarke, *From Grub Street to Fleet Street*, 26–7.
13 Williams, *The English Newspaper*, 13.
14 The authorities attempted to monitor what was sent through the post, regularly opening, reading, copying and resealing letters; see Whyman, S. 'Postal Censorship in England 1635–1844'.
15 Clarke, *From Grub Street to Fleet Street*, 29.
16 Sutherland, *The Restoration Newspaper*, 131.
17 Williams, *The English Newspaper*, 16.
18 Clarke, *From Grub Street to Fleet Street*, 29.
19 Curran, J. (1977) 'Capitalism and control of the press, 1800–1975' in Curran, J., Gurevitch, M. and Woollacott, J. (eds) *Mass Communication and Society* London: Arnold, 198.
20 Clarke, *From Grub Street to Fleet Street*, 31.
21 Emery, E. and Emery, M. (1984) *The Press and America: An Interpretive History of the Mass Media* Englewood Cliffs, NJ: Prentice-Hall, 5th edition, 12.
22 Rosenberg, M. (1953) 'The rise of England's first daily newspaper' *Journalism Quarterly* XXX (Winter), 3–14.

23 Fox Bourne, *English Newspapers*, 67.

24 Cited in Rosenberg, 'The rise of England's first daily newspaper', 4; Smith, 'The long road ... ', 159.

25 Smith, 'The long road ... ', 159.

26 Griffiths, D. (2006) *Fleet Street: Five Hundred Years of the British Press* London: The British Library, 26.

27 Williams, *The English Newspaper*, 20.

28 Cranfield, *The Press and Society*, 36.

29 Quoted in Conboy, M. (2004) *Journalism: A Critical History* London: Sage, 63.

30 In the various histories of journalism and the press written in the nineteenth century there is a dispute over whether *The Spectator* and other similar publications constituted a 'newspaper'. Andrews, writing in 1859, describes *The Spectator* as a 'series of essays', and not a newspaper as it did not contain news and politics. Fox Bourne states in 1887 that it was 'in no sense a newspaper ... only a varied and instructive series of short essays issued in daily pennyworths' and 'hardly here concerns us'. Hunt in 1850 describes publications such as *The Spectator* and *The Tatler* as 'journals' which 'cannot be described as newspapers'. These writers emphasise the centrality of news and politics in identifying a newspaper in the nineteenth century. However, many of the features of these 'essay papers' came to be incorporated into the press.

31 Griffiths, *Fleet Street*, 32.

32 Cranfield, *The Press and Society*, 37.

33 Brewer, J. (1997) *The Pleasures of the Imagination: English Culture in the Eighteenth Century*, London: HarperCollins, 100.

34 Quoted in Briggs and Burke, *A Social History of the Media*, 59.

35 Brewer, *The Pleasures of the Imagination*, 100.

36 Stephens, *A History of News*, 32.

37 Clarke, *From Grub Street to Fleet Street*, 55.

38 Brewer, *The Pleasures of the Imagination*, 34.

39 Barker, H. (2002) 'England 1760–1815' in Barker, H. and Burrows, S. (eds) *Press, Politics and the Public Sphere in Europe and North America, 1760–1820* Cambridge: Cambridge University Press, 107.

40 Brewer, *The Pleasures of the Imagination*, 35.

41 Quoted in Barker, 'England 1760–1815', 107.

42 Brewer, *The Pleasures of the Imagination*, 36–7.

43 Quoted in Barker, 'England 1760–1815', 107.

44 Black, *The English Press*, 12.

45 Stephens, *A History of News*, 35.

46 Quoted in Clarke, *From Grub Street to Fleet Street*, 45.

47 Brewer, *The Pleasures of the Imagination*, 104.

48 Griffiths, *Fleet Street*, 31.

49 Brewer, *The Pleasures of the Imagination*, 103.

50 Clarke, *From Grub Street to Fleet Street*, 45.

51 Cranfield, *The Press and Society*, 37.

52 Quoted in Williams, *Dangerous Estate*, 31.

53 Brewer, *The Pleasures of the Imagination*, 142.

54 Clarke, *From Grub Street to Fleet Street*, 46.

55 Quoted in Sutherland, *The Restoration Newspaper*, 4.

56 Griffiths, *Fleet Street*, 26; Williams, *Dangerous Estate*, 22; McKay, J. (2007) 'Defoe's The Storm as a model for contemporary reporting' in Keeble, R. and Wheeler, S. (eds) *The Journalistic Imagination: Literary Journalism from Defoe to Capote and Carter* London: Routledge, 24.

57 Marr, A. (2004) *My Trade: A Short History of British Journalism* London: Macmillan, 8.

58 Quoted in Williams, F. (1969) *The Right to Know: The Rise of the World Press* London: Longmans, 28.
59 Black, *The English Press*, 11.
60 Ibid.
61 Sutherland, *The Restoration Newspaper*, 225.
62 Smith, 'The long road ... ', 158.
63 Quoted in Smith, A. (1977) 'The long road to objectivity and back again: the kinds of truth we get in journalism' in Boyce, Curran and Wingate, *Newspaper History*, 159.
64 Marr, *My Trade*, 8.
65 Cited in McKay, J. (2007) 'Defoe's The Storm ... ', 22.
66 McKay, 'Defoe's The Storm ... '
67 Pottker, H. (2004) 'Objectivity as (self-)censorship: against the dogmatism of the professional ethics of journalism', *Public Janvost*, 87.
68 Clarke, *From Grub Street to Fleet Street*, 47.
69 Clarke, *From Grub Street to Fleet Street*, 48.
70 Quoted in Woolf, D. (2001) 'News, history and the construction of the present in early modern England' in Dooley and Baron, *The Politics of Information*, 107.
71 Fox Bourne, *English Newspapers*, 3.
72 Black, *The English Press*, 10.
73 Clarke, *From Grub Street to Fleet Street*, 45.
74 Griffiths, *Fleet Street*, 35.
75 Black, *The English Press*, 10.
76 Curran, 'Mass communication as a social force in history', 38.
77 Clarke, *From Grub Street to Fleet Street*, 49.
78 Black, *The English Press*, 9.
79 Quoted in Griffiths, *Fleet Street*, 36.
80 Harris, 'The structure, ownership and control of the press 1620–1780', 85.
81 Williams, *The English Newspaper*, 25.
82 Quoted in Marr, *My Trade*, 10.
83 Clarke, *From Grub Street to Fleet Street*, 66.
84 Quoted in Barker, 'England 1760–1815', 103.
85 Griffiths, *Fleet Street*, 29.
86 Clarke, *From Grub Street to Fleet Street*, 55.
87 Clarke, *From Grub Street to Fleet Street*, 53–4; Black, *The English Press*, 29–39.
88 Griffiths, *Fleet Street*, 29.
89 Barker, *Newspapers, Politics and English Society*, 98.
90 Ibid.
91 Winston, *Messages*, 73.
92 Harris, 'The structure, ownership and control of the press 1620–1780', 95.
93 Barker, *Newspapers, Politics and English Society*, 83.
94 Harris, B.(1996) *Politics and the Rise of the Press: Britain and France, 1620–1800* London: Routledge, 39.
95 Barker, *Newspapers, Politics and English Society*, 83–4.
96 Winston, *Messages*, 78.
97 Cranfield, *The Press and Society*, 75.
98 Cranfield, *The Press and Society*, 73.
99 Cranfield, *The Press and Society*, 76.
100 Clarke, *From Grub Street to Fleet Street*, 39.
101 Conboy, *Journalism*, 80.
102 Smith, 'The long road ... ', 157.
103 Cranfield, *The Press and Society*, 179.
104 Ibid.

105 Cranfield, G. (1962) *The Development of the Provincial Press, 1700–60* Oxford: Claredon Press, 65.

106 Quoted in Cranfield, *The Press and Society*, 182.

107 Cranfield, *The Press and Society*, 179.

108 Ibid.

109 See Black, *The English Press*; Cranfield, *The Press and Society*.

110 Griffiths, *Fleet Street*, 49.

111 Clarke, *From Grub Street to Fleet Street*, 77.

112 Above all by Harrison, S. (1974) *Poor Men's Guardians: A Survey of the Struggle for a Democratic Newspaper Press, 1763–1973* London: Lawrence & Wishart.

113 Harrison, *Poor Men's Guardians*, 17.

114 Cranfield, *The Press and Society*, 59.

115 Curran, 'Mass communication as a social force in history', 43.

116 Barker, *Newspapers, Politics and English Society*, 151.

117 Curran, 'Mass communication as a social force in history', 43.

118 See Habermas, J. (1989) *The Structural Transformation of the Public Sphere*, 64.

119 Clarke, *From Grub Street to Fleet Street*, 57.

120 Sparrow, A. (2003) *Obscure Scribblers: A History of Parliamentary Journalism* London: Politico's, 8.

121 Clarke, *From Grub Street to Fleet Street*, 91.

122 Barker, *Newspapers, Politics and English Society*, 77.

123 Griffiths, *Fleet Street*, 39.

124 Sparrow, *Obscure Scribblers*, 13.

125 Sparrow, *Obscure Scribblers*, 15.

126 Harris, *Politics and the Rise of the Press*, 41.

127 See Sparrow, *Obscure Scribblers*, Chapter 2; Thomas, P. (1959) 'The beginning of parliamentary reporting in the newspapers, 1768–74' *English Historical Review* 74: 623–36; Thomas, P. (1960) 'John Wilkes and Freedom of the Press' *Bulletin of the Institute of Historical Research* 33: 86–98.

128 Quoted in Black, *The English Press*, 130.

129 Harris, *Politics and the Rise of the Press*, 42.

130 Black, *The English Press*, 132.

131 Harrison, *Poor Men's Guardians*, 23.

3 KNOWLEDGE AND POWER

1 Quoted in Harrison, *Poor Men's Guardians*, 103.

2 Harrison, *Poor Men's Guardians*, 17.

3 Asquith, quoted in Curran and Seaton, *Power without Responsibility*, 4th edition, 7.

4 Hollis, P. (1970) *The Pauper Press* Oxford: Oxford University Press, viii.

5 Curran, J. (1980) 'Advertising as a patronage system' in Christian, H. (ed.) *The Sociology of Journalism and the Press* Keele: Keele University Press.

6 Anderson, P. (1994) *The Printed Image and the Transformation of Popular Culture 1790–1860* Oxford: Claredon Press, 2.

7 Quoted in Anderson, *The Printed Image*, 10.

8 Quoted in Curran, 'Mass communication as a social force in history', 45.

9 Quoted in Hartley *et al.*, 'The development of printing', 10.

10 Quoted in Hall, S. (1982) *Popular Culture*, Block 7, Unit 28, The State and Popular Culture 1, Milton Keynes: The Open University Press, 23.

11 Quoted in Barker, *Newspaper, Politics and English Society*, 52.

12 James, L. (1978) *Print and the People 1819–1851* London: Peregrine, 19; see also Davies, O. (1998) 'Newspapers and popular belief in witchcraft and magic in the modern period' *Journal of British Studies* 37(2): 139–65.

13 Hall, *Popular Culture*, 23.
14 Barker, *Newspaper, Politics and English Society*, 53.
15 Altick, *The English Common Reader*, 6.
16 James, *Print and the People*, 18.
17 Altick, *The English Common Reader*, 5.
18 Webb, R. (1955) *The British Working Class Reader 1790–1848* London: Allen & Unwin, 6–18.
19 Webb, *The British Working Class Reader*, 23.
20 James, *Print and the People*, 18.
21 Barker, *Newspaper, Politics and English Society*, 51; Webb, *The British Working Class Reader*, 13.
22 Hartley *et al.*, 'The development of printing', 11.
23 Barker, *Newspaper, Politics and English Society*, 54–5.
24 Webb, *The British Working Class Reader*, 14.
25 Webb, *The British Working Class Reader*, 18.
26 Webb, *The British Working Class Reader*, 24.
27 Hannah More, quoted in Donald, J. (1981) 'Language, literacy and schooling' in *Popular Culture*, Open University course Block 7, Unit 29 Milton Keynes: Open University Press, 51.
28 James, *Print and the People*, 29.
29 James, *Print and the People*, 32.
30 Jones, *Power of the Press: Newspapers*, 105.
31 Hollis, *The Pauper Press*, 139.
32 Fox, C. (1978) 'Political caricature and the freedom of the press in early nineteenth century England' in Boyce, Curran, and Wingate, *Newspaper History*, 227.
33 Quoted in Barker, *Newspaper, Politics and English Society*, 21.
34 Quoted in Anderson, *The Printed Image*, 53.
35 Anderson, *The Printed Image*, 52.
36 See Mountjoy, P. (1977) 'The working-class press and working-class conservatism' in Boyce, Curran, and Wingate, *Newspaper History*, 267.
37 For a comprehensive discussion of the unstamped press and the campaign to repeal the taxes on knowledge, see Weiner, J. (1969) *The War of the Unstamped: The Movement to Repeal the British Newspaper Tax 1830–1836* Cornell: Cornell University Press.
38 Barker, *Newspaper, Politics and English Society*, 95.
39 Quoted in Clarke, *From Grub Street to Fleet Street*, 99.
40 Smith, 'The long road ... ', 166.
41 Clarke, *From Grub Street to Fleet Street*, 100.
42 Cranfield, *The Press and Society*, 86.
43 Williams, *Dangerous Estate*, 92.
44 James, *Print and the People*, 42.
45 Cited in Cranfield, *The Press and Society*, 86.
46 Cranfield, *The Press and Society*, 86.
47 Barker, *Newspaper, Politics and English Society*, 34.
48 Cranfield, *The Press and Society*, 111.
49 Cited in Chibnall, S. (1980) 'Chronicles of the gallows: the social history of crime reporting' in Christian, *The Sociology of Journalism and the Press*, 199.
50 Cranfield, *The Press and Society*, 152.
51 Clarke, *From Grub Street to Fleet Street*, 227.
52 Clarke, *From Grub Street to Fleet Street*, 228.
53 Details of composition of *The Times* drawn from Clarke, *From Grub Street to Fleet Street*, 228.
54 Clarke, *From Grub Street to Fleet Street*, 227.
55 Harrison, *Poor Men's Guardians*, 28.
56 Curran, 'Capitalism and control of the press', 203.

57 Williams, 'Radical and/or respectable', 17.
58 Harrison, *Poor Men's Guardians*, 38.
59 Cranfield, *The Press and Society*, 91.
60 Williams, *Dangerous Estate*, 65.
61 Ibid.
62 Griffiths, *Fleet Street*, 79.
63 Quoted in Herd, H. (1951) *The March of Journalism* London: George Allen & Unwin, 22.
64 Cranfield, *The Press and Society*, 96.
65 Harrison, *Poor Men's Guardians*, 61.
66 Ibid.
67 James, *Print and the People*, 36.
68 Hollis, *The Pauper Press*, 123.
69 Wilson, C. (1985) *First with the News: The History of W.H. Smith 1792–1972* London: Guild Publishing.
70 Hollis, *The Pauper Press*, 121.
71 Ibid.
72 Quoted in Hollis, *The Pauper Press*, 122.
73 Griffiths, *Fleet Street*, 108; Rose, J. (1897) 'The unstamped press 1815–36' *English Historical Review* 12(48), October: 711–26.
74 Anderson, *The Printed Image*, 25.
75 James, *Print and the People*, 25.
76 Ibid.
77 Anderson, *The Printed Image*, 17.
78 Allen, J. and Ashton, O. (2005) *Papers for the People: A Study of the Chartist Press* London: Merlin Press, 1.
79 Yelland, C. (2003) 'Speech and writing in the *Northern Star*' in Roberts, S. (ed.) *The People's Charter: Democratic Agitation in Early Victorian Britain*, cited in Jones, A. (2005) 'Chartist journalism and print culture in Britain, 1830–55' in Allen and Ashton, *Papers for the People*, 2.
80 Cranfield, *The Press and Society*, 195.
81 Quoted in Herd, *The March of Journalism*, 149.
82 Quoted in Cranfield, *The Press and Society*, 194.
83 Chase, M. (2005) 'Building identity, building circulation: engraved portraiture and the *Northern Star*' in Allen and Ashton, *Papers for the People*, 25–54.
84 Harrison, *Poor Men's Guardians*, 123.
85 Cranfield, *The Press and Society*, 196.
86 Barker, *Newspaper, Politics and English Society*, 215.
87 Curran, 'Capitalism and control of the press', 207.
88 Curran, 'Capitalism and control of the press', 206–7.
89 Ibid.
90 Curran, 'The press as an agency of social control', 63.
91 Curran, 'Capitalism and control of the press', 210.
92 Asquith, I. (1978) 'The structure, ownership and control of the press 1780–1855' in Boyce, Curran, and Wingate, *Newspaper History*, 112.
93 Curran, 'The press as an agency of social control'. While this book subscribes to Curran's interpretation of the development of the press, and his argument that the market reforms of the mid-nineteenth century led to the integration of newspapers into the established power structure of British society, it is important to stress that this interpretation is disputed by other historians of the press, for example Stephen Koss (1991) *The Rise and Fall of the Political Press in Britain* London: Fontana.
94 Curran 'The press as an agency of social control', 55.
95 Ibid.

96 Curran and Seaton, *Power without Responsibility*, 4th edition, 29.
97 Curran, 'Capitalism and control of the press', 211.
98 Curran, 'The press as an agency of social control', 61.
99 Curran, 'The press as an agency of social control', 63.
100 Mountjoy, 'The working-class press ... ', 280.
101 Mountjoy, 'The working-class press ... ', 274.
102 Mountjoy, 'The working-class press ... ', 280.
103 Mackenzie, J. (1984) *Propaganda and Empire: The Manipulation of British Public Opinion 1880–1960* Manchester: Manchester University Press, 254.
104 Quoted in Harrison, *Poor Men's Guardians*, 158.
105 Curran, 'Capitalism and control of the press', 218.
106 Curran, 'Capitalism and control of the press', 221.

4 TRANSITION TO DEMOCRACY

1 This article is also attributed to Henry Reeve, the editor of the *Edinburgh Review* in which it was written. Reproduced in quoted in King, A. and Plunkett, J. (2005) *Victorian Print Media: A Reader* Oxford: Oxford University Press, 44–7.
2 Tulloch, 'The eternal recurrence of new journalism', 139.
3 Smith, *The Newspaper*, 126.
4 Boyce, D.G. (1978) 'The Fourth Estate: a reappraisal of a concept' in Boyce, Curran and Wingate, *Newspaper History*, 21.
5 Hampton, M. (2001) 'Understanding media: theories of the press in Britain 1850–1914' *Media, Culture & Society* 23: 217.
6 Morison, *The English Newspaper*, 279.
7 Hoyer, S. and Pottker, H. (eds) (2005) *Diffusion of the News Paradigm 1850–2000* Goteborg: Nordicom.
8 Lord Chancellor, 1834, quoted in Curran and Seaton, *Power without Responsibility*, 6th edition, 18.
9 Lee, A. (1976) *The Origins of the Popular Press 1855–1914* London: Croom Helm, 53–4; Lee 'The structure, ownership and control ...' , 117.
10 Griffiths, *Fleet Street*, 96.
11 Cranfield, *The Press and Society*, 206.
12 Cranfield, *The Press and Society*, 207.
13 Smith, *The Newspaper*, 122.
14 Quoted in Griffiths, *Fleet Street*, 98.
15 Smith, *The Newspaper*, 123.
16 Herd, *The March of Journalism*, 164.
17 Griffiths, *Fleet Street*, 98; Fyfe, *Sixty Years of Fleet Street*, 14; Herd, *The March of Journalism*, 164.
18 Herd, *The March of Journalism*, 164.
19 Hatton, J. (1998/1882) *Journalistic London* London: Routledge/Thoemmes Press, 118.
20 Interview in Hatton, *Journalistic London*, 115.
21 Fyfe, H. (1949) *Sixty Years of Fleet Street* London: W.H. Allen, 10.
22 Fyfe, *Sixty Years of Fleet Street*, 11.
23 Smith, 'The long road ... ', 161.
24 Smith, 'The long road ... ', 162.
25 Clarke, *From Grub Street to Fleet Street*, 255.
26 Sparrow, *Obscure Scribblers*, 27.
27 Sparrow, *Obscure Scribblers*, 30.
28 Clarke, *From Grub Street to Fleet Street*, 255.
29 Sparrow, *Obscure Scribblers*, 52.

30 Clarke, *From Grub Street to Fleet Street*, 255.

31 Clarke, *From Grub Street to Fleet Street*, 256.

32 Sparrow, *Obscure Scribblers*, 55; Cockerell, M., Hennessey, P. and Walker, D. (1988) *Sources Close to the Prime Minister: Inside the World of the Hidden Manipulators* London: Macmillan, 35.

33 Fyfe, *Sixty Years of Fleet Street*, 12.

34 Quoted in Bingham, A. (2005) 'Monitoring the Popular Press: a historical perspective', www.historyandpolicy.org/papers/policy-paper-27.html.

35 Quoted in Fyfe, *Sixty Years of Fleet Street*, 12.

36 Cockerell *et al.*, *Sources Close* ... , 6.

37 Cockerell *et al.*, *Sources Close* ... , 34.

38 Lee, *The Origins of the Popular Press*, 101.

39 Chapman, J. (1855) 'The London daily press' *Westminster Review* October, 492–521, reproduced in King and Plunkett (2005) *Victorian Print Media: A Reader*, 350–2.

40 Clarke, *From Grub Street to Fleet Street*, 230.

41 Cranfield, *The Press and Society*, 153.

42 Clarke, *From Grub Street to Fleet Street*, 230.

43 Steed, *The Press*, 75.

44 Knightley, P. (2003) *The First Casualty: The War Correspondent as Hero, Propagandist and Myth Maker from Crimea to Iraq* London: Andre Deutsch, Chapter 1.

45 Knightley, *The First Casualty*, 7.

46 Knightley, *The First Casualty*, 11.

47 Quoted in Clarke, *From Grub Street to Fleet Street*, 232.

48 Knightley, *The First Casualty*, 6.

49 Quoted in Clarke, *From Grub Street to Fleet Street*, 232.

50 Koss, *The Rise and Fall of the Political Press*, 413.

51 Quoted in Cranfield, *The Press and Society*, 155.

52 Cranfield, *The Press and Society*, 154.

53 Williams, *Dangerous Estate*, 84.

54 Williams, *Dangerous Estate*, 85.

55 Williams, *Dangerous Estate*, 89.

56 Griffiths, *Fleet Street*, 93.

57 Williams, *Dangerous Estate*, 81.

58 Williams, *Dangerous Estate*, 83.

59 Clarke, *From Grub Street to Fleet Street*, 241.

60 Smith, *The Newspaper*, 154.

61 Lee, A. (1973) 'Franklin Thomasson and the Tribune: a case-study in the history of the liberal press, 1906–8' *Historical Journal* 16(2): 342.

62 Conboy, *Journalism*, 126.

63 Herd, *The March of Journalism*, 134.

64 'Newspaper anonymity', *New York Times*, 26 May 1905.

65 Tunstall, 'Editorial sovereignty', 264.

66 Tunstall, 'Editorial sovereignty', 265.

67 Ibid.

68 Baistow, T. (1985) *Fourth Rate Estate: An Anatomy of Fleet Street* London: Comedia, 5.

69 Tunstall, 'Editorial sovereignty', 263.

70 Tunstall, 'Editorial sovereignty', 267.

71 Tunstall, 'Editorial sovereignty', 260.

72 Hampton, *Visions of the Press*, 135.

73 Brown, L. (1977) 'The treatment of news in mid-Victorian newspapers' *Transactions of the Royal Historical Society* Fifth Series 27, 25.

74 Brown, 'The treatment of news in mid-Victorian newspapers', 24.

75 For a detailed discussion of the relationship between the press and politics in this period, see Lee, *The Origins of the Popular Press*, Chapters 5 and 6.

76 Fyfe, *Sixty Years of Fleet Street*, 12.

77 Brown, 'The treatment of news in mid-Victorian newspapers', 29.

78 Brown, 'The treatment of news in mid-Victorian newspapers', 26.

79 Quoted in Morus, I. (2000) '"The nervous system of Britain": space, time and the electric telegraph in the Victorian age' *British Journal for the History of Science* 33(4): 459.

80 Palmer, M. (1977) 'The British press and international news, 1851–99: of agencies and newspaper' in Boyce, Curran and Wingate *Newspaper History*, 206. A detailed discussion of the history of Reuters is found in Read, D. (1992) *The Power of News: A History of Reuters* Oxford: Oxford University Press.

81 Brown, 'The treatment of news in mid-Victorian newspapers', 27.

82 Griffiths, *Fleet Street*, 122.

83 Palmer, 'The British press and international news ... ', 207.

84 Quoted in Hampton, *Visions of the Press*, 78.

85 Brown, 'The treatment of news in mid-Victorian newspapers', 33.

86 Brown, 'The treatment of news in mid-Victorian newspapers', 29.

87 Quoted in Palmer, 'The British press and international news ... ', 208.

88 Ibid.

89 Quoted in Knightley, *The First Casualty*, 47.

90 Knightley, *The First Casualty*, 47, 51.

91 Brown, 'The treatment of news in mid-Victorian newspapers', 37.

92 Chapman, 'The London daily press', 351.

93 Walker, 'The development of the provincial press in England', 377.

94 Lee, *The Origins of the Popular Press*, 69.

95 Clarke, *From Grub Street to Fleet Street*, 129.

96 Lee, *The Origins of the Popular Press*, 68.

97 Walker, 'The development of the provincial press in England', 379.

98 Ibid. For fuller discussion of the political economy of the provincial press in this period, see Lee, *The Origins of the Popular Press*, Chapter 5.

99 Lee, 'The structure, ownership and control ... ', 119.

100 Herd, *The March of Journalism*, 180.

101 Griffiths, *Fleet Street*, 385.

102 Herd, *The March of Journalism*, 181.

103 Lee, 'The structure, ownership and control ... ', 119.

104 Clarke, *From Grub Street to Fleet Street*, 128.

105 Walker, 'The development of the provincial press in England', 382.

106 Quoted in Herd, *The March of Journalism*, 184.

107 Griffiths, *Fleet Street*, 105.

108 Berridge, 'Popular Sunday newspapers and mid Victorian society', 257.

109 Ibid.

110 Griffiths, *Fleet Street*, 114.

111 Coulling, S. (1961) 'Matthew Arnold and the *Daily Telegraph*' *Review of English Studies* 12 (46), May: 173–9.

112 Clarke, *From Grub Street to Fleet Street*, 258.

113 Clarke, *From Grub Street to Fleet Street*, 259. For a discussion of Stead's earlier campaigning journalism in the provincial press, see Goldsworthy, S. (2006) 'English non-conformity and the pioneering of the modern newspaper campaign, including the strange case of W.T. Stead and the Bulgarian horrors' *Journalism Studies* 7(3): 387–402.

114 Cranfield, *The Press and Society*, 212.

115 Quoted in Cranfield, *The Press and Society*, 213.

116 Herd, *The March of Journalism*, 230.

117 Stead, W.T. (1886) 'Government by journalism' *Contemporary Review*, 653–74.

118 Herd, *The March of Journalism*, 228.

119 Hoyer, S. (2005) 'Old and new journalism in the London press. The 1880s and 1890s' in Hoyer and Pottker, *Diffusion of the News Paradigm*, 68.

120 Ibid.

121 Cranfield, *The Press and Society*, 215.

122 Herd, *The March of Journalism*, 225.

123 Boyce, 'The Fourth Estate ... ', 36.

124 Clarke, *From Grub Street to Fleet Street*, 263.

125 Griffiths, *Fleet Street*, 125.

126 Engel, M. (1999) *Tickle the Public: One Hundred Years of the Popular Press*, London: Victor Gollancz, 45.

127 Conboy, *The Press and Popular Culture*, 100.

128 Williams, *Dangerous Estate*, 117.

129 Conboy, *The Press and Popular Culture*, 100.

130 Williams, *Dangerous Estate*, 117.

5 THE NORTHCLIFFE REVOLUTION

1 Quoted in Jackson, K. (2000) 'George Newnes and the "loyal Tit-Bitites": editorial integrity and textual interaction in *Tit-Bits*' in Brake, Bell and Finkelstein, *Nineteenth Century Media and the Construction of Identities*, 11. For a more detailed discussion of Newnes, his magazines and their relationship with British journalism, see Jackson, K. (2001) *George Newnes and the New Journalism in Britain, 1880–1910: Culture and Profit* Aldershot: Ashgate.

2 Weiner, J. (1988) *Papers for the Millions: The New Journalism in Britain 1850s to 1914* New York: Greenwood Press, 4.

3 Variously described as 'rupture', 'paradigmatic shift' and 'revolution' – see Chalaby, J. (1998) *The Invention of Journalism* London: Macmillan; Hoyer and Pottker, *Diffusion of the News Paradigm*; Conboy, M. (2002) *The Press and Popular Culture* London: Sage.

4 Engel, 52.

5 Curran and Seaton, *Power without Responsibility*, 51.

6 Brendon, P. (1982) *The Life & Death of the Press Barons* London: Secker & Warburg, 116.

7 Herd, *The March of Journalism*, 241.

8 Le Mahieu, D.L. (1988) *A Culture for Democracy: Mass Communication and the Cultivated Mind in Britain Between the Wars* Oxford: Oxford University Press, 20.

9 Quoted in Brendon, *The Life & Death of the Press Barons*, 111.

10 Quoted in Fyfe, *Sixty Years of Fleet Street*, 76.

11 From now on referred to as Lord Northcliffe.

12 Taylor, S. (1996) *The Great Outsiders: Northcliffe, Rothermere and the Daily Mail* London: Weidenfeld & Nicholson, 11.

13 Taylor, *The Great Outsiders*, 13.

14 Jenkins, *Newspapers*, 19.

15 Griffiths, *Fleet Street*, 119.

16 Ibid.

17 Taylor, *The Great Outsiders*, 15.

18 Engel, *Tickle the Public*, 54; Taylor, *The Great Outsiders*, 16.

19 Clarke, *From Grub Street to Fleet Street*, 263.

20 Griffiths, *Fleet Street*, 127.

21 Taylor, *The Great Outsiders*, 27.

22 Taylor, *The Great Outsiders*, 28.

23 Herd, *The March of Journalism*, 239.

24 Williams, *The English Newspaper*, 75.

25 Quoted in Herd, *The March of Journalism*, 239.

26 Engel, *Tickle the Public*, 60.

27 Quoted in Engel, *Tickle the Public*, 63.

28 Engel, *Tickle the Public*, 63.

29 Herd, *The March of Journalism*, 241.

30 Herd, *The March of Journalism*, 240.

31 Engel, *Tickle the Public*, 64.

32 Jeffrey, T. and McClelland, K. (1987) 'A world fit to live in: the Daily Mail and the middle classes 1918–39' in Curran, J., Smith, A. and Wingate, P. (eds) *Impacts and Influences* London: Methuen.

33 Griffiths, *Fleet Street*, 153.

34 Fyfe, *Sixty Years of Fleet Street*, 95.

35 Griffiths, *Fleet Street*, 121.

36 Chisholm, A. and Davie, M. (1993) *Lord Beaverbrook: A Life* New York: Alfred Knopf, 211.

37 Chisholm and Davie, *Lord Beaverbrook*, 209.

38 Quoted in Koss, *The Rise and Fall of the Political Press*, 447.

39 Chisholm and Davie, *Lord Beaverbrook*, 212.

40 Conboy, *The Press and Popular Culture*, 108.

41 Chisholm and Davie, *Lord Beaverbrook*, 211.

42 Taylor, A.J.P (1974) *Beaverbrook*, Harmsondworth: Penguin, 9.

43 Ibid.

44 Brendon, *The Life & Death of the Press Barons*, 161.

45 Taylor, *The Great Outsiders*, 136–8.

46 Engel, *Tickle the Public*, 148.

47 Bourne, R. (1990) *Lords of Fleet Street: The Harmsworth Dynasty* London: Unwin & Hyman, 33.

48 Williams, *Dangerous Estate*, 194.

49 Fyfe, *Sixty Years of Fleet Street*, 114.

50 Griffiths, *Fleet Street*, 145.

51 Engel, *Tickle the Public*, 153; Griffiths, *Fleet Street*, 145.

52 Herd, *The March of Journalism*, 262.

53 Wright, J. (2003) 'The myth in the Mirror' *British Journalism Review* 14(3): 59–66.

54 Engel, *Tickle the Public*, 151.

55 Fyfe, H. (1935) *My Seven Selves* London: Allen & Unwin.

56 Engel, *Tickle the Public*, 151.

57 Twaites, P. (2000) 'Circles of confusion and sharp vision: British news photography, 1919–39' in Catterall, Seymour-Ure and Smith, *Northcliffe's Legacy*.

58 Quoted in Fyfe, *Sixty Years of Fleet Street*, 119.

59 Murdock and Golding, 'The structure, ownership and control of the press, 1914–76', 130.

60 Bourne, *Lords of Fleet Street*, 85.

61 Murdock and Golding, 'The structure, ownership and control of the press, 1914–76', 130.

62 Williams, *Dangerous Estate*, 151.

63 Engel, *Tickle the Public*, 76.

64 Taylor, *The Great Outsiders*, 78.

65 Chalaby, J. (1997) 'No ordinary press owners: press barons as a Weberian ideal type' *Media, Culture & Society* 19: 621–41.

66 Chalaby, 'No ordinary press owners … ', 633.

67 Lee, 'The structure, ownership and control of the press 1855–1914', 131.

68 Murdock and Golding, 'The structure, ownership and control of the press 1914–76', 132.

69 Smith, *The Newspaper*, 154.

70 Gliddon, P. (2003) 'The political importance of provincial newspapers 1903–45: the Rowntrees and the liberal press' *Twentieth Century British History* 14(1): 24–42.

71 Walker, 'The development of the provincial press in England', 384.

72 Morgan, K. (2002) 'The Boer War and the media (1899–1902)' *Twentieth Century British History* 13(1): 8.

73 Knightley, *The First Casualty*.

74 Morgan, 'The Boer War and the media', 1.

75 Knightley, *The First Casualty*, 68.

76 Morgan, 'The Boer War and the media', 9.

77 Kaul, C. (2000) 'Popular press and Empire: Northcliffe, India and the *Daily Mail*, 1896–1922' in Catterall, Seymour-Ure and Smith, *Northcliffe's Legacy*, 46.

78 Morgan, 'The Boer War and the media', 11.

79 Chalaby, 'No ordinary press owners … '

80 LeMahieu, *A Culture for Democracy*, 12.

81 Chalaby, 'No ordinary press owners … ', 627.

82 Fyfe, *Sixty Years of Fleet Street*.

83 Boyce, D. (1987) 'Crusaders without chains: power and the press barons' in Curran, J., Smith, A. and Wingate, P. (eds) *Impacts and Influences* London: Methuen, 100.

84 For a discussion, see McEwen, J. (1978) 'The press and the fall of Asquith' *Historical Journal* 21(4): 863–83; McEwen, J. (1981) 'Northcliffe and Lloyd George at War, 1914–18' *Historical Journal* 24 (3): 651–72.

85 Boyce, 'Crusaders without chains … ', 101.

86 Ramsay McDonald, quoted in Lee, *The Origins of the Popular Press*, 217.

87 Curran, J. (2000) 'Press reformism 1918–98: a study of failure' in Tumber, H. (ed.) *Media Power, Professionals and Policies* London: Routledge, 38.

88 Quoted in Tulloch, 'The eternal recurrence of new journalism', 135.

89 Tulloch, 'The eternal recurrence of new journalism', 135.

90 Lee, 'The structure, ownership and control of the press 1855–1914', 124.

91 Catterall, Seymour-Ure and Smith, *Northcliffe's Legacy*, 11.

92 Lee, *The Origins of the Popular Press*, 293.

93 Ibid.

94 Lee, 'The structure, ownership and control of the press 1855–1914', 126.

95 LeMahieu, *A Culture for Democracy*, 11.

96 Engel, *Tickle the Public*, 62.

97 Curran, 'Advertising as a patronage system'.

98 Engel, *Tickle the Public*, 63.

99 Curran, 'Advertising as a patronage system', 79.

100 Dibblee, *The Newspaper*, 200.

101 Quoted in Tulloch, 'The eternal recurrence of new journalism', 141.

102 Tulloch, 'The eternal recurrence of new journalism', 142.

103 Chalaby, J. (2000) 'Northcliffe: proprietor as journalist', in Catterall, Seymour-Ure and Smith, *Northcliffe's Legacy*, 30.

104 Northcliffe, quoted in Chalaby, 'Northcliffe: proprietor as journalist', 29.

105 Kaul, 'Popular press and Empire', 49.

106 Ibid.

107 Chalaby, 'Northcliffe: proprietor as journalist', 36.

108 Chalaby, 'Northcliffe: proprietor as journalist', 34.

109 Chalaby, 'Northcliffe: proprietor as journalist', 31

110 Ibid.

111 Ibid.

112 LeMahieu, *A Culture for Democracy*, 19.

113 Stubbs, 'Appearance and reality', 326–7.
114 LeMahieu, *A Culture for Democracy*, 19.
115 Mansfield, *The Complete Journalist*, 30.
116 Chalaby, 'Northcliffe: proprietor as journalist', 31.
117 Chalaby, 'Northcliffe: proprietor as journalist', 33.
118 Ibid.
119 Chalaby, 'Northcliffe: proprietor as journalist', 35.
120 LeMahieu, *A Culture for Democracy*, 67.
121 Ibid.
122 LeMahieu, *A Culture for Democracy*, 69.
123 Fyfe, quoted in LeMahieu, *A Culture for Democracy*, 68.
124 LeMahieu, *A Culture for Democracy*, 68.
125 Williams, *The English Newspaper*, 79.
126 LeMahieu, *A Culture for Democracy*, 73.
127 Seymour-Ure, C. (1975) 'How special are cartoonists?' *20th Century Studies*, 13/14, December: 8.
128 Fox, C. (1978) 'Political caricature and the freedom of the press in early nineteenth century Britain' in Boyce, Curran and Wingate, *Newspaper History*.
129 Seymour-Ure, 'How special are cartoonists?', 8–9.
130 LeMahieu, *A Culture for Democracy*, 71.
131 Ibid.
132 LeMahieu, *A Culture for Democracy*, 72.
133 Fyfe, *Sixty Years of Fleet Street*, 147.
134 Fyfe, *Sixty Years of Fleet Street*, 148.
135 Smith, 'The long road ... ', 168.
136 Fyfe, *Sixty Years of Fleet Street*, 154.
137 Steed, *The Press*, 205.
138 Fyfe, *Sixty Years of Fleet Street*, 153.
139 Ibid.
140 Quoted in Griffiths, *Fleet Street*, 132.
141 Chalaby, 'Northcliffe: proprietor as journalist', 33.
142 Koss, *The Rise and Fall of the Political Press*, 690.
143 Morris, A.J.A (1984) *The Scaremongers: The Advocacy of War and Rearmament 1896–1914* London: Routledge & Kegan Paul.

6 NEWSPAPER WARS

1 Quoted in Engel, *Tickle the Public*, 106.
2 Quoted in Bromley, M. (1999) 'Was it the Mirror wot won it? The development of the tabloid press during the Second World War' in Hayes, N. and Hill, J. (eds) *Millions Like Us: British Culture in the Second World War* Liverpool: Liverpool University Press, 95.
3 Stevenson, J. and Cook, C. (1977) *The Slump* London, Quartet Books.
4 Quoted in Stevenson and Cook, *The Slump*, 3.
5 Whitaker, B. (1981) *News Ltd.: Why You Can't Read All About It* London: Comedia, 68.
6 Curran, J., Douglas, A. and Whannel, G. (1981) 'The political economy of the human interest story' in Smith, A. (ed.) *Newspapers and Democracy* Cambridge, MA: MIT Press.
7 Cockett, R. (1989) *Twilight of Truth: Chamberlain, Appeasement and the Manipulation of the Press* London: Weidenfeld & Nicholson.
8 Williams, *Dangerous Estate*, 234.
9 Lunn, K. (1992) 'Reconsidering Britishness: the construction and significance of national identity in twentieth century Britain' in Jenkins, B. and Sofos, S. (eds) *Nation and Identity in Contemporary Europe* London: Routledge, 93.

10 Taylor, A.J.P., quoted in Richards, J. (1984) *The Age of the Dream Palace: Cinema and Society 1930–39* London: Routledge, 11.

11 LeMahieu, *A Culture for Democracy*, 69.

12 Nicholas, 'All the news that's fit to broadcast: the popular press versus the BBC, 1922-45' in Catterall, Seymour-Ure and Smith, *Northcliffe's Legacy*.

13 Nicholas, 'All the news', 137.

14 LeMahieu, *A Culture for Democracy*, 23.

15 Murdock, G. and Golding, P. (1978) 'The structure, ownership and control of the press 1914–76' in Boyce, Curran and Wingate, *Newspaper History*, 131.

16 Curran and Seaton, *Power without Responsibility*, 5th edition, 42.

17 Conboy, *The Press and Popular Culture*, 113.

18 Murdock and Golding, 'The structure, ownership and control of the press 1914–76', 130.

19 Richards, *The Bloody Circus*, 2.

20 Murdock and Golding, 'The structure, ownership and control of the press 1914–76', 130.

21 Murdock and Golding, 'The structure, ownership and control of the press 1914–76', 131; Williams, *The Right to Know*, 110.

22 Williams, *Dangerous Estate*, 176.

23 Statistics drawn from Murdock and Golding, 'The structure, ownership and control of the press 1914–76', 131; Williams, *Dangerous Estate*, 173.

24 Murdock and Golding, 'The structure, ownership and control of the press 1914–76', 131; Griffiths, *Fleet Street*, 240; Williams, *Dangerous Estate*, 177.

25 Murdock and Golding, 'The structure, ownership and control of the press 1914–76', 131.

26 Griffiths, *Fleet Street*, 240.

27 Williams, *Dangerous Estate*, 176.

28 Fyfe, *Sixty Years of Fleet Street*, 192.

29 Bromley, 'The development of the tabloid press', 104.

30 Williams, *The Right to Know*, 112.

31 Ibid.

32 Cummings, A.J. (1936) *The Press and a Changing Civilisation* London: Bodley Head, 1.

33 Stevenson, J. (1990) *British Society 1914–45* Harmondsworth, Penguin, 402.

34 Murdock and Golding, 'The structure, ownership and control of the press 1914–76', 134–5.

35 Murdock and Golding, 'The structure, ownership and control of the press 1914–76', 132.

36 Curran, Douglas and Whannel, 'The political economy of the human interest story', 295.

37 Hutt, *The Changing Newspaper*, 107.

38 Quoted in Hutt, *The Changing Newspaper*, 117.

39 Quoted in Griffiths, *Fleet Street*, 246.

40 LeMahieu, *A Culture for Democracy*, 261.

41 Griffiths, *Fleet Street*, 246.

42 LeMahieu, *A Culture for Democracy*, 261.

43 Baistow, *Fourth Rate Estate*, 43.

44 LeMahieu, *A Culture for Democracy*, 261; Hutt, *The Changing Newspaper*, 119–20.

45 LeMahieu, *A Culture for Democracy*, 261.

46 Hutt, *The Changing Newspaper*, 120.

47 LeMahieu, *A Culture for Democracy*, 262.

48 Quoted in Engel, *Tickle the Public*, 133.

49 Steed, *The Press*, 28.

50 Ibid.

51 Quoted in LeMahieu, *A Culture for Democracy*, 256.

52 LeMahieu, *A Culture for Democracy*, 257.

53 Hutt, *The Changing Newspaper*, 112.

54 LeMahieu, *A Culture for Democracy*, 260.

55 LeMahieu, *A Culture for Democracy*, 265.

56 Quoted in LeMahieu, *A Culture for Democracy*, 265.

57 Steed, *The Press*, 28.

58 Steed, *The Press*, 30.

59 Wallas, G. (1948) *Human Nature in Politics* London: Constable & Co.4th edition (first published in 1908).

60 Angell, N. (1922) *The Press and the Organisation of Society* London: Labour Publishing Company, 15.

61 Steed, *The Press*, 30.

62 Carey, J. (1992) *Intellectuals and the Masses* London: Penguin, 7.

63 Curran, Douglas and Whannel, 'The political economy of the human interest story', 295.

64 Fyfe, *Sixty Years of Fleet Street*, 198.

65 Negrine (1989, 71–5) disagrees with the broad conclusion that there was a depoliticisation of the popular newspapers during this period and seeks to stress that readers had access to 'substantial amounts of information about the outside world'.

66 Quoted in Williams, K. (1996) *British Writers and the Media 1930–45* London: Macmillan, 48.

67 Steed, *The Press*, 171.

68 Bromley, 'The development of the tabloid press', 101.

69 Quoted in Bromley, 'The development of the tabloid press', 100.

70 Orwell, G. 'A farthing newspaper' in Orwell, S. and Angus, I. (eds) *The Collected Essays, Journalism and Letters of George Orwell*, vol. 1 London: Penguin, 37.

71 Engel, *Tickle the Public*, 136.

72 C. Day Lewis, cited in Aldgate, A. 'The newsreels, public order and the projection of Britain' in Curran, J., Smith, A. and Wingate, P. (eds) (1987) *Impacts and Influences: Essays on Media Power in the Twentieth Century* London: Methuen, 145.

73 Graves, R. and Hodge, A. (1995 [1940]) *The Long Weekend* London: Abacus, 430.

74 Campion, N. (2008) 'Horoscopes and popular culture' in Franklin, B. (ed.) *Pulling Newspapers Apart* London: Routledge, 255.

75 Graves and Hodge, *The Long Weekend*, 431.

76 Hoyer, S. and Laup, E. (2003) 'The paradoxes of the journalistic profession: an historical perspective' *Nordicom Review* 20: 3–17.

77 Baxendale, J. and Pawling, C. (1996) *Narrating the Thirties: A Decade in the Making: 1930 to the Present* London: Macmillan, 3.

78 Nicholas, 'All the news', 142.

79 Nicholas, 'All the news'.

80 Scannell, P. and Cardiff, D., *A Social History of British Broadcasting* Oxford: Blackwell, 1991, 25.

81 Nicholas, 'All the news', 131.

82 Nicholas, 'All the news', 134.

83 Pegg, M. (1983) *Broadcasting and Society 1918–39* London: Croom Helm, 150.

84 Nicholas, 'All the news', 137.

85 Pegg, *Broadcasting and Society*, 151.

86 Graves and Hodge, *The Long Weekend*, 429.

87 Knightley, *The First Casualty*, Chapter 5.

88 Cockett, *Twilight of Truth*, 14.

89 Engel, *Tickle the Public*, 131; Taylor, A.J.P. (1970) *English History 1914–45* London: Pelican Books, 491.

90 Fyfe, *Sixty Years of Fleet Street*, 201.

91 Cockett, *Twilight of Truth*, 62–3; Griffiths, *Fleet Street*, 256.

92 Seymour-Ure, C. (1974) 'The Times and the appeasement of Hitler' in his book *The Political Impact of the Mass Media*, London: Constable.

93 Cockett, *Twilight of Truth*, 30–1.
94 Cockett, *Twilight of Truth*, 55.
95 Cockett, *Twilight of Truth*, 59.
96 Aldgate, 'The newsreels, public order and the projection of Britain', 147.
97 Williams, *British Writers*, 14.
98 Bromley, 'The Development of the Tabloid Press', 99.
99 Ibid.; Graves and Hodge, *The Long Weekend*, 428.
100 Angell, *The Press and the Organisation of Society*, 22.
101 Thompson, J. (2006) 'Fleet Street colossus: the rise and fall of Northcliffe, 1896–1922' in Schweizer, K. (ed.) *Parliament and the Press* Edinburgh: Edinburgh University Press, 113.
102 Pearson, Cadbury and Northcliffe's ownership of 67 per cent of national daily circulation in 1910 represents the highest degree of concentration of ownership that has ever existed.
103 Boyce, D. 'Crusaders without chains: power and the press barons 1896–1951' in Curran, Smith and Wingate, *Impacts and Influences*, 97.
104 Chalaby, 'No ordinary press owners … ', 635; Murdock and Golding, 'The structure, ownership and control of the press 1914–76', 136.
105 Hart-Davies, Duff (1990) *The House the Berrys Built: Inside the Telegraph 1928–1986* London: Hodder & Stoughton.
106 Chalaby, 'No ordinary press owners … ', 625.
107 Curran and Seaton, *Power without Responsibility*, 44.
108 Curran and Seaton, *Power without Responsibility*, 6th edition, 47.
109 Boyce, 'Crusaders without chains … ', 100.
110 Engel, *Tickle the Public*, 117.
111 Cockett, *Twilight of Truth*, 13, 118–19.
112 Boyce, 'Crusaders without chains … ', 105.
113 Taylor, *Beaverbrook*, 491.
114 Quoted in Boyce, 'Crusaders without chains … ', 99.
115 Both press barons joined the government.
116 Curran and Seaton, *Power without Responsibility*, 6th edition, 47.
117 Ferris, P. (1971) *The House of Northcliffe* London: Weidenfeld and Nicholson, 82.
118 Curran and Seaton, *Power without Responsibility*, 49.
119 Lee, 'The structure, ownership and control of the press 1855–1914', 126.
120 Curran and Seaton, *Power without Responsibility*, 6th edition, 39.
121 Ibid.
122 Bourne, *Lords of Fleet Street*, 96.
123 Bourne, *Lords of Fleet Street*, 97.
124 Curran and Seaton, *Power without Responsibility*, 40.
125 Hirsch, F. and Gordon, D. (1975) *Newspaper Money* London: Hutchinson.
126 Cockett, *Twilight of Truth*, 59.
127 Cockett, *Twilight of Truth*, 60.
128 Graves and Hodge, *The Lost Weekend*, 429.
129 Tulloch, J. (1998) 'Managing the press in a medium-sized European power' in Stephenson, H. and Bromley, M. (eds) *Sex, Lies and Democracy: The Press and the Public* London: Longman, 67. It was not until 1950 that provincial newspapers were allowed to have their own correspondents admitted to the Lobby – they had relied on the PA until then – and the Sundays came in 1961.
130 Sparrow, *Obscure Scribblers*.
131 Sparrow, *Obscure Scribblers*; Cockerell *et al.*, *Sources Close …*
132 Cockett, *Twilight of Truth*, 2.
133 Tulloch, 'Managing the press', 67.
134 Constantine, S. (1986) 'Bringing the Empire alive: the Empire Marketing Board and imperial propaganda' in Mackenzie, J. (ed.) *Imperialism and Popular Culture* Manchester: Manchester University Press, 202, 204.

135 Swann, P. (1983) 'John Grierson and the G.P.O. Film Unit 1933–39' *Historical Journal of Film, Radio and Television* 3(1): 19–34.
136 Taylor, *British Propaganda in the Twentieth Century*, 93.
137 Casey, R. (1939) 'The National Publicity Bureau and British party propaganda' *Public Opinion Quarterly* (October): 624.
138 Casey, 'The National Publicity Bureau', 625.

7 WAR, SOCIAL CHANGE AND RECONSTRUCTION

1 Curran and Seaton, *Power without Responsibility*, 128.
2 Marwick, A. (1982) 'Press, pictures and sound: the Second World War and the British experience' *Daedalus*, Fall: 135–55.
3 See Pronay, N. (1982) 'The news media at war' in Pronay, N. and Spring, D. *Propaganda, Politics and Film 1918–45* London: Macmillan.
4 Tunstall, J. (1983) *The Media in Britain* London: Constable, 80.
5 Ibid. A more detailed discussion of advertising and the post-war press is found in a number of pieces by James Curran: 'The impact of advertising on the British mass media' *Media, Culture & Society* (1981), 3: 43–69; 'Advertising and the press' in Curran, J. (ed.) (1978) *The British Press: A Manifesto* London: Macmillan.
6 For a discussion of the impact of television on the press in this period, see Curran, J. (1970) 'The impact of television on the audience for national newspapers 1945–68' in Tunstall, J. (ed.) *Media Sociology* London: Constable.
7 Marwick, 'Press, pictures and sound', 140.
8 Curran and Seaton, *Power without Responsibility*, 61; Richards, *The Bloody Circus*, 43. For a discussion of the Communist press in the inter-war years, see Ure-Smith, J (1985) 'The Communist press in Britain, 1920–24' *Media, Culture & Society* 7: 169–85, while insight into the *Daily Worker* is provided by Morgan, K. (1996) 'The miracle that failed' *British Journalism Review* 6(3): 48–53.
9 Curran and Seaton, *Power without Responsibility*, 61.
10 Williams, F. (1946) *Press, Parliament and the People* London: William Heinemann, 33–4.
11 Cited in BBC TV (1983) *Trumpets and Typewriters: A History of War Reporting*.
12 Griffiths, *Fleet Street*, 286–7.
13 Griffiths, *Fleet Street*, 291.
14 Griffiths, *Fleet Street*, 289.
15 Williams, *Dangerous Estate*, 178.
16 Curran and Seaton, *Power without Responsibility*, 65.
17 Curran and Seaton, *Power without Responsibility*, 69.
18 Jenkins, S. (1986) *The Market for Glory: Fleet Street Ownership in the 20th Century* London: Faber & Faber, 63.
19 Seymour-Ure, *The British Press and Broadcasting since 1945*.
20 Tunstall, *The Media in Britain*, 82.
21 Tunstall, *The Media in Britain*, 82–3; Seymour-Ure, *The British Press and Broadcasting since 1945*, 16–18.
22 Seymour-Ure, *The British Press and Broadcasting since 1945*, 17.
23 Curran and Seaton, *Power without Responsibility*, 91.
24 O'Malley, T. (1997) 'Labour and the 1947–49 Royal Commission on the Press' in Bromley, M. and O'Malley, T. *Journalism: A Reader* London: Routledge, 139.
25 O'Malley, 'Labour and the 1947–49 Royal Commission ... ', 142.
26 Ibid.
27 O'Malley, 'Labour and the 1947–49 Royal Commission ... ', 136–7.
28 O'Malley, 'Labour and the 1947–49 Royal Commission ... ', 142.
29 O'Malley, 'Labour and the 1947–49 Royal Commission ... ', 150.

30 Ibid.
31 Seymour-Ure, *The British Press and Broadcasting since 1945*, 257.
32 Ibid.
33 Ibid.
34 Tunstall, *Newspaper Power*, 184.
35 Ibid.
36 Curran, 'The impact of advertising on the British mass media', 47
37 Seymour-Ure, *The British Press and Broadcasting since 1945*, 142.
38 Curran, 'The impact of advertising on the British mass media', 49.
39 Seymour-Ure, *The British Press and Broadcasting since 1945*, 54.
40 Ibid.
41 Seymour-Ure, *The British Press and Broadcasting since 1945*, 27.
42 Williams, *The Right to Know*, 116.
43 Cudlipp, H. (1997) 'The godfather of the British tabloids' *British Journalism Review* 8(2): 32–44.
44 Williams, *Dangerous Estate*, 195.
45 Engel, *Tickle the Public*, 158.
46 Greenslade, *Press Gang*, 88.
47 Edelman, M. (1966) *The Mirror: A Political History* London: Hamish Hamilton, 45.
48 Conboy, *The Press and Popular Culture*, 127.
49 Conboy, *The Press and Popular Culture*, 128.
50 Edelman, *The Mirror*.
51 Smith, A.C.H. (1975) *Paper Voices: The Popular Press and Social Change 1935–1965* London: Chatto and Windus, 62.
52 Smith, *Paper Voices*, 63.
53 Edelman, *The Mirror*, 42.
54 Edelman, *The Mirror*, 111.
55 Quoted in Edelman, *The Mirror*, 114.
56 Bromley, 'Was it the Mirror wot won it?'
57 Bromley, 'Was it the Mirror wot won it?', 114
58 Quoted in Bromley, 'Was it the Mirror wot won it?', 104.
59 Ibid.
60 Richards, *The Bloody Circus*, 161; Smith, *Paper Voices*, 72.
61 Engel, *Tickle the Public*, 170.
62 Quoted in Edelman, *The Mirror*, 142.
63 See Conboy, *The Press and Popular Culture*, 128.
64 Bromley, 'Was it the Mirror wot won it?', 105; Conboy, *The Press and Popular Culture*, 129.
65 Edelman, *The Mirror*, 151.
66 Edelman, *The Mirror*, 149.
67 Richards, *The Bloody Circus*, 162.
68 Engel, *Tickle the Public*, 175.
69 Horrie, C. (2003) *Tabloid Nation: From the Birth of the Daily Mirror to the Death of the Tabloid*, London: Andre Deutsch, 63.
70 Engel, *Tickle the Public*, 179.
71 Ibid.
72 Conboy, *The Press and Popular Culture*, 133.
73 Engel, *Tickle the Public*, 181.
74 Engel, *Tickle the Public*, 200.
75 Engel, *Tickle the Public*, 194.
76 Jenkins, *The Market for Glory*, 112.
77 Murdock and Golding, 'The structure, ownership and control of the press 1914–76', 138.
78 Jenkins, *The Market for Glory*, 113.

79 Murdock and Golding, 'The structure, ownership and control of the press 1914–76', 142.
80 Jenkins, *The Market for Glory*, 113.
81 Jenkins, *The Market for Glory*, 114.
82 Jenkins, *The Market for Glory*, 113.
83 Greenslade, *Press Gang*, 201.
84 Greenslade, *Press Gang*, 202.
85 Jenkins, *The Market for Glory*, 116.
86 Jenkins, *The Market for Glory*, 50.
87 Greenslade, *Press Gang*, 209.
88 Cleverley, G. (1976) *The Great Fleet Street Disaster* London: Constable.
89 Whale, J. (1980) *The Politics of the Media* London: Fontana, 2nd edition, 73.
90 Quoted in Tunstall, *Newspaper Power*, 89.
91 Edelman, *The Mirror*, 164.
92 Jenkins, S. (1979) *Newspapers: The Power and the Money* London: Faber & Faber, 48.
93 Greenslade, *Press Gang*, 246.
94 Jenkins, *Newspapers*, 49.
95 Jenkins, *Newspapers*, 55.
96 Baistow, *Fourth Rate Estate*, 80.
97 Jenkins, *Newspapers*, 49.
98 Jenkins, *Newspapers*, 57.
99 Joe Wade, Secretary-General NGA (1976–84), quoted in Baistow, *Fourth Rate Estate*, 85.
100 Tunstall, *Newspaper Power*, 156.
101 Tunstall, *Newspaper Power*, 157.
102 Tunstall, J. (1971) *Journalists at Work. Specialist Correspondents: Their News Organisations, News Sources & Competitor-colleagues* London: Constable.
103 Marr, *My Trade*, 113.
104 Seymour-Ure, *The British Press and Broadcasting since 1945*, 148.
105 Curran and Seaton, *Power without Responsibility*, 96.
106 Curran, Douglas and Whannel, 'The political economy of the human interest story'.
107 Hirsch and Gordon, *Newspaper Money*, 45; Seymour-Ure, C. (1974) *The Political Impact of the Mass Media* London: Constable, Chapter 8, cited in Murdock and Golding, 'The structure, ownership and control of the press, 1914–76', 147.

8 THE LAND OF THE RISING SUN

1 Quoted in Snoddy, R. (1992) *The Good, the Bad and the Unacceptable* London: Faber & Faber, 121.
2 Horrie, *Tabloid Nation*, 142.
3 Quoted in McLachlan, S. and Golding, P. (2000) 'Tabloidisation in the British press: a quantitative investigation into changes in British newspapers, 1952–97' in Sparks and Tulloch, *Tabloid Tales*, 75.
4 Tunstall, *The Media in Britain*, 87.
5 Franklin and Murphy, *Making the Local News: Local Journalism in Context*, 13.
6 Griffiths, *Fleet Street*, 339.
7 Horrie, *Tabloid Nation*, 117.
8 Horrie, *Tabloid Nation*, 115.
9 Baistow, *Fourth Rate Estate*, 11.
10 Horrie, *Tabloid Nation*, 116.
11 Engel, *Tickle the Public*, 251.
12 Horrie, *Tabloid Nation*, 140.
13 Baistow, *Fourth Rate Estate*, 11.
14 Horrie, *Tabloid Nation*, 141.

15 Lamb, L. (1983) *Sunrise: The Remarkable Rise and Rise of the Best-selling Soaraway Sun* London: Papermac, 64.

16 Baistow, *Fourth Rate Estate*, 42.

17 Horrie, *Tabloid Nation*, 140.

18 Horrie, *Tabloid Nation*, 138.

19 Horrie, *Tabloid Nation*, 40.

20 Horrie, *Tabloid Nation*, 139.

21 Griffiths, *Fleet Street*, 335.

22 Horrie, *Tabloid Nation*, 141.

23 Greenslade, *Press Gang*, 216.

24 Molloy quoted in Engel, *Tickle the Public*, 259.

25 Griffiths, *Fleet Street*, 328.

26 Engel, *Tickle the Public*, 258.

27 Baistow, *Fourth Rate Estate*, 21.

28 Pilger, J. (1998) 'Breaking the Mirror' in his book *Hidden Agendas* London: Vintage, 410–44.

29 Tunstall, *The Media in Britain*, 86.

30 Chester, L. and Fenby, J. (1979) *The Fall of the House of Beaverbrook* London: Andre Deutsch, 13.

31 Jenkins, *The Market for Glory*, 62.

32 Tunstall, *Newspaper Power*, 54.

33 Greenslade, *Press Gang*, 259.

34 Greenslade, *Press Gang*, 262.

35 Griffiths, *Fleet Street*, 350.

36 Baistow, *Fourth Rate Estate*, 29.

37 Quoted in Griffiths, *Fleet Street*, 350.

38 Greenslade, *Press Gang*, 406.

39 Greenslade, *Press Gang*, 405.

40 Seymour-Ure, *The British Press and Broadcasting since 1945*, 266.

41 Seymour-Ure, *The British Press and Broadcasting since 1945*, 265.

42 Greenslade, *Press Gang*, 331.

43 Franklin, *Pulling Newspapers Apart*, 8.

44 Griffiths, *Fleet Street*, 233.

45 Griffiths, *Fleet Street*, 235.

46 Jenkins, *The Market for Glory*, 69.

47 Tunstall, *Newspaper Power*, 53.

48 Seymour-Ure, *The British Press and Broadcasting since 1945*, 28–9.

49 Franklin, *Pulling Newspapers Apart*, 9.

50 Tunstall, *Newspaper Power*, 48.

51 De Burgh, H. (2000) *Investigative Journalism: Context and Practice* London: Routledge, 50–1; Knightley, P. (2005) 'The Thalidomide scandal: where we went wrong?' in Pilger, J. (ed.) *Tell Me No Lies: Investigative Journalism and Its Triumphs* London: Vintage.

52 Melvern, L. (1986) *The End of the Street* London: Methuen, 95.

53 Franklin, *Pulling Newspapers Apart*, 9.

54 Leapman, M. (1983) *Barefaced Cheek: Rupert Murdoch* London: Hodder & Stoughton, 13–14. For detailed accounts of the rise of Rupert Murdoch, see Shawcross, W. (1992) *Rupert Murdoch* London: Chatto & Windus; Wolff, M. (2008) *The Man Who Owns the News: Inside the Secret World of Rupert Murdoch*, London: Bodley Head.

55 Baistow, *Fourth Rate Estate*, 5.

56 Curran and Seaton, *Power without Responsibility*, 85.

57 Murdock and Golding, 'The structure, ownership and control of the press 1914–76', 145.

58 Murdock and Golding, 'The structure, ownership and control of the press 1914–76', 143.

59 Ibid.

60 Tunstall, *Newspaper Power*, 85.

61 Seymour-Ure, *The British Press and Broadcasting since 1945*, 125.

62 Curran and Seaton, *Power without Responsibility*, 82.

63 Curran and Seaton, *Power without Responsibility*, 86.

64 Curran and Seaton, *Power without Responsibility*, 82.

65 Greenslade, *Press Gang*, 505.

66 Quoted in Hargreaves, I. (2003) *Journalism: Truth or Dare* Oxford: Oxford University Press, 13.

67 Rooney, D. (2000) 'Thirty years of competition in the British tabloid press: the *Mirror* and the *Sun* 1968–98' in Sparks and Tulloch, *Tabloid Tales*, 93.

68 Franklin, B. (1997) *Newszak and News Media* London: Arnold, 4.

69 Ward, G. (2007) 'UK national newspapers' in Anderson, P. and Ward, G. (eds) *The Future of Journalism in Advanced Democracies* Aldershot: Ashgate, 83–4.

70 Franklin, *Newszak and News Media*, 98.

71 Greenslade, *Press Gang*, 620; Pilger, 'Breaking the Mirror', 437.

72 Stephenson, H. (1999) 'Tickle the public: consumerism rules' in Stephenson and Bromley *Sex, Lies and Democracy*, 21.

73 For a full discussion, see Thomas, J. (2007) *Popular Newspapers, the Labour Party and the British Press* London: Routledge.

74 Tunstall, *Newspaper Power*, Chapter 15.

75 Tunstall, *Newspaper Power*, 240.

76 See Hollingsworth, M. (1986) *The Press and Political Dissent* London: Pluto Press. Not all the efforts were successful; see, for example, Curran, J. (1987) 'The boomerang effect: the press and the battle for London, 1981–86' in Curran, Smith and Wingate, *Impacts and Influences*, 113–40.

77 Seymour-Ure, *The British Press and Broadcasting since 1945*, 220.

78 Eldridge, J., Kitzinger, J. and Williams, K. (1999) *The Mass Media and Power in Modern Britain* Oxford: Oxford University Press, Chapter 3.

79 Quoted in Tunstall, *Newspaper Power*, 18.

80 Seymour-Ure, *The Press and Broadcasting since 1945*, 22.

81 Baistow, *Fourth Rate Estate*, 90.

82 Stephenson and Bromley, *Sex, Lies and Democracy*, 5.

83 Shawcross, *Rupert Murdoch*, 343.

84 Tunstall, *Newspaper Power*, 22.

85 Greenslade, *Press Gang*, 475.

86 Quoted in Shawcross, *Rupert Murdoch*, 347.

87 Seymour-Ure, *The British Press and Broadcasting since 1945*, 23; Greenslade, *Press Gang*, 477.

88 Greenslade, *Press Gang*, 477.

89 Benton, S. (1987) 'The remarkably rapid death of hope, idealism & £6.5m.' *New Statesman*, 26 June.

90 Chippindale, P. and Horrie, C. (1988) *Disaster: The Story of News on Sunday* London: Sphere.

91 Greenslade, *Press Gang*, 484–5.

92 Greenslade, *Press Gang*, 485.

93 Greenslade, *Press Gang*, 496.

94 Stephenson and Bromley, *Sex, Lies and Democracy*, 5.

95 Franklin and Murphy, *Making the Local News: Local Journalism in Context*, 214.

96 Quoted in Freer, J. (2007) 'UK regional and local newspapers' in Anderson, P. and Ward, G. (eds) *The Future of Journalism in the Advanced Democracies* Aldershot: Ashgate, 91.

97 Aldridge, M. (2007) *Understanding the Local Media* Maidenhead: Open University Press, 34.

98 Seymour-Ure, *The British Press and Broadcasting since 1945*, 52.

99 Aldridge, *Understanding the Local Media*, 27.

100 Franklin, B. (2006) 'A right free for all!: Competition, soundbite journalism and the local free press' in Franklin, *Local Journalism and Local Media*, 153.

101 McNair, B. (1999) *News and Journalism in the UK* London: Routledge, 200.

102 Aldridge, *Understanding the Local Media*, 31–2.

103 Franklin, 'A right free for all!', 151.

104 Aldridge, *Understanding the Local Media*, 31.

105 Cited in Aldridge, *Understanding the Local Media*, 32.

106 Franklin, 'A right free for all!', 152; Aldridge, *Understanding the Local Media*, 32.

107 Quoted in Franklin, 'A right free for all!', 150.

9 THE LONG GOODBYE

1 Murdoch, R. (2006) 'Newspapers will change, not die' *Independent*, 20 March.

2 Tunstall, *Newspaper Power*, Chapter 3.

3 *The Economist* (2006) 'Who killed the newspaper?', 24 August, www.economist.com/opinion/cfm?story_id = 7830218 (accessed 21 February 2008).

4 Murdoch, 'Newspapers will change, not die'.

5 Quoted in Farey-Jones, D. (2008) ' Lords say more regulation is answer to concerns over news provision' *Brand Republic*, 27 June.

6 Greenslade, *Press Gang*, 628; Franklin, *Pulling Newspapers Apart*, 15.

7 Franklin, *Pulling Newspapers Apart*, 18.

8 Davies, N. (2008) *Flat Earth News* London: Chatto & Windus.

9 Cited in Harrison, J. (2004) *News* London: Routledge, 117.

10 Franklin, *Pulling Newspapers Apart*, 13.

11 The figures in this paragraph are drawn from the tables in Franklin, *Pulling Newspapers Apart*, 8–9.

12 Franklin, *Pulling Newspapers Apart*.

13 Franklin, *Pulling Newspapers Apart*, 8–9.

14 Greenslade, *Press Gang*, 629.

15 Greenslade, *Press Gang*, 630.

16 Franklin, *Pulling Newspapers Apart*, 9.

17 Greenslade, *Press Gang*, 625.

18 Franklin, B. (2006) 'Attacking the devil' in Franklin, B. (ed.) *Local Journalism and Local Media: Making the Local News* London: Routledge, 5.

19 Franklin, *Pulling Newspapers Apart*, 9.

20 Brook, S. (2006) 'London paper hits the streets' *Guardian*, 4 September.

21 Hargreaves, I. and Thomas, J. (2002) *New News, Old News* London: ITC and BSC, 5.

22 Greenslade, *Press Gang*, 558.

23 Buckingham, L. (1994) 'Only one winner in the battle of media moguls' *Guardian*, 9 July.

24 Greenslade, *Press Gang*, 559.

25 Griffiths, *Fleet Street*, 396.

26 Griffiths, *Fleet Street*, 390.

27 Griffiths, *Fleet Street*, 392.

28 Horrie, *Tabloid Nation*, 196.

29 Greenslade, *Press Gang*, 564.

30 Ibid.

31 Greenslade, *Press Gang*, 664.

32 Griffiths, *Fleet Street*, 379.

33 Greenslade, *Press Gang*, 665, notes that the *Express on Sunday* had only 26 staff compared to 200 on the *Mail on Sunday*.

34 Greenslade, *Press Gang*, 565.
35 See Marr, *My Trade*, Chapter 4.
36 Marr, *My Trade*, 201.
37 Griffiths, *Fleet Street*, 398.
38 Quoted in Griffiths, *Fleet Street*, 400.
39 Quoted in Griffiths, *Fleet Street*, 401; see also Hastings, M. (2002) *Editor: An Inside Story of Newspapers* London: Pan Books, 350–63.
40 Petley, J. (1997) 'Faces for spaces' in Bromley, M. and O'Malley, T. *Journalism: A Reader* London: Routledge
41 Quoted in McNair, B. (2008) 'I, columnist' in Franklin, *Pulling Newspapers Apart*, 118.
42 Glover, S. (1999) 'What are columnists for?' in Glover, S. (ed.) *Secrets of the Press* London: Allen Lane, 295.
43 Waterhouse, K. (1995) 'Climbing the column' *British Journalism Review* 6(3): 12–15.
44 Watkins, A. (2005) 'Called to the bar' *British Journalism Review* 16 (2): 37–4. For a detailed discussion of the political columnists, see Duff, A. (2008) 'Powers in the land? British political columnists in the information era' *Journalism Practice* 2(2): 230–44.
45 Tunstall, *Newspaper Power*, 155.
46 Tunstall, *Newspaper Power*, 166.
47 Franklin, *Pulling Newspapers Apart*, 11.
48 Tunstall, *Newspaper Power*, 164.
49 Brett, N. and Holmes, T. (2008) 'Supplements' in Franklin, *Pulling Newspapers Apart*, 201.
50 Sampson, A. (1996) 'The crisis at the heart of our media' *British Journalism Review* 7(3): 45.
51 Brett and Holmes, 'Supplements', 199.
52 Much of this discussion is drawn from Chapter 6, 'Page Power', of Tunstall, *Newspaper Power*.
53 Tunstall, *Newspaper Power*, 168.
54 Sampson, 'The crisis … ', 44.
55 Franklin, *Pulling Newspapers Apart*, 15.
56 Hastings, *Editor*, 354.
57 Franklin, *Pulling Newspapers Apart*; 15; Bromley, M. (1998) 'The "tabloidising" of Britain: "quality" newspapers in the 1990s' in Stephenson and Bromley, *Sex, Lies and Democracy*.
58 Marr, *My Trade*, 245.
59 Ward, 'UK National Newspapers', 82
60 Franklin, B. and Murphy, D. (1998) 'Changing times: local newspapers, technology and markets' in Franklin, B. and Murphy, D. (eds) *Making the Local News: Local Journalism in Context* London: Routledge, 17.
61 Franklin and Murphy, 'Changing times … ', 13.
62 Freer, J. (2007) 'UK regional and local newspapers' in Anderson, P. and Ward, G. (eds) *The Future of Journalism in Advanced Democracies* Aldershot: Ashgate, 90–1.
63 Franklin, 'Attacking the devil', 9.
64 The sector as a whole has experienced a decline in circulation but this is not evenly spread across the local press, with a significant number of weekly titles celebrating a small rise in sales in the early 2000s.
65 Freer, 'UK regional and local newspapers', 91.
66 Franklin, 'Attacking the devil', 13.
67 Williams, G. (2005) 'Profits before product: ownership and economics of the local press' in Franklin, *Local Journalism and Local Media*, 90.
68 Rooney, D. (1999) 'Thirty years of competition in the British tabloid press: the *Sun* and the *Mirror* 1968–98' in Sparks and Tulloch, *Tabloid Tales*, 101.
69 Quoted in Ward, 'UK national newspapers', 82.
70 Greenslade, *Press Gang*, 671; Ward, 'UK national newspapers', 82.
71 British Social Attitudes survey, 2008.

72 See Engel, *Tickle the Public*, 284–9; Greenslade, *Press Gang*, 509–11.

73 Engel, *Tickle the Public*, 288.

74 Greenslade, *Press Gang*, 510.

75 Snoddy, *The Good, the Bad and the Unacceptable*, 11.

76 Sweeney, J. (1989) 'The Sun and the Star' *Independent* magazine, 11 February.

77 Greenslade, *Press Gang*, 500.

78 Chippindale, P. and Horrie, C. (1992) *Stick It Up Your Punter: The Rise and Fall of the Sun* London: Mandarin, 292.

79 Greenslade, *Press Gang*, 461; Engel, *Tickle the Public*, 299.

80 Snoddy, *The Good, the Bad and the Unacceptable*, 69. See also Porter, H. (1985) *Lies, Damn Lies and Some Exclusives: Fleet St. Exposed* London: Coronet Books.

81 Ibid.

82 Tunstall, *Newspaper Power*, 267.

83 Baistow, *Fourth Rate Estate*, 53–5.

84 Tunstall, *Newspaper Power*, 398.

85 McNair, B. (2003) *News and Journalism in the UK* London: Routledge, 187.

86 Cited in Snoddy, *The Good, the Bad and the Unacceptable*, 101.

87 Snoddy, *The Good, the Bad and the Unacceptable*, 211.

88 Quoted in McNair, *News and Journalism in the UK*, 191.

89 Tulloch, J., 'Managing the press in a medium-sized European power' in Bromley and Stephenson, *Sex, Lies and Democracy*, 74.

90 Kemp quoted in McNair, *News and Journalism in the UK*, 193.

91 Engel, *Tickle the Public*, 304.

92 Greenslade, *Press Gang*, 571.

93 Coward, R. (2008) 'The monarchy' in Franklin, *Pulling Newspapers Apart*, 139.

94 Coward, 'The monarchy', 136–7.

95 Tench, D. (2008) 'Max Mosley: the media feels the whip', *Guardian.co.uk*, 24 July, http://www.guardian.co.uk/media/2008/jul/24/mosley.newsoftheworld.

96 For a wide ranging discussion of the case and its implications for press freedom and individual privacy, see *Guardian*, 'Privacy & the media: Max Mosley case', http://www.guardian.co.uk/media/privacy.

97 Horrie, C. (2008) 'A canny kiss and tell' *Guardian*, 28 July.

98 Franklin, *Pulling Newspapers Apart*, 11.

99 Franklin, *Pulling Newspapers Apart*, 12.

100 Davies, *Flat Earth News*, 74.

101 Lewis, J., Williams, A., Franklin, B., Thomas, J. and Mosdell, N. (2006) *The Quality and Independence of British Journalism* Cardiff: Cardiff University. See also note 105.

102 Davies, *Flat Earth News*, 84.

103 Davies, *Flat Earth News*, 75–84.

104 Miller, D. and Dinan, W. (2000) 'The rise of the PR industry in Britain, 1979–98' *European Journal of Communication* 15(1): 5–35.

105 Michie, D. (1998) *The Invisible Persuaders* London: Bantam, 17.

106 Quoted in Franklin, *Pulling Newspapers Apart*, 17

107 Cited in Davies, *Flat Earth News*, 84. This data is drawn from research undertaken by academics at Cardiff University, who discuss their findings and the reasons for the reliance of the quality press on news agency and PR copy in Lewis, J., Williams, A. and Franklin, B. (2008) 'Four rumours and an explanation: a political economic account of journalists' changing newsgathering and reporting practices' *Journalism Practice* 2(1): 27–45.

108 Cited in Franklin, 'Attacking the devil', 12.

109 Marr, *My Trade*, 115.

110 Gandy, O. (1982) *Beyond Agenda Setting: Information Subsidies and Public Policy* Norwood, NJ: Ablex Publishing.

111 For example, McNair, B. (2004) 'PR must die: spin, anti-spin and political public relations in the UK, 1997–2004' *Journalism Studies* 5(3): 325–38. For a broader discussion of the role of PR, see Davies, A. (2002) *Public Relations Democracy: Public Relations, Politics and the Mass Media in Britain* London: Routledge; Franklin, B. (2004) *Packaging Politics: Political Communications in Britain's Media Democracy* London: Arnold; Hobsbawm, J. (2006) *Where the Truth Lies: Trust and Morality in PR and Journalism* London: Atlantic Books.

112 Franklin, *Pulling Newspapers Apart*, 23.

113 Harrison, *News*, 77.

114 Ibid.

115 Herbert and Thurman, 'Paid content strategies for news websites', 216.

116 See Herbert and Thurman, 'Paid content strategies for news websites'.

117 Crosbie, V. (2004) 'What newspapers and their websites must do to survive' *Online Journalism Review*, 4 March, cited in Franklin, B. 'The future of newspapers' *Journalism Studies* 9: 5, 636. See also Franklin, *Pulling Newspapers Apart*, 25–7.

118 BBC NEWS, http://news.bbc.co.uk/go/pr/fr/-/1/hi/business/6502773.stm, published 28 March 2007.

119 Williams, A. and Franklin, B. (2007) *Turning the Tanker Around: Implementing Trinity–Mirror's Online Strategy* Cardiff: Cardiff University, 14.

120 Kiss, J. (2008) 'Newspaper website audits come under close scrutiny' *Guardian*, 26 May.

121 McNair, 'I, columnist', 119.

122 Wahl-Jorgensen, K. (2008) 'Op-ed pages' in Franklin, *Pulling Newspapers Apart*, 76.

123 Quoted in McNair, 'I, columnist', 119.

124 Aldridge, *Understanding the Local Media*, 35.

125 Franklin, *Pulling Newspapers Apart*, 13.

126 Toynbee, P. (2007) 'We need a rebellion against a press that's damaging our national psyche' *Guardian*, 15 June.

127 Quoted in Wintour, P. (2007) 'Blair: media is feral beast obsessed with impact' *Guardian*, 13 June.

128 Marsh K. (2004) 'Power, but scant responsibility' *British Journalism Review* 15(4): 17.

129 Lloyd, J. (2004) *What the Media Are Doing to Our Politics* London: Constable.

130 Curtice, J., quoted in Greenslade, R. (2008) 'Who wants newspapers in a society that no longer bothers with news?' *Guardian*, 23 January. For a discussion of the future of newspapers, see the special issue of *Journalism Studies*, 'The Future of Newspapers', 9(5) (2008).

BIBLIOGRAPHY

GENERAL HISTORIES

Andrews, A. (1859/1998) *The History of British Journalism* London: Routledge/Thoemmes Press.

Boston, R. (1990) *The Essential Fleet Street: Its History and Influence* London: Blandford.

Boyce, D.G. (1978) 'The Fourth Estate: a reappraisal of a concept' in Boyce, D., Curran, J. and Wingate, G. (eds) *Newspaper History: From the 17th Century to the Present Day* London: Constable.

Boyce, D., Curran, J. and Wingate, P. (1978) *Newspaper History: From the 17th Century to the Present Day* London: Constable.

Briggs, A. and Burke, P. (2005) *A Social History of the Media: From Gutenberg to the Internet* London: Polity.

Chalaby, J. (1998) *The Invention of Journalism* London: Macmillan.

Christian, H. (1980) *The Sociology of Journalism and the Press* Keele: University of Keele.

Clarke, B. (2004) *From Grub Street to Fleet Street: An Illustrated History of English Newspapers to 1899* Aldershot: Ashgate.

Conboy, M. (2003) *The Press and Popular Culture* London: Sage.

——(2004) *Journalism: A Critical History* London: Sage.

Cranfield, G. (1978) *The Press and Society* London: Longman.

Curran, J. (1977) 'Capitalism and Control of the Press, 1800–1975' in Curran, J., Gurevitch, M. and Woollacott, J. (eds) *Mass Communication and Society* London: Arnold.

——(1977) 'Mass communication as a social force' *Mass Communication and Society* Block 1, Unit 2 Open University.

——(1978) 'The press as an agency of social control: an historical perspective' in Boyce, D., Curran, J. and Wingate, G. (eds) *Newspaper History: From the 17th Century to the Present Day* London: Constable.

Curran, J. and Seaton, J. (2003) *Power without Responsibility: A History o f Press and Broadcasting in Britain* London: Routledge, 6th edition.

Feather, J. (1988) *A History of British Publishing* London; Routledge.

Fox Bourne, H. (1887/1998) *English Newspapers* London: Routledge/Thoemmes Press, 2 vols.

Griffiths, D. (2006) *Fleet Street: Five Hundred Years of the British Press* London: The British Library.

Habermas, J. (1989) *The Structural Transformation of the Public Sphere* London: Polity Press.

Hampton, M. (2004) *Visions of the Press in Britain, 1850–1950* Urbana and Chicago: University of Illinois Press.

Harrison, S. (1974) *Poor Men's Guardians: A Survey of the Struggle for a Democratic Newspaper Press, 1763–1973* London: Lawrence & Wishart.

Herd, H. (1951) *The March of Journalism* London: George Allen & Unwin.

Hunt, F. (1850/1998) *The Fourth Estate* London: Routledge/Thoemmes Press, 2 vols.

Hutt, A. (1973) *The Changing Newspaper: Typographical Trends in Britain and America 1622–1972* London: Gordon Fraser Ltd.

Innis, H. (1942) 'The newspaper in economic development' *Journal of Economic History* 2, Supplement, 1–33.

Keeble, R. and Wheeler, S. (eds) (2007) *The Journalistic Imagination: Literary Journalism from Defoe to Capote and Carter* London: Routledge.

Knightley, P. (2003) *The First Casualty: The War Correspondent as Hero, Propagandist and Myth Maker from Crimea to Iraq* London: Andre Deutsch.

Koss, S. (1990) *The Rise and Fall of the Political Press in Britain* London: Fontana Press.

Marr, A. (2004) *My Trade: A Short History of British Journalism* London: Macmillan.

Morison, S. (1932) *The English Newspaper* Cambridge: Cambridge University Press.

Nevett, T. (1982) *Advertising in Britain: A History* London: Heinemann.

Read, D. (1992) *The Power of News: A History of Reuters* Oxford: Oxford University Press.

Scott, G. (1968) *Reporters Anonymous: The Story of the Press Association* London: Hutchinson.

Siebert, F. (1965) *Freedom of the Press in England 1476–1776: The Rise and Decline of Government Control* Urbana, IL: University of Illinois Press.

Smith, A. (1979) *The Newspaper: An International History* London: Thames & Hudson.

Snoddy, R. (1993) *The Good, the Bad and the Unacceptable: The Hard News About the British Press* London: Faber & Faber.

Sparrow, A. (2003) *Obscure Scribblers: A History of Parliamentary Journalism* London: Politico's.

Steed, H.W. (1938) *The Press* Harmondsworth: Penguin.

Stephens, M. (1997) *A History of News* Fort Worth, TX: Harcourt Brace.

Tulloch, J. (1999) 'The eternal recurrence of new journalism' in Sparks, C. and Tulloch, J. (eds) *Tabloid Tales: Global Debates over Media Standards* Lanham, MD: Rowman & Littlefield.

Williams, F. (1959) *Dangerous Estate: The Anatomy of Newspapers* London: Arrow Books.

——(1969) *The Right to Know: The Rise of the World Press* London: Longmans.

Williams, K. (1977) *The English Newspaper: An Illustrated History to 1900* London: Springwood Books.

Williams, R. (1978) 'The press and popular culture: an historical perspective' in Boyce, D., Curran, J. and Wingate, G. (eds) *Newspaper History: From the 17th Century to the Present Day* London: Constable.

——(1980) *The Long Revolution* Harmondsworth: Penguin.

Wilson, C. (1985) *First with the News: The History of W.H. Smith 1792–1972* London: Cape.

Winston, B. (1998) *Media, Technology and Society: A History from the Telegraph to the Internet* London: Routledge.

——(2005) *Messages: Free Expression, Media and the West from Gutenberg to Google* London: Routledge.

EARLY NEWSPAPERS

Arblaster, P. (2005) 'Posts, newsletters, newspapers: England in a European system of communications' *Media History* 11(1/2): 21–36.

Atherton, I. (1999) 'The itch grown a disease: manuscript transmission of news in the seventeenth century' in Raymond, J. (ed.) *News, Newspapers and Society in Early Modern Britain* London: Frank Cass.

Brownlees, N. (2005) 'Spoken discourse in early English newspapers' *Media History* 11(1/2): 69–85.

Clyde, W. (1934) *The Struggle for the Freedom of the Press* New York: Burt Franklin.

Curran, J. (1982) 'Communications, power and social order' in Gurevitch, M., Bennett, T., Curran, J. and Woollacott, J. (eds) *Culture, Society and the Media* London: Methuen.

Cust, R. (1986) 'News and politics in early seventeenth century England' *Past & Present* 112, August: 60–90.

Dooley, B. and Baron, S. (eds) *The Politics of Information in Early Modern Europe* London: Routledge.

Eisenstein, E. (1983) *The Printing Revolution in Early Modern Europe* Cambridge: Cambridge University Press.

Frank, J. (1961) *The Beginnings of the English Newspaper* Boston, MA: Harvard University Press.

Gerard, D. (1982) 'The Impact of the First Newsmen on Jacobean London' *Journalism Studies* 7 July.

Hartley, J, Goulden, H. and O'Sullivan, T. (1985) 'The development of printing', Block Two, Unit Three 'Media Institutions' in *Making Sense of the Media* London: Comedia.

Lambert, S. (1992) 'Coranto printing in England: the first newsbooks' *Journal of Newspaper and Periodical History* 3(1): 3–19.

Lebvre, L. and Martin, H.-J. (1976) *The Coming of the Book* London: Verso.

Mendle, M. (2001) 'News and pamphlet culture of mid-seventeenth-century England' in Dooley, B. and Baron, S. (eds) *The Politics of Information in Early Modern Europe* London: Routledge.

Muggli, M. (1992) 'Ben Jonson and the business of news' *Studies in English Literature 1500–1900* 32(2): 323–40.

Peachey, J. (2005) 'The struggle for *Mercurius Britannicus*: factional politics and the parliamentarian press, 1643–46' *Huntington Library Quarterly* 68(3): 517–43.

Raymond, J. (1996) *The Invention of the Newspaper: English Newsbooks 1640–49* Oxford: Clarendon Press.

——(ed.) (1999) *News, Newspapers and Society in Early Modern Britain* London: Frank Cass.

Rosenberg, M. (1953) 'The rise of England's first daily newspaper' *Journalism Quarterly* XXX (Winter): 3–14.

Shaaber, M. (1966) *Some Forerunners of the Newspaper in Britain 1476–1622* London: Frank Cass.

Skeaping, L. (2005) *Broadsides Ballads* London: Faber Music.

Sommerville, C.J. (1996) *The News Revolution in England: Cultural Dynamics of Daily Information* Oxford: Oxford University Press.

Sutherland, J. (2004) *The Restoration Newspaper and Its Development* Cambridge: Cambridge University Press, 2nd edition.

Williams, J. (1908) *A History of English Journalism to the Foundation of the Gazette* London: Longmans, Green & Co.

Woolf, D. (2001) 'News, history and the construction of the present in early modern England' in Dooley, B. and Baron, S. (eds) *The Politics of Information in Early Modern Europe* London: Routledge.

EIGHTEENTH-CENTURY NEWSPAPERS

Asquith, I. (1975) 'Advertising and the press in the late eighteenth and early nineteenth centuries: James Perry and the *Morning Chronicle* 1790–1821' *Historical Journal* 18(4): 703–24.

Barker, H. (2001) *Newspaper, Politics and English Society 1695–1855* London: Longman.

Barker, H. and Burrows, S. (2002) *Press, Politics and the Public Sphere in Europe and North America, 1760–1820* Cambridge: Cambridge University Press.

Black, J. (2001) *The English Press 1621–1861* Stroud: Sutton Publishing.

Bond, D. and McLeod, W. (1977) *Newsletters to Newspapers: Eighteenth-Century Journalism* Morgantown, WV: Department of Journalism, West Virginia University.

Brewer, J. (1997) *The Pleasures of the Imagination: English Culture in the Eighteenth Century* London: HarperCollins.

Cranfield, G. (1962) *The Development of the Provincial Press, 1700–60* Oxford: Clarendon Press.

Harris, B. (1996) *Politics and the Rise of the Press: Britain and France, 1620–1800* London: Routledge.

Harris, M. (1978) 'The structure, ownership and control of the press 1620–1780' in Boyce, D., Curran, J. and Wingate, G. (eds) *Newspaper History: From the 17th Century to the Present Day* London: Constable.

——(1988) *London Newspapers in the Age of Walpole* London: Associated University Presses.

McKay, J. (2007) 'Defoe's The Storm as a model for contemporary reporting' in Keeble, R. and Wheeler, S. (eds) *The Journalistic Imagination: Literary Journalism from Defoe to Capote and Carter* London: Routledge.

Schweizer, K. (2006) 'Newspapers, politics and public opinion in the later Hanoverian era' in Schweizer, K. (ed.) *Parliament and the Press 1689-c1939* Edinburgh: Edinburgh University Press.

Targett, S. (1994) 'Government and ideology during the age of Whig supremacy: the political argument of Sir Robert Walpole's newspaper propagandists' *Historical Journal* 37(2): 289–317.

Thomas, P. (1959) 'The beginning of parliamentary reporting in the newspapers, 1768–74' *English Historical Review* 74: 623–36.

——(1960) 'John Wilkes and freedom of the press' *Bulletin of the Institute of Historical Research* 33: 86–98.

Walker, R. (1974) 'The newspaper press in the reign of William III' *Historical Journal* 17(4): 691–709.

NINETEENTH-CENTURY NEWSPAPERS

Allen, J. and Ashton, O. (2005) *Papers for the People: A Study of the Chartist Press* London: Merlin Press.

Anderson, P. (1994) *The Printed Image and the Transformation of Popular Culture 1790–1860* Oxford: Clarendon Press.

Aspinall, A. (1973) *Politics and the Press 1780–1850* Brighton: Harvester Press.

Asquith, I. (1978) 'The structure, ownership and control of the press 1780–1855' in Boyce, D., Curran, J. and Wingate, G. (eds) *Newspaper History: From the 17th Century to the Present Day* London: Constable.

Berridge, V. (1977) 'Popular Sundays and mid-Victorian society' in Boyce, D., Curran, J. and Wingate, G. (eds) *Newspaper History: From the 17th Century to the Present Day* London: Constable.

Brake, L., Bell, B. and Finkelstein, D. (eds) (2000) *Nineteenth Century Media and the Construction of Identities* London: Palgrave.

Brake, L, Jones, A. and Madden, L. (eds) (1990) *Investigating Victorian Journalism* London: Macmillan.

Brown, L. (1977) 'The treatment of news in mid-Victorian newspapers' *Transactions of the Royal Historical Society* Fifth Series 27: 23–39.

——(1985) *Victorian News and Newspapers* Oxford: Clarendon Press.

Coulling, S. (1916) 'Matthew Arnold and the *Daily Telegraph*' *Review of English Studies* 12(46), May: 173–9.

Epstein, J.A. (1976) 'Feargus O'Connor and the *Northern Star*' *International Review of Social History* 21(1): 51–97.

Fox, C. (1978) 'Political caricature and the freedom of the press in early nineteenth century England' in Boyce, D., Curran, J. and Wingate, G. (eds) *Newspaper History: From the 17th Century to the Present Day* London: Constable.

Gilmartin, K. (1996) *Print Politics: The Press and Radical Opposition in Early Nineteenth Century England* Cambridge: Cambridge University Press.

Gliddon, P. (2003) 'The political importance of provincial newspapers 1903–45: the Rowntrees and the liberal press' *Twentieth Century British History* 14(1): 24–42.

Hampton, M. (1999) 'Journalists and the "professional ideal" in Britain: the Institute of Journalists, 1884–1907' *Historical Research* 72(178): 183–201.

——(2001) 'Understanding media: theories of the press in Britain' *Media, Culture & Society* 23: 213–31.

——(2005) 'Defining journalism in late nineteenth century Britain' *Critical Studies in Media Communication* 22(2): 138–55.

——(2008) 'The "objectivity" ideal and its limitations in 20th-century British journalism' *Journalism Studies* 9(4): 477–93.

Hatton, J. (1998/1882) *Journalistic London* London: Routledge/Thoemmes Press.

Hollis, P. (1970) *The Pauper Press* Oxford: Oxford University Press.

Hoyer, S. and Pottker, H. (eds) (2005) *Diffusion of the News Paradigm 1850–2000* Goteborg: Nordicom.

James, L. (1978) *Print and the People 1819–1851* London: Peregrine.

Jones, A. (1996) *Powers of the Press: Newspapers, Power and the Public in Nineteenth-Century England* Aldershot: Scolar Press.

King, A. and Plunkett, J. (2005) *Victorian Print Media: A Reader* Oxford: Oxford University Press.

Lee, A. (1973) 'Franklin Thomasson and the Tribune: a case-study in the history of the liberal press, 1906–8' *Historical Journal* 16(2): 341–60.

——(1976) *The Origins of the Popular Press 1855–1914* London: Croom Helm.

——(1978) 'The structure, ownership and control of the press 1855–1914' in Boyce, D., Curran, J. and Wingate, G. (eds) *Newspaper History: From the 17th Century to the Present Day* London: Constable.

Mountjoy, P. (1977) 'The working-class press and working-class conservatism' in Boyce, D., Curran, J. and Wingate, G. (eds) *Newspaper History: From the 17th Century to the Present Day* London: Constable.

Morus, I. (2000) '"The nervous system of Britain": space, time and the electric telegraph in the Victorian age' *British Journal for the History of Science* 33(4): 455–75.

O'Malley, P. (1981) 'Capital accumulation and press freedom 1800–850' *Media, Culture & Society* 3: 71–83.

Palmer, M. (1977) 'The British press and international news, 1851–99: of agencies and newspaper' in Boyce, D., Curran, J. and Wingate, G. (eds) *Newspaper History: From the 17th Century to the Present Day* London: Constable.

Walker, A. (2006) 'The development of the provincial press in England c1780–1914' *Journalism Studies* 7(3): 373–86.

Weiner, J. (1969) *The War of the Unstamped: The Movement to Repeal the British Newspaper Tax, 1830–1836* Ithaca, NY: Cornell University Press.

——(1988) *Papers for the Millions: The New Journalism in Britain 1850s to 1914* New York: Greenwood Press.

TWENTIETH-CENTURY AND CONTEMPORARY NEWSPAPERS

Aldridge, M. (2007) *Understanding the Local Media* Maidenhead: Open University Press.

Andrews, L. and Taylor, H.A. (1970) *Lords and Labourers of the Press: Men Who Fashioned the Modern British Newspaper* Carbondale, IL: South Illinois University Press.

Angell, N. (1922) *The Press and the Organisation of Society* London: Labour Publishing Co.

Baistow, T. (1985) *Fourth Rate Estate: An Anatomy of Fleet Street* London: Comedia.

Boyce, D. (1987) 'Crusaders without chains: power and the press barons' in Curran, J., Smith, A. and Wingate, P. (eds) *Impacts and Influences* London: Methuen.

Boyd-Barrett, O., Seymour-Ure, C. and Tunstall, J. (1977) *Studies on the Press*, Royal Commission on the Press Working Paper 3 London: HMSO.

Brendon, P. (1982) *The Life & Death of the Press Barons* London: Secker & Warburg.

Broersma, M. (2008) *Form and Style in Journalism: European Newspapers and the Representation of News 1880–2005* Leuven: Peeters.

Bromley, M. (1999) 'Was it the Mirror wot won it? The development of the tabloid press during the Second World War' in Hayes, N. and Hill, J. (eds) *Millions Like Us: British Culture in the Second World War* Liverpool: Liverpool University Press.

Camrose, V. (1947) *Newspapers and Their Controllers* London: Cassell & Co. Ltd.

Catterall, P., Seymour-Ure, C. and Smith, A. (eds) (2000) *Northcliffe's Legacy: Aspects of the British Popular Press, 1896–1996* London: Macmillan.

Chalaby, J. (1997) 'No ordinary press owners: press barons as a Weberian ideal type' *Media, Culture & Society* 19: 621–41.

——(2000) 'Northcliffe: proprietor as journalist' in Catterall, P., Seymour-Ure, C. and Smith, A. (eds) *Northcliffe's Legacy: Aspects of the British Popular Press, 1896–1996* London: Macmillan.

Cleverley, G. (1976) *The Great Fleet Street Disaster* London: Constable.

Curran, J. (1980) 'Advertising as a patronage system' in Christian, H. (ed.) *The Sociology of Journalism and the Press* Keele, Keele University Monograph 29.

——(2000) 'Press reformism 1918–98: a study of failure' in Tumber, H. (ed.) *Media Power. Professionals and Policies* London: Routledge.

Curran, J., Douglas, A. and Whannel, G. (1980) 'The political economy of the human interest story' in Smith, A. (ed.) *Newspapers and Democracy* Cambridge, MA: MIT Press.

Davies, N. (2008) *Flat Earth News* London: Chatto & Windus.

Eldridge, J., Kitzinger, J. and Williams, K. (1999) *The Mass Media and Power in Modern Britain* Oxford: Oxford University Press.

Engel, M. (1996) *Tickle the Public: One Hundred Years of the Popular Press* London: Victor Gollancz.

Franklin, B. (1997) *Newszak and the News Media* London: Arnold.

——(ed.) (2006) *Local Journalism and Local Media: Making the Local News* London: Routledge.

——(ed.) (2008) *Pulling Newspapers Apart* London: Routledge.

Franklin, B. and Murphy, D. (1991) *What News? The Market, Politics and the Local Press* London: Routledge.

——(1998) *Making the Local News: Local Journalism in Context* London: Routledge.

Gliddon, P. (2003) 'The political importance of provincial newspapers 1903–45: the Rowntrees and the liberal press' *Twentieth Century British History* 14(1): 24–42.

Glover, S. (ed.) (1999) *Secrets of the Press* London: Allen Lane.

Greenslade, R. (2003) *Press Gang: How Newspapers Make Profits from Propaganda* London: Macmillan.

Hambro, C.J. (1958) *Newspaper Lords in British Politics* London: Macdonald.

Hargreaves, I. (2003) *Journalism: Truth or Dare* Oxford: Oxford University Press.

Hastings, M. (2002) *Editor: An Inside Story of Newspapers* London: Pan Books.

Herbert, J. and Thurman, N. (2007) 'Paid content strategies for news websites' *Journalism Practice* 1(2): 208–26.

Hirsch, F. and Gordon, D. (1975) *Newspaper Money* London: Hutchinson.

Hollingsworth, M. (1986) *The Press and Political Dissent* London: Pluto Press.

Horrie, C. (2003) *Tabloid Nation: From the Birth of the Daily Mirror to the Death of the Tabloid* London: Andre Deutsch.

Hutcheson, D. (2008) 'The history of the press' in Blain, N. and Hutcheson, D. (eds) *The Media in Scotland* Edinburgh: Edinburgh University Press.

Jackson, I. (1971) *The Provincial Press and the Community* Manchester: Manchester University Press.

Jeffrey, T. and McClelland, K. (1987) 'A world fit to live in: the *Daily Mail* and the middle classes 1918–39' in Curran, J., Smith, A. and Wingate, P. (eds) *Impacts and Influences* London: Methuen.

Jenkins, S. (1979) *Newspapers: The Power and the Money* London: Faber & Faber.

——(1986) *The Market for Glory: Fleet Street Ownership in the 20th Century* London: Faber & Faber.

Kaul, C. (2000) 'Popular press and empire: Northcliffe, India and the *Daily Mail*, 1896–1922' in Catterall, P., Seymour-Ure, C. and Smith, A. (eds) *Northcliffe's Legacy: Aspects of the British Popular Press, 1896–1996* London: Macmillan.

LeMahieu, D.L. (1988) *A Culture for Democracy: Mass Communication and the Cultivated Mind in Britain between the Wars* Oxford: Clarendon Press.

McLachlan, S. and Golding, P. (1999) 'Tabloidization and the British press: a quantitative investigation into changes in British newspapers, 1952–97' in Sparks, C. and Tulloch, J. (eds) *Tabloid Tales: Global Debates over Media Standards* Lanham, MD: Rowman & Littlefield.

McNair, B. (1999) *News and Journalism in the UK* London: Routledge.

Marwick, A. (1982) 'Press, pictures and sound: the Second World War and the British experience' *Daedalus* Fall: 135–55.

Melvern, L. (1986) *The End of the Street* London: Methuen.

Morgan, K. (2002) 'The Boer War and the media (1899–1902)' *Twentieth Century British History* 13(1): 1–16.

Murdock, G. and Golding, P. (1978) 'The structure, ownership and control of the press 1914–76' in Boyce, D., Curran, J. and Wingate, G. (eds) *Newspaper History: From the 17th Century to the Present Day* London: Constable.

Murphy, D. (1976) *The Silent Watchdog: The Press in Local Politics* London: Constable.

Negrine, R. (1989) *Politics and the Mass Media in Britain* London: Routledge, 2nd edition.

O'Malley, T. (1997) 'Labour and the 1947–49 Royal Commission on the Press' in Bromley, M. and O'Malley, T. *Journalism: A Reader* London: Routledge.

O'Malley, T. and Soley, C. (2000) *Regulating the Press* London: Pluto Press.

Rance, N. (1993) 'British newspapers in the early twentieth century' in Bloom, C. (ed.) *Literature and Culture in Modern Britain 1920–29* London: Longman.

Rooney, D. (1999) 'Thirty years of competition in the British tabloid press: the *Mirror* and the *Sun* 1968–98' in Sparks, C. and Tulloch, J. (eds) *Tabloid Tales: Global Debates over Media Standards* Lanham, MA: Rowman & Littlefield.

Sampson, A. (1996) 'The crisis at the heart of our media' *British Journalism Review* 7(3): 45–51.

Seymour-Ure, C. (1975) 'How special are cartoonists?' *Twentieth Century Studies* 13/14: 6–21.

——(1995) *The British Press and Broadcasting since 1945* London: Blackwell, 2nd edition.

Smith, A.C.H. (1975) *Paper Voices: The Popular Press and Social Change 1935–1965* London: Chatto & Windus.

Smith, M. (1994) *Paper Lions: The Scottish Press and National Identity* Edinburgh: Polygon.

Snoddy, R. (1993) *The Good, the Bad and the Unacceptable: The Hard News about the British Press* London: Faber & Faber.

Sparks, C. (1991) 'Goodbye, Hildy Johnson: the vanishing "serious" press' in Dahlgren, P. and Sparks, C. (eds) *Communication and Citizenship: Journalism and the Public Sphere* London: Routledge.

Sparks, C. and Tulloch, J. (1999) *Tabloid Tales: Global Debates over Media Standards* Lanham, MA: Rowman & Littlefield.

Stephenson, H. and Bromley, M. (1999) *Sex, Lies and Democracy: The Press and the Public* London: Longman.

Stubbs, J. (1977) 'Appearance and reality: a case study of the Observer and J.L. Garvin, 1914–42' in Boyce, D., Curran, J. and Wingate, G. (eds) *Newspaper History: From the 17th Century to the Present Day* London: Constable.

Thompson, J. (2006) 'Fleet Street colossus: the rise and fall of Northcliffe, 1896–1922' in Schweizer, K. (ed.) *Parliament and the Press* Edinburgh: Edinburgh University Press,

Tunstall, J. (1971) *Journalists at Work. Specialist Correspondents: Their News Organisations, News Sources & Competitor-Colleagues* London: Constable.

——(1980) 'The British press in the age of television' in Christian, H. (ed.) *The Sociology of Journalism and the Press* Keele, Keele University Monograph 29.

——(1983) *The Media in Britain* London: Constable.

——(1996) *Newspaper Power: The New National Press in Britain* Oxford: Oxford University Press.

Tunstall, J. and Palmer, M. (1991) *Media Moguls* London: Routledge.

Twaites, P. (2000) 'Circles of confusion and sharp vision: British news photography, 1919–39' in Catterall, P., Seymour-Ure, C. and Smith, A. (eds) *Northcliffe's Legacy: Aspects of the British Popular Press, 1896–1996* London: Macmillan.

Ward, G. (2007) 'UK national newspapers' in Anderson, P. and Ward, G. (eds) *The Future of Journalism in Advanced Democracies* Aldershot: Ashgate.

Whale, J. (1980) *The Politics of the Media* London: Fontana, 2nd edition.

Whitaker, B. (1981) *News Ltd.: Why You Can't Read All About It* London: Comedia.

Williams, F. (1946) *Press, Parliament and People* London: William Heinemann.

Wright, J. (2003) 'The myth in the Mirror' *British Journalism Review* 14(3): 59–66.

HISTORY OF READING, WRITING AND LEISURE

Altick, R. (1957) *The English Common Reader; A Social History of the Mass Reading Public 1800–1900* Chicago: University of Chicago Press.

Burke, P. (2000) *The Social History of Knowledge* London: Polity Press.

Carey, J. (1992) *Intellectuals and the Masses: Pride and Prejudice among the Literary Intelligentsia, 1880–1939* London: Faber & Faber.

Cavallo, G. and Chartier, R. (1999) *A History of Reading in the West* London: Polity Press.

Curran, J. and Tunstall, J. (1983) 'Mass media and leisure' in Smith, M., Parker, S. and Smith, C. (eds) *Leisure and Society in Britain* London: Allen Lane.

Matheson, D. (2000) 'The birth of news discourse: changes in news language in British newspapers, 1880–1930' *Media, Culture & Society* 22: 557–73.

Swingewood, A. (1977) *The Myth of Mass Culture* London: Macmillan.

Thompson, E.P. (1968) *The Making of the English Working Class* London: Pelican.

Vincent, D. (1989) *Literacy and Popular Culture 1790–1840* Cambridge: Cambridge University Press.

Wahrman, D. (1992) 'Virtual representation: parliamentary reporting and language of class in the 1790s' *Past & Present* 136: 83–113.

Webb, R. (1955) *The British Working Class Reader 1790–1848* London: Allen & Unwin.

NEWSPAPER BIOGRAPHIES AND PERSONAL RECOLLECTIONS

Bourne, R. (1990) *Lords of Fleet Street: The Harmsworth Dynasty* London: Unwin & Hyman.

Chester, L. and Fenby, J. (1979) *The Fall of the House of Beaverbrook* London: Andre Deutsch.

Chippindale, P. and Horrie, C. (1988) *Disaster: The Story of News on Sunday* London: Sphere.

——(1992) *Stick It up Your Punter: The Rise and Fall of the Sun* London: Mandarin.

Chisholm, A. and Davie, M. (1993) *Lord Beaverbrook: A Life* New York: Alfred Knopf.

Christansen, A. (1961) *Headlines All My Life* London: Heinemann.

Connor, R. (1969) *Cassandra: Reflections in a Mirror* London: Cassell.

Cudlipp, H. (1953) *Publish and Be Damned* London: Hamlyn.

Dibblee, G. (1913) *The Newspaper* London: Williams and Norgate.

Edelman, M. (1966) *The Mirror: A Political History* London: Hamish Hamilton.

Evans, H. (1983) *Good Times, Bad Times* London: Weidenfeld & Nicholson.

Ferris, P. (1971) *The House of Northcliffe* London: Weidenfeld & Nicholson.

Fyfe, H. (1949) *Sixty Years of Fleet Street* London: W.H. Allen.

Gibbs, P. (1923) *Adventures in Journalism* London: Harper.

Hart-Davies, Duff (1990) *The House the Berry's Built: Inside the Telegraph 1928–1986* London: Hodder & Stoughton.

Hobson, H., Knightley, P. and Russell, L. (1972) *The Pearl of Days: An Intimate History of the Sunday Times 1822–1972* London: Hamish Hamilton.

Jackson, K. (2001) *George Newnes and the New Journalism in Britain, 1880–1910: Culture and Profit* Aldershot: Ashgate.

Leapman, M. (1983) *Barefaced Cheek: Rupert Murdoch* London: Hodder & Stoughton.

MacArthur, B. (1988) *Eddie Shah: Today and the Newspaper Revolution* Newton Abbot: David & Charles.

Mansfield, F. (1944) *The Complete Journalist* London: Isaac Pitman & Sons.

Richards, H. (1997) *The Bloody Circus: the Daily Herald and the Left* London: Pluto Press.

Shawcross, W. (1992) *Rupert Murdoch* London: Chatto & Windus.

Simonis, H. (1917) *The Street of Ink: An Intimate History of Journalism* London: Cassell & Co. Ltd.

Spender, J. (1927) *Life, Journalism and Politics* London: Cassell & Co. Ltd.

Stead, W.T. (1886) 'Government by journalism' *Contemporary Review*: 653–74.

Taylor, A.J.P. (1974) *Beaverbrook* Harmsondworth: Penguin.

Taylor, S. (1996) *The Great Outsiders: Northcliffe, Rothermere and the Daily Mail* London: Weidenfeld & Nicholson.

Wintour, C. (1972) *Pressures on the Press: An Editor Looks at Fleet Street* London: Andre Deutsch.

Wolff, M. (2008) *The Man Who Owns the News: Inside the Secret World of Rupert Murdoch* London: Bodley Head.

PROPAGANDA, PUBLIC RELATIONS AND INFORMATION MANAGEMENT

Balfour, M. (1979) *Propaganda in War, 1940–45: Organisations, Policies and Publics* London: Routledge & Kegan Paul.

Cockerell, M., Hennessy, P. and Walker, D. (1986) *Sources Close to the Prime Minister* London: Macmillan.

Cockett, R. (1989) *Twilight of Truth: Chamberlain, Appeasement and the Manipulation of the Press* London: Weidenfeld & Nicholson.

Constantine, S. 'Bringing the Empire alive: the Empire Marketing Board and imperial propaganda' in Mackenzie, J. (ed.) *Imperialism and Popular Culture* Manchester: Manchester University Press.

Davies, A. (2002) *Public Relations Democracy: Public Relations, Politics and the Mass Media in Britain* London: Routledge.

Fletcher, R. (1982) 'British propaganda since World War II – a case study' *Media Culture & Society* 4: 97–107.

Franklin, B. (1994) *Packaging Politics: Political Communications in Britain's Media Democracy* London: Arnold.

Grant, M. (1994) *Propaganda and the Role of the State in Inter-War Britain* Oxford: Oxford University Press.

Hobsbawm, J. (2006) *Where the Truth Lies: Trust and Morality in PR and Journalism* London: Atlantic Books.

L'Etang, J. (2004) *Public Relations in Britain: A History of Professional Practice in the Twentieth Century* Mahwah, NJ: Lawrence Erlbaum Associates.

Mackenzie, John (1984) *Propaganda and Empire: The Manipulation of British Public Opinion 1880–1960* Manchester: Manchester University Press.

McNair, B. (2004) 'PR must die: spin, anti-spin and political public relations in the UK, 1997–2004' *Journalism Studies* 5(3): 325–38.

Margach, J. (1978) *The Abuse of Power: The War between Downing Street and the Media from Lloyd George to Callaghan* London: W.H. Allen.

Michie, D. (1998) *The Invisible Persuaders* London: Bantam.

Miller, D. and Dinan, W. (2000) 'The rise of the PR industry in Britain, 1979–98' *European Journal of Communication* 15(1): 5–35.

——(2007) *Thinker, Faker, Spinner, Spy: Corporate PR and the Assault on Democracy* London: Pluto Press.

——(2008) *A Century of Spin: How Public Relations Became the Cutting Edge of Corporate Power* London: Pluto Press.

Moore, M. (2006) *The Origins of Modern Spin: Democratic Government and the Media in Britain, 1945–51* London: Palgrave.

Scammell, M. (1995) *Designer Politics: How Elections Are Won* Basingstoke: Macmillan.

Seymour-Ure, C. (1968) *The Press, Politics and the Public* London: Methuen.

Taylor, P. (1995) *Munitions of the Mind* Manchester: Manchester University Press.

——(1999) *British Propaganda in the Twentieth Century: Selling Democracy* Edinburgh: Edinburgh University Press.

Tunstall, J. (1970) *The Westminster Lobby Correspondents* London: Routledge Kegan & Paul.

INDEX